THE COMPLETE IDIOT'S GUIDE TO

Hinduism

Second Edition

by Linda Johnsen

ALPHA

A member of Penguin Group (USA) Inc.

To Hindus everywhere, with affection and respect.

ALPHA BOOKS

Published by Penguin Group (USA) Inc.

Penguin Group (USA) Inc., 375 Hudson Street, New York, New York 10014, USA • Penguin Group (Canada), 90 Eglinton Avenue East, Suite 700, Toronto, Ontario M4P 2Y3, Canada (a division of Pearson Penguin Canada Inc.) • Penguin Books Ltd., 80 Strand, London WC2R 0RL, England • Penguin Ireland, 25 St. Stephen's Green, Dublin 2, Ireland (a division of Penguin Books Ltd.) • Penguin Group (Australia), 250 Camberwell Road, Camberwell, Victoria 3124, Australia (a division of Pearson Australia Group Pty. Ltd.) • Penguin Books India Pvt. Ltd., 11 Community Centre, Panchsheel Park, New Delhi—110 017, India • Penguin Group (NZ), 67 Apollo Drive, Rosedale, North Shore, Auckland 1311, New Zealand (a division of Pearson New Zealand Ltd.) • Penguin Books (South Africa) (Pty.) Ltd., 24 Sturdee Avenue, Rosebank, Johannesburg 2196, South Africa • Penguin Books Ltd., Registered Offices: 80 Strand, London WC2R 0RL, England

Copyright © 2009 by Linda Johnsen

International Standard Book Number: 978-1-59257-905-1
Library of Congress Catalog Card Number: 2008941489

16 15 14   8 7 6

Interpretation of the printing code: The rightmost number of the first series of numbers is the year of the book's printing; the rightmost number of the second series of numbers is the number of the book's printing. For example, a printing code of 09-1 shows that the first printing occurred in 2009.

Printed in the United States of America

Note: This publication contains the opinions and ideas of its author. It is intended to provide helpful and informative material on the subject matter covered. It is sold with the understanding that the author and publisher are not engaged in rendering professional services in the book. If the reader requires personal assistance or advice, a competent professional should be consulted.

The author and publisher specifically disclaim any responsibility for any liability, loss, or risk, personal or otherwise, which is incurred as a consequence, directly or indirectly, of the use and application of any of the contents of this book.

Most Alpha books are available at special quantity discounts for bulk purchases for sales promotions, premiums, fund-raising, or educational use. Special books, or book excerpts, can also be created to fit specific needs.

For details, write: Special Markets, Alpha Books, 375 Hudson Street, New York, NY 10014.

Publisher: *Marie Butler-Knight*
Editorial Director: *Mike Sanders*
Senior Managing Editor: *Billy Fields*
Senior Acquisitions Editor: *Paul Dinas*
Development Editor: *Jennifer Moore*
Production Editor: *Kayla Dugger*

Copy Editor: *Nancy Wagner*
Cover Designer: *Bill Thomas*
Book Designer: *Trina Wurst*
Indexer: *Johnna Vanhoose Dinse*
Layout: *Ayanna Lacey*
Proofreader: *Mary Hunt*

Contents at a Glance

Contents

Appendixes

Foreword

The Hindu religion is an ocean of spiritual teachings about all aspects of life and consciousness. It's the world's oldest religion, going back to the very dawn of history. It sees its origin in the cosmic mind itself. Yet Hinduism is perhaps the world's youngest religion because it emphasizes the authority of living teachers and allows for correction and evolution over time.

Hinduism is the most diverse religious tradition in the world. It could be said that there are probably more religions inside of Hinduism than outside of it. It has numerous saints, sages, and yogis, both male and female, from ancient to modern times, and today still has what is probably the largest number of monks and renunciates (including a number of Westerners). Tens of millions of Hindus showed up in Allahabad for the Kumbha Mela festival in January 2001. It was the largest gathering of any type and the largest religious gathering in the history of the world.

Hinduism is the world's largest non-biblical tradition, with nearly a billion followers worldwide. It could be called the world's largest non-organized religion as it emphasizes individual spiritual experience, the realization of the higher Self over any religious institution, book, dogma, or savior. It's also the world's largest native or pagan tradition, reflecting the ancient spiritual traditions that once existed all over the world. Like native traditions everywhere, it honors God or the sacred throughout all of nature. It has many insights in harmony with the ecological age, as it affords reverence to the Earth as a conscious and loving presence and asks us to respect our environment.

Hinduism contains the world's oldest and largest tradition of Goddess worship—worshipping the Divine not only as father but also as mother. It recognizes all the diverse forms of the Goddess and her powers of wisdom, beauty, strength, love, and compassion.

Perhaps most notably, Hinduism is the world's largest pluralistic tradition, recognizing One Truth—an eternal reality of Being-Consciousness Bliss in all beings—but also many paths to realize it. Hinduism recognizes theism (the belief in One Creator) but only as one portion of the human religious experience that includes polytheism, pantheism, monism, and even atheism. As the most inclusive of the world's great religions, Hinduism has room for all these views and yet guides us through these to Self-realization that transcends them all.

Hinduism has probably the world's oldest and largest literature of spirituality, mysticism, and yoga. It provides a complete spiritual culture including art, dance, sculpture, medicine, and science, with all these subjects explained according to a science of consciousness.

Hinduism has a view of the universe in time and space that is compatible with modern science. Aspects of the Hindu tradition such as Yoga, Vedanta, Ayurveda, and Vedic astrology are already popular in the West. Hindu terms such as guru, mantra, shakti, prana, kundalini, and chakra have entered into the English language. Great gurus from the Hindu tradition such as Ramana Maharshi, Yogananda, Ramakrishna, Shivananda, Aurobindo, and Mahatma Gandhi have extensive followings and much respect in the West today.

There are now nearly two million Hindus of Indian origin in the United States, as well as significant numbers in Canada, the United Kingdom, and the Caribbean, with Hindu temples in most of the main cities of the United States. This Hindu group is one of the wealthiest and best-educated in the West and contains many successful scientists, computer engineers, and doctors. India itself, the home of most Hindus, is the second largest country in the world and is expected to be a major superpower in the coming century.

The New Age Movement in the West honors Hindu gurus and teachings. Most New Age followers believe in a higher Self, God as both Father and Mother, karma and rebirth, and spiritual practices such as Yoga, much like the Hindu religion.

Clearly examining Hinduism will geometrically expand your ideas of religion and spirituality. *The Complete Idiot's Guide to Hinduism, Second Edition*, is the best place to begin such an adventure in consciousness. Linda Johnsen—herself a practitioner in the tradition—does a superb job of making this very different religion relevant, understandable, and appealing to the modern mind. Her book is remarkably refreshing and dynamic, showing the living beauty and profundity of this great spiritual tradition. It makes an excellent, engaging textbook for teaching Hinduism.

As one who has traveled throughout the world, including all over India, teaching aspects of the Hindu tradition to both Hindus and Westerners, I can attest that Johnsen's book is probably the best introduction and overview of the Hindu religion available in English today. The book is written with humor, love, consciousness, and inspiration. It shows the Hindu religion alive and expressive today, so that we can easily access it in our own life-experience. I doubt that a single serious reader will come away without finding his view of Hinduism challenged, expanded, and transformed—and along with it his view of the entire universe, humanity, and all of history.

—Dr. David Frawley (Pandit Vamadeva Shastri)

Author, *Yoga and Ayurveda, Hinduism, the Eternal Tradition*; Director, American Institute of Vedic Studies

Introduction

Many of us in the West think of India as a poor and backward country. We forget that for at least 4,000 years the Hindus were recognized (and envied) as some of the richest, best-educated, most scientifically advanced, and most profoundly religious people on the planet. History shows that Hinduism has provided the spiritual foundation for one of the most successful and enduring cultures in the world.

The Sumerians dominated the Middle East in the third millennium B.C.E. At one time, they were believed to be the founders of civilization. Today we know they imported goods by the ton from equally civilized trading partners in India. They even adopted the system of weights and measures used by the Hindus. The Sumerians' most famous myth is the amazing tale of a flood that wiped out almost all life on Earth. This same story is found in India's earliest scriptures and may date as far back as 4000 B.C.E.

Manetho, the Egyptian priest who wrote a history of his country in the third century B.C.E., counts the immigration of a colony of Hindus to Egypt around 1400 B.C.E. as one of the most significant events in Egyptian history. Apollonius of Tyana, a traveler from Turkey who visited both India and Egypt during the time of Christ, noted the amazing similarities between the Egyptian desert ascetics and the Hindu mystics. He was convinced that Hindu immigrants centuries earlier had trained the Egyptians.

Alexander the Great, during his brief military foray into India, was fascinated by the Hindu holy men. His troops brought home incredible stories about the wisdom and incorruptibility of these Indian sages.

A major problem in the Roman Empire from the time of Caesar Augustus through Emperor Hadrian was Rome's massive trade imbalance with India. It brought Rome to the verge of an economic meltdown! Hindu philosophers were teaching in Rome by the third century C.E. at the latest. Some scholars believe they profoundly influenced Neoplatonic thinkers like Plotinus (who tried to get to India) and, through them, the Western and Kabbalistic mystical systems.

In medieval times, the Arabs praised the Hindus as the world's leading astronomers, mathematicians, and philosophers.

In the fifteenth century, Christopher Columbus risked his neck (and the lives of the rest of the sailors on the *Nina*, the *Pinta*, and the *Santa Maria*) trying to reach India. He mistakenly thought he'd gotten there, too, which is the reason many people call Native Americans "Indians" to this day. The monarchies of northern Europe were the backwater states of the time and desperately needed trade with the prosperous Hindus to jumpstart their sputtering economies.

And when the British conquered India in the seventeenth century, they hailed the vast wealth of the subcontinent as "the jewel in the crown" of the British Empire. The English made off with much of India's riches, leaving the country bankrupt when they finally granted it independence in 1947. For the most part, though, they missed its greatest treasure, the spiritual knowledge hoarded by brahmin priests in their carefully guarded scriptures and secretly practiced by yogis and yoginis in the caves and forests of Hindustan.

Today, we see a resurgence of interest in "the wisdom of the East." Many of us in the West flounder spiritually, confused by the inability of our religions to square with scientific reality and craving actual spiritual experience of which our lives seem so devoid. We're impressed by the ability of Eastern religions like Hinduism to meet science head on, agreeing in many respects about important topics, such as the age and size of the universe. Hindu yogis have gone into the laboratory and proven that at least some of their alleged superhuman powers—like the ability to control their brainwaves and heartbeat and to stop breathing for extended periods—are for real.

Hinduism is the one world religion that reaches out to embrace other faiths with respect, a welcome change from groups who expend enormous amounts of energy condemning the sincere beliefs of others. Hinduism holds no eternal damnation because Hindus believe absolutely no one is excluded from divine grace.

The Hindu tradition has held the culture of greater India together for thousands of years, through fair times and foul. Increasingly, we in the West are looking to Hinduism with the respect and appreciation it deserves, realizing we modern people have a great deal to learn from the oldest religion on Earth.

What We'll Be Looking At

The Complete Idiot's Guide to Hinduism, Second Edition, is divided into six parts so we can look at the many facets of Hinduism from several different perspectives.

Part 1, "The Eternal Religion," explains how Hindus look at time and space. Westerners who've been to India sometimes admit that it was like visiting another planet, the worldview there being so radically different from our own. The Hindus' cyclical view of time leads to a unique understanding of human history and of our role in the divine plan.

We'll look at the beginnings of a religion its adherents themselves believe is beginningless, pausing to explore how nineteenth-century European scholars actually created a history for India out of thin air—because the true story struck them as unbelievable!

In its multimillennial development, Hinduism has collected so many scriptures that no one person can become familiar with even a fraction of them in the course of a lifetime. We'll examine some of the most important ones, the ones Hindus admit were composed by human authors and the ones they say came from the heart of the universe itself!

Part 2, "What Hindus Believe," introduces you to the Hindus' amazingly liberal ideas about God and the value of other faiths.

It also takes you into the realm of karma and reincarnation, ideas that seem very New Age to us but are age-old to Hindus. For those who find that incarnating again and again gets tiresome after a while, there is a way out. You'll see what enlightenment really means and what it takes to be "liberated."

There are six major schools of thought about the divine reality in Hinduism. We'll look at how each major school of Hindu theology contributes its piece of the puzzle to the complete picture.

Part 3, "Who Hindus Worship," will, I hope, clear the air about some mistaken ideas Westerners often have about Hindu polytheism and "idol worship." I introduce you to some of India's more popular deities, the gods and goddesses who still inhabit the inner world of the Hindu people. You'll also see what an "avatar" actually is, another concept that's gotten somewhat garbled in its translation into Western New Age thought! I also introduce the main Hindu denominations as well as a few especially important breakaway sects.

Part 4, "How Hindus Live," details the caste system and the stages of life orthodox Hindus go through. We'll examine Indian ethics, take a look at some of Hinduism's many sacraments and holy days, and visit some of the temples and sacred sites of the tradition.

Part 5, "God's House Has Many Doors," examines the paths to God in Hinduism: the paths of action, of love, of the intellect, and of meditation. We'll also look at Tantra, perhaps the single most misunderstood aspect of Hinduism.

Part 6, "A Timeless Tradition," offers a look at the issues Hindus face today as they endeavor to reconcile a very ancient religion with a rapidly changing world.

I've also included three appendixes to help you get a handle on Hinduism. Appendix A is a glossary of commonly used Sanskrit terms. If you're interested in learning more about this ancient tradition, Appendix B offers a list of outstanding books for further reading, and Appendix C refers you to some organizations and websites you'll find useful in future explorations.

India is poised to surpass China as the most populated country on Earth. As it continues to pull itself up by the bootstraps economically, what Hindus believe and practice is becoming increasingly important for others to understand. Hopefully this book will help you gain a clearer concept of what Hinduism, "the eternal religion," is all about.

A Few Extra Points

Scattered throughout this book, you'll find a number of special messages to help speed you on your way.

The Hindu View

Factoid time! These boxes contain extra information I believe you'll find especially interesting.

Guidepost

Here I post suggestions to help prevent embarrassing mistakes when you interact with Hindus.

Sages Say

These boxes contain words from the wise, valuable quotes from holy texts and holy people—and a few regular folks, too—that I think you'll enjoy.

def•i•ni•tion

I promise to keep the foreign words you need to learn to a minimum, and I help you keep the few key Sanskrit terms we'll use straight by providing clear definitions in these boxes.

In each chapter, you'll also find a "Quick Quiz" to ensure that you remember some key points from the discussion. I'm hoping you'll find these quizzes more fun than the ones you took in school!

Acknowledgments

I'd like to thank the editors and staff at Alpha Books, who helped materialize this book, especially Mike Sanders, Michael Thomas, and Katherin Bidwell. Thanks also to Jessica Faust at BookEnds, who made the connections that made the book happen.

I want to acknowledge all my friends and teachers in the Hindu community who invited me into their profoundly wise tradition, but the list is way too long! My *pranams* to you all!

Thanks also to my husband, Johnathan Brown, who held my hand on all my journeys through India.

Trademarks

All terms mentioned in this book that are known to be or are suspected of being trademarks or service marks have been appropriately capitalized. Alpha Books and Penguin Group (USA) Inc. cannot attest to the accuracy of this information. Use of a term in this book should not be regarded as affecting the validity of any trademark or service mark.

Part 1

The Eternal Religion

Hinduism is so ancient its origins are lost in the mist of prehistory. Many sages are associated with it, but none claim to be its first prophet. Hindus believe their religion has existed forever, even before the universe came into being. They say the truths of their faith are inherent in the nature of reality itself—and that all men and women peering into the depths of their inner nature will rediscover these same truths for themselves.

The image too many outsiders have of the Hindu tradition is of superstitious villagers worshipping idols. However, as we get to know the Hindus better, we'll see that their understanding of who and what God is, is incredibly sophisticated. In fact, their view of the world and our place in it is so stunningly cosmic in scope that it can boggle our Western minds!

So let's enter the universe of Hinduism, an amazing world where inner and outer realities reflect each other like images in a mirror and the loving presence of the divine is as close as the stillness behind your thoughts.

Time for God

In This Chapter

♦ Hinduism: the vital statistics

♦ The Hindu worldview

♦ A religion that began before time

♦ What it's like being God

I've spent the past 30 years shuttling back and forth between two universes: India and the West. My friends from India live on the same planet I do, yet in some ways we're from different planets.

Here in the West we see things as either true or false, black or white, animate or inanimate—we're either logged on or we're logged off. But when I ask one of my Hindu friends a straightforward question and she shakes her head in that characteristic way that means both yes and no, my Western mind bows in defeat. For Hindus, life is multidimensional, and to nail things down to yea or nay is to miss the bigger picture.

For us in the West, the universe is a material object that evolved out of random combinations of atomic particles. For the Hindu, though, the universe is rooted not in matter but in consciousness. Nothing is random—there is life everywhere and meaning in everything. Divine intelligence is present wherever we look. The universe is held together by God's constant, loving attention.

The Hindu Universe

The universe of a traditional Hindu differs from the world of an average educated Westerner in several ways:

◆ Hindus believe all things, from trees and butterflies to inanimate objects like mountains and bridges, are in some sense living entities. Those great beings that are more powerful than us, like the ocean or the wind, are called gods.

◆ Time circles back around on itself in cycles large and small. Just as a year returns to its beginning on January 1st, everything in nature dies and starts afresh, its body ever changing, its spirit ever the same.

◆ Hindus have enormous respect for the lineages of spiritual masters who pass the wisdom of the ancient sages down from one generation to the next, like runners in a relay race. They keep Hinduism fresh—their living connection with spirit never lets it get stale.

◆ The reality of psychic phenomena, like telepathy and precognition, poo-pooed by scientists here in the West, is taken for granted in Hindu culture. These experiences are accepted as evidence that everyone in the universe is interconnected in a vast inner network of consciousness called *Mahat*, "the Great One."

Hindus believe the mind is the sixth sense, that the mind is able to perceive entities, objects, and fields of energy the other five senses don't register. So for them the living spirits in fire and flowers and ocean froth, as well as the souls of the dearly departed, are just as real as hammers and nails. We can sense their presence even if we don't actually see them.

The laws of physics are different for Hindus, whose world includes subtle dimensions we in the West can barely imagine. Unlike us, they haven't been taught that miracles can't really happen. To them the laws of consciousness, as understood by saints and yogis, allow miracles to happen routinely!

I'll tell you more about all this later, since understanding the subtler dimensions of life is an important

Sages Say

You must realize that it is Pure Consciousness which projects this universe like images in the mirror of its own unlimited awareness. Merge in that Supreme Consciousness and you will experience limitless bliss.

—Tripura Rahasya

part of Hindu spirituality. But first we need to define some terms and learn a little more about the conceptual cosmos Hindus inhabit.

Who's a Hindu?

A billion Hindus inhabit this planet; one out of every six people on Earth is Hindu. A Hindu is basically any person born into the indigenous religion of Greater India. By Greater India I mean the region where Hindu culture flourished in full force till the advent of Buddhism and Islam. This includes the country we call India now, as well as Afghanistan, Pakistan, Bangladesh, Nepal, Bhutan, Ladakh, Sri Lanka, and even parts of Tibet. Indonesia and Malaysia became predominantly Hindu around 1400 C.E.

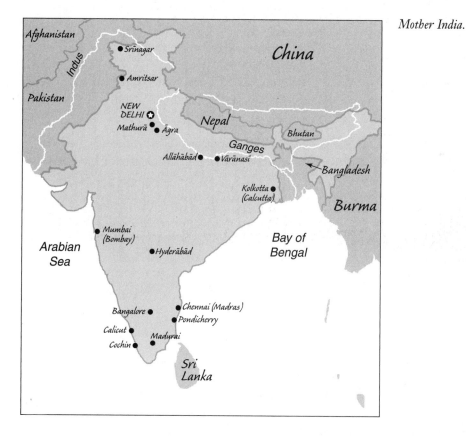

Mother India.

Today, Hinduism is still practiced by over 80 percent of the population of India. Nepal and Bali are largely Hindu, while Malaysia is home to over a million Hindus. Eleven million more live in Bangladesh.

In the past few decades, the population explosion in India has motivated millions of Hindus to emigrate to other countries like Great Britain, the United States, Canada, Reunion Island, Mauritius, and some parts of Africa. Well over a million Hindus live in South Africa, the country where Mahatma Gandhi first started his campaign for social justice.

The Hindu View

India's population of some one billion souls is made up of about 82 percent Hindus—that's over 800 million people! There are around 80 million Muslims in India, 14 million Sikhs, and 14 million Christians. Small pockets of Parsis (Zoroastrians), Jews, Jains, and Tibetan Buddhists also make their home in the Indian subcontinent.

Today, more than 60 million Hindus are living outside India. You'll find nearly two million of them in North America. Very rapidly, Hinduism is becoming less an exotic Eastern religion and more a familiar global presence.

Generally speaking, Hindus are born, not made. For the most part, Hindus are not interested in converting anyone else to their religion. "If all roads lead to Rome," one of my Hindu teachers told me, "all religions lead to God. Why should I insult your beliefs by saying God can't use your religion to call you to Him? Whatever your faith, God will still find a way to illuminate your life."

Technically, a Hindu is any person born into a Hindu family who accepts the Veda (the Hindu Bible) as the source of his tradition and who participates in the Hindu sacraments (see Chapter 17).

def•i•ni•tion

In India, **guru** means "teacher." It also specifically means your spiritual master, the man or woman guiding you to enlightenment.

A **swami** is an ordained Hindu monk.

In the last half of the twentieth century, as Western fascination with India increased, some outsiders asked to be initiated into the Hindu faith. Several of my friends, born Christians or Jews, have formally entered the fold of Hinduism. This ancient religion is gradually expanding its self-definition to accommodate foreigners, and today Hinduism includes some well-known *gurus* and *swamis* who were not born Hindu.

The word Hindu actually came from Persians who mispronounced *Sindhu* (Persians thought of Hindus as the people living to the east of the Sindhu River). Europeans picked up the term when they began setting up shop in India in the eighteenth century. Most Hindus are now so used to being called Hindu that they've started calling themselves that. The more traditional term for the native Indian spiritual tradition is *Sanatana Dharma*, "the eternal religion."

Beginningless Truth

You might think it takes a lot of chutzpah (if I may borrow a Jewish term) to claim one's religion is eternal. What Hindus mean when they say this is their tradition doesn't come from any one founding father or mother, from any single prophet towering over the bastion of hoary antiquity. In fact, the first few verses of the Veda—an incredibly old book, parts of which were composed over 5,000 years ago—acknowledge even earlier sages who lived long before!

Very old Hindu texts speak of a time when it became almost impossible to survive on Earth because of ice and snow. Some Hindu scholars believe this could be a reference to the last Ice Age. Archeologists have unearthed small goddess figurines in India dating from 10,000 years ago (about the time the Ice Age was ending). They're just like ones still being worshipped in Indian villages today. So even if we're not willing to grant that Hinduism is eternal, we still have to admit it got the jump on the other major religions.

But even more fundamental than the question of how Hinduism first got rolling (a very complicated and surprisingly interesting issue we explore in Chapter 2) is the fact that Hindus consider their tradition eternal because it's not based on the words of any one inspired man or woman. Instead, it's based on the eternal laws of nature.

The Hindu View

Between the first and eleventh centuries C.E., India produced 30 percent of the planet's Gross Domestic Product. From at least Sumerian times (2500 B.C.E.), Hindu culture was famous for its prosperity, comparative peacefulness, and spiritual science.

Guidepost

Don't automatically assume any person you meet from India is a Hindu. Most Indians are, but a substantial minority (about 10 percent) are Muslim.

Scientists of the Spirit

The Hindu sages were scientists of the spirit. In olden times before people had better things to do, like watch reality TV, these men and women conducted investigations into the nature of reality itself. They looked to the living universe as their teacher and guide. If there were spiritual laws we ought to be following, they should be apparent in the cycles of the stars, the flow of mountain streams, and the way the mind operates.

Natural law is called *Rita* in Sanskrit. There were a number of basic laws these early scientists observed:

♦ Pure awareness is always the same; everything else changes.

♦ Everything that dies is re-created in another form.

♦ Everything in the universe is directly or indirectly related to everything else.

♦ The consequences of an action always return to the person who performed it.

♦ The only lasting peace we experience comes when we rest our awareness in the lucid stillness hidden behind our thoughts.

Observations like these became the basis of Hindu beliefs about karma and reincarnation, ritual practice, and meditation.

The Hindu View

Sanskrit is the sacred language of Hinduism, much as Latin is the sacred language of Roman Catholicism. Like Latin, Sanskrit is a very old language that is no longer widely spoken, except by some orthodox priestly families. In South India, Tamil ranks alongside Sanskrit in importance as the language of religion.

Hindus believe that any truth worth setting up as a foundation of a religion has to be *akriti*—that is, it has to ultimately come from beyond space and time. It has to be true forever. In other words, billions of years from now, after this solar system has disintegrated and a whole new universe has taken shape, the things that were true in our world must be equally true in the cosmos to come.

Hindus believe that the messages of the sages preserved in the Veda are eternally true in just this manner. That's why they call Hinduism "the eternal religion." A trillion years from now in some other world system, inquiring minds will look to nature and rediscover the same truths Hindus believe today.

A Recyclable Universe

From the Hindu perspective, universes come and go.

Hindus experience time as cyclical, not progressing forward toward a final point as folks believe in Judaism, Christianity, and Islam. This concept is important because it leads to a completely different understanding of human history and of our role in the divine plan.

Hindus have been around for a long time, so it's not surprising that a cyclical model makes more sense to them. They have watched other civilizations, their erstwhile trading partners, rise and fall. Sumer was a great civilization in its heyday, but it's long gone now. Ancient Egypt rivaled India in the depth of its spiritual knowledge, but all that remains are some dusty old pyramids. The Greeks and Romans strutted around like peacocks once, but their empires crumbled, too. Not very long ago the British controlled much of the world; today, their empire is a fading memory. In India itself, great cities like Harrapa and Mohenjo Daro saw the light of day almost 5,000 years ago. Then they, too, disappeared into the darkness beneath the Earth.

Hindus believe time is circular because they're attuned to seasonal and agricultural cycles, as well as to the cycles of the planets and stars. But medieval Hindu texts also mention the cycles of mountains, growing incrementally over the millennia and then sinking back into the earth. (In fact, the Himalayas are getting higher and the Vindhya mountain range in central India is getting shorter. But you'd have to watch them carefully for a *very* long time to notice.)

The texts mention the changing course of rivers. They notice how lush and fertile lands like the grazing grounds of their ancient homeland slowly turned to sand, transforming into the Thar Desert in Rajasthan and the Sindh today. They describe cities, like ancient Dvaraka, disappearing into the sea, and whole branches of advanced technology that were lost long, long ago. Hindus have been kicking around a long time, and they've seen it all!

The Hindu View

For most of the last 2,000 years, the Judeo-Christian-Islamic traditions taught that our world started quite recently (around 4000 B.C.E.) and will come to a complete end when God stops the flow of time and establishes us in eternity. Hindus don't believe this. In 4000 B.C.E., their culture was already ancient.

It's not only empires that eventually bite the dust. Very old Hindu compendiums called the *Puranas* say that in the end (and here modern astrophysicists agree) the very atoms that form the universe will dissolve away. And then slowly, incredibly slowly, the universe will reform. In Hinduism, everything is recycled. Even the universe itself!

Hatching a World

In India, there are many different versions of the re-creation of our universe. This is Hinduism, where when you shake your head you mean both yes and no, so we're not going to ask which of the versions is most authoritative. Instead we're going to assume, as many Hindus do, that all the different stories refract some light of a reality far too vast to be reflected exclusively in just one tale.

Here is one version. Keep in mind that Brahma is the creator of our local world system; today we might call it our solar system. Vishnu is lord of our local universe; today, we might say that's our galaxy. (The modern name for the milky ocean Vishnu sleeps on is the Milky Way.) And the Goddess is the one in control of all the universes in all dimensions of being forever.

In a beginning (not in *the* beginning because there have been numberless previous beginnings), Vishnu is lying asleep on an ocean of milk. If you object that no self-respecting god would be caught napping, remember that even the Judeo-Christian God rested on the seventh day.

Vishnu's bed is an enormous cobra called Ananta, whose coils serve as his mattress and whose numerous hoods form a canopy over the slumbering deity. Vishnu's wife, the Goddess who never sleeps (a woman's work is never done!), sits lovingly massaging his feet.

Sages Say _____

Divine Being, like a sea, surges upward in a wave of creation, then subsides again into its own essence. Waves of universes rise incessantly, in infinite numbers, one after another.

—Yoga Vasishtha

In the course of Vishnu's dream, a lotus grows out of his navel, and lying there in the petals is a shiny golden egg. This egg will hatch into our solar system if everything proceeds according to plan.

Guiding the egg's development is Brahma. He's the mastermind behind our local universe, the intelligence who put our world together. He wants to shape a Sun and Moon and several planets, which shouldn't be too hard because debris from the previous solar system is still floating around in space.

Getting God Out of Bed

Finding people to inhabit this new world won't be hard either. Plenty of souls are left over from the last incarnation of the solar system, who didn't manage to find their way back to God before the world dissolved out from under them. They've been sound asleep in their subtle bodies for eons, just like Vishnu. Once a physical planet is in place, Brahma will toss these souls back into physical bodies, so they can complete their unfinished business from previous lives.

Brahma needs to resolve a number of problems before he can proceed, but he can't do it all himself. So he tries to wake up Vishnu since support from an even higher power would be incredibly helpful. But Vishnu is dead asleep.

At this point, Brahma turns to Vishnu's wife, the Goddess, and pleads, "You are the supreme, primeval power, the limitless store of energy that continues to exist even after the material worlds fade away. You remain active even when God, the primordial intelligence, passes into an unconscious state. He sleeps on the snake Ananta, whose name means infinite time, who floats in the milky ocean of primordial matter. Please remove the inertia from the Lord's awareness, so he can wake up!"

Having been asked so nicely, the Goddess lifts the veil of unconsciousness from the cosmic intelligence, her husband Vishnu. He leaps up, refreshed and invigorated, and he and Brahma set about clearing away the negative energies obstructing manifestation. Now Brahma can spend the next few days building our cosmos.

A Day in God's Life

Consider the vastness of the time scale Hindus are talking about here! Hinduism and the Judeo-Christian tradition agree that at the moment we're in the seventh day of creation. But according to the Hindu sages, a day for God is a bit longer than our human day of 24 hours.

Swami Veda Bharati, a mahamandaleshvara, or eminent religious leader who presides over an *ashram* in Rishikesh in northern India, taught me the following timetable. He's a devotee of the Divine Mother, as you'll probably be able to guess. (The Goddess is a major league player in Hinduism, you'll soon see.)

The Hindu View

Think you've got just one body? Hindus believe there's a subtle body made of energy that underlies our physical body. Treatments like homeopathy and acupuncture work on the energies in this nonmaterial body, according to both Hindu and Chinese medical systems.

def•i•ni•tion

An **ashram** is a house where a group of Hindus who have completely devoted themselves to spiritual life live together under the guidance of their guru.

Shiva is one of the main Hindu names for the Supreme Consciousness, the ultimate reality. Shiva is also one of the three main gods of Hinduism, the one who absorbs the universe back into himself at the end of each cycle of creation.

Swami Veda Bharati's timeframe starts with a day and a night in the life of our local creator god.

♦ One day and night in the life of Brahma is 8,640,000,000 human years.

♦ The lifetime of Brahma is 311,040,000,000,000 human years.

♦ One day and night in the life of Vishnu equals 37,324,800,000,000,000,000 human years.

♦ The life of Vishnu is 671,846,400,000,000,000,000,000 human years long.

♦ One day and night in the life of *Shiva* lasts 4,837,294,080,000,000,000,000,000,000 human years.

♦ Shiva's lifetime corresponds to 87,071,293,440,000,000,000,000,000,000,000 human years.

♦ One glance from the Mother of the Universe equals 87,071,293,440,000,000,000,000,000,000,000,000 human years.

It might surprise you that Hinduism speaks of gods dying. Not to worry—they're reborn again later like the rest of us! According to Swami Veda Bharati's tradition, at any one moment there are trillions upon trillions of Brahmas, Vishnus, and Shivas manifesting their universes within the endless expanse of the Divine Mother's awareness.

This, folks, is Hinduism's Big Picture.

Quick Quiz

1. India is …

   a. Mostly Hindu.

   b. Half Hindu, half Muslim.

   c. Home of the lost tribes of Israel.

2. The word Hindu comes from …

   a. A mispronunciation of the name of the river Sindhu.

   b. A misspelling of "Indian."

   c. The Sanskrit word for curry.

3. Sanatana Dharma is the name of …

   a. A famous Hispanic rock star.

   b. A character from a popular American sitcom.

   c. The Hindu religion.

4. For Hindus, time …

   a. Began about 6,000 years ago, when the world was created.

   b. Is without beginning or end.

   c. Starts with a hot cup of chai.

   Answers: 1 (a). 2 (a). 3 (c). 4 (b).

The Boy Who Lived Between Universes

Many of us in the Western world are so proud of what our scientists and technologists have achieved that we're tempted to laugh at the insights of other cultures, particularly if we don't understand them! Let's pause a minute to look a little more closely at one of the fables from Hinduism's supposedly primitive past.

Markandeya was not born in our world. He was actually born (according to this famous myth) in a previous world cycle, the last incarnation of our planet.

One day Markandeya noticed his parents were extremely upset. When he asked what was wrong, his father tearfully admitted that when Markandeya was born, the village astrologer predicted the boy would die on his sixteenth birthday.

Well, that very day was his sixteenth birthday. So now it was Markandeya who was upset! He ran to the nearby temple and threw his arms around the image of the god Shiva.

At that very moment the god of death entered the temple, ready to slip his noose around Markandeya's neck and drag him out of his body. But just as Death reached for the young boy, Shiva materialized in front of them both, and he didn't look happy. In fact, Shiva was furious that Death

Sages Say _____

At the end of the cosmic night, that Great Being who sleeps on the primeval ocean awakens. He finds a vast void where previously there had been a world filled with living beings. Then that most excellent soul begins to re-create the world.

—Linga Purana

would disturb a devotee who was worshipping him. Death was so terrified at Shiva's angry gaze that he ran away and never dared approach Markandeya again.

That was fine for the time being, but after a few billion years, a problem developed. The Sun eventually flickered out of existence; the Earth passed away; and Markandeya floated around in empty space for eons. Finally the Earth reshaped itself back into existence, and Markandeya was able to walk on terra firma once more. He reported what he'd experienced between worlds to anyone who asked.

What happens when the solar system dies, he explained, is that the Sun slowly turns red and expands to many times its present size. The surface of the Earth eventually becomes so hot no living thing can survive, and the planet becomes as bare as a turtle's back. Then the Sun explodes, emitting a burning wind that blasts the planet to ashes.

Rather startlingly, this extremely old Hindu myth describes the end of the world exactly as our own astrophysicists do. Carl Sagan, the well-known twentieth-century scientist from Cornell University, noted that the parallels between Hindu teachings and new scientific findings about the evolution of the universe were "an astonishing coincidence." Indeed!

Inner Vision

I'm not suggesting there really was a boy who survived the death of the last solar system. (Though, just as we have Elvis sightings here in America, Hindus from time to time do report catching a glimpse of Markandeya.) But the thought I'd like to leave with you is that for many millennia the Hindu sages have claimed that if we purify our minds with spiritual practices and open our hearts to learn from her, the Mother of the Universe begins to share her secrets with us.

In the West, we peer into space with powerful telescopes hoping to learn the origin of the universe. The Hindu approach is to couple astute observation of the world outside us with a self-disciplined inner journey. Peering into the depths of consciousness in our own minds, we connect with the consciousness that underlies the entire cosmos. Truths, which other cultures need radio telescopes to ferret out, simply present themselves to our concentrated inward attention.

To India's mystics, Brahma, Vishnu, and Shiva are not just characters in a story. They represent actual states of divine awareness that are available to devotees, provided the devotee is prepared to do the hard spiritual work necessary to access them.

In fact, in Hinduism the point of doing spiritual practices is to attain *jnana*, living knowledge of Divine Being. It's an ambitious agenda!

The Hindu View _____

Indian theologians called the Vaisheshikas developed the atomic theory long before Democritus, who's considered the founding father of atomism in the West. According to the ancient Greek historian Diogenes Laertius, Democritus sold everything he owned (he was filthy rich) to travel around the world. One of his stops was India. Could he have picked up the atomic theory there?

Cycles Within Cycles

God's agenda plays out across vast panoramas of space and time, or at least what seem like eons to us even if they're only an eyeblink to God.

Hindu theologians speak of yugas, great expanses of time through which the course of spiritual evolution runs. On our planet specifically, there are four great yugas, which roll by one after another within even larger repeating cycles:

- ◆ Krita Yuga: 1,728,000 years

- ◆ Treta Yuga: 1,296,000 years

- ◆ Dvapara Yuga: 864,000 years

- ◆ Kali Yuga: 432,000 years

The cycles are named after dice throws. Krita means you win. Treta means you don't win, but you do better than simply breaking even. Dvapara means you're barely still in the game. And Kali means you lose big time!

In the Krita era, people are pure-hearted, so everyone lives together in peace. When the Treta period rolls around, folks lose one fourth of their good qualities. By the time the Dvapara Yuga begins, we're only half as good as humans originally were. And in the Kali age, people are just plain bad. Only about a fourth of altruism and spiritual light is left in us; the rest is selfishness, hatred, and self-delusion.

def•i•ni•tion _____

Jnana means knowledge, specifically knowledge that you know in your soul, not just in your brain. It's related to the English words "gnosis" and "gnostic."

A **pandit** is a Hindu scholar.

The bad news is that the Kali Yuga began on February 18, 3102 B.C.E. That means we've got a *long* way left to go at our worst behavior! The good news is that there are cycles within cycles within the Kali Yuga, and in some of them things start looking up.

Dr. Rajmani Tigunait, a *pandit* from Allahabad, told me, "Don't be discouraged we're in the Kali Yuga. If you do your spiritual practices and purify your heart, it's as if you are living in the Golden Age. In your home it's still the Krita Yuga." In other words, you can live in the Garden of Eden if you prefer, but you have to plant it yourself.

Sages Say

He who experiences the whole of creation as his very own Self, who sees everything around him as the limbs of his own body, although he appears like an ordinary man to others, I consider him truly blessed. Strive to experience this sense of unity with all things. Feel yourself in the universe and the universe in you. I'm telling you again and again: There is no greater experience than perfect oneness.

—Jnaneshvari

The BIG Picture

Why did God create the universe? Hinduism offers several suggestions:

♦ He was lonely. He looked around and saw He was by Himself. He desired to become many. And whatever God wants, God gets. The moment that wish entered His mind, an infinite number of souls emerged from His limitless intelligence to keep Him company.

♦ She likes to play. The Goddess can't sit still for a moment. All the dramas in all the worlds are Her game or "Her sport" as Hindus like to say.

♦ The Divine Being is so brimming with bliss, He/She spills over. Shiva/Shakti (God and Goddess who are both two and one in Hinduism) spontaneously generate cosmos after cosmos. Creative energy simply pours out of the Divine. It's the nature of the Supreme One to create as it's the nature of light to shine.

In the Western religious traditions, God creates us out of nothing. In Hinduism, the Divine Being creates us out of himself/herself. This means we are literally one with the divine, one with everything else in the universe, and one with each other.

Hinduism is about finding our place in an immense universe. It shows us how to deal with suffering and where to find joy. It reveals that knowing our own inner Self is the key to entering the consciousness of God.

In the Western world, until very recently, there's been a tendency to consider Hindus "primitive" because they believe there is living spirit everywhere. What I hope you see now is that Hindu thought isn't primitive at all! In fact it's fantastically sophisticated. Hindus look at reality through a different lens than Westerners do, yet their understanding of who God is, how His laws operate, and where we stand in relation to Him, is just as insightful as the Western viewpoint.

The Least You Need to Know

- The Hindu tradition is extremely mystical.
- Hindus call their faith "the eternal religion."
- Time doesn't end; it spins on in cycles through eternity.
- Direct personal experience of God is the purpose of life.
- Everything arises out of consciousness.

Chapter 2

Hindus in History

In This Chapter

♦ An advanced civilization in ancient India

♦ Correcting ancient Hindu history

♦ North and South India get to know each other

♦ Implications for European prehistory

If you had been around in the third millennium B.C.E. (and if the Hindu theory of reincarnation is correct, you might have been!), India is where you would have wanted to be. The quality of life was higher there than practically anywhere else in the world. In fact, the towns of North India in 2600 B.C.E. were more comfortable and technologically advanced than most European cities till nearly the time of the Renaissance!

Religious life was vibrant in ancient India. Some of the oldest surviving spiritual texts come from this part of the world. They reveal a religion that was both boisterously earthy and transcendently mystical—not unlike Hinduism today.

But somewhere between then and now the history of these deeply religious people was erased. What happened?

The History That Vanished

Since the early 1920s, archeologists have been unearthing an astonishing ancient civilization in northwestern India, now called the Indus-Sarasvati culture. It was enormous, at least 700 miles from north to south and 800 miles from east to west. If you dropped the entire Egyptian civilization along with all of Sumer (two high cultures which were flourishing at about the same time) into that same geographical area, you would still have room for a few more civilizations!

Sages Say

The *dumbest* thing in this impermanent world is to delude yourself that *anything* in this impermanent world will last forever.

—Tirukural, a Tamil scripture, circa 130 B.C.E.

Here researchers have found the best-planned cities anywhere on the planet. The neatly arranged gridiron pattern of streets and houses revealed organizational and construction skills unparalleled in the ancient world and not always equaled in the world today. The cities were gargantuan for the time—3 miles in diameter, which isn't a bad size for a town even today.

The quality of the drainage system in these towns, which included brick-lined sewers complete with manholes, was not seen again until Roman engineers set up shop 2,000 years later.

The people who lived here had many of the trappings of civilization as we know it today (except maybe High Definition TV). They had nicely appointed bathrooms where they took bucket showers. They had one of the earliest written languages in the world. They had a sophisticated system of weights and measures that the business people of Mesopotamia liked so much they adopted it for their own use.

They had seaports, but those excavated docks are eerie to look at these days because the river tributaries they once serviced have evaporated away. The long-abandoned piers now overlook the bleak Thar Desert.

Messing with the Past

These findings astounded Western archeologists, but orthodox Hindus weren't surprised at all. Their ancient chronicles—enormous religious anthologies like the Puranas and the *Mahabharata* (see Chapter 5)—often mentioned glorious cities of the distant past. They even mentioned legendary architects like Asura Maya who could whip up spectacular buildings with beautiful gardens and lotus-laden pools and mirrored walls.

But Western scholars never took those ancient chronicles seriously. The surprising thing is that even as they dug up more and more evidence that the Hindus' own version of their history was more or less correct, Western scholars *still* couldn't believe it!

Here's why. In nineteenth-century European intellectual circles, Oxford University scholar Frederick Max Müller was held in only slightly less esteem than God. One day Müller announced that the Veda, India's most ancient spiritual classic and the very foundation of its faith, had been composed between 1200 to 1000 B.C.E. As far as Western scholars were concerned, God had spoken. This in spite of the fact that some of the positions of the stars mentioned in the Veda could only have occurred sometime between 3000 and 4000 B.C.E.!

The Hindu View

The majestic Sarasvati River ran through northwestern India until it dried up 4,000 years ago. To this day, the Indian name for the goddess of learning is Sarasvati. Could this be because the people of this region were once among the best educated in the world?

Tampering with Time

Where did Müller come up with a date as late as 1000 B.C.E. for a scripture Hindus themselves considered much older? It turns out that unlike Hindus, who believed the universe was billions of years old, as a Christian, Müller believed the world had been created in 4004 B.C.E. By adding the ages of the patriarchs listed in the Bible who lived between Adam and Noah, Müller could calculate the number of years that had passed since the creation and the Great Flood. This brought him to 2448 B.C.E.

Now, Müller was no fool. He knew it would take time for Noah's descendants to immigrate to India, repopulate the subcontinent, and create the hundreds of different languages and distinctive cultures flourishing there. This, he figured, must have taken at least 1,200 years, maybe as much as 1,400. Ergo, the earliest Hindu scripture could not have been written earlier than 1200 B.C.E. University textbooks uncritically repeated this date through the mid-1990s!

Guidepost

Scholarship on Indian chronology is currently in a state of uproar. In any book on Hindu history you look at—including this one—dates for events occurring before about 1000 C.E. should be approached with plenty of healthy skepticism.

To give the man credit, later in life Müller had second thoughts about his guesstimate, admitting, "Whatever may be the date of the Vedic hymns, whether 1500 or 15,000 B.C.E., they have their own unique place and stand by themselves in the literature of the world." But the damage was done. Everyone believed that when he'd given out the date of 1200 B.C.E., he had known what he was talking about!

Müller's mistake had catastrophic consequences for the study of Indian history. Saints, who, according to the Hindus, had lived before 3000 B.C.E., were downshifted to 1000 B.C.E. The Buddha, who, according to Northern Buddhist schools, lived closer to 1000 B.C.E., got shuffled to somewhere around 400 B.C.E. No less an authority than the sixteenth Dalai Lama has appealed to Western scholars to get together, clear their minds, and straighten out this mess once and for all!

"There is no more absorbing story than that of the discovery and interpretation of India by Western consciousness," noted the renowned Rumanian professor of religion, Mircea Eliade. You can say that again, Mircea!

Chronological Conundrums

But let's get back to our intrepid archeologists. They'd discovered a high civilization that flourished in northwestern India between 2900 and 1900 B.C.E. Since the Veda wasn't composed till maybe 1000 B.C.E. (according to Max Müller), these city dwellers couldn't have been Hindu. They supposedly lived nearly 2,000 years before the Veda, the sourcebook of Hinduism, even existed! Who were these amazingly advanced city people, and where did they go?

Enter the Aryan Invasion Theory. It was decided that the original inhabitants of India were the Dravidians, the people who fill up much of South India today. They speak a totally different language than most north Indians, and some of them have skin that's a little darker in color. Till 1000 B.C.E., they must have inhabited the whole of India, Müller's twentieth-century disciples decreed, and built the fabulous ancient cities in the north.

Then, the Western experts concluded, somewhere between 1500 and 1000 B.C.E., the primitive barbarians who composed the Veda invaded northern India, driving the helpless Dravidians into the southern part of the subcontinent where they flourish today. There were two difficulties with this popular theory:

1. Today's northern Hindus have absolutely no memory of having ever driven the Dravidians out of north India. None of their ancient histories mentions any such thing.

2. Today's Dravidians have absolutely no memory of ever having lived in North India. In fact, their ancient traditions suggest that their forebears came from the south, not from the north.

There are no Indus-Sarasvati-like artifacts or architecture in South India, while the archeological record in North India shows unbroken development. And early Hindu texts speak of North Indians emigrating *out* of India toward the west, not east *into* India as Western historians imagined.

The Aryan Non-Invaders

Minor problems like these did not discourage European and American scholars of the time. Thousands of pages of the Hindus' own historical records were simply dismissed as fiction.

These white scholars were certain a virile race of white warriors, much like themselves, had invaded India. The Veda mentioned a people called the *Aryans,* "the noble ones." They spoke a language related to German, Russian, Italian, and English. They worshipped deities who sounded quite a bit like some of the gods in the old European pagan tradition. Obviously then, they were proto-Europeans! And one of the symbols they frequently used in their religious art was a twisted cross called a swastika. These must have been the invaders who destroyed the ancient cities!

This theory of ancient white-skinned proto-Europeans sweeping across the eastern world establishing a vibrant new culture appealed to many Europeans in the 1930s—Adolph Hitler, for example. Hitler borrowed the term "Aryan" from the Veda and adopted the swastika, too, for his own campaign of world domination.

def•i•ni•tion

Arya is the Sanskrit word for noble or virtuous. An Aryan was a refined and civilized person who accepted the rites and ethical standards of the Veda.

The Hindu View

The swastika was originally a Hindu symbol representing happiness and good luck. You'll still find swastikas everywhere you travel in India. Hitler, however, flipped the swastika over on its side and adopted it as the symbol of the Nazis, which has given it a very different meaning in the West.

Back to the Beginning

Let's go back to the top and start over again. This time we'll tell the story as it appears in the Aryans' and Dravidians' own records—the Hindu version of Hindu history.

The descendants of the Vedic Aryans, that is, the people who live mostly in northern India today and speak languages related to Sanskrit, believe they have been right where they are today since time immemorial. The Veda, their ancient Bible, describes the landscape of northern India and Pakistan. It never mentions countryside like the area in the Caucasus near the Caspian Sea that Western scholars thought was the Aryans' original home.

The Veda portrays a temple-free religion where priests officiate at outdoor fire sacrifices. Yet it mentions the religious traditions of neighbors who worshipped images of deities inside temples, too. The indoor worshippers and the outdoor worshippers sometimes squabbled, but they were all indigenous people, natives of India.

The Veda talks about various groups who left India, but it never mentions invaders arriving from the outside. Instead it describes a rural culture where the wealthiest man was the one with the most cows! That's much the same as villages in India up until modern times. It talks about boats and seafaring, too, which would be pretty weird if the Western scholars were correct and these people were nomads from central Asia!

Meanwhile, the Dravidians of South India, who mostly speak languages related to Tamil rather than Sanskrit, have always been extremely proud of their own native traditions. They had gods like Vel, their warrior deity and loving protector. Their legends also place their distant ancestors where they still are today: smack dab in South India.

The Mountains Bowed Before Him

Enter Agastya. Agastya lived long ago—so long ago, in fact, that by the time the Veda was composed, he was already a legendary figure. Agastya decided it was time for his fellow Aryans in the north and those mysterious Dravidians in the south to get together. So he crossed the Vindhya mountain range in central India to meet the Tamil-speaking neighbors on the other side.

There's a famous story about this. The Vindhyas were extremely jealous of the Himalayas because the Himalayan mountains were much higher and kept getting even taller century by century. (Centuries seem like an eyeblink to a mountain.) So the

Vindhyas started working out, increasing their own size, too. This disturbed the balance of the Earth, and Agastya decided somebody had to do something about it.

So when he arrived at the Vindhyas on his journey south, Agastya said to them, "You're getting so tall these days, it will take weeks for a short guy like me to climb over you. Would you mind bowing down so I can cross you faster?"

Now, the Vindhyas were very spiritually advanced mountains. They knew how to treat a sage with respect! So they bowed low, and Agastya quickly scrambled over. If you visit central India today, you'll see the Vindhyas are not that imposing—they're more like hills, actually. That's because Agastya never went back north. The Vindhyas are still lying low so Agastya can cross easily when he returns home.

Agastya helped establish the Vedic religion in South India, teaching people there the outdoor fire sacrifice and the beautiful hymns of the Aryan people. Over thousands of years, the southerners were profoundly influenced by Aryan religion, while the Aryans were deeply affected by Dravidian religious concepts and practices as well. These two great peoples—along with a number of other minorities, like the Austro-Asiatic groups who also inhabit India—gradually mixed their philosophies and myths like different delicious spices combining to form a tasty curry. This eventually created the rich and complex religion we call Hinduism today.

Reclaiming the Hindu Heritage

From the Hindu perspective, by the time sophisticated cities like Mohenjo Daro and Harrapa came up in the middle of the third millennium B.C.E., the religion of the Veda was already incredibly ancient in India. In fact, the Veda refers to hundreds of towns existing even way back then.

This makes sense when you think about it. It's hard to believe well-designed towns like those the archeologists dug up in the northwest just shot up out of nowhere. You would think the Indians had had plenty of experience with urban planning before they created classy towns like Mohenjo Daro. In fact, the ancient Vedic word for "man" is *purusha*, which may originally have meant "town dweller."

def•i•ni•tion

Purusha means a man. It also can mean an individual soul or even God, the greatest soul of all.

Remember how I said in Chapter 1 that we're now in the Kali Yuga, the era where people are the least intelligent and least spiritually inclined of all? The Kali Yuga began in 3102 B.C.E., with things getting worse by the day since then. It's not hard for Hindus to believe that the more intelligent people of the past built incredible cities or even that they had advanced technologies like those described in the *Mahabharata* and *Ramayana*.

 The Hindu View _____

> An ancient Indian epic called the *Mahabharata* describes weapons of mass destruction unlike anything seen on Earth again till the twentieth century. So many people were killed in a massively destructive war in North India, says the text, that no one was left alive who knew how to build more of the weapons! The *Ramayana* even claims that in ancient times engineers knew how to build flying machines called *vimanas*.

Western scholars had trouble wrapping their minds around the Hindu version of history because folks in the West believe in linear time. History started from zero around 5,000 years ago in Mesopotamia. It's been progressing from there, continually improving until we reach the most intelligent, most enlightened creatures who ever lived on Earth: us.

Hindus believe time is cyclical. Yeah, there are some smart, technologically advanced people around today. But it's happened before. History repeats itself. Civilizations arise, work their way toward greatness, and eventually (and inevitably!) are destroyed. History hits the "restart" button, and the process begins again. But Western archeologists wanted to believe civilization began in the Middle East because that's where the Bible hints the Garden of Eden had been. That advanced cultures had existed elsewhere before Eden was first landscaped was not what they wanted to hear.

A River Runs Through It

The Veda often mentions a mighty river called the Sarasvati, where Aryan communities flourished and Vedic priests sang the hymns of glorious gods, like Indra, slayer of the terrifying dragon Vritra, and Agni, lord of fire who transports prayers to heaven on billows of smoke. Western scholars speculated that the Sarasvati might have been one of the rivers to the east of the Aral Sea in Soviet Central Asia. Perhaps, some even said, it had never existed at all! Hindus insist the river was real but disappeared over the course of time, just like the ancient cities.

In the early 1980s, proponents of the Aryan Invasion Theory got a terrible shock. Satellite photos of the Punjab, in far northwestern India and into Pakistan, revealed the dry bed of an enormous river, so huge it may have been 5 miles across at one site. While that river was in business, it was one of the largest and most spectacular in the entire world.

So there it was, the Sarasvati River the Veda had been talking about—just exactly where the Veda had always said it was. Geologists quickly established the river had dried up around 1900 B.C.E. Yet according to our friend Max Müller, the Veda hadn't been composed till, at the very least, 700 years after the river disappeared. What was this? Poets pretending they still lived alongside a river that vanished centuries before? How likely is that?

Sages Say _____

May Sarasvati, mother of abundance, guide and protect us, inspiring us to noble thoughts! Her unlimited waters rush past us in a constant flood, racing onward with a deafening roar!

—Rig Veda

This was the first nail in the coffin of the Western version of Hindu history. More nails quickly sealed the lid shut. After 60 years of searching, archeologists had not been able to find a shard of evidence that northern India's ancient urban culture had been destroyed by violent Aryan invaders. Instead it appeared the culture petered out as geographic and climatic conditions gradually changed.

Furthermore, the bulk of the physical evidence pointed to a continuity of culture, not the abrupt break you'd expect if nomadic warriors had replaced an older city-based culture. In fact, researchers unearthed numerous images of the god Shiva and various household goddesses, all still immensely popular in India today. It appears Shiva and Indra were both worshiped in ancient times much as they are today.

Meanwhile, evidence for a substantial Dravidian presence in the north never materialized. And most impressive of all, recent DNA evidence shows barely any difference between the Indians of the north or south. The proof is stacking up. Max Müller and his colleagues were seriously mistaken. The religion of the Vedas is thousands of years older than Western scholars originally thought, and no bloody invasion by merciless Aryan hordes ever occurred.

It turned out the Hindus had the history of their religion right all along!

Quick Quiz

1. The North Indian Aryans were ...

   a. Blond-haired, blue-eyed, white-skinned super-racists.

   b. Devotees of Vedic gods like Indra and Agni.

   c. A cricket team from New Delhi.

2. The Dravidians ...

   a. Were the original authors of the holy Veda.

   b. Claimed they were run out of North India by marauding blond-haired, blue-eyed Aryans.

   c. Were a South Indian culture speaking Tamil or languages related to it.

3. Max Müller was ...

   a. The greatest German composer who ever lived.

   b. Owner of the most successful brewery in Munich.

   c. An Oxford professor of immense stature.

4. The Sarasvati River ...

   a. Bowed before the Aryan sage Agastya.

   b. Dried up around 1900 B.C.E.

   c. Provides a scenic backdrop for many Bollywood blockbusters.

Answers: 1 (b). 2 (c). 3 (c). 4 (b).

A Crisis of Self-Identity

In the late twentieth century, news about new findings vindicating old truths sent shockwaves through the Indian intellectual community. Since the British took over India in the late eighteenth century, many of India's elite had been educated in European-style universities where they had been taught to sneer at their own ancient traditions.

The majority of Hindus clung to the old beliefs. But lots of prominent Indians had swallowed the Western retelling of their past, hook, line, and sinker. Important

Hindus like Jawaharlal Nehru, independent India's first Prime Minister, had undergone painful crises of self-identity, rejecting much of their Hindu heritage and identifying instead with their British conquerors. After all, the Europeans were men of science. India, they had been told, was a backwater of superstition that substituted myth for reality.

Now it turned out it was the European view of Hindu history that was the myth! Disillusioned Hindus quickly began to form influential new academic organizations designed to sort out the truth about their Vedic legacy. Their exciting work is reshaping the way educated Hindus think about themselves and their ancient sciences and religion.

Our Hindu Connections

If you're wondering why I've gone on for an entire chapter about the ancient history of the Hindus, there are two important reasons.

Reason #1. Most of the books you'll find written on Hinduism contain badly outdated material. Be advised that early Hindu history is being seriously reevaluated by Western academics at this very moment. A few still cling to the old theories, and some are struggling to adapt them so that they'll somehow stretch to fit the newly uncovered facts. But most researchers versed in the latest archeological findings acknowledge the crying need for an overhaul of modern Western ideas about ancient Hinduism.

Reason #2. The new archeological information, it turns out, has huge implications, not just for Hindus but also for the whole history of Western civilization.

"East is East and West is West/The twain shall never meet," wrote Rudyard Kipling, who spent a good chunk of his life in India. He was wrong, though. You've probably noticed the majority of Indian people are Caucasian, like the majority of people with ethnic European backgrounds. They have somewhat darker skin, but their skull shape and facial features are purely Caucasian. This is an important tip-off: many Indians are actually quite closely racially related to most Europeans.

That's not the only surprising connection Europeans have with Hindus. Most of the languages of North India, like Hindi, Bengali, Gujarati, Marathi, and Bihari, are related to the majority of European languages, such as English, French, German, Italian, Greek, and Spanish. In fact, when British scholars first started studying Sanskrit in the eighteenth century, they were dumbstruck at how closely it paralleled European languages.

Let's compare a few Sanskrit words and their English equivalents to see why the scholars were bowled over. There's *matri* and mother, *bratri* and brother, *duhitri* and daughter. There's *dvi* and two (think of duo and duet), *tri* and three. And there's *deva* and divine, *yoga* and yoke, *mrityu* and mortality. Clearly, the North Indians are related to most people of European descent, not only racially but also linguistically.

The Hindu View

Sir William Jones's discovery in 1786 of the link between Sanskrit and many European languages led to the founding of the science of comparative linguistics in the West. Linguistics, a fairly new science in the Western world, has been a major preoccupation of Indian pandits like Panini and Patanjali since at least the first millennium B.C.E.

Next consider this. Somewhere in the hoary past, the ancient Vedic sky god Dyaus Pitar (literally "Sky Father") seems to have hooked up with the Latins. How else can you explain why the ancient Romans called their sky god Jupiter (and pronounced his name "Dyu-piter")?

Sages Say

Imagine this universe as a tree. Its root reaches far above, its branches spread out below. The branches are these many worlds. The root is the Supreme Being from whom all these worlds receive life, who is their innermost being, who is the everlasting transcendent reality.

—Yajur Veda

The most important god in the Veda is Indra, the thunder god who wields a lightning bolt. He's an invincible warrior who sometimes has a bit too much to drink. His main job is to kill the serpent Vritra. Since I'm Norwegian, I immediately flash on Thor, the Norse thunder god who wields a lightning bolt, drinks too much, and has to be congratulated for his victory over a gigantic snake.

I'm also struck when I hear one of the oldest names for the gods used in the Veda is *asura* since I know the old Norse name for the ancient Scandinavian gods is *aesir*. The myths I learned as a child in Norway speak of a great world tree along whose roots and branches the entire cosmos is arranged. So do Vedic myths.

If you're beginning to suspect the North Indians are somehow culturally related to the Europeans, you hit the nail right on the head. Those of us of European descent for the most part threw out our old gods when Christianity came to town. The Hindus never got on board with Christianity; they're still worshipping *our* old gods.

The North Indian and European civilizations are definitely related. Their common culture is called Indo-European by academics today. Apparently, most Hindus of North India and most Europeans came from the same root stock. It's not "East is East and West is West." It's "East is West and West is East!"

The clearer we can get on early Hindu history, the nearer we'll be to solving the puzzle of our own past.

The Hindu Homeland

One of the most baffling mysteries of prehistory is where to find the original homeland of the Indo-European people. Where did our common ancestors come from?

Over the last two centuries an incredible number of locations for the Indo-European Garden of Eden have been offered, including the North Pole!

 The Hindu View _____

> B. G. Tilak, a close associate of Mahatma Gandhi, suggested the Indo-Europeans may have originated in the far north. He pointed out that ancient Hindu texts mention a divine land where one day and night is equal to an entire year for the rest of humanity. The only places on Earth where 24 hours literally equal a year are the North and South Poles. Antarctica is uninhabitable, so he concluded the ancient Indo-Europeans might have immigrated southward from latitudes near the North Pole.

Just about everywhere from Germany to Kazakhstan has been considered a viable homeland site, with Turkey being a current favorite. The issue remains highly controversial and evidence for new contenders continues to surface every few years.

Recently a number of authorities have raised an intriguing new possibility. The Veda is the oldest surviving record of the Indo-European people or at least the only one of any length. So wouldn't it be interesting to see if the Veda has anything to say on the topic, they wondered.

It turns out the Veda has plenty to offer in this connection. According to some Hindu researchers, tribes the Veda calls the Prithus, Parsus, Druhyus, and Alinas may be the forbears of the Parthians, Persians, Druids, and Hellenes (the Greeks). The Veda says all these groups lived in India at one time. It also explains that many communities migrated out of India. Might northern India be the original homeland of the Indo-Europeans peoples?

It will take years to sort out the complex historical issues involved here. For now, no one knows for sure. Still, it's intriguing to think there's a slim possibility that the fascination some Westerners feel for India may be an unconscious attraction toward their own original spiritual homeland.

The Least You Need to Know

- A highly advanced culture existed in northwestern India in antiquity.

- The Aryans of North India were the authors of the Veda.

- Aryan religion spread into South India and was, in turn, influenced by Dravidian (South Indian) spirituality.

- Errors by prominent European scholars have led to massive confusion about early Hindu history.

- The North Indians and many European cultures are culturally, racially, and linguistically related.

Chapter 3

The World Discovers Hinduism

In This Chapter

- ◆ Alexander the Great admits defeat
- ◆ Apollonius of Tyana and the Hindu "god-men"
- ◆ A Hindu Goddess protects Rome
- ◆ Chinese pilgrims in India
- ◆ A Muslim scholar checks out Hinduism

"India has created a mystique about itself. It is the sacred land for which everyone seeks." So wrote the German philosopher George W. Hegel.

Since time immemorial, India has been synonymous with spiritual knowledge. Merchants from as far west as Egypt traveled to India routinely to benefit from its fabulous wealth, but pilgrims also made the difficult journey to sit at the feet of Hinduism's fabled spiritual masters.

Until recently, most modern Western scholars were reluctant to believe there'd been much contact between India and the ancient West. Recent archeological finds, like the site of a Roman colony at Arikamedu in South

India, prove them wrong. We now know that Rome imported so many luxury items from India, it developed a massive trade deficit and nearly went bankrupt!

Heading East

Educated people in the ancient West had at least some basic knowledge of the Hindu tradition. After all, following Alexander the Great's foray into the part of Greater India we call Pakistan today, Greek soldiers who set down roots in India were sending news about Hindu culture to relatives back home in Europe.

But reports about India went back further than Alexander. If you look at a world map, you'll see the Middle East is just a hop, skip, and a jump from India. Take a boat down the Persian Gulf, then sail a few hundred miles along the coast of Persia, and you're in the Indus Valley. If you could get to Babylon, India was actually quite accessible.

Sages Say

For the man who has conquered it, the mind becomes his greatest friend. For the man who has failed to conquer it, the mind becomes his own worst enemy.

—Bhagavad Gita

We read in ancient Greek biographies that a number of important Greek intellectuals, such as Pythagoras, studied in Persia. Even if Pythagoras never visited India himself (as some students of history have speculated), he would have learned some of the doctrines of India's yogis and brahmins in Babylon, where he lived for 12 years.

The Hindu View

Ancient Hellenistic biographers mention a number of famous Greek philosophers who made the trip to India. One was Pyrrho, who returned to Greece and founded a philosophical tradition emphasizing inner tranquility and self-control, the chief virtues practiced by Hindu sages.

Conquering Alexander the Great

Some 2,300 years ago, a fellow by the name of Alexander conquered the world, or at least just about all the world he and his fellow Greeks had ever heard of. Egypt fell to the overachiever from Macedonia, then Persia. Alexander fans will tell you he conquered India, too, but that's a slight exaggeration. In 327 B.C.E., he made a few incursions into what we'd call Pakistan, but the Greco-Indian kingdom he left behind, called Bactria, was really more in Afghanistan than India.

As far as Alexander knew, India was the final frontier, the end of the world. To his shock, India turned out to be a heck of a lot bigger than he'd figured. This excited Alexander; there were still more worlds to conquer!

Sages Say

The wisdom of the ancients has been taught by the philosophers of Greece, but also by a people in Syria called the Jews, and by the brahmins in India.

—Megasthenes, Greek ambassador to India, writing around 300 B.C.E.

The Hindu View

In India, Alexander the Great excitedly announced he'd found the source of the Nile River. This says something about the ancient Greeks' grasp of world geography! In fact they'd arrived at the Indus, which Indians called "the blue river." Blue is pronounced *nila* in the native tongue, which is probably what confused Alexander.

Indian Surprises

Alexander made a number of other truly astonishing discoveries. The first was that there were Greek-speaking communities in India. (Imagine if Columbus had landed in America and found Native Americans speaking Spanish!)

It turns out these were descendants of Greek citizens from Turkey who had been repatriated to India by the Persians. Some of their ancestors had sold out to Persian rulers in the distant past. When Alexander found out what their forefathers had done, he had them all slaughtered. Maybe he wasn't that "great" after all!

Another surprise was that people this far from home were worshipping the familiar Greek gods. The Vedic deity Bhaga was practically the same as Bacchus back home, for example. Today we know the reason these deities seemed so familiar to Alexander was that, like his own gods and goddesses, they were part of the ancient Indo-European pantheon.

Alexander Meets His Match

It was in India that Alexander met the only men on Earth he couldn't conquer: the yogis. Greek historians traveling with the feisty commander brought back a record of the encounter.

In the woods, lying on a bed of leaves, Greek soldiers stumbled across a brahmin sage named Dandamis. Alexander was intensely curious about the fabled wisdom of the holy men of India. He sent Dandamis a message: "Alexander, Son of God and Lord of the Earth, invites you into his presence. If you come, you will be richly rewarded. If you don't, you will be killed."

Dandamis was not impressed. His answer to Alexander is worth quoting in full:

> There is only one king, the one who created light and life. He's the only king I obey, and he abhors war.

> How can this Alexander be the greatest king on Earth since he himself is subject to the king of death? And what can he offer me when my mother the Earth already supplies everything I need? I have no possessions I need to protect, so I sleep peacefully at night. Alexander may kill my body, but he can't touch my soul.

> Tell your king that at the time of death, each of us will be asked to account for our actions in this life. Ask him how he's going to explain the agony of those he has murdered and oppressed.

> Your king can tempt those who crave gold. He can terrify those who fear death. But we brahmins care for neither. Go tell Alexander he has nothing I want, and I will not come to him.

When Alexander heard Dandamis's answer, he admitted that he, the conqueror of the world, had been conquered by a naked old man.

The Hindu View

In his classic work, the Enneads, the Egyptian-born philosopher Plotinus (205–270 C.E.) explains how to shift your awareness from mental objects into a deeper state of meditative absorption focused on a reality transcending words and images. He explains the process exactly the same way Hindu yogis do! In his 30s Plotinus had set out for India to study with the Hindu sages but was forced to turn back in Persia.

A Visit from Apollonius

Apollonius of Tyana was a physician living in Turkey in the first century C.E. He'd heard stories about the sages of India and eagerly wanted to meet them.

Apollonius was a follower of Pythagoras, a remarkable Greek sage who had lived six centuries earlier. Apollonius knew that many Pythagorean teachings, such as the beliefs in reincarnation, vegetarianism, and keeping silent for years at a time as a form of spiritual discipline, were part and parcel of the Hindu tradition, too.

We know what happened next from a biography of Apollonius written by Philostratus, a leading literary light of his era, who carefully researched his subject. The book was commissioned by Julia Domna, the empress of Rome.

With a small group of devotees, Apollonius set out for India, pausing in Babylon to study with the Magi, Zoroastrian priests whose scriptures were historically related to the Veda. Then they headed on through Afghanistan, crossing the Khyber Pass into India.

Apollonius in the Ashram

With the help of a local maharaja, Apollonius was ushered into the ashram of a yogi named Iarchas. Before Apollonius could open his mouth, Iarchas greeted him by name, told him his parents' names as well, and mentioned a few salient details from Apollonius's life, including some incidents that had occurred during his long journey to India.

Needless to say, Apollonius was dumbfounded. (Many of us who have had run-ins with the yogis' amazing powers have felt the same way!) "How can you know all these things?" he demanded.

"We begin," Iarchas explained, "by knowing ourselves."

In the ensuing months, Iarchas taught Apollonius to know himself. He put him through intensive yogic training and introduced him to the Vedic method of performing *pujas* and other Hindu occult techniques. Apollonius learned to work with *mantras* and how to empower *yantras*. For centuries after his death, the yantras empowered by

def•i•ni•tion

Puja is a religious ritual, usually involving making offerings to an image of a deity.

A **mantra** is a sacred sound, word, or phrase that leads the mind to a higher state of consciousness.

A **yantra** is a geometric diagram into which divine energy is infused.

Apollonius were famous throughout the Western world for their alleged miraculous properties.

As he left for home, Apollonius told his guru, "I came to you by land, and you poured over me an ocean of knowledge which enables mortal men to rise to heaven. When I return to the West, I will tell the entire world of your wisdom. I will honor you till the last breath of my life."

Egypt and India

Apollonius traveled throughout the Roman Empire, from Spain to Rome to Africa, relating his experiences in India. "I have seen men dwelling on the Earth but not of the Earth. I saw them well-defended without fortifications. I saw they owned nothing, yet possessed all things."

Apollonius eventually also decided to visit Egypt, the other ancient civilization famous for its spiritual science. There he was bitterly disappointed. Apollonius found the religious institutions of Egypt in decay and the Egyptian priests' knowledge of their inner tradition in sad decline.

Apollonius made the long pilgrimage south along the Nile to see for himself the Ethiopian gymnosophists, the famous desert ascetics. He was stunned at how similar their spiritual beliefs and practices were to those of the ascetics he'd studied with in India. Inquiring into Egyptian history and legend, Apollonius concluded that the ancestors of these Ethiopians had emigrated from India in remote antiquity. Ancient authors frequently confused India and Ethiopia. This helps explain why.

Apollonius visited many Egyptian temples where he couldn't resist offering helpful suggestions to the staff on how to spiritually enliven their practices. "Who dares teach Egyptian priests their own religion?" one hierophant thundered.

"Anyone," Apollonius answered calmly, "who comes from India."

Guidepost

There are two kinds of wonder-working yogis in India: the genuine article and the clever fraud. Frauds use tricks not unlike those of stage magicians to delude you into thinking they can read your mind and know your past and future. The real McCoy may offer words of advice but will never demand money or try to manipulate you.

A Tribute to India's Sages

Apollonius was on the road much of his life, traveling virtually the whole of the civilized Western world as well as to Egypt and Persia. Yet he insisted that he never found such great wisdom anywhere else as that he experienced in India. He went so far as to claim that many of the mystery schools of the West had originated in India in the distant past. He called the yogis "god-men" both because of their miraculous powers and because of their profound spirituality and extraordinary compassion.

Apollonius wrote a four-volume book about the teachings of the Hindu spiritual masters, which unfortunately has been lost. But we know that for the first several centuries of the Common Era, Apollonius of Tyana was one of the most celebrated and respected spiritual teachers of the Western world. During his lifetime, the Roman emperors Nerva and Titus counted themselves among his devotees.

Emperor Severus Alexander, who reigned from 222 to 235, considered Apollonius one of the greatest men in world history. And in 271, when Emperor Lucius Aurelian set out with an army to destroy the city of Tyana, Apollonius appeared to him in a vision and commanded him to show mercy. Shaken by this vision, Aurelian instantly stopped the attack.

A Hindu Goddess in Rome

Another surprising connection exists between the Hindu tradition and ancient Rome. When the Romans were fighting the Carthaginian Empire for control of the Mediterranean (and in the beginning, pretty much losing), they appealed for help from an oracle. It advised them to seek the aid of Magna Mater, a ferocious goddess who had been worshipped in Turkey since at least the eighth century B.C.E. So in 204 B.C.E., a Roman delegation was sent to Phrygia in Asia Minor to beg, borrow, or steal a sacred image of the goddess. After a considerable amount of wheeling and dealing, they finally brought the image back to Rome.

Now, Magna Mater knew the Romans didn't have much confidence in her abilities yet, so just before the boat carrying her image was about to enter the city, she

Sages Say

We bow to the Goddess Durga, Who illumines the mind immersed in meditation, Who bestows the results of our actions, and Who removes all our difficulties. We bow to the Supreme Goddess who clears the mind of thought so the brilliant light of pure spirit can shine through.

—Sri Devyatharvashirsham

grounded it in the Tiber River. It was completely stuck—it absolutely wouldn't budge. It wasn't a good omen that the Goddess of Victory refused to enter Rome!

A priestess of the goddess, whose name was Claudia, was summoned to the scene. Tying her belt around the ship's prow, Claudia respectfully requested Magna Mater to enter Rome. The boat instantly lurched forward.

Shortly afterward, the Romans finally got the better of Hannibal and gleefully sacked the city of Carthage. Until Rome's conversion to Christianity, Magna Mater remained the presiding deity of Rome, divine protectress of the cradle of Western civilization.

The Great Mother

But who was Magna Mater? Her religion at one time extended all the way from Turkey to India. Three hundred feet up the north face of Mount Sipylus in Turkey travelers today can still find an ancient 30-foot-high image of the goddess carved into solid rock. But in India, portraits of this same goddess riding her lion into battle are present everywhere. You'll find posters of her hanging in people's living rooms. You'll even see her painted on truck boxes and lunch boxes.

Magna Mater, her Latin name, means "Great Mother," which is surprisingly reminiscent of her age-old titles in India: Sri Mata (Great Mother) and Maha Devi (Great Goddess). In ancient Turkey, she was also called Truqas, which some scholars believe is related to her Indian name, Durga.

In ancient Turkey, a small number of her more zealous male devotees would castrate themselves in her honor, a practice which shocked the Romans—who didn't shock easily. Amazingly this unique way of propitiating the Great Mother survived in some areas of India until quite recently (see Chapter 12).

Hindu Gods Abroad

The worship of Magna Mater in Turkey leads to an important point. For the most part, we think of Hinduism as being confined to India. However, the further we go back in time, the fuzzier the borders of Hindu culture become. That's because the North Indians, as I explained in Chapter 2, are related to many of the European peoples. When you understand this, it becomes less surprising that a goddess we unmistakably recognize as Hindu today was being worshipped in Turkey in the first millennium B.C.E.

In fact, a thousand years earlier, the Mitanni people of Turkey are known to have pro-pitiated Indra, Mitra, Varuna, and the Ashvins—gods straight out of the Veda. Mitra, whose worship was already ancient in India in 3000 B.C.E., reincarnated as Mithras, one of the Persians' most important deities, and eventually found work as the patron deity of the Roman army!

Chinese Pilgrims Check It Out

Two other famous pilgrims to India whose travel accounts have survived to the present day were Chinese Buddhists. Faxian passed through India in the fourth century C.E., and Xuanzang made the 10,000-mile round trip journey three centuries later, follow-ing along the Silk Road trade route up through Kashmir and then down into north central India where Buddha had lived and taught.

Faxian marveled at the peace, prosperity, and high culture of the Hindus, though his primary focus was on the Buddhist sites he had come to see. Having grown up in China, war-torn through much of its history, Faxian was deeply impressed by a land whose leaders were more concerned with promoting commerce and religion than with slaughtering substantial portions of the population.

Faxian noted that it was possible to travel from one end of India to the other without fear of crime and even without a passport! The culture was safe, stable, and deeply spiritual. By the time Xuanzang showed up, however, the effects of the Kali Yuga were setting in more firmly. (Remember the Kali era from Chapter 1, in which human behavior degenerates to its worst possible point?) He was robbed twice and almost murdered on another occasion!

Xuanzang spent several extended periods studying at Nalanda Buddhist University in Bihar. Buddhism was in serious decline in India by the mid-600s, but Xuanzang was still able to study Sanskrit, grammar, and logic as well as weighty Buddhist philo-sophical tomes.

About 3,000 Buddhist monks and 150 faculty lived at the university, but non-Buddhist students were welcome, too. Hindu fields of study were included in the curriculum. One could learn the Vedas

Guidepost

Don't mix up Hinduism and Buddhism! You should be aware that just as Christianity broke away from Judaism to become a completely distinct faith, the Buddhists broke off from the Hindu tradition. Buddhists do not accept the Hindu Veda as divine revelation and claim not to believe in an individual soul—though they do believe in reincarnation.

there or study Vedic mathematics and astronomy as well as the Hindu medical arts and Indian literature.

Ironically, the concentration of Buddhist talent at large centers like Nalanda was a major contributing reason to the fall of Buddhism in India. Hindu students usually studied in small groups in the homes of their teachers, while Buddhist students congregated at large centers like Nalanda. Buddhist practices, too, were generally carried out at the monasteries. Hindus performed their spiritual practices in their homes or in the woods or mountains.

When the Muslims came to town around 1000 C.E., they simply burned down the Buddhist university-monasteries and killed all the monks. Poof!—Buddhism was gone. The only way the Muslims could have wiped out Hinduism was to burn down every Hindu home in the country. Not even the most fanatical Muslim invader was capable of that!

Al Biruni Takes Notes

Al Biruni was born in Khwarizm (today's Khiva in Uzbekistan) in 973 C.E. He was a brilliant scholar who published books on optics, mineralogy, chemistry, mechanics, astronomy, mathematics, and the calendars and dating systems of many different cultures.

The Muslim despot Abu-Said Mahmud raided Khwarizm in 1017. Al Biruni was taken to India as one of Mahmud's reluctant human prizes and lived there for 13 years.

Al Biruni despised Mahmud, who he complained wrecked northern India economically as well as killing Hindus "like specks of dust scattered every which way." The scholar found a good use for his time, however, in purchasing all the Sanskrit manuscripts he could find and consulting endlessly with Indian pandits about Hindu science and spirituality. The result was *India*, Al Biruni's monumental study of Hindu culture and spirituality.

Notes on the Hindu God

Al Biruni was a good Muslim and was by no means always sympathetic to Hindu ideas or culture. He thought the Hindus' claim that the universe was billions of years old was ludicrous and mocked their tendency to think in terms of incredibly long cosmic cycles. But he made a sincere effort to report Hindu beliefs objectively, so that Muslims interested in India could clearly understand the Hindu perspective.

In *India*, Al Biruni described the Hindu view of God:

> There is one God only who is without beginning or end. He cannot be reached by thought but is sublime beyond our ability to conceive. He is infinitely vast, but not in the spatial sense since he exists outside of time and space.
>
> How can we worship this one whom we cannot perceive? He lies beyond the grasp of the physical senses, but the soul feels his presence and the mind understands his divine qualities.
>
> Meditating on him one-pointedly is true worship. When meditation is practiced for a long time without interruption, one attains the highest state of blissfulness.

 The Hindu View _____

No image is more closely identified with India than the Taj Mahal. Ironically this is not a Hindu temple but a Persian mausoleum built by the Muslim emperor Shah Jahan for his late wife in 1648. Shah Jahan's fanatical son Aurangzeb was notorious for persecuting Hindus and destroyed tens of thousands of sacred Hindu sites. Not surprisingly, the beauty of the Taj Mahal is bittersweet for many Hindus.

Notes on Reincarnation

Al Biruni's description of the Hindu view of reincarnation is particularly interesting:

> Until it reaches the highest state of consciousness, the soul is not able to experience all things at once, as if there were no space or time. Therefore it has to experience the universe piecemeal, one thing at a time, until it has been through all possible experiences. An awfully lot of experiences are possible, so this process takes a very long time.
>
> So immortal souls range through the universe in mortal bodies, which have good or bad experiences depending on whether their behavior has been virtuous or evil. The purpose of experiencing heavenly states in the time between physical incarnations is so that the soul learns what is truly good and wants to become as good as possible. The purpose of experiencing hellish states in the time between lives is so that the soul learns what evil is and determines to avoid it all together.
>
> The process of reincarnation begins at very low levels of consciousness, like minerals, plants, or animals, and slowly winds its way upward toward very elevated states of awareness.

The process ends when the soul no longer desires to explore new worlds but gains insight into the sublime nature of its own being and rests content in itself. At that point the soul turns away from matter, and its links with physical existence are broken. It returns to its true home, carrying with it the knowledge it has gained during its many journeys.

Having closely studied all their systems, Al Biruni noted that the Greek, Indian, and Sufi mystics taught the very same thing.

Quick Quiz

1. Alexander the Great ...

    a. Was deeply impressed by the sages of India.

    b. Conquered the entire Indian subcontinent.

    c. Shaved his head, converted to Hinduism, and spent the last years of his life chanting "Hare Krishna."

2. Apollonius of Tyana ...

    a. Was the god of the Sun in ancient Greece.

    b. Moved to New Delhi where he made a living franchising Tandori fast food outlets.

    c. Concluded that the Indian and Egyptian mystical traditions were related.

3. Faxian and Xuanzang ...

    a. Were legendary Taoist martial arts masters.

    b. Were two Chinese Buddhist pilgrims who visited India.

    c. Were star-crossed lovers torn apart by their feuding families.

4. Al Biruni ...

    a. Was a brilliant Muslim scholar living in India around the year 1000.

    b. Is a type of Arabic board game related to chess.

    c. Are the first two letters in the Arabic alphabet.

Answers: 1 (a). 2 (c). 3 (b). 4 (a).

Transcendentalists Get the Gita

European powers gained control of some parts of India in the late eighteenth century. Like zealous Muslims before them, Christian missionaries were determined to convert all India to their own faith. In their minds, replacing Hinduism with the Judeo-Christian tradition was the greatest possible blessing they could bestow on India's heathens. But some open-minded and sensitive Western artists and intellectuals had a very different response.

Emerson Encounters the Bhagavad Gita

Ralph Waldo Emerson, a nineteenth-century Unitarian minister who lectured on theology at Harvard University, was becoming increasingly disillusioned with aspects of Christian teaching that just didn't make sense to his active and inquiring intellect. When he first began reading newly translated Indian scriptures like the Bhagavad Gita, the Hindu tradition hit him with the force of revelation. He wrote:

> I owed a magnificent day to the Bhagavad Gita. It was the first of books, it was as if an empire spake to us, nothing small or unworthy, but large, serene, consistent, the voice of an old intelligence which in another age and climate had pondered and thus disposed of the same questions that exercise us.

In part due to the mind-expanding influence of mystical Hinduism, Emerson went on to found the Transcendentalist movement in America. The Transcendentalists turned from unquestioning faith in the religious doctrines of their own culture to a more open and honest inquiry into direct spiritual experience.

Sages Say _____

Standing on the bare ground, my head bathed by the blithe air, and uplifted into infinite space, all mean egotism vanishes. I become a transparent eye-ball; I am nothing; I see all; the currents of the Universal Being circulate through me; I am part or particle of God.

—Ralph Waldo Emerson

Thoreau Joins the Club

Emerson excitedly introduced other Americans to Hinduism, perhaps most notably his young protégé, Henry David Thoreau. Thoreau was not busy earning a living or raising a family like Emerson. Instead he was living in the woods outside Concord, composing some of the greatest classics of American literature, such as *Walden*, and reading the Bhagavad Gita.

"What extracts from the Veda I have read fall on me like the light of a higher and purer luminary, which describes a loftier course through a purer stratum," Thoreau wrote enthusiastically. "In the morning I bathe my intellect in the stupendous and cosmogonal philosophy of the Bhagavad Gita, since whose composition, years of the gods have elapsed and in comparison with which our modern world and its literature seem puny and trivial."

If Hinduism influenced Thoreau, he certainly returned the favor! Thoreau's great essay, "On Civil Disobedience," had a profound effect on a Hindu born a century later. Mahatma Gandhi acknowledged Thoreau as a major inspiration for the movement he founded calling for nonviolent resistance to British rule in India.

The Least You Need to Know

- Alexander the Great's encounter with a yogi became legendary.

- Apollonius of Tyana brought back from India fabulous stories of the Hindu sages' wisdom and supernatural abilities.

- Chinese pilgrims visited India to observe Buddhism and Hinduism first-hand.

- The Muslim scholar Al Biruni wrote extensively on Hindu beliefs.

- Hindu wisdom greatly inspired the American Transcendentalists.

Chapter 4

Matrix of the Hindu Tradition

In This Chapter

- ◆ The Bible of Hinduism
- ◆ Enlightened sages of India
- ◆ Offering prayers into a fire
- ◆ Gods as interlinking divine forces
- ◆ The quintessence of Hindu thought

Hinduism is a living lineage of enlightenment. It is very much an oral tradition, passed on from guru to disciple. The Veda, the Bible of Hinduism, was transmitted by word of mouth for thousands of years before finally being committed to writing.

But once the Hindus did start writing down their holy scriptures, well, they never stopped! All the sacred texts of the other great world religions put together would form scarcely a chapter or two in the immensity of Hindu sacred literature.

Veda: The Hindu Bible

The Veda, the massive holy book of Hinduism, has existed from before the beginning of time. Brahma, the creator god, carefully preserved it during the dissolution of the last universe and then gave it to humanity once again when the world was recreated.

Hindus do not believe the Veda was written by a group of authors. Rather, the great sages of antiquity "heard" the verses of the Veda in deep states of meditation (today we might say they "channeled" them) and passed them along to other brahmins, the priests who have been custodians of the Veda from time immemorial.

Other authorities, such as the great yogi Patanjali, had a slightly different perspective. Patanjali said it was not the words of the Veda that were eternal but the wisdom contained in them.

Either way, because the Veda was so holy, it was imperative that it be preserved exactly as it was first spoken by the original sages. Therefore, to this day brahmin priests memorize the Veda backward and forward, then backward and forward again skipping every other word, and even backward and forward in other combinations as well.

They also used other memorization techniques, such as chanting the Veda to particular rhythms and bopping their hands up and down according to prescribed rules as the inflection of the words changed. Brahmins from different villages would meet regularly to check each others' mastery of the text. These methods helped ensure that when we hear the verses being chanted today, they are still pronounced exactly as they were thousands of years ago, with not one word or even one syllable lost due to the passage of time. The Veda is a time machine in which the insights of India's great ancient masters have been transmitted to us today.

What's in the Veda?

The Veda is actually four different books, which is why you'll often hear it called "the Vedas," plural. They are in a language called Vedic, an archaic form of Sanskrit.

Though the Vedic hymns had been known for a long, long time, the great sage Vyasa finally compiled them into one large oral text and further organized them into the four books. Traditionally it's said he worked over 5,100 years ago, concerned that otherwise this wisdom might be lost during the upcoming Kali Yuga, the age of spiritual darkness.

The most important of these four texts is the Rig Veda, a collection of 1,017 hymns to a wide assortment of gods, arranged in 10 sections. The Sama Veda is mostly a selection of hymns taken straight from the Rig Veda. The big difference is that the

Sama Veda is specially notated with melodies so that rather than just chanting these hymns, one can sing them. Want to hear what the favorite tunes of 5,000 years ago sounded like? Listen to the Sama Veda!

The Hindu View _____

Vyasa, who compiled the four Vedas into their current format, is also credited with writing the *Mahabharata*, a book four times the length of the Christian Bible, and the 18 Puranas, many of which are over 400 pages long. Cooler heads believe that although there probably was an original Vyasa involved in collecting the hymns in the Vedas, his name was later applied to other men and women who authored or edited voluminous sacred texts.

The Yajur Veda hymns, on the other hand, are used specifically for certain types of sacrifices, not just for singing or chanting. The Atharva Veda, in some ways the most practical of all the Vedas, contains hymns for a variety of useful purposes including attracting lovers, subduing enemies, regulating the weather, and curing diseases, such as urinary tract infections!

Vedic Appendixes

Three very special compendiums of texts are considered part of the Veda but consist of discussions and explanatory material rather than hymns.

The Brahmanas are a huge mass of writings that explain how to perform the Vedic rituals. They throw in some great myths, which help make these detailed instructions livelier to read. The Aranyakas and Upanishads are philosophy texts that discuss the inner significance of the Vedic rites. (The Upanishads are so important I've dealt with them in a separate section, "Upanishads: Liberating Literature," later in this chapter.)

Who Were the Vedic Sages?

The sages who composed the Vedas, capturing eternal truths and shaping them into beautiful hymns, are called *rishis*. A rishi is someone who sees the divine reality for himself or herself. These sages weren't content to rely on the testimony of others but gained direct personal experience of divinity.

Hinduism acknowledges that seers come in a wide spectrum of types. There are advanced

def•i•ni•tion _____

Rishi means seer. The Vedic seers were saints and sages of the highest caliber.

seers who see everything and beginning-level seers, great souls for sure, but who have only just begun to glimpse the full majesty of the Supreme Reality. V. Madhusudan Reddy, a disciple of the twentieth-century sage Sri Aurobindo, outlines them in this way, based on ancient traditions:

- **Deva rishis** means god-like seers. The level of consciousness of these sages is beyond human imagination. Their awareness extends to all worlds and through-out the past and the future. These great beings live in a much higher plane of reality than ours, but when they will to do so, they can enter our world. To us they're practically like gods. The sage Narada is an example. During various crises in India's history he would materialize to advise just the right people at just the right place in order to tweak the course of events back toward the underlying divine plan.

- **Brahma rishis** means god-realized seers. These are fully enlightened men and women who exist here on Earth in physical bodies. They could move into higher worlds if they wanted to, but remain here to serve humanity. Babaji, the eighteenth-century Kriya Yoga master who initiated the famous Bengali saint Lahiri Mahasaya, belonged in this category. So did Bengali Baba, the twentieth-century adept who was known for transferring his consciousness from one body to another and even raising the dead!

- **Raja rishis** are "royal seers"—those who have gained mastery in both the physi-cal and the spiritual worlds. The legendary King Janaka, who successfully gov-erned the prosperous and cultured kingdom of Videha while remaining in a continuous state of divine awareness, is a famous example.

- **Maha rishis** are "great seers" who may not be fully enlightened like the Brahma rishis but have a deep and authentic understanding of the divine and work tire-lessly to help raise humanity to higher levels of consciousness. Mahatma Gandhi belonged to this group.

- **Parama rishis** are "advanced adepts" who are well along the road to enlighten-ment but have not yet completely purified their minds. The seer Daksha is a case in point. He was such a great saint that the Divine Mother agreed to be born as his daughter. But while he sincerely honored the god of his own tradition, he held the god of another tradition in contempt. This wound up completely under-mining his spiritual life.

- **Shruta rishis** means "learned seers"—those souls who have grasped the truths at the core of their spiritual tradition and are now working hard to translate that knowledge into living experience.

 ◆ **Kanda rishis** are "striving seers"—the beginners on the path who don't have much technical knowledge about spirituality yet feel a complete commitment to spiritual life and a burning desire for spiritual truth. They make their best effort to live ethically, discipline themselves, and raise their level of awareness.

The men and women who "channeled" the Vedic hymns thousands of years ago were only able to do so because of their advanced stage of spiritual development. Hindus universally hail them as Brahma rishis, seers of the highest order possible for mortal beings.

Who Reads the Veda?

Not everyone benefited from the Veda. Because the priests considered these hymns so holy, they were very careful about who was allowed access to them. They permitted only members of the three top classes of Indian society to hear the four Vedas and participate in Vedic sacrifices. Over the centuries, women's access to the Vedas, even if they were high class, became increasingly limited, which is pretty ironic since women composed some of the Vedic hymns!

Today, the four Vedas have been translated into many different languages, and just about anyone who wants to read them, can. However, reading them and understanding them are two different projects. Vedic knowledge remains an oral, initiatory tradition. Without a guru to lead you through the complex symbolism and hidden mystical meaning, many of the hymns don't make a lot of sense. Fortunately for me, my guru showed me how, using the keys given in the Brahmanas. I can actually see how brilliantly the rishis crafted the hymns to reveal their spiritual and astronomical science to students who were properly initiated, while concealing it from everyone else.

The Vedas are so important in the Hindu tradition, even after 5,000+ years, that the word "Vedic" is often used as a synonym for anything Hindu, as in "Vedic literature" or "Vedic science."

How Is the Veda Used?

If you required help from a specific god or goddess or wanted to express your gratitude to a particular deity, you could go to a Vedic priest who would perform a fire ritual for you, chanting the appropriate sacred hymns. Some of the earliest fire priests were called angirasas, the specialists who mediated between gods and humans, relaying messages transdimensionally. (Over the millennia, the word *angirasa* evolved into our English word angel!)

In olden times, the fire rituals sometimes involved blood sacrifices. Animals like goats were commonly sacrificed; on rarer occasions other creatures, such as a horse, might be offered.

Guidepost

Today many of us are shocked and disgusted to hear people in ancient cultures sacrificed animals. We forget the animals were killed humanely, their spirits blessed with holy mantras, and their flesh eaten as a source of protein. Was this worse than what goes on in our modern-day slaughterhouses? These days, however, animal sacrifice has been largely abandoned in India, and many Hindus are vegetarian.

Most Hindus abandoned animal sacrifice centuries ago. Today, priests offer objects such as flowers, grains, clarified butter, fragrant-smelling wood, and herbs into the sacred fire. The Vedic fire rituals are no longer practiced as widely as they used to be, but at certain major life events, like marriage, brahmin priests are called in, the ritual fire is lit, and once again the ancient mantras are chanted exactly as they have been at Hindu weddings for thousands of years.

Incidentally, I've attended numerous Vedic rituals and seen their effects for myself. It's not unusual following one of these ceremonies for fantastically unlikely results to occur. The individual asking for financial help immediately receives a lucrative job offer, right out of the blue; health dramatically improves; business suddenly starts to boom. We in the West are trained to call these events coincidences. However, I have to admit I've seen some of the best-timed coincidences in the world right after a traditional Vedic fire offering is performed!

For the Western scientific mind, consciousness is rooted in matter. For the priest performing the fire ceremony, though, matter is rooted in consciousness. Therefore, according to the Hindu laws of physics, if the priest sends out a message into the cosmic mind, "Kumar Sharma needs work!" it's not surprising to him when a job offer quickly materializes. It's par for the course.

Who Are the Vedic Gods?

Very few Hindus worship the gods mentioned in the Veda anymore because these deities go back to an era so incredibly long ago. Other more popular gods who've shown up over the years have gradually replaced them. Still, reading the hymns to these gods provides important insights into the spirituality of the ancient Indo-Europeans, the ancestors of the North Indians and many of us Western peoples, too.

These are some of the most important gods and goddesses of the Veda:

- Indra, the dragon slayer

- Agni, fire in all its forms

- Varuna, the Moon, ruler of celestial and terrestrial seas

- Mitra, the sun as our celestial friend

- Savitar, source of life and light

- Ashvins, twin gods of healing and vitality

- Ushas, gorgeous goddess of the dawn

- Sarasvati, source of intelligence and creativity

- Rudra, giver and remover of disease

- Bhaga, dispenser of good fortune

About one fourth of the hymns in the Rig Veda go to Indra, with Agni running a close second in terms of popularity.

You'd be mistaken to think of these gods as a pantheon like the hierarchy of deities we're familiar with from Greek and Roman mythology. In the Vedas, the gods are surprisingly indistinct, blending easily into one another. Indra and Agni even become Indragni, two gods in one! Savitar is hailed as the sun god, but so is Mitra, and so is Agni and Vishnu and Surya and Bhaga and Pushan, and so on.

What's going on? It's important to remember that Hindus live in a different conceptual universe than Westerners. These gods aren't colorful personalities running around having affairs like the Greco-Roman deities. They're personifications of natural forces, which are considered actual fields of intelligence in Hindu cosmology. They work in a unified manner, integrating their functions and dissolving their identities into each other just as clouds lose themselves in rain and rain loses itself in the Earth and sea.

Many Gods in One

Many Westerners and most Muslims are raised with the firm conviction that there is only one God (theirs) and every other deity is a false god. Hindu belief is exactly the opposite. The Veda consistently portrays all the different gods as ultimately just different faces of the one Supreme Being. They are the various ways its will acts in nature. As the late sage Sri Aurobindo put it, it is the "one central idea of the Vedic religion, the idea of the One Being with the [gods] expressing in numerous names and forms the many-sidedness of His unity."

This is why Al Biruni, living in India at the beginning of the second millennium and surrounded by temples to dozens of different Hindu deities, could honestly report to his fellow Muslims that the Hindus believe in only one God.

Hidden Meanings

Many of the verses in the Vedas have hidden yogic and astronomical significance. The twin Ashvins, for example, represent the two nostrils through which the breath or life force is regulated. In fact, the twins were often called Nasatyas, related to our word nasal! They also stand for the twin stars alpha and beta Arietis. In ancient India these stars represented the nostrils of a celestial horse head, which Hindus picture in the part of the sky we call Aries. There are many important myths about the Ashvins since they're placed at the beginning point of the zodiac, where the circle of the sky renews itself. At the same time their connection with life energy makes them heavenly healers!

Many ancient Vedic myths that sound silly or bizarre when we read them today turn out to be deeply meaningful once we understand the science behind them.

Sampling the Veda

Let's take a tiny taste of this enormous literature, sampling portions of some of the hymns from the Rig Veda. Here are several verses from a typical hymn to Indra, the dragon slayer:

> Indra is the lord of all things living and inanimate, of all creatures wild and tame. He contains all beings in himself like spokes in a felly.

The sophisticated understanding of the rishis is evident in many of the hymns, such as the following:

> He to whom the priests sacrifice, what do they know of him? Though set burning in many different fire pits, Agni, lord of fire, is only one. Though his light extends in every direction, Surya, the sun, is only one. That one being has become all this. All this is only one.
>
> They call him Indra, Mitra, Varuna, Agni. They call him Garutman, Yama and Matarishvan. There is one God; he is known by many names.

The Hindu View

A story about the Vedic god Indra appears in the Bible in disguise! Ancient Indo-Europeans (such as the early Hindus) and ancient Semitic peoples shared many myths in common. Just as Indra was called on to kill the monster of the cosmic sea, in Assyrian and Babylonian mythology, Marduk had to slay the serpent demon Tiamat. The job eventually passed to Yahweh (see Isaiah 27:1), who killed Leviathan, "the dragon that is in the sea."

Many portions of the Veda are extremely mystical. The seer Ambrini related the following hymn. In it she celebrates the goddess Vak, Queen of the Universe, with whom she mystically identifies. This is one of the most ancient surviving accounts of the experience of cosmic consciousness:

> I move with the winds and the destructive powers, with the divisions of the sky, and with all the gods I travel.
>
> I hold up the day sky and the night sky, the Sun, the constellations, and the planets.
>
> I love and hold aloft the Moon and the Sun in their many courses.
>
> I shower wealth on those who honor the gods with sacred rites.
>
> I am the Queen, dispenser of treasure, the source of thought, most worthy of those who deserve to be worshipped!
>
> I am established everywhere, I abide in many places.
>
> Your breath, your speech, all your actions are performed through my power alone. I am the force of movement and will.
>
> I celebrate myself, the splendor of my power!

I make those who love me great, I give them spiritual knowledge.

Destruction I bestow on those who have no gratitude.

I pervade heaven and earth! From the summit of the world I gave birth to the Creator!

I dwell in the sea, my forehead grazes the sky.

I breathe in all living beings. My breath is the life of all the worlds!

Larger than the earth, wider than the sky, my majesty has no ending!

The Inner Veda

Beginning with Sri Aurobindo, the twentieth-century "sage of Pondicherry," Hindu researchers have made an effort to reconnect with the original mystical significance of the Veda. Many of the Western scholars who initially looked into the Veda had dismissed it as primitive nature worship. Aurobindo looked a little deeper and in Indra, for example, found not a mere weather deity but a king of heaven who "symbolizes the Power of Mind and especially the divine or self-luminous Mind in the human being."

The Hindu View

The Sanskrit word *veda* literally means "knowledge." It is related to the English words wisdom, wit, and even witch! (Witch used to mean a wise woman, not a scary lady.)

Aurobindo was probably on the right track. From remote antiquity, the first singers of the Veda were known as Brahma rishis, the highest human type of meditation adepts. That advanced meditation masters just sat around making up chants about how pretty the dawn is and how refreshing the rain feels seems quite unlikely.

Over and over the Veda retells the story of how Indra smashed the mountain with his thunderbolt, loosening the waters. Yogis often note that the Sanskrit word for the senses is *indriya*. To them, Indra is therefore "the lord of the senses," a master of the body and mind. The thunderbolt he controls is the *kundalini*, psycho-physical energy which yogis learn to draw up the spine into the brain, sparking genuine mystical experience.

In Hindu mysticism to this day, a mountain represents the spine because mediators are supposed to sit as quietly and solidly as a mountain does. In heightened states of consciousness, yogis experience the *dharma megha*, the rain cloud of divine knowledge, which when it begins to pour, fills the mind with wisdom and bliss. Indra is therefore a yogi who has mastered the kundalini and contacted the life-giving waters of living spiritual awareness in deep states of meditation.

def•i•ni•tion

The **indriyas** are the five senses.

Kundalini is a subtle form of psychic energy. When it rises through the spine into the brain, extraordinary states of mystical awareness are produced.

The **dharma megha** is the last obstacle a yogi must confront before achieving enlightenment. When it is pierced by the kundalini, it releases a torrent of divine knowledge and bliss.

A Map to Higher Consciousness

With this understanding, the Veda becomes not just a collection of nature hymns but also a map to higher consciousness. A yogi from Dehra Dun told me, "If you don't understand a Vedic myth on at least seven different levels, you don't understand the myth." Remember, everything in Indian spirituality is multi-dimensional.

Those who are privy to the jealously guarded oral tradition learn about many levels of meaning compacted into the Veda much like data compression in computer technology, where a small number of variables are configured so they contain massive amounts of information. There is the ritual significance of the Vedic verses and another level of meaning corresponding to the intelligent energies inherent in nature. An astronomical level keys different deities to various planets and constellations. In the psychological level of interpretation, Indra fighting the dragon is each one of us grappling with our own inner demons. And the yogic interpretation has to do with vectors of awareness moving through the subtle body.

Sages Say

The Vedic experience may perhaps disclose, not an alternative to the modern view of life and the world … but an already existing, although often hidden, dimension of Man himself.

—Raimundo Panikkar

Recently, several Hindu scholars have made a number of fascinating suggestions about yet more information encoded in the Veda. It seemed like overkill to these researchers that the Vedic rishis made such a point of ensuring that the hymns would be reproduced exactly correctly for millennia to come. It now appears that certain mathematical, geometric, and astronomical information essential to the ancient Hindus' concept of sacred space was encoded in the very rhythm, meter, and pronunciation of the verses! The evidence for this hypothesis is surprisingly strong.

If this seems unlikely to you, remember that much of the Indian population has been illiterate for most of India's history. Using mnemonic devices, such as rhythmic chants which are easy to remember, would be an excellent way to preserve technical information in the absence of writing.

Upanishads: Liberating Literature

The German philosopher Arthur Schopenhauer once said, "The study of the Upanishads has been the solace of my life. It will be the solace of my death."

The Upanishads are the philosophical portion of the Veda, written as prose rather than in the form of hymns. While many authorities count 108 of them, 11 are most important. These are the Aitareya, Mandukya, Brihadaranyaka, Mundaka, Chhandogya, Prashna, Isha, Shvetashvatara, Katha, Taittiriya, and Kena Upanishads.

Quick Quiz

1. The Veda is …

   a. The holiest book of the Hindus.

   b. A line of expensive hair care products.

   c. The bad guy in the *Star Wars* trilogy.

2. The Vedic god Indra is …

   a. The god India is named after.

   b. Famous for destroying a serpent demon.

   c. Founder of a Silicon Valley software dynasty.

3. Today, the offerings made at Vedic fire sacrifices often include …

   a. Flowers, grain, clarified butter, herbs, and fragrant woods.

   b. Horses and goats.

   c. Screaming virgins.

Answers: 1 (a). 2 (b). 3 (a).

The Something in Nothing

The following is a story from the Chhandogya Upanishad:

> After years away at school, Shvetaketu returned home to his father, Uddalaka. Uddalaka could tell from his son's boasting about how much he'd learned, that he hadn't learned anything at all! Or at least nothing really worth knowing.
>
> "Did your teacher teach you how to hear that which can't be heard or know what can't be known?" Uddalaka asked.
>
> "Oh-oh. That wasn't in the curriculum."
>
> "Go outside and get me a fruit from the banyan tree." Shvetaketu ran outside for the fruit.
>
> "Now cut it in half," his father instructed. "What do you see?"
>
> "I see the seeds, dad."
>
> "Cut one of those in half." This wasn't easy—banyan seeds are extremely small. Finally Shvetaketu managed to slice one evenly. "What do you see?" Uddalaka asked.
>
> The boy was baffled. "What do you mean, dad? There's nothing there."
>
> Uddalaka looked his son in the eye. "An enormous tree grows out of that 'nothing.' When you understand what that 'nothing' is, you will understand yourself. The nothing you can't see is the creative potency out of which the tree grows. That unperceivable essence of being is also what you are. You are that, Shvetaketu.
>
> "Pour some salt into this bucket of water," Uddalaka continued. Shvetaketu obeyed. "Now give me the salt back."
>
> "I can't do that!" Shvetaketu objected. "There's none left!"
>
> "Take a sip of the water. You taste the salt, don't you? You can't see it, yet it's there. Just as salt pervades the water, so the subtle essence of reality pervades your body. That subtle essence is your true being. You are that, Shvetaketu."

Uddalaka is talking about the intelligence inherent in nature—innate in us, too—an all-pervading living presence underlying everything. This story is typical of the way the Upanishads teach.

Lighting the Way

If Vedic hymns represent the heart's response to the divine, the Upanishads represent the intellect's attempt to fathom the depths of spirit. These texts are not naive about the mind's ability to encompass the infinite. "Into a blind darkness enter those devoted to ignorance, but into an even greater darkness enter those devoted to knowledge," admits the Isha Upanishad. Too often intellectuals are like the blind leading the blind, caught in a web of words and mental paradigms.

The purpose of the Upanishads is not to give you enlightenment. Words can't do that. Their purpose is to light your way, helping you discriminate between experiences that have only passing value and the living knowledge of divine being which is the supreme and everlasting value.

Vedic rituals have two purposes: to help us obtain the things we need and want in life, and to propel us toward heavenly states after death. The Upanishadic seers noted that worldly success and enjoyment never last very long. Also no matter how exalted the soul's condition might be in heaven, eventually the cosmic wheel will turn again, the soul's good karma which carried it to heaven will run out, and the soul will find itself back in the physical world, starting from scratch.

There had to be a way off the wheel, a way to happiness that never ends, ever. The Upanishads taught a way of wisdom that steers away from the seeming truths presented to us by our senses toward the unchanging, self-luminous world of consciousness itself.

We'll return to the Upanishads in Chapter 22. We'll learn how we can actually experience the Upanishadic insight, "You are that seeming nothingness that in reality is *everything*."

The Least You Need to Know

- For millennia, Hinduism's sacred knowledge was preserved in its oral tradition.
- Enlightened seers composed the Vedic hymns.
- The primary use of the Vedic hymns is to sanctify religious rituals.
- The Vedic gods represented different facets of the one God.
- The Upanishads preserve the highest philosophical thought of the ancient Hindu sages.

Chapter 5

The People's Religion

In This Chapter

- ◆ Colorful stories highlight Hindu principles
- ◆ The ideal way to live
- ◆ The appropriate response to injustice
- ◆ God's advice to humanity
- ◆ Encyclopedias of Hindu lore

The Veda is India's most sacred book, but almost no one reads it anymore. Because it was reserved for the exclusive use of certain classes of society, many people never had access to it anyway.

Besides, the Veda is very, very long. Most people shy away from reading such a thick book, just as most Christians believe in the Bible but hesitate to sit down and actually read a book that's over 1,000 pages long. Plus, the style of Sanskrit in which the Veda is written is now so ancient that even people who are top authorities on Hinduism have trouble understanding it all!

User-Friendly Scriptures

Fortunately, Hinduism has many other fully authorized scriptures that are open to the public and easy and fun to read. Like the Vedas, they were originally passed on through the generations by word of mouth. There were people whose job it was to memorize these huge oral texts and then travel around reciting them. When one of these people showed up in a village, everyone would come running. Work was called off, and folks would sit for days listening to the expert chant the scripture. It was like going to the movies, except they imagined the scenes in their minds.

Sages Say _____

Ancient India, like ancient Greece, boasts of two great Epics. One of them, the *Mahabharata*, relates to a great war in which all the warlike races of Northern India took a share, and may therefore be compared to the *Iliad*. The other, the *Ramayana*, relates mainly to the adventures of its hero, banished from his country and wandering for long years in the wilderness of Southern India, and may therefore be compared to the *Odyssey*.

—Romesh C. Dutta

Epics: The Hindu Homer

Move over Homer! Homer's *Iliad* and *Odyssey* are often considered the greatest epics in the Western world. Homer has serious competition in India, however, where the great Hindu epics, the *Mahabharata* and *Ramayana*, have stirred hearts and exalted the spirit for thousands of years.

Does size matter? The *Ramayana* is as big as the Bible. The *Mahabharata* is four times bigger and eight times as long as the *Iliad* and the *Odyssey* put together! The *Mahabharata* contains so much material its author couldn't resist a little bragging. "If it's anywhere else, it's here too," he said. "And if it ain't here, it ain't nowhere!"

No, size doesn't really matter; it's the content that counts. If you're wondering about the quality of the content, consider this. When television producers ran a series of hour-long episodes dramatizing these two epics on Indian TV in the 1980s, the entire country shut down! During the hour the program was being broadcast no one could get a taxi, get a meal in a restaurant, or find an open shop; airline pilots wouldn't even take off. Every Hindu in the country had somehow, somewhere, found a TV and was sitting transfixed, watching the great sagas of Hinduism gamely portrayed on the small screen.

Both epics have been around since at least 700 B.C.E. but not in their present form. The original texts were undoubtedly much shorter, but they were so popular that succeeding generations kept tacking on more and more of their own contributions. Like a snowball rolling down a snowy hill, by the time the two epics had careened down the hill of history, they'd grown to glacier size. You'd practically need a shopping cart to carry around all the volumes of the *Mahabharata*, much less the *Ramayana!*

Guidepost

The chanting of mantras is an excellent way to cleanse and focus the mind. Since mantras can have dramatic effects both subtle and profound, it's not necessarily a good idea to just pick one out of a book and try practicing it. It's better to be initiated in a mantra by an authorized teacher of a spiritual lineage, who is well versed in a mantra's effects.

Sages Say

Keep the name of Rama always in your mind, remembering it with love. It will feed you when you're hungry, be your friend when you're alone, bless you when you feel cursed, and protect you when you're abandoned. To the crippled it's another limb. To the blind it's another eye. To the orphaned it's a loving parent. Whenever I remember Rama's name, the desert of my heart blooms lush and green.

—Tulsi Das, sixteenth-century Hindu poet

Ramayana: The Great Rescue

Valmiki was a thief who plied his trade in northern India many a century ago. After a string of unsuccessful robberies, he was getting so desperate, he actually tried robbing a *sadhu*, a Hindu holy man. Now sadhus own absolutely nothing but the cloth they have wrapped around their private parts. "I don't have anything to give you," the holy man pointed out.

"Give me *something* or I'll kill you!" Valmiki cried in desperation.

"Okay, okay, how about this? I'll give you a mantra that will make you the richest man in the world. But it will only work if you repeat it constantly, day in and day out."

def•i•ni•tion

A **sadhu** is a man who has renounced the material world and wanders from place to place without any possessions, immersed in meditation and spiritual practice.

Mara means evil.

Valmiki knew that sadhus don't lie. Because they've devoted their lives to God, they would rather die than tell an untruth. So he trusted the sadhu completely. "What's the mantra?"

"*Mara*," the holy man answered.

An Evil Mantra

This set well with Valmiki. Mara is the Sanskrit word for evil, and it fit his disposition. So, crazed with desire for wealth, Valmiki sat down and started chanting the mantra over and over, day and night. "Mara, mara, mara."

As he sat there, Valmiki's heart began to feel lighter. Tremendous peace filled his mind, and he experienced real joy for the first time in many, many years. Then he realized with a shock that the sadhu, in having him chant "Mara, Mara," had tricked him into chanting "Rama, Rama" as the syllables ran together. Rama, of course, is the name of God. While Valmiki had been sitting there lusting for gold, the divine vibrations of God's name had been purifying his mind.

Valmiki had become the wealthiest man in the world. He now had the most valuable thing a person could possibly possess: the living presence of God in his heart.

Valmiki gave up his evil ways and went on to become India's most famous poet. He composed the *Ramayana*, the story of how Rama, Hinduism's perfect son, husband, and king, rescued his wife, Sita, from the evil king of Lanka.

The Perfect Son

Long, long ago, the *Ramayana* goes, the king of Ayodhya had a very special son named Rama who was intelligent, courageous, compassionate, and virtuous. The people of Ayodhya adored the prince and his lovely wife, Sita. More than once Rama demonstrated both his wisdom in guiding them and his valor in protecting them.

Finally the happy day arrived when the old king decided to retire and hand over the reins of the kingdom to his beloved eldest son. But something always has to go wrong or there's no story, right? So the youngest of the king's three wives decided she wanted *her* son to rule instead.

The youngest wife was able to pull off a coup because many years earlier the king had promised her any two wishes she desired. Now she went to the king and demanded that her son, not Rama, receive the coronation. Secondly, she wanted Rama banished into the forest for 14 years. Life in the forest in those days was extremely dangerous, what with the lions and tigers and bears. Perhaps she hoped Rama would get eaten by some large, furry, carnivorous animal.

When Rama heard the news, he immediately prepared to leave for the forest, without losing his composure or complaining. And he was not just being a goody-goody. Rama understood that people look to their leaders for examples of how to live. Long ago, his father had made a promise to his youngest wife, and if he broke it now, it would signal to the people that keeping your word was not important. Kings must keep their promises even if it caused them grief.

The Hindu View

In the sixteenth century, the beloved Hindu poet Tulsi Das composed a new, Hindi version of the *Ramayana* called the *Rama Charita Manasa*. An updated version was necessary because most people could no longer understand Sanskrit, the language of the original poem. Mahatma Gandhi considered the *Rama Charita Manasa* the single greatest book in the world.

The Perfect Husband

Sita insisted on accompanying her husband into the forest, and they roamed through the woods for many happy years, together with Rama's devoted half-brother, Lakshman. Their numerous adventures, some harrowing, others hysterically funny, are lovingly described in the *Ramayana*.

Rama was very protective of Sita, whom he adored, and Sita was completely devoted to Rama. To this day, Rama and Sita are held up as the best possible example of a loving Hindu marriage.

But something's always got to go wrong. Sure enough, tragedy struck again. Rama and Lakshman were lured away from their campsite, and when they returned, Sita had vanished into thin air!

The bulk of the *Ramayana* is about Rama's desperate search for his missing wife and the amazingly daring rescue when he finally found her. It turned out she was kidnapped by the tyrannical king of Lanka (that's today's Sri Lanka). I tell you more about how Rama wins Sita back in Chapter 13.

The Hindu View _____

J. Robert Oppenheimer, the theoretical physicist best known as the director of the Manhattan Project and father of the atomic bomb, was an avid student of Sanskrit. When his Los Alamos team exploded its first nuclear weapon at a test site in New Mexico, he quoted Krishna's words in the Bhagavad Gita to express his feelings: "If the radiance of a thousand suns were to burst at once into the sky, that would be like the splendor of the Mighty One. Now I am become Death, the shatterer of worlds."

The Perfect King

After 14 years, Rama, Sita, and Lakshman returned to their home kingdom of Ayodhya in triumph. And to the citizens' infinite delight, Rama assumed his rightful role as king. To this very day, Hindus use the expression "the reign of Rama" to mean an ideal government. During "the reign of Rama" the king ruled with complete integrity and absolute commitment to the welfare of his beloved subjects. It was a time of peace, prosperity, justice, and joy. This is something of a contrast with government in India today, which may be why Indians speak of "Rama's reign" with such nostalgia!

Mahabharata: The Great War

The *Mahabharata* is attributed to the sage Vyasa, who also appears as a character in the story. (This is the same Vyasa we met in Chapter 4, who compiled the hymns of the ancient seers, shaping the Veda into its present format.) The *Mahabharata* is based on a war that probably really happened. The war is traditionally—and very controversially—dated to the thirty-second century B.C.E.! It was fought at a battlefield called Kurukshetra, which isn't too far from present-day New Delhi.

If the account given in the *Mahabharata* is literally accurate—okay, that's a big if—it wouldn't be much of an exaggeration to call this the real World War I. The story goes that the Indian warriors involved called in help from all their allies, all the way from Turkey in the west to Java in the east. That's pretty outrageous, but not as outrageous as it seems at first.

Remember that India was a major world trade center going back to Sumerian times at the least, and the area around Delhi would have been an important trade capital for international merchants. So plenty of foreign leaders may well have had a vested interest in who won the war.

So is this a holy text or a war story? The *Mahabharata* is considered a scripture because it illustrates in dramatic form how good Hindus should live. The characters are constantly facing tough moral issues and having to make difficult choices. This gives their spiritual mentors an opportunity to advise them about Hindu ethics and spirituality, sometimes for a hundred pages at a stretch! Then we learn from the wise or foolish decisions of the main characters and the consequences of their actions, what happens when people choose to follow *dharma* (righteousness) or *adharma* (unrighteousness).

def•i•ni•tion

Dharma is the best possible course, righteousness, the fulfillment of one's true purpose, virtue.

Adharma means behaving unethically, unrighteous action.

Feuding Cousins

The *Mahabharata* is brimming with entertaining and enlightening tales about many different sets of characters. But the main storyline is about two sets of brothers, who are cousins. The 5 Pandavas are the good brothers, and the 100 Kauravas are the bad brothers.

The Pandavas are raised in the forest, where they learn virtue and respect. Their cousins, the Kauravas, are raised at court where they become cynical and corrupt. If you're wondering how there could be a hundred Kaurava brothers, it's because the Hindus had already developed cloning (if we can believe the story)! We're told that when the Kauravas' mother miscarried, a yogi placed the fetus in a pot filled with nutrients. Later he separated it into a hundred healthy baby boys!

The eldest of the good set of brothers, Yudhisthira, is supposed to become the next king when he comes of age. But the acting king's eldest son, the oldest of the bad 100 brothers, feels *he* ought to be the next king. After all, his dad has been the de facto ruler since the legal king—Yudhisthira's dad—died years ago.

So when Yudhisthira comes of age, his scheming cousin Duryodhana refuses to relinquish the throne. In fact, he experiments with various schemes to get rid of Yudhisthira and his four brothers once and for all. For example, he builds a super-flammable house, invites them to move into it, and then sets it on fire with them inside. Fortunately, his nefarious plans fail. (If you think this plot line is complicated, believe me, you don't know the half of it!)

After numerous attempts to resolve the dispute peacefully, Yudhisthira regretfully realizes the only way he can assume his rightful role as king is to go to war with Duryodhana. This is an extremely painful choice because it means having to fight, and maybe kill, many people he sincerely loves, like former teachers and some of his own relatives. But at this point, it's becoming increasingly clear how truly evil Duryodhana is and that somebody must stop him.

Picking Sides

The Pandavas and Kauravas prepare for battle. As both sides call in their allies, Yudhisthira sends his younger brother Arjuna to ask their friend Krishna if he'll help them. Arjuna is one of the greatest warriors of his time and also a really good guy. Take note: he's the main hero of the *Mahabharata*. When he shows up at Krishna's palace, he finds that the evil Duryodhana has shown up, too, also hoping to enlist Krishna's large army and gold-laden treasury.

Sages Say

The *Mahabharata* has moulded the character and civilisation of one of the most numerous of the world's people. How? By its gospel of dharma, which like a golden thread runs through all the complex movements in the epic; by its lesson that hatred breeds hatred, that covetousness and violence lead inevitably to ruin, that the only real conquest is in the battle against one's lower nature.

—C. Rajagopalachari

Now there's something very special about this fellow Krishna. The long and short of it is, he's God. Hindus believe in divine incarnations (see Chapter 13), and Krishna is God in human form, though Duryodhana's vision is too clouded with hatred and greed to see this.

Krishna tells the two cousins, "You're both my relatives. I can't choose sides. What I will do is this. I'll give one of you all my soldiers, my horses and elephants, my artillery and my gold. The other, well, I'll come along with you as an advisor, but I won't fight. Whichever of you shows up first tomorrow morning, I'll let him choose which of the two options he prefers."

Choosing God

Duryodhana came rushing in the next morning before the break of dawn and sat anxiously at the head of Krishna's bed, waiting for him to wake up. Arjuna got up at his usual time, took his morning bath, and sat for worship and meditation. Then he headed over to Krishna's house, where he stood humbly by the foot of Krishna's bed.

Krishna finally woke up. Even though Duryodhana got there first, Arjuna was the first one Krishna laid eyes on since he was standing respectfully at the end of the bed, not sitting behind Krishna's head like Duryodhana. So Krishna gave Arjuna the choice. "My army or me?"

"I choose you, Lord," was Arjuna's very, very famous reply.

Duryodhana walked away a happy man, with all the military power, the money, and the horses and elephants at Krishna's command. But guess who won the war?

Arjuna had a much smaller army, but with Krishna's advice he was able to outwit his evil cousins and win back the kingdom for his brother, the legitimate heir. The point, which I don't think anyone who's ever heard the story has missed, is that when we choose God over all the strengths and all the temptations of the world, we make the right decision.

Bhagavad Gita: The Song of God

The war between the Pandavas and the Kauravas was about to begin. Arjuna asked his friend Krishna to drive him to the center of the battlefield so he could get his bearings. But sitting in his chariot between the two armies, the full enormity of what was about to occur hit Arjuna like a ton of bricks. Tens of thousands of good men on both sides, including many of Arjuna's friends and relatives, were about to die. Innocent women would lose their husbands and sons. A whole generation would grow up without fathers. It would take decades for the kingdom to recover from the staggering losses about to ensue.

Was it really worth it—so many deaths for control of a piece of land? Arjuna sank to the floor of the chariot in a state of emotional paralysis. He couldn't do it. He couldn't fight these people. Then Krishna turned to him, and the two of them had a little chat.

A Conversation with God

The *Bhagavad Gita* (which means "Song of God") is the conversation between Krishna, who is God in human form come to guide and protect the good, and Arjuna, who is the rest of us in human form, confused about what course of action to take and sickened by the horror we see in the world around us.

The Gita, as most Hindus call it, actually consists of 18 short chapters lifted right out of the *Mahabharata.* Many Hindus can recite the entire Gita, the most loved holy book in Hinduism, from memory. Most have memorized at least a few lines.

def•i•ni•tion

Bhagavan means God. In the Rig Vedas, Bhaga is the deity who nourishes and protects His devotees.

Gita is a song or chant. There are many thousands of religious gitas in Hinduism, like the Avadhuta Gita or the Ribhu Gita, but when Hindus say simply "Gita," they mean the Bhagavad Gita, "The Song of God," the most famous song of them all.

Sages Say

When doubts haunt me, when disappointments stare me in the face, and I see not one ray of hope on the horizon, I turn to Bhagavad Gita and find a verse to comfort me; and I immediately begin to smile in the midst of overwhelming sorrow. Those who meditate on the Gita will derive fresh joy and new meanings from it every day.
—Mahatma Gandhi

Krishna has already explained that in the battle against evil, when all peaceful options are exhausted, men of good conscience must get up and fight. Control of the world cannot be handed over to evil men by good people too weak-willed to stand against them.

Now, in the face of death and catastrophe, Krishna urges Arjuna to look at the Big Picture. Everyone dies. From the perspective of eternity, these men gathered on the battlefield are dead already. Since death is inevitable, why not die nobly, fighting for justice?

During the day, we change clothes several times. Death, Krishna says, is when the soul changes its clothes. It takes off a body that's worn out or damaged and puts on a new one. But the inner Self never dies. It is wrong to identify ourselves with our perishable body. We need to realize that we are immortal spirits, ultimately unaffected by death.

Arjuna may win the battle, or he may lose. He may live, or he may die. The outcome of the events ahead is in the hands of God. Krishna advises his friend not to be concerned with how things will turn out. He should focus instead on fighting for truth and justice simply because, under the present tragic circumstances, it's the right thing to do.

The Vision of God

Arjuna is persuaded by Krishna but asks for a favor. He's not content with the Big Picture—he wants to see the *Really* Big Picture. He knows Krishna is God in disguise and wants to see what God really looks like.

Krishna shows him. Arjuna sees universes without end, galaxies spinning in and out of existence. He sees trillions and trillions and trillions of souls trapped in the cycle of birth and death, being born, suffering, dying.

For a mind that has not yet been completely purified by spiritual practice, the vision is too much to bear. Arjuna screams for Krishna to stop, and the Lord resumes his human form.

"I have taught you the secret of secrets," Krishna concludes. "Now surrender to me, worship me in all your words and thoughts, and offer your actions to me as a sacrifice of love. You cannot even begin to conceive how much I care for you. I am your eternal refuge. Don't be afraid! I promise, I will save you."

For 2,500 years, Hindus have clung with unshakable faith to Krishna's loving promise.

Very often Westerners, when they're first exposed to the Gita, complain that it condones war. At one level, there's some truth to this. At another, they miss the point completely. Mahatma Gandhi, the quintessential man of peace, kept a copy of the Bhagavad Gita with him at all times. Hindus understand that the battlefield Kurukshetra, where Arjuna and Duryodhana are facing off, is not really near Delhi but rather in the human heart. All of us are at war with the Duryodhanas inside ourselves: greed, hatred, ignorance. In the Gita, God himself shows us the way to victory.

Quick Quiz

1. India's two great epics are …

   a. The *Ramayana* and the Vedas.

   b. The *Ramayana* and the *Mahabharata*.

   c. The *Ramayana* and *The Complete Idiot's Guide to Hinduism.*

continues

continued

2. The war between the Pandavas and the Kauravas is fought because …

   a. The kingship is in dispute.

   b. They're trying to rescue Sita from the evil king of Lanka.

   c. The Kauravas stole the Pandavas' iPod and won't give it back.

3. The Bhagavad Gita is a conversation between …

   a. Rama and Sita, about who cooks dinner tonight.

   b. The Pandavas and the Kauravas, about whether there should be pepperoni or calamari olives on the pizza.

   c. God and Arjuna, who stands in for the rest of us.

Answers: 1 (b). 2 (a). 3 (c).

Puranas: Encyclopedias of Spirit

I mentioned earlier that most Hindus today don't really worship the gods in the Vedas anymore. If you want to connect with the living gods of India, you should turn to any of the 18 major *Puranas*. (Or else turn to Chapters 11 and 12, where I introduce the most popular gods and goddesses from the Puranas, one by one.)

def•i•ni•tion

Purana means "ancient chronicle" or "account of the ancient times."

The Puranas are often called the fifth Vedas. While the first four Vedas are reserved for particular classes of people, the Puranas are for everyone. They're the average person's Vedas.

How to Become a Purana

A book has to cover certain ground if it wants to be a Purana. It has to include …

◆ An explanation of how the Supreme Being projected the universe out of its limitless awareness. Not just our world, but all planes of existence must be accounted for.

◆ Details of how the multi-billion year cycles of the manifestation and dissolution of the universe actually work.

- Cycles of the different types of humanity that have appeared and disappeared on our planet since it originally formed.

- Historical information about the original lineages of our present humanity.

- Genealogies of important early Hindu rulers.

Optional elements you may also find in a Purana include …

- Information about especially spiritually supercharged pilgrimage sites.

- Broad outlines of powerful spiritual practices your guru will explain to you in more detail.

- Reports of God's and the Goddess's activities when they visit Earth.

- Stunningly beautiful hymns in praise of the divinity.

- News about the saints' and sages' efforts to get to know the Supreme Being better.

A Continuing Tradition

Dating the Puranas, for all practical purposes, is impossible. Some of the material in them is certainly older than the Vedas itself. But unlike the Vedas, which priests were entrusted to pass to their children without altering even one syllable, succeeding generations felt free to reshape the Puranas according to present needs. So in all the Puranas, you'll find something old and something new.

More Puranas are continually being written. In fact, the swami at my local Kali temple just wrote a new one a few years ago. But they're always based on the same ancient principles, and none of the new ones have quite the same impact as the 18 VIPs (Very Important Puranas).

The Hindu View

Manu is the forefather of the present race of humankind, according to the Puranas. He survived the great flood that wiped out the last humanity and began repopulating the world. The name Manu is related to the Sanskrit word *manas*, which means "the thinking mind." Etymologically related English words are human, man, and woman. We are the beings who have manas, who think!

An Expanding Library

As a living tradition, Hinduism is continually generating more spiritual classics. Unlike Christianity and Islam, where the Bible or Koran represent God's word once and for all, in Hinduism God speaks afresh to every generation. Hindu saints and sages constantly create new scriptures, keeping the Vedic vision dynamic and directly relevant to people's present concerns.

During the European Middle Ages, Hindus produced such timeless spiritual master-pieces as the *Yoga Vasishtha* and the *Tripura Rahasya*. Closer to our own time, classics of such exceptional merit as *The Gospel of Sri Ramakrishna* by Mohendranath Gupta and *Adoration of the Divine Mother* by Vasistha Ganapati Muni have taken on the stature of holy scripture in some circles.

Nevertheless, because Hindus believe that men and women of eras long past were actually more illumined than most of us are today, the spiritual preeminence of Hinduism's earliest scriptures, the Vedas, Puranas, and Upanishads, remains unsur-passed.

The Least You Need to Know

- Ordinary Hindus rarely read the Vedas—they turn to easier-to-digest, popular texts for inspiration.
- The *Ramayana* is the story of the perfect Hindu man and woman.
- The *Mahabharata* is the tale of the battle between light and darkness.
- The Bhagavad Gita is the most popular scripture in Hinduism.
- The Puranas are the layperson's Vedas.
- Hinduism continually spawns new scriptures.

Part 2

What Hindus Believe

Hinduism is, in many ways, the most open-minded of the world's great religions. Maybe this is because India is composed of so many different people and cultures and languages. Respect, or at least tolerance, for other traditions grew gradually over the centuries. People borrowed each other's gods and goddesses, spiritual practices, and even saints. In the end, India merged into one more or less unified Hindu culture.

In this part, we look at the defining beliefs most Hindus share in common: reincarnation, karma, and an immortal soul. They also believe in an infinite ocean of divine energy that underlies the universe we perceive with our senses and an inner universe of consciousness through which we connect with the whole.

Chapter 6

One God with Many Names

In This Chapter

- ◆ How Hinduism differs from Western religions
- ◆ The roots of Hindu tolerance
- ◆ Hindu gods worship each other
- ◆ Keeping tolerance alive
- ◆ A visit from Jesus

"God is one. Men call Him by various names," is the eternal truth voiced by the Veda. It doesn't matter what address you send your prayer to. Whether you mail it to Indra or Agni, God or Goddess, Allah or Buddha, Mary or Jehovah, your letter ends up in the same mailbox. The one God always gets your message, no matter who you are, no matter what religion you belong to.

To use another metaphor: Christians say that to access the hard drive, you have to click on the Jesus icon. No other icon will take you to the hard drive.

Muslims say it's a spiritual crime to use any icons at all. Never confuse the hard drive with any of the silly icons on the desktop. Access the drive directly, with the code Mohammed provided.

Hindus say, hey, click on any icon. Every icon on the screen will connect you with the hard drive. Don't see any icon you like? Make up a new one—it will work just as well.

My God's Not Better Than Yours

According to the Veda, it's a serious mistake to confuse your name for God with the Supreme Being himself. The Big Guy is bigger than you think. In fact, he's not necessarily even a guy at all! It's just as valid to call Him Her or It. If words like "God" or "Goddess" or "Supreme Reality" point you in the right direction, use them by all means.

But the point is not to choose a name for God and then claim that anyone who calls God by a different name is going to hell. For Hindus the point is to enter into a living relationship with the Supreme Being till you feel its breath in your breath, till you feel enveloped in the all-encompassing embrace of the infinite wisdom out of which this universe emerged.

> **Sages Say**
>
> This universe is the outpouring of the majesty of God, the auspicious one, radiant love. Every face you see belongs to him. He is present in everyone without exception.
>
> —Yajur Veda

According to Hinduism, there are no false gods, at least not if your prayer to that god is sincere. Whatever form of the divine you worship, even if it's a man with an elephant's head, the one all-pervading Being who loves you more than you can possibly imagine will use that form to guide you to Her.

Begging to Differ

There is no minimizing the fact that Hindu belief differs dramatically from the Judeo-Christian-Islamic tradition. Before I begin explaining in detail what Hindus do believe, let me clarify what they do *not* believe.

Jews believe they have a very special relationship with God. God has selected them for his special loving attention and created laws for them that set them apart from the rest of humanity. Hindus do not accept the concept of a chosen people. For Hindus, God's relationship with *every* soul is equally special.

A metaphor repeated by Hindu saints is that God is like the sun. The sun shines equally on everyone, no matter what social class you belong to, no matter whether you're male or female, a good person or a not-so-good person. And certainly no matter what religion you subscribe to.

The Jewish idea of what it means to be a prophet and the Hindu idea of what it means to be a seer are also radically different. In Judaism, Yahweh speaks to His prophets, and they deliver God's message to the Jewish people. In Hinduism, the consciousness of the seer merges into the consciousness of God. For Jews, the Creator and His creation—us—are radically distinct. But in Hinduism, the Divine Being emanated us out of its own all-pervading awareness. It makes sense that our awareness can merge back into its source, like a wave subsiding into the sea.

The Hindu View

Jews and Muslims believe God is completely transcendent and has never appeared on Earth in human form. Christians believe God took a human birth once as Jesus Christ. Hindus believe that whenever humanity calls out to God and the Goddess for help, He and She appear here in physical form to guide and protect us.

Christian Beliefs

Orthodox Christians believe Jesus took on the sins of the entire world. (Hindus also believe saints can take on the karma of their disciples.) To access the saving grace of Jesus, it's absolutely essential to have faith in him.

A Hindu would find this idea perplexing. Many Hindu saints devoted every breath of their lives to the love of God and service of humanity. Why would someone be sent to hell for eternity because they hadn't heard of Jesus?

In Hinduism, two great principles are at work in the universe: *karma* and *kripa*, justice and grace. Despite huge campaigns and the outlay of hundreds of millions of dollars, Christian missionaries have made little headway in converting Hindus. This is largely because Hindus see little justice *or* grace in a god who would damn all their ancestors for no fault of their own.

Hindus believe very literally that "As you sow, so shall you reap." But in Hinduism there is no eternal damnation. No being can have sown enough bad karma that in the vast stretches of eternity, God can't find a way to bring that lost soul back into the light.

def•i•ni•tion

Karma is the law of action and reaction at work in the moral universe. Every thought, word, and action produces an effect that rebounds on the person who generated it.

Kripa is divine grace.

The Image of God

Probably no two religions are as radically opposed in their fundamental beliefs as Hinduism and Islam. The meeting of Muslim and Hindu cultures led to catastrophic historical consequences still playing out in South Asia today.

Muslims feel it is a spiritual crime to make an image of God. Hindus feel that, used with proper understanding, images of God, such as the statues of various deities found in Hindu temples, are an excellent way to focus the mind on the divine. Some Muslims feel they are called upon by their faith to destroy any images of God they come across. During the first few centuries of the Muslim occupation of North India, many thousands of Hindu temples were destroyed. The destruction was so complete that today you must travel to South India, where the Muslims didn't penetrate, to find a truly ancient Hindu temple.

Using an image as a focus for worship is a defining characteristic of Hinduism (see Chapter 10).

The Hindu View

The monuments of ancient cultures are filled with images of kings crushing their enemies and enslaving their neighbors. Not so in the ancient Indus-Sarasvati civilization. Hardly any evidence of violence appears in the ancient Indians' art or in archeological strata for that era, and few weapons have been found. In this peaceful and well-ordered society, philosophy, mathematics, science, and inner life were free to flourish without fear of disruption from war.

Inner Religion

One of the great ironies of religious history is that, although the religions that came out of the Near East—Judaism, Islam, Christianity—adamantly reject most of Hinduism's fundamental teachings, their mystical traditions—the *Kabbalah*, *Sufism*, and Christian *Gnosticism*—reflect Hindu insights in almost every detail. Numerous students of comparative religion, from Muslim scholar Al Biruni in 1000 C.E. to the world famous writer Aldous Huxley nearer our own time, have expressed their amazement at the parallels between the major mystical traditions of the world and Hinduism.

def•i•ni•tion

The **Kabbalah** is a system of Jewish mysticism explaining how the universe emanated from the one transcendental reality.

Sufism is a form of Islamic mysticism which teaches yoga-like techniques leading to higher states of awareness.

Gnosticism was a system of highly mystical beliefs embraced by many early Christians (perhaps—some scholars believe—even by St. Paul, author of portions of the New Testament).

The Tolerant Religion

Christianity and Islam are aggressive missionary religions. In Hinduism, missionary efforts have traditionally been the exception rather than the rule. For the most part, the Hindu attitude toward other faiths is "Live and let live."

This does not mean Hindus always look at what goes on in other traditions, or even within their own tradition, with unblinking acceptance. Even in the Veda, the rishis rolled their eyes at what they felt were the excesses of some of the tribal practices and urged Hindus to live nobly, abiding by the highest ideals and practicing some rudiments of self-control. How did Hinduism develop this tolerant spirit?

One Culture, Many Traditions

Westerners today tend to think of India in monolithic terms: one country, one culture. In reality, at very few times and for very brief periods in its history has most of the Indian subcontinent been unified—at least until 1947 when the modern state of Bharat (the Indian name for India) was created. Instead, for most of its long history, India has been home to an amazingly large number of distinct subcultures.

About 80,000 subcultures exist in India today. That's not a misprint—the correct figure is 80,000. Over 325 languages are spoken there, not to mention thousands of dialects. There are also 25 commonly used written scripts. And we think of America as a melting pot of different cultures!

Hinduism is by far the most complex religion in the world, shading under its enormous parasol an incredibly diverse array of contrasting beliefs, practices, and denominations. Hinduism is, by far, the oldest major religion and has had more than enough time to develop a diversity of opinions and approaches to spirituality unmatched in any other tradition.

A Peaceable People

Generally speaking, the Hindus are a peaceable people. Whether or not different communities liked each other, they made an effort to get along. The *caste system*, considered evil in the West, assured that different subcultures, whether they ranked high or low in the pecking order, survived relatively unmolested within the framework of India's highly structured society.

def•i•ni•tion

The **caste system** is the basis of Hindu social hierarchy. Priests and kings are at the top of the social order, manual laborers at the bottom. Foreigners, renunciates, and nonconformists are outside the system altogether.

The Hindus are perhaps the most peaceful of the major world cultures. Think about it: for at least the last 2,500 years, the only significant military foray Hindus have made outside India was the South Indian conquest of Indonesia, Malaysia, and the Philippines around 1400 C.E. Hindus may fight with each other, but they've had very little interest in conquering anyone else—though many of the world's other cultures have certainly had a crack at conquering India!

A Test of Tolerance

Before the arrival of the Muslims around 1000 C.E., Hindus handily assimilated all the would-be conquerors who came storming over its northern borders. The Kushans (Mongolians), the Parthians (Persians), and the Huns all eventually melted into India's embrace, disappearing into the sea of Hindu culture.

The broad-minded Hindus were able to accommodate just about everybody who came knocking on their door—until the Muslims. For the first time, foreign invaders left wounds so deep they refused to heal. Hindu tolerance was put to the ultimate test.

In ancient times, however, religious tolerance was the norm throughout much of the world. The ancient Greeks and Romans, for example, were astonishingly tolerant of other religions, at least by today's standards. As the monotheistic religions began to dominate world culture, respect for other cultures' religious beliefs largely disappeared. Today Hindu culture is one of the last remaining enclaves of a universal-minded religion.

Exceptions Prove the Rule

I would love to tell you that Hindus have *always* been shining examples of a people who consistently respect other religious traditions, but I'd be fooling you and myself if

I did. Human nature is human nature, and the tendency to believe that one's own faith is not only the best—but also perhaps the only valid one—has raised its head in Indian history, too.

If you have a look at the Puranas, you'll find that while some of them are quite universalistic in outlook, others are notably sectarian. Some of their authors poke fun at their neighbors' gods in a fairly lighthearted manner, but in others the insults get edgier.

At times, friction between different Hindu denominations has gotten out of hand. At some points, the devotees of Vishnu have actively persecuted the devotees of Shiva. At other points, the devotees of Shiva have persecuted the devotees of Vishnu. Non-Hindus living in India, such as Jains, Sikhs, Buddhists, and more recently Muslims, have occasionally taken some serious hits from fanatical Hindus.

> **Sages Say** _____
>
> Everything in the outside world changes constantly. But the Lord of Love in the inner world never changes. He rules both inner and the outer realities. Meditate on Him. Merge in Him. Wake up from the dream that you exist apart from Him.
>
> —Shvetashvatara Upanishad

The Vedic Vision

Yet religious tolerance is more the norm. A man may be devoted to Lord Vishnu, but when his bride moves into the household, she may place her image of Lord Shiva on the family altar. Their daughter, however, may be more attracted to the goddess Lakshmi and place *her* image in the family shrine. And no one blinks an eye!

We can trace this open attitude all the way back to the Veda itself. Still, throughout the centuries, Hindu saints and even India's famous divine incarnations have had to make the point over and over again: "God is one. Men call him by various names."

In one very well-known story, a yogi named Narada got so fed up with the devotees of Shiva and Rama squabbling with each other about which of their gods was higher that he decided to resolve the question once and for all.

Who the Gods Worship

At this juncture in history, many long years ago, Rama was wandering in the forest with his wife, Sita. Rama was God incarnate; he's still passionately worshipped in India even today.

So Narada teleported to the forest to talk to Rama. He wound up having to wait several hours to get his attention, however. Rama was in the middle of making offerings into the sacred fire, an age-old religious ritual. When he finally finished, he ran over to Narada and apologized. "Sir, I'm so sorry I kept you waiting! I was performing my daily worship to Shiva."

Narada was delighted! Here was his answer without even having to ask. Rama considered Shiva a greater god than himself!

Narada immediately teleported to heaven to tell Shiva the exciting news. But there he had to wait, too, as Shiva doesn't like to be disturbed when he is in meditation. Sometimes he meditates for years without a break, which can make getting an appointment with him intensely frustrating. Fortunately, Shiva soon opened His three eyes and noticed the yogi. "Oh Narada, I'm sorry I kept you waiting!" Shiva quickly apologized. "I just couldn't tear myself away from meditating on the lotus feet of Rama!"

Enough Miracles for Everyone

Again and again Hindu scriptures repeat the same point. Before Rama fights the evil king Ravana, Rama worships Durga, the goddess of victory. No matter how much their devotees favor one deity over another, the Hindu gods themselves have nothing but respect for each other.

In the Bhagavad Gita, Krishna—the voice of the Supreme Being itself—assures us, "To whatever god you direct your prayer, by whatever name you call the Supreme, your prayer immediately comes to me." Call God Harry if you want. Call him Joe. If your prayer is sincere, it goes right to the heart of the universe, and God responds. This is why miracles don't only happen in the lives of Roman Catholics or for Sunni Muslims or for Hindus. People everywhere experience miracles because God attends to the prayers of all.

The Smartas: A Smart Faith

One of the most famous Hindu sages of historical times, Shankaracharya (his name was really Shankara; *acharya* means teacher), was so disgusted with the petty disputes of the different Hindu sects that he formed his own denomination, the Smartas. The Smartas, he directed, would worship all the major gods of both North and South India! To this day, Smarta swamis honor Hinduism's great gods: Vishnu (the one who keeps the universe in good running order and incarnates on Earth from time to time to deal with emergencies), Shiva (the one who's always meditating), Devi (the Mother of the Universe), Ganesha (the one with the elephant head), Murugan (the young warrior god of the Tamils), and Surya (the sun god).

Sages Say

Realizing who you really are, discovering your spiritual identity, is your true purpose in life. If you fritter away your time stoking the fires of your body's endless cravings, you are committing spiritual suicide. The body is nothing more than the vehicle of the immortal spirit. You are living spirit, not the perishable body!

—Shankaracharya

Shankaracharya was an advanced yogi who believed that ultimately God doesn't have any shape or form; he's pure being, consciousness and bliss. Yet Shankaracharya was wise enough to appreciate that the tremendous faith simple people had in their beloved deities, like Krishna or the Divine Mother, could be mobilized for their spiritual benefit. If people avoided squabbling about whose god was the greatest, their love for their chosen deity would propel them toward the actual experience of the unity of all gods in the one Supreme Being. Then they could discover for themselves their unity with God and with each other.

In this way throughout its history, spiritual masters like Shankaracharya guided Hindus to temper their enthusiastic devotion with mature reflection.

Ramakrishna Samples Religions

Ramakrishna Paramahansa, one of the most influential saints of recent times, was born into a brahmin family in the tiny village of Kamarpukur in Bengal in 1836. As he entered young adulthood, he was handed a plum of a job. He would be a priest at Dakshineshvar, the beautiful new temple complex in Kolkata (a.k.a. Calcutta), right at the bank of the Ganges.

Ramakrishna soon distinguished himself as a saint of the highest order. He was able to spontaneously enter high states of consciousness it usually took yogis a lifetime to master. His ecstatic devotion to the goddess Kali enchanted visitors and soon created a community of disciples who loved to be near the Goddess-intoxicated master.

Then a disaster of unimaginable proportions occurred. Ramakrishna converted to Islam! During a conversation with a Sufi who had come to see the temple,

Ramakrishna was so impressed by the beautiful teachings at the heart of Islam that he decided, "Islam is also a way to reach God. I must practice this path."

Ramakrishna Paramahansa, champion of religious tolerance.

(Vedanta Society of Saint Louis)

Trying On Islam

To the unrestrained horror of his family and friends, Ramakrishna refused to even approach the main Kali temple. He started dressing like a Muslim, performed Islamic prayers while bowing toward Mecca five times a day as Muslims do, and wouldn't even look at the image of a Hindu god.

Ramakrishna insisted he was going to eat like a Muslim, too. This meant eating beef, which to a Hindu is the virtual equivalent of eating human flesh. This was just too much. His disciples hired a Muslim cook who prepared a vegetarian meal cooked in the Muslim style. Ramakrishna, who had no idea what beef tasted like, ate the dish in all good faith.

After three days of total commitment to Islam, Ramakrishna had a vision of Mohammed. He saw the Muslim prophet, shining with spiritual luminosity, dissolve into God and then God dissolve into the Absolute Reality. Ramakrishna went into such ecstasy his disciples were hard pressed to bring him back to this plane of reality.

Guidepost _____

If you're having Hindus over for dinner, please don't serve beef! Cows are beloved in India, and no practicing Hindu would consider eating one. Cows are the only mothers that freely share their milk with any creature that suckles from them. Cows represent the Divine Mother and the bounteous grace of the Earth itself.

When he did touch down, the master announced, "Islam is a true path. I experienced the highest reality by practicing it." Then, to his family's immense relief, he went back to being a good Hindu. But more trouble lay ahead.

The Radiant Stranger

One day another visitor to the temple started telling Ramakrishna about Jesus. Ramakrishna was tremendously inspired by the story of Jesus' life and felt his commitment to Hinduism slipping away. From now on he would be a Christian! He sat in front of a painting of the Virgin Mary holding the infant Christ in her lap and went into ecstasy.

One day shortly after adopting this new religion, Ramakrishna was astonished to see a foreigner with a glowing face coming straight toward him. "This is Jesus Christ!" he realized. The radiant man walked right up to him and then merged into his heart, throwing the master once more into unspeakable states of bliss.

Ramakrishna resumed his duties as a priest of Kali, but now he also told people, "Christianity is a true faith, too. If you practice Christianity sincerely, it will take you to God."

In his life, Ramakrishna tested three great faiths, Hinduism, Islam, and Christianity. He found, through direct personal experience, that although each religion differed drastically in doctrine, they all were legitimate spiritual paths. Any one of them could do the job of bringing an individual home to God.

Sages Say _____

God's grace is like a strong wind that's always blowing. All we have to do is raise our sails.

—Ramakrishna Paramahansa

What Missionaries Are Missing

Christian missionaries have often complained about the intractability of the Hindus. They're very tough to convert. Hindus may listen with great interest and enthusiasm to the story of Jesus' life and then go home and lovingly place a picture of Jesus on their home altars, right next to the pictures of Shiva and Krishna and the Goddess! They have a hard time grasping that Jesus is supposed to be the *only* God whose picture is on the altar!

Hindus worship God not only in temple images but also in special trees and stones and rivers. For Hindus, God is literally omnipresent and His grace is literally limitless. Divine Being never turns away from any soul who turns to It with sincerity, no matter whether he calls It Isis or Allah, Rama, or Jesus.

And if Jesus really blesses and protects as the missionaries say he does, then by all means, Hindus feel, put his portrait on the altar, too!

Quick Quiz

1. Shankaracharya asked the monks in his monasteries …

    a. To honor all Hindu gods.

    b. To lead a holy war against the Muslims.

    c. To sponsor Bingo games on Saturday evenings.

2. Ramakrishna converted to Christianity …

    a. And became a Dominican monk.

    b. To see whether Christianity would lead him to God.

    c. So he could attend Bingo games on Saturday evenings.

3. The Indian subcontinent …

    a. Is home to 80,000 subcultures.

    b. Has been one unified country throughout most of its history.

    c. Was discovered by Christopher Columbus in 1492.

Answers: 1 (a). 2 (b). 3 (a).

Did Jesus Visit India?

Recently, independent investigators have raised the issue of whether Jesus might have studied with the sages of India. Since this question has caught the attention of many New Agers, you and I might as well deal with it here.

We know very little about most of Jesus' life. His entire teenage and young adulthood years are missing from the historical record, investigators have pointed out. Could this be because he was absent from Palestine all those years, perhaps on a pilgrimage to the Himalayas?

The question intrigues people because so many of the miracles attributed to Christ—healing the sick, materializing objects like extra food to feed large crowds, controlling the weather, performing clairvoyance, and showing mastery over death—are identical to the powers attributed to the greatest of the Hindu masters even today. Could Jesus have learned these techniques from Hindu gurus?

A number of surprising pieces of evidence have been well-publicized.

The Tibetan Evidence

In the late 1880s, a Russian explorer named Nicolas Notovitch fell off his horse while he was riding in Ladakh, near the Tibetan border, and monks in a nearby Buddhist monastery cared for him. To help him pass the time, a sympathetic monk translated for him a fascinating Tibetan manuscript that described a long ago visit to Kashmir by a young man from the Middle East. The man's name was Issa (very close to Isha or Yeshu, the Indian pronunciations of Jesus' name).

According to the text, Issa ran away from home at the age of 13 and made his way along the well-traveled Silk Road to India, where he spent 12 years studying with both Hindu and Buddhist teachers. By the time he completed the long trek back to Palestine, he was 29 years old. The manuscript offers various fascinating details about Issa's stay in the east.

The Hindu View

In 1925, the famous Russian painter Nicolas Roerich arrived in Ladakh and made some inquiries about Norovitch's Jesus manuscript. He was unable to locate it but confirmed that the legend of Saint Issa from Palestine was well known among the local people.

In 1922, Swami Abhedananda, an Indian monk from the Oriental Seminary in Calcutta, visited Tibet and saw the manuscript. He brought back a translation he had worked on with the help of a Tibetan lama.

Before Western scholars heard about the stunning find and could reach the monastery to examine it for themselves, the Chinese army invaded Tibet. During the devastating destruction of Buddhist monasteries that followed, this amazing manuscript vanished completely.

A Tomb in Kashmir

Other evidence has been brought forward, such as a tomb in Srinagar, the capital city of Kashmir, where legend claims Jesus is buried. Another tomb near Taxila in Afghanistan (Taxila is near the border of Kashmir) has long been recognized by locals as the final resting place of the Mother Mary.

The Acts of Thomas, an astonishing early Christian text, describes how Jesus commanded his disciple, the famous Doubting Thomas, to sail to India to teach. Then it suggests that Jesus himself visited Thomas in North India.

That Christian missionaries established a church in India not long after Jesus' crucifixion is an uncontested historical fact. But we need to approach the rest of the evidence presented here very cautiously. The resting places of saints have always been big business, and what is now called the tomb of Jesus might just as well have been called the tomb of Mohammed a few centuries ago, depending on what pilgrims were passing through town and how much they were willing to pay to see the tomb.

A Doubting Thomas myself, at the back of my mind lies the nagging concern that the famous Tibetan manuscript could be a modern forgery or, to put it more generously, a well-meaning work of historical fiction. It's extremely unfortunate that the manuscript has vanished, so we'll probably never have an opportunity to examine it directly.

Guidepost

Be advised that the Jewish Talmud reports that Jesus spent his missing years in Egypt, not India, studying Egyptian spiritual science as Moses had done. Apollonius of Tyana, who visited both India and Egypt in the first century, believed the Egyptian desert ascetics had actually been initiated by Hindu immigrants centuries earlier. If this is true, Jesus may well have learned the secrets of the Hindu masters, but he learned them in Egypt!

"Come, Lord"

Since proof that Jesus visited India would have enormous historical implications, I've looked into the issue in far more detail than I have space to outline here. I would love to tell you the evidence is strong. But when I look at it clearheadedly, I can't honestly say that's true. Still, I haven't completely closed my mind to the possibility.

A colleague of mine, the president of the Himalayan Institute, pointed out that the oldest Christian prayer (used by St. Paul in I Corinthians and by John in the Book of Revelation) is Maranatha, which in Aramaic means "Come, Lord."

In Sanskrit, Maranatha means "Lord of Love."

Oh, and one more thing. The name of the area near Srinagar, Kashmir where Jesus is supposed to have lived is Amaranatha.

The Least You Need to Know

- According to the Veda, there's only one God, no matter what we call him.

- Hindus do not believe in eternal damnation.

- Hindus accept the worship of images of God as a useful form of devotional practice.

- Throughout Indian history, numerous saints have continually reminded Hindus of the value of religious tolerance.

- In the nineteenth century, Ramakrishna Paramahansa practiced each major world religion in turn to confirm its validity.

- Some Hindus believe that Jesus may have visited India.

Chapter 7

Born Again!

In This Chapter

- ◆ The cycle of birth, death, and rebirth
- ◆ Memories of previous lives
- ◆ Karma drives the cycle of reincarnation
- ◆ Paying off karmic debts
- ◆ After-death states

You've just learned about Hindu history. You heard about the holy books that define the Hindu tradition and read a whole chapter on the fundamental Hindu attitude toward religious life, a view based on tolerance and mutual respect. Now it's time to look at Hinduism's two most fundamental beliefs: karma and reincarnation.

We can't understand the purpose of the soul's journey till we realize we don't just go around once in life. According to Hinduism, we are *all* born again.

Caught in the Spin Cycle

"The Supreme Being is present in everyone's heart," says Krishna in the Bhagavad Gita. "He directs the comings and goings of all living beings. It's as if they're strapped in a spinning machine. That machine is the material universe."

Imagine a gigantic Ferris wheel with only the top half above ground. It rotates upward from beneath the Earth: a child is born. It reaches its zenith: full adulthood is attained. It starts to turn downward: old age kicks in. It disappears beneath the Earth: death comes.

The Hindu View

Did Jesus believe in reincarnation? He mentions several times that John the Baptist was the prophet Elijah in a previous life (Matthew 11:2–15, Matthew 17:10–13, and Mark 9:9–13). Many early Christians—including Origen, the most famous Church Father of them all—accepted reincarnation as a fact. In 553, however, Christian theologians at the Fifth Ecumenical Council in Constantinople formally banned the doctrine of reincarnation.

But the cycle doesn't stop there. It continues through after-death experiences that those of us still standing on the surface of Earth can't see. Then it swings back up again from beneath the ground: the soul is reborn in another body.

We meet a person we've never laid eyes on before and instantly we feel like we've known her forever. We meet another person and immediately distrust him. Why?

Some of us are born with exceptional talents. We may be gifted singers, musicians, scientists, or business people. We're attracted from early childhood to fields in which we already seem to have notable abilities. How can this be?

The Western scientific answer would be that at some point in our embryonic development the molecule in an unidentified enzyme shifted slightly and shaped our brain chemistry a certain way. Hindus offer an alternative answer that makes at least as much sense as that. They say we're attracted and repelled by new people we meet because we've met them before, and at some level of our awareness, we already know whether they're friend or foe. We have skills in certain areas because we developed them through plain hard work in previous lives.

"This Is Not My Real Home!"

Shanti Devi, a young girl growing up in Delhi in the 1930s, spoke very little till she was four years old. When she did start talking, she shocked everyone in her family. "This is not my real home! I have a husband and son in Mathura! I must return to them!"

This was India, so instead of taking their daughter to a psychiatrist, her parents told her, "That was then. This is now. Forget your past life. You're with us this time."

But Shanti Devi wouldn't give up. She talked about her former family to anyone who would listen. One of her teachers at school sent a letter to the address Shanti Devi gave as her "real home" in Mathura, inquiring if a woman had died there not too many years ago. To his astonishment, he soon received a reply from Shanti Devi's previous husband, admitting that his young wife Lugdi Devi had passed away some years previously, after giving birth to their son. The details Shanti Devi had given about her old house and members of her previous family were all confirmed.

Guidepost _____

Young children have vivid imaginations and will often make up the wildest stories. But perhaps not all their wild stories are fiction! In Hindu, Buddhist, and shamanic cultures, when young children describe things that happened to them "before," their parents understand they may be relating real events, but events that occurred in previous lives. Perhaps parents in the West should not be so quick to shrug off similar stories from their own offspring!

This launched the most thoroughly researched investigation of a case of reincarnation in modern history. Everyone got in on the act, including Mahatma Gandhi and several prominent members of the Indian government. A team of researchers, working under stringent conditions to ensure that Shanti Devi couldn't possibly be getting her information from any other source, accompanied the little girl to Mathura. On her own, she lead them to her previous home and correctly described what it had looked like years earlier before its recent refurbishing. She also related extremely intimate information, such as extramarital affairs of family members, that no one outside the family could possibly have known.

The award-winning Swedish journalist Sture Lönnerstrand spent several weeks with Shanti Devi later in her life, recording her story and verifying information about the famous government investigation. If you have any interest in reincarnation at all, I highly recommend his book, *I Have Lived Before: The True Story of the Reincarnation of Shanti Devi*. In it this remarkable woman describes what it's like to live two lives at once—the one going on now and another that's supposed to be over. She also describes her experiences in the transition period between her death as Lugdi Devi and her rebirth as Shanti Devi.

Why Don't I Remember?

You don't have to say it. I know you're thinking, "If we lived before, how come we don't remember?" Shanti Devi may have recalled her previous life, but most of us don't.

Actually we do, according to the Hindus. The very fact that we're drawn to certain people and certain places is a reflection of the dim memory of previous lives we all possess. The fact that most of us don't remember our last life in detail like Shanti Devi is due to the nature of the soul.

In the West, those of us who believe in a soul at all think of it in a very straightforward way. We have a body. It dies. We have a soul. It lives forever. For Hindus the topic is not so simple. Hindus believe the universe is multidimensional and so is the soul. What the soul is and how it operates is a critically important subject for anyone who wants to understand Hinduism (see Chapter 8).

Now, to answer your question about why we don't remember our past lives. At the moment of rebirth, Hindus believe, the infant takes its first gulp of air and becomes a breathing being. This jolts the brain and subtle body, causing a force called *vaishnava shakti* to act. In most people, this force cuts off detailed memories of the past life.

def•i•ni•tion

Vaishnava shakti is the force that stuns the soul at the time of rebirth so that it loses conscious memory of its past life.

The **karmashaya** is the karmic residue we carry from past lives, our old memories and habits and desires, which are stored in our subtle body. It's our karmic DNA.

In fact, it also cuts off detailed memories of *this* life, which is why most people don't remember much of what happened in the first three or four years of their current life either. The soul is still completing its "hook up" to the new physical brain, and not all the data from the previous file is downloaded. It's still there, though, preserved on an internal drive called the *karmashaya*, a storage bin of previous thoughts and actions that's a little hard for us to access because it's buried deep in the subtle body, not the physical brain.

Presence of Mind

I'm guessing your next question is, "Well, then how did Shanti Devi remember *her* past life?" This is where it gets interesting.

You may have heard of the *Tibetan Book of the Dead*. Perhaps you've even heard of the *Egyptian Book of the Dead*. Numbers of ancient, spiritually advanced cultures carefully trained people so they would know how to go through the process of death consciously. Often—as in the Egyptian texts and in some early Christian books, too—this involved memorizing lots of key phrases and detailed imagery.

The point in all these traditions is that if you don't want to lose yourself, if you want to attain the type of immortality that comes from the ability to hang on to your present identity from life to life, then during the process of death you must *keep your presence of mind!* All those elaborate memorizations and visualizations in the various Books of the Dead are designed to help the newly deceased soul stay focused and conscious.

Lugdi Devi, Shanti Devi's previous self, had been using an old trick recommended by yogis for thousands of years. During her Lugdi life she had constantly repeated the name of God, with full devotion, day and night. At the time of her death, her mind stayed with the divine name. It helped her remain calm and alert through a process where most people lose consciousness. As she was being reborn, her awareness remained with the name of God rather than locking into her new physical brain. So she didn't forget her previous identity. Shanti Devi actually describes this procedure in Lönnerstrand's book.

Well, you may believe this story or you may not. But now you know how it's explained in the Hindu tradition.

Guidepost

Don't assume that reincarnation takes place in linear time. Remember, to the Hindu, time and space are multidimensional. According to a Hindu classic called the *Yoga Vasishtha*, your next incarnation, or your last incarnation for that matter, may be happening *right now*. Your next life may actually occur in the past! This is because your innermost spirit exists outside of time and space and can travel to wherever and to whenever it wants!

What's My Karma?

Karma drives the process of reincarnation. Karma, to borrow from St. Paul in the Bible, means "As you sow, so shall you reap." Where, when, and in what circumstances we next incarnate is due, in large measure, to our thoughts, words, and actions in the past and present.

Sages Say

Do not be deceived; God is not mocked, for whatever a man sows, that he will also reap. ... And let us not grow weary in well-doing, for in due season we shall reap.

—Galatians 6:7–9

To be reborn into a human body is a great blessing. Human bodies, far more so than animal and plant bodies, are capable of devoting themselves to spiritual life. Most animals answer primarily to the dictates of nature, but humans have a capacity for self-reflection rarely seen in animals. Vistas of unlimited spiritual growth lie spread before the men and women who turn their attention to inner life.

The capacity to make decisions for ourselves rather than automatically doing what our natural drives tell us to do gives humans our special status. We have free will. With free will comes responsibility, however. We can't blame a tiger if it kills a deer. But if one man kills another out of greed, delusion, or hatred, very serious karmic consequences ensue. Then again, if a person selflessly helps others, superb karmic results will ultimately follow.

We can lose our human status, Hindu sages warn. If we don't take advantage of our human birth but continue living like animals, we may return to an animal body in our next life. (Perhaps some people would be more comfortable in animal bodies anyway. Then they can just eat, sleep, have sex, and never have to fill out tax forms.) Particularly pernicious people, one holy text warns, could even be reborn as "flies, gnats and biting insects"!

Three Kinds of Karma

There are three kinds of karma:

♦ **Sanchita:** All the karma we've accrued during all our previous lives.

♦ **Prarabdha:** That portion of our karma destined to play out in our present lifetime.

♦ **Kriyamana:** The fresh karma we're producing in this incarnation.

Sanchita karma includes all the debits and credits in our soul's entire karmic portfolio. Prarabdha karma only includes the debits and credits coming due in this present incarnation, and kriyamana karma is the store of merit and demerit we've been adding to our karmic account since we were born in this particular body.

Due to the constraints of time and space, only a small portion of the total karma we've collected over many incarnations can manifest in any one lifetime. In a previous life, we may have intensely desired to live on Mars. But in this life, only our karma to live near Cape Canaveral may play out. The space colonizer karma will have to wait till another lifetime. That's the distinction between sanchita and prarabdha karmas.

However, by working incredibly hard in this incarnation, we may qualify as a U.S. astronaut and get to fly the Space Shuttle—if not to Mars, then at least to NASA's orbiting space station. That's due to our kriyamana karma, our present earnest efforts.

Collective Karma

Here are another three ways to look at karma:

- **Adyatmika:** The karma we incur in our own right, as an individual soul.

- **Adhibhautika:** The karma we incur as a member of a group, our collective karma.

- **Adhidaivika:** The karma we experience due to living on this particular planet, the karma of nature itself.

Adyatmika karma is the most important because it's the one form of karma that's completely under our control. It consists of our thoughts, words, and actions. If we treat others with kindness and respect, the universe will reflect similar qualities back to us. If we treat others contemptuously, their hatred reflects our own behavior onto us.

Yet if we imagine we're in total control of our own destiny, we're mistaken. Many events that profoundly influence our lives are completely out of our control. Many Americans voted for Al Gore during the 2000 U.S. presidential election, yet they experienced the social and economic consequences of having George W. Bush in the presidency on September 11, 2001, just as

Guidepost

Never assume that when something bad happens to a person, then because of the law of karma "he had it coming." Only great spiritual masters are in a position to know all the complex karmic factors involved. It is not up to us to pass judgment.

much as the Americans who voted for Bush. Adhibhauktika or group karma can override our own karma.

When I was growing up in Norway, violent crime was a rare occurrence. If it was your karma to have a bad day in Norway, you might fall off your skis and break your leg. Living in Chicago, however, I soon discovered how different things were in America. In the United States if it's your karma to have a bad day, you may get mugged in an alley or shot in your classroom. The collective karma of your culture influences the way you'll experience your own karmic deserts.

That's why it's wrong to judge someone who's been the victim of a crime or other disaster. You can't justly "blame the victim" because he may never have done anything to bring a violent act down on himself other than happen to live in a dangerous neighborhood. Nature holds us responsible not only for our own behavior but also for the activities of the people with whom we're interconnected—our family members, neighbors, community, clubs and organizations, city, state, and nation. That's because whether we're aware of it or not, our thoughts and activities contribute to the current state of our collective affairs.

Cosmic Karma

Hindus believe nature itself is a living thing. The Earth, Wind, Water, and Fire are living intelligences called devatas. They have their own karma, which we experience in the form of earthquakes, hurricanes and tornadoes, floods and tsunamis, fire storms and volcanoes. The global warming we're experiencing now is a result of the devatas' karmic cycles, exacerbated unfortunately by our own unwise management of our environment. In India priests perform rituals not only for the good of individuals but for the community as a whole and also to harmonize relations with the living intelligences in nature. Karma is extremely complex, interlinking everyone and everything in the world! We're like a cell in a body, influenced not only by its own DNA but also by the activity of the organs around it and by the thoughts and actions of the soul inhabiting the body as a whole.

Your Fate Is Your Choice

The *Mahabharata* says that just as a lost calf can always find its mother, no matter how large the herd, so the karmic results of actions we performed in past lives will inevitably seek us out.

Hindus definitely believe in fate. The paradox is that, for the most part, we create our own fate through the use of our free will.

Yet some karmic outcomes can be prevented. Here's another three ways to understand karma:

- **Adridha:** Flexible karma we can easily deflect.

- **Dridhadridha:** Karmic patterns we can alter if we make a substantial effort.

- **Dridha:** Inflexible karma. We can do nothing to prevent this karma from playing out. Only God and a guru can change fixed karma.

Maybe you paid $120 for tickets to the *American Idol* Summer Tour, but on the night of the concert you have to stay up late studying if you're going to be prepared for an important exam the next day in medical school. You hate to throw away the $120, but you study through the night anyway. The karma you set in motion—to see your *American Idol* favorites perform in person—was flexible. You could easily change your plans when your priorities shifted.

Now suppose you spend 12 years in medical school learning to be a doctor. Then just as you're about to graduate, you decide you hate dealing with whiney sick people and you'd rather take vocal lessons and try out for *American Idol*. Now you have to lay out more money and more time learning to sing at a professional level. It takes a lot of effort to modify the flow of your karma, but if you have the will, you'll find a way.

And now let's imagine you're so captivated by *The Complete Idiot's Guide to Hinduism* that you decide you want to visit India. But after you board the jet to Delhi, you have a change of heart; maybe you should go to the *American Idol* audition after all. Problem is, your plane has already taken off. You're on your way to Delhi whether you like it or not. This is inflexible karma, representing the events and experiences you're definitely scheduled to undergo in this life due to the overwhelming karmic momentum of your choices in the past.

If the karma we've got coming to us is good, everybody's happy. But if we're experiencing a spate of bad karma, we may want

Guidepost

Does fate rule the world? According to Hinduism, almost all karma can be altered, at least to some extent, through sincere, sustained effort. You control your own fate!

Sages Say

Love God and serve others selflessly, and your bad karma will have no more power than a cancelled check.

—Mata Amritanandamayi

to look into some of the traditional Hindu methods for paying off our karmic debts on an accelerated plan so that we can get our lives back on the right track as quickly as possible.

Redirecting the Flow of Destiny

Here are some of the most popular Hindu methods for clearing out our negative karma:

- **Pilgrimage.** Hindus make long and difficult journeys to sacred sites. The journey itself is a form of spiritual practice, strengthening your faith and reliance on spirit to help see you safely through to the journey's end. At Prayag, where the Ganges and Yamuna rivers meet, pilgrims bathe in the holy waters to wash away their sins. I don't know if you can literally wash off bad karma with water, but the tremendous faith of the pilgrims I've seen at Prayag must have some effect!

- **Charitable Donations.** Since much "bad karma" is the result of debts we've incurred in previous lives, making generous donations helps us balance our karmic accounts. Hindus struggling with their health may make donations to medical research. Poverty-stricken Hindu families may go out into the woods or meadows near their homes each morning and offer food to wild animals.

- **Rituals.** By making offerings to the gods, Hindus hope to restore a positive balance in the karmic forces at work in their lives. They hope to make peace with the forces of nature and request the gods' gracious intervention.

- **Selfless Service.** Offering one's time and energy for the benefit of others without any expectation of reward is considered one of the most effective means of defusing bad karma.

- **Self-Discipline.** By undertaking vows to perform a certain type of austerity for a certain length of time, Hindus hope to overcome various karmic complexes. An example of a common vow is fasting for a predetermined period or on certain days of the week.

The Hindu View

One way of dealing with bad karma is to do breathing exercises. You read right—I said breathing exercises. Some Hindus use breathing techniques to help manage stress and promote mental calmness and clarity. When you're in a tranquil state of mind, bad karma just rolls over you—it can't really hit you in the gut.

Washing Out Your Mind

Other methods of making amends for misdeeds of the past are more internal:

- ◆ **Meditation.** Deep meditation can actually release karmic complexes buried in the subtle body. When an "inner demon" is recognized and released in meditation, it loses its ability to wreak havoc in your life.

- ◆ **Prayer.** Many Hindus chant stotras, or sacred prayers, as part of their daily worship. Often these prayers involve listing the many divine qualities of a favorite deity. Regularly contemplating all these good qualities helps elevate your consciousness and transform your personality.

- ◆ **Mantras.** Chanting the resonant divine sounds prescribed by a meditation master helps purify the field of one's consciousness and neutralizes the effect of bad karmas. Hindus use a rosary of 108 beads and make a promise to repeat a mantra many hundreds of thousands, or even millions, of times. Your mind is not supposed to wander during this practice, which is called japa. It's a form of sacrifice. You sacrifice your time and attention to God as well as all the thought energy that would otherwise be expended on romantic fantasies and inner chatter.

- ◆ **Self-Inquiry.** Self-knowledge is the greatest cure for what ails us. Some Hindus use various techniques of self-analysis to diagnose and correct the problems in their thinking and behavior that are reflected onto them as difficult karma.

- ◆ **Devotion.** In India, you will often encounter Hindus as devoted to God as many of us are to our closest friends and relatives. Developing a living relationship with the divine takes the sting out of the problems life throws your way and turns life into a love affair with a higher power.

- ◆ **Self-Surrender.** If all else fails, surrender to the Divine Will may be the last and best prescription for ameliorating bad karma. Sometimes the best we can do is surrender to God and His will for our lives, with gratitude and humility.

Sages Say _____

Reincarnation is a series of dreams within a dream: man's individual dreams within the greater dream of God.

—Paramahansa Yogananda

Life Between Lives

Let's talk about what happens when the Ferris wheel of karma rotates down where we can't see it anymore. What happens after death?

Hindus believe in heaven and hell. But while Christians believe heaven and hell are forever, Hindus see these as temporary after-death states.

The Veda talks about the paths most human souls take after death. The first is the path of the misty light to Pitri Loka, the world of the ancestors. This is where most of us average folk go, hanging out with friends and relatives who've gone on before.

The second is the path of the bright light into the heaven world called *Deva Loka*. Only very pure souls can enter this realm. It's a high heaven where we experience incredible knowledge and joy. Here we get to dwell with the devas, divine or angelic beings.

The third path, which some texts don't even mention because they assume you're a basically good person and aren't heading there, is the path of no light at all. This leads to Patala, a very turbulent after-death existence. You want to be a kind person, a decent person, a spiritually oriented person, so you don't wind up in this nasty place.

Designer Heavens

Here is an important twist you need to understand. God doesn't create heaven and hell. We do. Whatever plane of consciousness we find ourselves in after the body drops away is a world of our own making, according to the Hindu seers. If our thoughts have been predominantly cheerful and benevolent, our after-death experience is similar. If our thoughts have been filled with violence and anger, our afterlife will be, too.

The climate in the life after death is the atmosphere of our own minds. Our karma—the mental vectors we've created by our thoughts and actions—carries us to a high state, a low state, or an okay in-between state. We're in control—if we're living life consciously. If we're not directing our lives with awareness, then the unconscious tendencies stored in our subtle body take control when we die.

For many Hindus, a long stay in heaven is just what the doctor ordered, and some Hindus devote considerable effort to building up enough karmic velocity to transport them into a higher world after they jettison their bodies.

Eventually, the karmic forces that propelled you into a disembodied realm peters out. Your stay in that world is up—it's time to return to a physical body. You remember how much you enjoyed sex. You remember how much you enjoyed whipped cream puffs. You remember how much you wanted to go to Mars. You remember that your brother-in-law owes you $3,000.

Your unfulfilled desires draw you back to an appropriate physical body and—*poof!*—here you are again. The obstetrician is cutting your umbilical cord and slapping your bottom while you wail helplessly at the indignity. You traded the old model in for a new vehicle. Hopefully, thanks to good karma, you've traded up.

Quick Quiz

1. Karma and reincarnation are …

   a. Fundamental beliefs of Hinduism.

   b. Fundamental beliefs of Islam.

   c. Fundamental rights guaranteed in the United States' constitution.

2. According to Hinduism, going on a pilgrimage is a good way to …

   a. Burn off bad karma.

   b. Meet potential romantic partners.

   c. Sample India's varied cuisine.

3. Sanchita karma is …

   a. All the karma in the universe.

   b. All the karma you've accumulated over the course of your lifetimes.

   c. All the karma you can eat.

4. Hindus say you go to heaven …

   a. Forever to be with Jesus.

   b. For a while, if you've been very good.

   c. If you know the right password.

Answers: 1 (a). 2 (a). 3 (b). 4 (b).

Breaking the Cycle

A pandit once told me that yogis don't fear death because "They know where they're going." They have, in effect, practiced being dead in deep meditative states where they were completely disengaged from their bodies. They know how to remain fully conscious, alert and awake, in the after-death state, and can direct their out-of-body journey in full awareness.

The great saints and sages aren't driven around in karmic circles by the thoughts and desires stored in their subconscious, as happens to most of the rest of us in life and in death. They're like lucid dreamers, awake while everyone else is asleep. In fact, that's why some enlightened people are called buddhas. Buddha means "somebody who's awake."

You can spend a lot of time cycling through the universe. The cosmos is a long highway—there are plenty of campsites where you can pitch your tent. But when you finally tire of "exploring new worlds and new civilizations" like the heroes in *Star Trek*, there is a way to get off the wheel.

"Stop the universe! I want to get off!" In the next chapter, India's spiritual masters show you how.

The Least You Need to Know

- ◆ Hindus believe in karma and reincarnation.
- ◆ Only a portion of our total karma manifests in any one lifetime.
- ◆ Our present thoughts and actions affect the course of our destiny.
- ◆ Hindus use methods like meditation and pilgrimage to clean up their bad karma.
- ◆ Our karma leads us to pleasant or unpleasant after-death states.
- ◆ Heaven and hell are temporary; sooner or later we're reborn.

Chapter 8

Turning On Your Inner Light

In This Chapter

- Cloaking the soul
- What dies and what doesn't
- The guru's job
- Recognizing your Self
- Getting off the karmic wheel

If karma and reincarnation form the spinning wheel of the cosmic process, the Inner Self is the stable axle around which the wheel turns.

"Know Thyself" was the advice chiseled over the portico at the Oracle of Delphi in ancient Greece. No religion has ever taken the quest for self-knowledge as seriously as Hinduism. At its core, Hinduism is not about believing what somebody else tells you about the nature of your soul or accepting what other people claim about God. Ultimately, Hinduism is about exploring the very depths of your own soul yourself and getting to know God personally.

Secrets of the Subtle Body

In the West, a minority of people are interested in weird stuff like astral bodies and out-of-body travel. They're often looked at as harmless New Age flakes. But in Hinduism, coming to grips with the mechanics of what the soul actually is and how it operates are fundamental to understanding karma and reincarnation. If you want to learn how to control your reincarnational cycle, you have to understand this stuff.

Inner realities are legitimate realities to Hindus. They're not cavalierly dismissed as outdated superstitions like they are in the West. Those of us with a Christian background hear primarily about miracles that happened in Palestine 2,000 years ago. In India, however, every generation of Hindu has been exposed to living saints and yogis who demonstrate what seem like super-human abilities to the uninitiated.

In India, science and religion have always worked hand in hand. No scientist was ever burned at the stake in India! There the exploration of inner dimensions is considered just as valid as research into biochemistry or geology. While India has produced great scientists and mathematicians, it also has excelled in the science of spirit, pioneered by inner researchers called yogis.

The Hindu View _____

Hindu contributions to science have been exceptional. Very ancient Sanskrit texts called the Sulva Sutras demonstrate advanced mastery of mathematics and geometry in ancient times. The Iron Pillar of Delhi, an iron post that hasn't rusted after standing in all weather conditions for centuries, attests the Hindus' skill in metallurgy. A very old scientific manual called the Aryabhatiya demonstrates advanced knowledge of astronomy. The brilliant work of Panini on linguistics was unmatched in Europe for millennia.

Your Five Bodies

According to the yogis, you don't have just one body. You have five! Just as you wear layers of clothes—underwear, a shirt or blouse, a sweater, a coat—so your innermost spirit wears layers of increasingly subtle energies, with which it can operate in increasingly subtle dimensions of the universe.

The Taittiriya Upanishad describes five "sheaths" worn by the spirit, like a sword in a scabbard that's in a box that's in a chest that's in a closet that's in a house:

1. **Anna maya kosha:** the physical body or sheath made of physical matter

2. **Prana maya kosha:** the energy body or sheath made of life force

3. **Mano maya kosha:** the mental body or sheath consisting of thought energy

4. **Vijnana maya kosha:** the wisdom body or sheath of higher intelligence

5. **Ananda maya kosha:** the spiritual body or sheath of mystical awareness

The anna maya kosha, or physical body, is made from anna, or food. You eat; you grow. The physical matter in food becomes the physical matter of your body. This one's a no-brainer. But now let's look at ourselves a little more deeply than they taught us in high school biology.

Hindus believe there's also something called the prana maya kosha, a deeper dimension of our being made up of life energy. This is the subtle energy medieval physicians in Europe used to call the vital force. In China it's called *chi*, and learning to manipulate it is the basis of acupuncture and the martial arts. In the Western esoteric tradition, this sheath is sometimes called the etheric body.

Homeopathic medicines do not act directly on the physical body but are used to balance the pranic fields. These form the energy substrate around which the physical matter of our material body takes shape, like iron filings arranging themselves along the lines of force emanating from a magnet.

But when it comes to exploring our subtle nature, that's not even half of it! To find out more, get in line.

def•i•ni•tion

Homeopathy is a system of medicine widely practiced in Europe and India that uses very minute, potent amounts of medicine to help balance the subtle energies underlying the physical body.

Coats of Living Energy

You're standing in line at the health food store waiting to buy a half dozen organic apples. The man in front of you takes a bite of an apple and falls down dead. (It was probably an aneurysm, but you still reconsider purchasing the apples.) How is the dead man so different from you, anyway? You're both made of physical matter, and since he just died a few seconds ago, the matter in his body is pretty much as good as the matter in yours.

The major difference between a living person and a dead one, according to the yogis, is the dead one isn't breathing. When the breath stops cranking, the life force can no longer animate the body or keep the mind and body connected. The man's mind may still actually be present, perhaps hovering over his body wondering why the lady ahead of him in line is taking so dang long to pay for a carton of soymilk. But he can no longer manipulate his fingers or toes because the energy link between his mind and body has been severed.

Sages Say

All of the body is in the mind, but not all of the mind is in the body.

—Swami Rama of the Himalayas

But suppose the man doesn't die. Suppose he just goes into a coma. This means his life force is still operating. His physical body keeps breathing and doesn't start to decompose. But now the mental body has gone missing. You're shouting, "Sir! Sir! Can you hear me?" But he can't because his ability to think or to connect with his body through his sense organs has shut down.

Let's consider another scenario. An agitated man runs into the health food store and shoots another patron who's complaining the tofu isn't fresh. How could any human being kill another without the slightest twinge of remorse? In the killer's case, his wisdom body isn't working properly. This very subtle body of living intelligence is responsible for making judgments and moral decisions. When it operates normally, it works as the conscience, the will, and the higher intellectual and intuitive functions. A sociopath has no conscience. His wisdom body is barely functioning.

The Body of Bliss

Let's look at the rest of the folks standing in line at the store. Most of them are decent, hard-working people. Some are passionately interested in sports. Some love to cook. Others want nothing more than to go home, plop down on the sofa, and watch *CSI: Miami* on their high-definition TV. Very few of the people here are seriously interested in spiritual life.

This doesn't mean they're bad people—it just means they have other priorities. Their spiritual body is underdeveloped. They've never tasted the ananda, the divine bliss, of deeper meditative states. The possibility of expanding their awareness to experience higher states of consciousness has probably never occurred to them. In these people, the body of mystical awareness is not enlivened. If a person doesn't exercise and eat right, her physical body is unlikely to be in good shape. If people don't meditate or spend some time praying and contemplating a higher reality, then the spiritual sheath, our subtlest body, atrophies.

I studied the Taittiriya Upanishad, the source of this doctrine, many years ago with a yoga master named Swami Rama. I can't emphasize strongly enough that to the adepts of the Hindu tradition, the five distinct yet interlinking bodies are just as real as the circulatory or respiratory systems are to us in the West. The yogis say they use these different bodies as vehicles for traveling through different dimensions.

Life in the Three Worlds

Let's swing around and come back at this stuff from another angle that compacts the five bodies down into three:

1. **Sthula sharira:** the physical body

2. **Sukshma sharira:** the subtle body

3. **Karana sharira:** the causal body

The physical level includes both the material body and vital force. Why? Because at death, when the material body starts to disintegrate, so does the life force. According to the yogis, the "wreaths" some people claim to see floating over graves are decaying pranic fields. There no longer is a material body for them to animate, so their energy field gradually dissipates.

The subtle body represents both the wisdom sheath and the mental sheath from the previous scheme. It continues to exist after death. Each of us still experiences ourselves as the same entity who used to live in a physical body. We may temporarily lose consciousness after death, as if we were sinking into deep sleep, but when we wake up in our subtle body, we're our same old selves. Yogic adepts are said to be able to travel outside their physical bodies in this ball of mental energy.

For most people, at the time of rebirth, the subtle body from the last life now also passes away and the causal body reincarnates. The causal body contains the very essence of who you are as an individual. The habits and attitudes developed in your previous lives, your likes and dislikes, talents and liabilities, are carried with the causal body like a piece of luggage. But specific memories from past lives often slip away. (If that sounds disturbing, consider that

 The Hindu View

The three bodies or shariras known to the Hindus were familiar to the ancient Greeks as well. The Greeks called the physical, subtle, and causal bodies the *soma*, *psyche*, and *nous*.

most of your specific memories from this life are already forgotten! What did you have for breakfast ten years ago today? What did your social studies teacher tell you was the capital of Costa Rica?)

Spiritual masters, because they have aligned their awareness with their causal body, retain full awareness of their previous lives when they are reborn. Most of us identify with our physical or mental bodies, which don't necessarily travel with us into the next life, so we don't have detailed past life recall. Instead we begin evolving a new personality and fresh memories, which develop along with our new physical body.

If you begin exploring Hindu sacred literature, you will find numerous references to "the three worlds." Western scholars often interpret these as the surface of the Earth, the atmosphere, and the upper sky. But to Hindu spiritual practitioners, they refer to the physical world accessible to our five senses, the mental world accessible to our mind, and the causal or formless realm beyond the reach of thought. We can travel in the formless world only with the highest intuitive powers inherent in our causal body. In that world we don't travel from place to place but from insight to insight.

 The Hindu View

Texts like the Vedantasara explain that just as numerous trees are considered one forest, in the same way the totality of everyone's subtle bodies can be understood as one great, collective soul. This is called the *sutratma*, the World Soul, which experiences itself through all our individual souls.

The mental and physical worlds were originally projected out of the causal or "seed" world, the world of concepts or archetypal patterns, and will eventually dissolve back into it. This is the extra-dimensional world of "ideas" the Greek philosopher Plato wrote about.

"Who Am I?"

If you have some familiarity with the mystical traditions of the world, bells are clanging in your head like crazy. You recognize the breakdown of the soul into the five sheaths as strikingly similar to the fivefold soul of the ancient Egyptian tradition. And the threefold scheme of the physical, subtle, and causal bodies is exactly paralleled in the ancient Greek tradition. Plutarch, a first century priest from the temple of Apollo at Delphi, described it explicitly in his essays.

When you start to recognize the amazing links between different spiritual traditions, you can understand why, in the first century C.E., Apollonius of Tyana expressed his opinion that India was the motherland of the world's mystical knowledge!

"Okay," you may be wondering. "So I have all these different bodies. Which one of them is *me*?"

Ramana Maharshi Finds Himself

Ramana Maharshi was born in Tiruchuli, Tamil Nadu, in 1879. He impressed no one. He was a mediocre student and something of a bully on the playground. He felt no draw to spiritual life at all.

Ramana Maharshi, sage of Arunachala.

Then, at the age of 17, Ramana Maharshi woke up. "I was sitting alone in a room on the first floor of my uncle's house," Ramana later related. "There was nothing wrong with my health, but a sudden violent fear of death overtook me. I felt, 'I am going to die' and began thinking what to do about it. I felt I had to solve the problem myself, there and then."

Ramana lay down on the floor and acted out the process of death. He stiffened his body as if rigor mortis had set in and held his breath as if his heart and lungs had stopped. "Okay, the body is dead. But am I dead?" he inquired.

At that moment, he experienced an overwhelmingly powerful sense of the deathless spirit within himself. "This was not a dull thought but flashed through me vividly as living truth which I perceived directly, almost without thinking. 'I' was something real."

Sages Say _____

The only enquiry leading to Self-realization is seeking the source of the "I" with an in-turned mind.

—Ramana Maharshi

From then on, Ramana was obsessed with his Inner Self. He left home and hid in a small storage cell in the Shiva temple near Mount Arunachala. There he did intense spiritual practice, learning to maintain his focus continually on the deathless reality he felt inside himself. Eventually he experienced the conscious root of his being constantly, even while talking or reading. Ramana had become an enlightened sage, living in the unflickering light of spirit.

Remember how I said earlier that Hindus call their tradition "the eternal religion" because anyone who explores the laws of consciousness will rediscover Hinduism's fundamental truths? Ramana was an average 17-year-old boy with no formal religious training whatever. Yet by lying down and focusing intently inward, he had rediscovered the ancient truths of the Upanishadic seers. "That thou art. You are that undying inner awareness."

Ramana had traveled beyond the physical body, beyond the subtle body, and even through the causal body. Underlying them all he discovered the true Self.

The Inner Self

Ramana Maharshi went on to become one of the best-known and best-loved saints of modern India. Hindus (and later foreigners) would come from thousands of miles away merely to sit in the presence of the master. By remaining fully centered in his Inner Self, he radiated a tranquil luminosity. Those sitting near him reported their minds immediately became still. Some experienced inner peace for the first time in their lives.

Scientists in the West consider consciousness a by-product of the nervous system that ends with death. The sages of India don't buy that. During out-of-body travel they experience their consciousness moving independently of their body. The great masters have also reported remaining conscious and alert after their previous bodies died and journeying through other inner worlds. To them the physical body is the by-product of consciousness, not the other way around!

The Inner Self is called Atman in Sanskrit. The Atman is who you really are—not your physical and subtle bodies, all of which are perishable. The Atman exists beyond space and time. It is the undying reality, your fundamental inner being and truth.

Sages Say _____

There is an eternal, all pervading intelligence in which all individual souls are rooted. That Supreme Awareness is the final truth. That is your innermost being. You are that.

—Chhandogya Upanishad

Entering the Inner World

Many people have experienced the Inner Self at some point in their lives. If you haven't—if what I'm talking about here sounds to you like it comes from another planet—let's try a short exercise and maybe you can get a glimpse of the inner world Ramana discovered in yourself.

1. Sit up comfortably with your head, neck, and spine straight. Close your eyes and relax deeply.

2. Breathe naturally. Your breath should be even, slow, and continuous. No jerky or shallow breathing, please! (The subtle currents you're feeling coursing through your system is your energy body.)

3. Don't feel stupid! This is just an experiment. (The part of you that's tell you this is silly is your mental body.)

4. Bring your full awareness to the point between your eyebrows. Then shift your awareness about three inches behind this point, inside your brain. If any visual images or mental chatter appear, ignore them.

5. Rest your attention in the silent darkness in your mind. Ask yourself, "Who is aware of the silent darkness?" Focus attentively. (The part of you asking this subtle, discerning question is your wisdom body.)

6. Be fully aware of your own awareness. (The silent force of intuitive attention in you, reaching for pure awareness, is your spiritual body.)

7. The pure awareness itself is your true nature, your authentic Self. You are now resting in your immortal spirit.

Good job! Open your eyes and relax!

Did you experience an intense inner lucidity, a sort of primordial awareness that wasn't thinking or doing anything, just kind of watching?

If you connected, even for a second, with your Atman, you would have felt vividly alive, intensely focused, and very clear-headed. In the Hindu tradition, it's believed that people who visit this state regularly experience dramatic healing and become much more creative and successful and much less fearful.

Great saints live continually in this state. They gain from it the ability to help others with tangible blessing power, as Ramana Maharshi did.

The Inner Sun

Let me state the obvious. Most of our lives we do not walk around experiencing ourselves as a being of pure, radiant consciousness. We experience ourselves as harried housewives, aggressive salesmen, bored students, starving musicians, or just about anything but God-centered saints. We're just standing in line at the health food store waiting to buy some apples.

An athlete or a sick person or a high-fashion model may remain intensely identified with her physical body. Her attention is most often directed toward her health or strength or appearance. That is her reality. Hinduism says that no matter how well she cares for her body, one day it will die. But the Inner Self hidden behind her self-image will not.

A scientist or intellectual or computer programmer may be very intensely focused at the level of thought. A lover or a new mother or a neurotic may be very intensely focused on her emotions. But eventually the field of experience with which they're identifying will pass away. Their Higher Self will not.

def·i·ni·tion

Prakriti is the primeval energy from which the universe is shaped. It's the stuff of which matter is made.

You may feel who you really are is your familiar mental body—your work-a-day thoughts and emotions. You may feel your real identity is your trusty, tangible material body. Hinduism says that all our bodies, including the physical one, are nothing more than fields of energy, called *prakriti* in Sanskrit. They reflect the light of spirit and, because of this, appear to be independent and conscious, just as the Moon appears to shine with its own light but actually only reflects the Sun's.

What you experience as your mind has no more independent reality than your body. When you enter the state of deep sleep, for example, the light of spirit withdraws from your mental body and for all practical purposes your mind ceases to exist!

The Tripura Rahasya compares the Inner Self to a splendid gem locked in a chest that's fallen into the sea and sunk into the mud. You have to find the chest, clean off the mud, and break open the lock. Then you'll see for yourself the shining gem of incalculable value. All Hindu spiritual practices are designed with the ultimate goal of helping us find the "pearl of great price" that lies buried in our minds and encrusted with the mud of our generally petty, run-of-the-mill thoughts. That gem is the pure, undying awareness that illuminates our lives.

Spiritual Mentoring

"There are some especially pure souls who have attained Self-realization, establishing their awareness permanently in their Inner Self," wrote the famous Hindu adept Shankaracharya. "They bring blessings to all humanity, like the coming of spring. They have crossed the ocean of birth and death, yet selflessly remain here among us and help others cross, too. It is the very nature of these great men and women to help others."

In Hinduism, the guru—your spiritual mentor—ranks in stature second only to God. In fact, in some traditions the guru is valued even more than God. After all, it's the guru who introduces you to God in the first place. Without the assistance of this guide, you may never find your way into the divine presence!

The Upanishads put it this way. If someone hits you over the head, blindfolds you, carries you away God knows where, then dumps you off in the middle of nowhere, you have a problem. Many of us may have the sense of being spiritually lost, dropped here in the material world, blundering around cluelessly. Now, if someone comes up to you and says, "Oh, you're from Duluth? Duluth is that way!" Suddenly you're not so lost. You're headed in the right direction, and with a little effort and resourcefulness on your part, you'll find your way back to Duluth.

The guru shows you the way home. He or she teaches you the wisdom of the ancients and guides your moral and spiritual development. And most important, the guru prescribes the specific spiritual exercises you need to grow in self-awareness.

A guru is a very useful resource if you have begun a meditation practice. It's amazing, the crazy content thrown up by your subconscious and the confusion it can lead to. The guru helps you distinguish between the seductive but ultimately not very productive images streaming out of your subconscious and the genuine insights pouring out of your superconscious. The guru has been through the process and knows how to distinguish what's spiritually legitimate.

The Guru Hook-Up

Advanced gurus transmit the enlightening energy of their spiritual tradition. They don't generate it—they serve as conduits through which the living knowledge flows. This is the famous process of *shaktipat*, the "descent of spiritual power." You work very hard, making every sincere effort to attain higher states of divine awareness. When you can't go any further by yourself, the guru does the hook-up, plugging you into the cosmic circuit box and—*zap!*—you spontaneously rocket into a higher orbit of being.

def·i·ni·tion

Shaktipat is the transmission of spiritual knowledge and power.

Swami Rama told me about his own experience. He was so discouraged with his lack of progress in meditation after years of sincere effort that he actually felt suicidal. His guru, the great master Bengali Baba, touched his forehead, and for the next nine hours, Swami Rama sat motionless in the highest state of bliss he had ever experienced.

My own experiences with Hindu gurus have often been intensely frustrating. This is because I come from the Western academic tradition where teachers exist to give information. You ask a straightforward question, you get a straight answer. I'll tell you right now that if you want to get a straight answer out of a Hindu guru, you're better off going to dental school and learning to pull teeth.

Sages Say

The spiritual aspirant controls his senses. He controls his life force. He controls his mind. He gains lordship over the faculties of his higher intelligence. Then he becomes one with the Supreme One, Whose body is space, Who is ever tranquil, Who is immortal.

—Taittiriya Upanishad

In the Hindu tradition, gurus don't see their role as imparters of information. Their goal isn't simply to help you get a Ph.D. Their goal is to make you a sage, to awaken your intuitive powers so that you can find the answers in the inner world yourself. In Hinduism, it's said that a guru's greatest achievement is to propel a disciple to even greater heights than the guru herself has reached.

Into the Pressure Cooker

Gurus do convey information. But a larger portion of the training they impart involves character building and purification of the ego. So they throw you into awful situations, like starting a medical center to help the poor and then putting completely incompetent people in charge. Can you maintain your spiritual center and your focus on serving others when your bosses are continually making irrational decisions that irritate the heck out of you? Can you stay calm when your guru, who was always so loving to you before, suddenly starts accusing you of something you didn't even do?

These are the kinds of tricks of the trade the Hindu guru has traditionally used to help disciples clearly see the play of their egos and to test the strength of their commitment to spiritual life.

Very few, very special people have attained Self-realization without the help of a guru. Recent historical examples include Ramana Maharshi, Anandamayi Ma, and Amritanandamayi Ma. Hindus believe exceptional people like these either had spectacularly good karma from the past, when they *did* work with a guru, or else they are incarnations of great sages of the past or even of deities, who entered our world to serve humanity.

Quick Quiz

1. For Hindus, a human being is made up of …

    a. Physical, subtle, and causal bodies.

    b. Slugs and snails and puppy dog tails.

    c. Pizza, Pepsi, and potato chips.

2. When he was 17 years old, Ramana Maharshi realized …

    a. He was deeply attracted to girls.

    b. He needed to buy some apples.

    c. Within his soul lay a deathless Inner Self.

continues

continued

3. The guru's job is to …

   a. Separate us from the contents of our wallets.

   b. Align us with our real nature.

   c. Teach us how to win friends and influence people.

4. The Inner Self …

   a. Is the deathless awareness hidden behind our thoughts.

   b. Can be experienced with the help of antidepressants.

   c. Is the result of enzymatic activity in the brain.

Answers: 1 (a). 2 (c). 3 (b). 4 (a).

Getting On the Innernet

For many Hindus, Self-realization is God-realization. "The air inside an empty jar is the same as the air outside the jar," wrote the sage Shankaracharya. "In exactly the same way, your Inner Self is identical with the Self of all. Smash the jar, and the air inside it merges seamlessly with the air outside. Smash the illusion that you exist apart from God, and you merge in that divine reality."

The jars we are locked into are the physical, subtle, and causal bodies. The physical body is smashed at death. The subtle body is smashed at rebirth. But the causal body, the subtlemost vortex of energy in which our Inner Self reincarnates, is smashed only at the moment of final liberation, when the Inner Self merges in the Divine Self.

Think about it. Just as your five fingers are not really separate because they are linked to the same hand, so the Self in you and the Self in me and the Self in the person ahead of you in line at the bank are not really separate because they are linked in the Supreme Self, the consciousness of God.

When you harm someone else, you are literally harming your Self. When you love someone else, you are literally loving your Self.

At the innermost level of our being we are all intimately linked. Apollonius of Tyana was amazed when he arrived in Kashmir and found yogis who knew everything about him. "How can you possibly know me?" he demanded. "We begin by knowing ourselves," was their reply.

The advanced adepts of the Hindu tradition move into a space in consciousness where there is no space between us. They explain that that is how they know their disciples' very thoughts. Hindus assume Jesus was expressing exactly the same concept when he said, "I am the vine, you are the branches." (John 15:5) We are linked at the root with God.

The Hindu View

Many Christians are puzzled by Jesus' words, "I am the vine, you are the branches." These words are adopted from the ancient Orphic mysteries in which the god Dionysus uses the same phrase, referring to the mystic identity of his disciples with himself. The Hindu doctrine of our unity with God and each other appears in mystical traditions throughout the world.

Getting Off the Wheel

The goal of every Hindu life is to eventually shift one's awareness to the inner world of divine union. Hindu life is actually structured so that even average lay people can spend the last portion of their lives devoted solely to spiritual practice. (I'll explain how this actually works in Chapter 15.)

As long as you continue to wear a body, whether it's a physical one or a body of subtler energy, you're on the wheel of rebirth. Your identification with a body, your desire to explore a realm of existence whether material or astral, will keep tugging you into the round of birth and death.

In Hinduism, the spiritual master is the one who is no longer tied to any body. From the realm of pure consciousness, this being can choose voluntarily to reenter the world and can just as effortlessly exit again when the mission that soul has chosen to complete in the world is done. These are the liberated souls of Hinduism, the great enlightened masters. What they've mastered is themselves. Now they live in God-consciousness.

The Least You Need to Know

- In addition to the physical body, we have increasingly subtler bodies.
- The true Self is none of these bodies but the consciousness that operates through them.

- The guru helps us connect with our Inner Self.

- Self-realization is ultimately God-realization because God is the Self of all.

9

Blind Men Describe an Elephant

In This Chapter

- ◆ A reasonable path to God
- ◆ Hindu atomic theory
- ◆ Ritual road to heaven
- ◆ Counting out reality
- ◆ Truth and illusion

Warning: You are about to launch into the dizzying world of Hindu theology. If your "Boring!" light is switching on, let me reassure you that the Hindus have some of the most interesting theology on the planet, if I may say so myself.

And I think if you get some of this stuff down, then later when we see how Hindus live their daily lives and what spiritual practices they actually perform, it will seem a lot less like "heathen superstition" and more like something truly beautiful, meaningful, and profound.

Six Views of One Reality

There's a famous story in India about six blind men who try to understand what an elephant looks like by running their hands over its body. One feels its trunk, another its ears, another its leg. A fourth man fingers its tail, a fifth its belly, and the sixth balances himself on its back. Not surprisingly, they come to completely different conclusions about what an elephant must look like.

Hindus believe God is like that. He's so big and so multidimensional and so impossible to grasp with the human mind that everyone who has something to say about His nature may be absolutely correct, but only about the one small part of His nature they are able to understand.

Imagine we're standing together in a dark room. I hold up a sheet of paper. You shine a flashlight on it and see that it's white. Okay, that was a no-brainer.

Now imagine your flashlight has a yellow bulb instead of a white one. This time the paper looks yellow. If your flashlight had a blue bulb, it would look blue. If you turn off your flashlight, you won't see the paper at all. It's merged in the darkness. So what color is the sheet of paper, *really?*

def•i•ni•tion

Darshana means "seeing." It refers to Hinduism's schools of theology, which are different ways of "seeing" God. It can also mean having the direct vision of the Supreme Being yourself—for example, when you see his or her image in a temple.

There are many thousands of different *darshanas*, ways of looking at reality, in Hinduism. But six are most important. They're all looking at the same divine reality, but they see it in different colors.

Please note that in summarizing these complex systems of Indian thought for you, I will be shamelessly oversimplifying.

Nyaya: The Logical Approach

When I was in college, oh, it seems like a century ago, in world history we were taught that the ancient Greeks were the first people to think logically. This always seemed suspicious to me. The Egyptians built the pyramids without being able to think logically? Humans have lived on this planet for hundreds of thousands of years at least, and Thales of Miletus was the first person ever to have a logical thought? Frankly, my professors thought the Greeks were the only ancient culture capable of logic because the Greeks were the only ancient culture they'd ever studied.

Today, more knowledgeable scholars admit that until very recently, the Nyaya philosophers of India were probably the most skilled logicians in history. These guys had nitpicking down to a science.

Nyaya was founded by a sage named Gotama a long, long time ago. He noted that anyone could run around claiming anything, so how do we decide whom to believe? We have to reason clearly and methodically, Gotama said, so we don't inadvertently delude ourselves and everyone else at the same time.

The Hindu View

People often think scientific materialism is a modern phenomenon. But India's ancient school of Lokayata was wholly materialistic. It taught that there is no reality beyond what we see with our five senses and that human consciousness ends at death. This school never gained much credibility in India because it failed to explain the extrasensory or psychic phenomena so many people experience and that saints and advanced yogis exhibit all the time.

When we analyze nature critically, we're forced to the conclusion that the objective universe is composed of individual atoms and the subjective universe is composed of individual souls. But how can we souls be sure that our ideas about the world outside ourselves are correct? We can rely on four sources of information if we're careful:

♦ Data we perceive with our senses.

♦ Inferences we make based on this data. ("If there's smoke, there's fire.")

♦ Careful comparisons. ("A tiger is like a big lion with stripes.")

♦ Reliable testimony. (Like the statements of enlightened masters.)

Nyaya theologians determined that God must exist for a number of logical reasons. Here are two:

♦ Atoms can't coordinate themselves into an intelligible universe. Everywhere you look, the cosmos shows evidence of intelligent planning and purpose.

♦ Karma doesn't run itself. Some higher intelligence apportions to each soul the karma it deserves.

The Nyayas worked out their arguments with painstaking attention to detail and logical consistency. They set the standard for clear thinking in Hinduism.

Vaisheshika: The Atomic Theory

My professors in college also told me the Greeks were the first people to come up with the atomic theory, but that wasn't true either.

The Vaisheshikas formulated the Indian atomic theory sometime before the beginning of Buddhism and Jainism, both of which incorporated some ideas about atoms into their worldviews. This takes Vaisheshika back to, at the very latest, 500 B.C.E. It's attributed to a brilliant founding sage named Kanada.

According to the Vaisheshikas, we can say some specific things definitely exist. Atoms do, as do the space and time in which they move. So does God, and so do we, in the form of immortal souls who put on bodies to play out our karma during the cycles of universal manifestation.

Sages Say

After a cycle of universal dissolution, the Supreme Being decides to recreate the cosmos so that we souls can experience a solid world. Very subtle atoms begin to combine, eventually generating a cosmic wind that blows heavier and heavier atoms together. Souls, depending on their karma earned in previous world systems, spontaneously draw to themselves atoms that coalesce into an appropriate body.

—Prashasta Pada

Here comes an important point. (Prepare not to be confused.) Remember that six blind men can describe an elephant completely differently and still be talking about the same animal.

Remember how I mentioned that Hinduism says we're all one? That our souls all connect in the divine consciousness? Well, the Vaisheshikas don't believe this. But that doesn't mean they're not Hindus! Nor does it mean they don't believe in the Veda. It just means they're reading the Veda from a slightly different perspective that makes more sense to them. It's like Christians reading the Bible. Some say the Bible tells us we should follow the pope. Others insist the Bible doesn't breathe a word about the pope.

The Vaisheshikas believe each soul is an eternally separate unit that exists as a whole in itself. When it disengages from involvement with the universe, becoming a liberated soul, it enters a state much like unconsciousness because it doesn't perceive or interact with anything outside itself. It's not happy. It's not unhappy. It just exists. It's something like the state of your awareness during deep sleep. After millions of years of reincarnating in one challenging lifetime after another, a good long sleep may be just what the doctor ordered!

Mimamsa: The Way to Heaven

Mimamsa is the system of theology favored by many orthodox brahmins who devote their lives to performing Vedic rituals.

Mimamsa is attributed to the ancient sage Jaimini. It emphasizes the performance of duty as the structural law that holds families, nations, and the universe itself together. Literally from their first waking moment, Hindus who follow this tradition devote each moment of the day to the conscientious performance of religious duties, from chanting sacred mantras before getting out of bed, chanting other prayers the moment their feet touch the floor, and so on throughout the day.

The Mimamsas are not deeply interested in defining the nature of God or in spiritual liberation. Their preoccupation is with the performance of sacred ritual in the effort to live righteously here on Earth and to obtain a heavenly state after death. They're not interested in getting off the wheel of rebirth but in living ethically in the here and now.

To the Mimamsas, the universe itself is an unending fire sacrifice. Life is offered back to life as one creature dies to feed another. By aligning ourselves with the self-sacrificial nature of the universe, we live in accord with eternal law.

Sankhya: Spirit and Matter

Here comes a totally mind blowing one. Sankhya is one of the most ancient, most interesting, and most influential philosophies of all time. Thinkers from other schools would do their best to debunk Sankhya, but in the end, they'd incorporate parts of it into their own systems. If you can grasp the fundamental insights of Sankhya, you'll have a firm handle on the mystical traditions of cultures all over the world.

The yogis and pandits I've studied with claim Sankhya is the oldest known philosophical system in existence. They may be right. The system was founded by the sage

> **Sages Say**
>
> The followers of Sankhya put their trust in the words of the sages. The followers of Yoga put their trust in their own experience. There is no other wisdom equal to Sankhya. There is no other power equal to Yoga.
>
> —*Mahabharata*

Kapila in prehistory. Sankhya terminology already appears in the Veda, particularly the Upanishads.

Sankhya literally means "number." Sankhya enumerates the categories that make up physical and mental reality. In prehistory, the great minds of India didn't have particle accelerators to help them analyze different types of atoms. Instead they used astute observation of nature and of their own minds to analyze the components of human experience. These components added up to 25.

Let's start at ground zero, the most physical of physical matter, and work our way up the ladder of reality:

1. **Prithivi:** Dense physical matter (like Earth).

2. **Apas:** Fluid physical matter (like Water).

3. **Agni:** Combustive physical matter (like Fire).

4. **Vayu:** Gaseous matter (like Air).

5. **Akasha:** Extremely attenuated physical matter (like space).

6. **Gandha:** That which is smelled.

7. **Rasa:** That which is tasted.

8. **Rupa:** That which is seen.

9. **Sparsha:** That which is felt.

10. **Shabda:** That which is heard.

11. **Payu:** The ability to excrete.

12. **Upastha:** The ability to procreate.

13. **Pada:** The ability to locomote.

14. **Pani:** The ability to handle objects.

15. **Vak:** The ability to speak.

16. **Ghrana:** The sense of smell.

17. **Jinva:** The sense of taste.

18. **Chakshu:** The sense of sight.

19. **Tvak:** The sense of touch.

20. **Stotra:** The sense of hearing.

21. **Manas:** Thought processes.

22. **Ahankara:** Self-identity.

23. **Buddhi:** Judgment, intellect and intuition.

24. **Prakriti:** The material matrix. Primordial matter.

25. **Purusha:** The individual spirit.

Guidepost _____

Is our Western way of categorizing reality the only legitimate way? We say there are 100-plus elements and 4 or so basic forms of energy. Other cultures—such as the Hindus and Chinese—described nature in ways that initially appear odd to us. Westerners who have taken the trouble to learn these foreign systems have expressed amazement at their level of insight and sophistication.

Ordering Reality

To put it all together, Sankhya lists five physical elements, five subtle elements, five organs of action, five sense organs, three faculties of mind, then matter and spirit per se.

Note that items 1 through 4 on the list are often mistranslated as Earth, Water, Fire, and Air. These four concepts, as they're actually applied in Hindu physics and medicine, are far more complex than such simplistic translations would suggest. Hindus understand them as energy states, as the way matter behaves in its densest forms.

Akasha, item 5, is a super fine form of matter that fills space and in a sense actually *is* space. Atomic particles are created from it. Nuclear physicists have actually admitted that such a field of "super matter" or "zero point energy" must indeed exist to explain the appearance of particles "out of nowhere" during their experiments!

Note that only the first five categories on the list are physical! Items 5 through 10 are *not* physical. These subtle elements refer to matter *as you experience it in your mind,* not as it exists outside your body. After all, when you see a fire in a dream, your skull doesn't burst into flames! According to the Hindu tradition, the substance of your dreams and inner visions is just as real as the substance of the external world. In fact, whole other dimensions exist of this immaterial matter. This is an important point that may help you understand how visualizations and ritual magic—important components of Hindu spiritual practice—actually work.

Hold on to your hat, because the next major point is totally counterintuitive to our Western conditioning. Sankhya holds that the sense organs and organs of action are not physical either. When you glanced over items 11 through 20 in the list, you probably assumed they were referring to hands and feet, ears and eyes. If you did, you were mistaken.

The Sankhya masters noted that we see and move not only in the physical world but also in our dreams and out-of-body experiences. So our ability to interface with the stuff around us must exist in our subtle body. They operate through our physical organs while we're in a physical body, interacting with the solid world accessible to our waking consciousness. But they operate through our subtle body in lucid dream states, "astral travel," and after death.

The Nature of Mind

Your brain is a valuable apparatus, but ultimately it's not the brain that sees and hears. The brain registers sound waves and photons from the physical world, but these are transmitted to a receiving station that's not *in* the brain, though it operates *through* the brain. This receiving station is called manas, the processing port of the mind. It's item 21 on the Sankhya list.

The renegade Western physicist Rupert Sheldrake pointed out that a person who doesn't understand how a television set works might believe Simon Cowell and Paula Abdul live inside the TV. So if the TV set breaks, Simon and Paula no longer exist. In reality, of course, Simon and Paula (and Randy Jackson, too) film *American Idol* in a studio in Los Angeles, and their program is routed to your TV via the wonders of modern technology.

According to Sheldrake, we in the West have a very primitive understanding of the brain. When the brain is switched on, images appear. When the brain switches off, the images vanish. Ergo, scientists assume the images exist only in the brain. But our thought processes may be generated in another dimension entirely and may only be *routed* through the physical brain when we engage with the external world and our physical body. In Chapter 25, I explain what happened when Western scientists put yogis to the test in the laboratory to see whether wild claims like these could possibly hold up. (Spoiler alert: The yogis passed with flying colors!)

In addition to manas, which receives, transmits, and interprets sense data, there's the ahankara, or "me" awareness (item 22 on our list). This is the lens that focuses thoughts and reactions on a single point we identify as "me." Problems arise when this "me" sense gets out of hand and we start claiming not only our thoughts and perceptions as our own, but also objects around us ("That's *my* doll, you can't have it!") and even other people as exclusively our own.

Buddhi (item 23) is the part of the mind in which will power and the ability to make decisions kicks in. Manas senses Rum Raisin premium ice cream. Ahankara declares, "That's for me!" Buddhi is the part of the intelligence that then deliberates: "I'm already 25 pounds overweight. What does another pound or two matter?" And then makes the decision to go ahead and pork down a pint of ice cream. Animals have manas and ahankara, but buddhi, or the capacity to make wise or foolish judgments based on reason, exists primarily in humans.

The real Self, consciousness, called *purusha* (related to the English word *person*) in this system, exists outside the range of mind and matter all together. The mind is the apparatus through which consciousness interfaces with the inner and outer worlds. But the mind is made of perishable patterns of energy and will dissolve away sooner or later (item 24), unlike the real conscious Self within, which is eternal (item 25).

 Sages Say _____

Mental states are not conscious in themselves. Mind has a knower. The Self is that knower; it is the real man.

—Swami Satparakashananda

How do the Sankhya masters know this? Because they've been doing yoga!

Yoga: Techniques for Higher Awareness

In the West, yoga means standing on your head. In Hinduism, it means meditation. Yoga literally means "union." It's about uniting your attention with its source, your everyday awareness with the fountain of consciousness from which it springs.

Hindu thinkers were not into philosophy just to show how smart they were. Even the driest Hindu thinkers of them all, the Nyaya logicians, had a sacred purpose in mind. That was to use their knowledge as a means to *moksha*, spiritual liberation. To Hindus, philosophy is never just an intellectual exercise as it so often is in the West. It's a door to the living experience of divine reality.

def•i•ni•tion _____

Moksha means "freedom." The liberated man and woman are freed from the wheel of death and rebirth and from the destiny enforced by their karma.

Yoga is the practical branch of Sankhya, the spiritual techniques used to move from talking about higher levels of reality to actually experiencing them.

Sankhya says that everything in the ever-changing universe, including the subtle matter out of which our minds are made, comes from prakriti, primordial energy. Prakriti is the ocean of energy that exists forever in all dimensions of eternity. Its grossest manifestation is the physical matter we see and touch.

Prakriti has three modes called gunas:

◆ **Rajas:** Motion. Active, energetic, hot. Kinetic energy.

◆ **Tamas:** Inertia. Heaviness, dullness. Potential energy.

◆ **Sattva:** Harmony. Lightness, clarity. Balanced energy.

When all three gunas balance each other, the universe melts away. It's like the mathematical equation $[-1] + 0 + 1 = 0$. But when the gunas fall out of equilibrium, a motion rolls through the cosmic ocean of primeval energy, and a new universe begins to take shape.

The Hindu View

The word *yoga* comes from the Sanskrit root *yuj.* It's related to the English word *yoke* and signifies union with divine consciousness, whether you see it as your own Inner Self or as union with the Supreme Being.

Yogis actively work to balance the gunas in their personalities so that they can disengage from matter completely and shift their awareness fully back into pure consciousness itself. When that happens, the sack of past life karma the causal body carries around with it falls away along with the causal body itself. The yogi is now liberated—free from karma and the cycles of rebirth. She has shifted her awareness totally into the twenty-fifth category of reality, purusha, the Inner Self.

The Sankhya masters say an infinite number of purushas are floating around the universe, trillions upon trillions of souls. The yoga system adds one more special purusha: God. According to yoga, God is the divine consciousness that never fell into matter when the universe first formed. God has always existed outside time and space but is so gracious he occasionally lends us a hand in our efforts to escape the eternal treadmill.

Purusha and prakriti, spirit and matter, never come into contact with each other in this system. Purusha doesn't act in matter. It can't because the power to act, our organs of action, belong to the sphere of prakriti. The purusha is a ball of consciousness that merely observes. Have you been in an accident where your car was spinning out of control? During emergencies, many people report they were thrust into a state of calm clarity where they weren't afraid at all but were simply observing what was happening. That tranquil inner observer is the purusha.

While purusha never does anything, its mere proximity to prakriti causes matter to do everything. It's like a magnet under a sheet of paper covered with iron filings. The magnet never touches the bits of metal, yet they all spontaneously align themselves in accord with the magnet's fields. In the same way, nature, which is not conscious in itself, automatically serves the Inner Self. The chaos of primordial energy becomes the ordered cosmos perceived by consciousness.

Vedanta: It's All an Illusion!

For many of the educated Westerners who know anything about Hinduism, Hinduism means Vedanta. That's because the first Hindu spiritual leaders to teach widely in the West were Vedantists. If you hear people say, "Hindus believe this world is just an illusion," you're hearing a rather jumbled version of Vedanta.

Vedanta means both "the last portion of the Veda," referring to the Upanishads, and "the fulfillment of the Veda," meaning the most enlightening portion of the Veda. For over a thousand years, Vedanta has been the most important theological force in India. This is due largely to the immense impact of Shankaracharya, and to the incredible strength of the reaction against him by other Vedanta masters, such as Ramanuja and Madhva.

Guidepost _____

It's not true that Hindus believe the world is "just an illusion." Shankaracharya, the famous master who is supposed to have taught this, in fact admitted that the world is fully real to those of us living in it. It appears like an illusion only from the point of view of enlightened awareness because it is constantly changing and finally disappears. The consciousness from which the universe was projected is the *real* reality, Shankaracharya said, not the ever-changing world.

One, Not Two!

Shankaracharya was one of those staggering geniuses the world too rarely sees. He was not just a brilliant intellectual but a highly advanced yogi with a living experience of the unity of all reality. He appeared at a time in history when Hinduism was in a slump, having taken some big hits from alternative religions, like Buddhism and Jainism. He traveled all over India, reinvigorating Hinduism through the force of his luminous personality, his impeccable logic, and his yogic power.

Shankaracharya carried the doctrine of Advaita Vedanta throughout the subcontinent. Advaita means nondual, "not two." Shankaracharya disagreed with the Sankhya masters that reality is dual, that spirit and matter exist separately. To Shankaracharya, spirit—by which he means pure consciousness—is the only reality.

Shankaracharya uses the Vedic name for the one reality, Brahman. Atman, our innermost Self, is identical in essence to Brahman, the divine consciousness, just as a drop of water is essentially identical with the ocean. When we achieve moksha, spiritual liberation, we merge back into that ocean of consciousness, as a drop of water merges seamlessly into the sea.

There is no way to describe Brahman. It is far beyond human conception. But if we had to use words to give us a hazy idea of the greatness of that vast reality, Shankaracharya would use the words *sat*, *chit*, and *ananda*: being, consciousness, and bliss. To him, the highest state of awareness was not the unconscious state the Vaisheshikas described. It was a luminous and lucid state full of divine knowledge and blissfulness.

If all that exists is pure being, consciousness, and bliss, why do we have to deal with rent payments, incompetent supervisors, and dead car batteries? Shankaracharya would be the first to acknowledge the practical realities we face in day-to-day life. But from the point of view of the deepest states of meditation, where one actually experiences one's own Atman merging in Brahman, the external world is *maya*, the superimposition of our own ideas about the world on an unchanging and ever-perfect underlying reality.

If you see a coiled rope on the road in the dark, you may think it's a snake. Your heart starts pounding; your hands get sweaty and clammy. For you, at the moment, that's really a poisonous snake. But when you shine a flashlight at it and see it's just a rope, your fear disappears instantly, and you recognize the fear was groundless from the very beginning. When the flashlight of genuine meditative experience shines in our awareness, we recognize that there is not and never has been anything, anywhere, anytime, but Brahman—pure, perfect divinity.

One, But Two, Too!

Ramanuja caught hold of a different part of the elephant. Ramanuja, who may have lived somewhere around 1000 C.E., couldn't quite accept that we individual souls are in some sense equal in essence with God. He started his own brand of Vedanta called Vishishta Advaita, which roughly translates as "almost but not quite not two."

For Ramanuja, we souls can experience union, not unity, with Brahman. The world is not an idea superimposed on reality but has a real existence of its own. It is the body of Brahman, while Brahman is the innermost soul of the world. We exist as beings distinct from Brahman and will forever, though our innermost essence is rooted in that Supreme Reality. We can recognize our unity in Brahman, but we'll never lose our identity in it.

While Shankaracharya emphasized using the discriminating intellect to contemplate the inner reality, Ramanuja, like the Mimamsas, emphasized the importance of rituals and religious and social duties. While Shankaracharya promoted a mental approach to the truth, Ramanuja felt devotion was a more appropriate way to approach the Supreme Being.

Two, Not One!

Madhva, who lived around 1200 C.E., rejected both points of view. He created a third major school called Dvaita Vedanta, the Vedanta of duality. Some scholars have speculated that Christianity influenced his views because he is the only major Hindu thinker who believed in eternal damnation!

Madhva taught that the world is real, we're real, and God is real, and we're all eternally separate. We're not united or in union or anything to that effect, thank you!

During Madhva's lifetime, the Muslims were creating havoc in India, actively trying to extinguish the Hindu religion. It's possible he felt the need to arouse Hindus from the other-worldliness that other schools of Vedanta tended to produce and to inspire them to deal with real life emergencies in the material world, like homicidal Islamic armies.

The Whole Elephant

Most of my Hindu teachers are not in the least disturbed by the dramatic differences in the teachings of Hindu masters like Kapila, Shankaracharya, and Jaimini. To my gurus, these different philosophers were just hanging on to different parts of the elephant. In some respects, their differing doctrines say more about where they were in their meditation practice than about reality itself.

There comes a point in one's meditation where you enter a state much like unconsciousness. There comes a deeper state where you feel yourself to be pure conscious awareness alone, an observer of the material world that seems somehow "outside" you.

Continuing the journey inward, there comes a still deeper state where the distinction between you, the world, and God fades away, and you experience an expansive state of unity. So these different teachers aren't contradicting each other. They're all correct, based on the level of meditation they attained.

Very influential schools like Kashmir Shaivism and Shakta Advaita, led by spiritual geniuses like Abhinava Gupta (eleventh century C.E.), have beautifully integrated the six classical theologies into breathtakingly elegant, philosophically consistent systems.

Quick Quiz

1. Hindu theologians are …

    a. Completely incapable of thinking logically.

    b. Among the best logicians in the world.

    c. The original inventors of sudoku.

2. Kapila taught that …

    a. There are 25 components of reality.

    b. Brahman is the only reality.

    c. The Beatles are the greatest rock group of all time.

3. Shankaracharya is famous for …

    a. Sitting without blinking for 20 years.

    b. Playing sitar.

    c. Spreading nondual Vedanta throughout India.

Answers: 1 (b). 2 (a). 3 (c).

The Least You Need to Know

◆ Ancient Hindus mastered logic and the atomic theory.

◆ Sankhya summarized the levels of physical and nonmaterial realities.

◆ Yoga teaches techniques leading to actual experience of divine reality.

◆ Vedanta has three main schools defining the soul's relation to the Supreme Spirit.

Part 3

Who Hindus Worship

"The one God wears many masks," wrote mythologist Joseph Campbell. In no other religion does the Supreme Being wear so many masks and invite worship in so many different forms as the Eternal Religion of Hinduism.

Hindus love to worship. Every aspect of life is worship. "Let my walking be circumambulation of You," wrote Shankaracharya. "Let my speech be the recitation of Your holy mantras. When I lie down to sleep, may it be prostrating to You."

The Supreme Being has no form at all and yet is inherent in all forms. In the following chapters, you'll meet the most popular forms in which the Eternal One is honored. Among the thousands of different Hindu sects, you'll also meet the three largest denominations—the devotees of Vishnu, Shiva, and Shakti.

This is the universe of Hinduism, in which any chance encounter can be a meeting with God.

Chapter 10

"Can You Show Me God?"

In This Chapter

- A God beyond imagination
- Going Om
- Hindu "idols"
- The root of all evil
- Lenses to the infinite

Naren Datta was born in Kolkata in 1863. His parents, visualizing a brilliant future for their precocious son, arranged for a good British education. His future would be bright indeed. In fact, the future of Hindus everywhere would improve radically thanks to Naren Datta, but not because of his British training.

Naren's European schoolmasters bequeathed to him the same gift they gave almost every Hindu schoolchild entrusted to their care: complete contempt for Hinduism. Naren would roll his eyes when he saw Hindu holy men on the streets. Or the bhairavis, the women yogis. How sad that these people lived in complete superstition, never having benefited, as he had, from an enlightened European education!

A Divine Challenge

To express his disdain, Naren would go to Hindu pandits—men who spent a great deal of time talking about God—and ask, "Can you show me God?" Inevitably they would regretfully admit they couldn't.

Then one day a friend took Naren to visit a local priest at the Kali temple in Kolkata. "Can you show me God?" Naren haughtily demanded.

"Of course!" Ramakrishna Paramahansa instantly replied.

Naren Datta, a.k.a. Swami Vivekananda.

(Vedanta Society of Saint Louis)

God Is Mind-Blowing!

I don't think there's any schoolchild in the state of Bengal who doesn't know the rest of the story.

Naren was sitting on the floor when he posed his challenge to the temple priest.

Ramakrishna lifted his foot and brushed Naren's forehead with his toe. Remember in Chapter 8, when I told you about shaktipat, the shot of energy some disciples get from their gurus? Well, Naren got a dose of shaktipat. A *big* dose. He was pitched into cosmic consciousness, his awareness merging into the living universe all around him. It was ecstatic!

Then, Naren suddenly remembered his poor widowed mother, who would starve if he wasn't on hand to support her. In that moment, his consciousness imploded back into his body. He was Naren Datta again. Or rather, he had just become the man history would remember as Swami Vivekananda, the leading disciple of one of the greatest Hindu masters of recent centuries, Ramakrishna Paramahansa.

Sages Say _____

Although almost every one of us can speak most wonderfully on spiritual matters, when it comes to action and the living of a spiritual life, we find ourselves awfully deficient. To quicken the spirit, the impulse must come from another soul. The person from whose soul such an impulse comes is called the guru.

—Swami Vivekananda

Naren—called Swami Vivekananda after he took the vows of a Hindu renunciate—would turn the tables on his schoolmasters. He would be the first swami in modern times to visit Europe and America, teaching the Sanatana Dharma, the eternal religion of Hinduism. He would meet with spectacular success abroad, introducing tens of thousands of eager Western students to yoga and meditation.

But for our purpose here we need to understand exactly what happened in that extraordinary moment when the master touched Naren's forehead. And to do that we need to understand Ramakrishna's own spiritual history.

A Rock in the Eye

Ramakrishna was a priest of the Hindu goddess Kali. It was his responsibility to care for the statue of the goddess in the Dakshineshvar Temple, to bring offerings and chant beautiful hymns in praise of her.

Ramakrishna took his duties very seriously (his brief forays into other religions, which I mentioned in Chapter 6, notwithstanding). He hardly had a life apart from the goddess. He would speak about her, sing about her, meditate on her, and worship her in virtually every waking moment. He experienced the statue of Kali as actually alive and would see her leap down from the altar to dance ecstatically around the temple.

A *tantric* master named *Bhairavi* Ma noticed Ramakrishna's extraordinary devotion and began calling people's attention to the presence of the great saint among them. As an advanced adept, she could see that his intense devotion was not only giving Ramakrishna divine visions but also carrying him into very high meditative states.

def•i•ni•tion

A **tantric** uses the techniques of Tantra—an advanced system of yogic practices—to expand his or her mystical awareness.

A **bhairavi** is a female tantric practitioner.

Then a master named Tota Puri visited the Kali temple. He was an adept in the Advaita Vedanta tradition. This, to remind you, is the tradition of Shankaracharya which encourages meditators to go beyond every trace of duality (see Chapter 9). Tota Puri scolded Ramakrishna for his attachment to Kali's form. He explained that if Ramakrishna really wanted to know the goddess's true nature, he must go beyond the image of her he cherished so dearly.

Tota Puri took a sharp rock and pierced Ramakrishna's forehead at the "third eye," the point between his eyebrows. "Next time you go into meditation," the Vedantin instructed, "focus behind this point. If a picture of Kali appears in your mind, take a sword and hack her to pieces."

Ramakrishna was shocked at this advice, but he obeyed. When he next sat for meditation, he brought his full awareness to his ajna chakra, the center behind the eyebrows. When he saw his beloved Kali approach, he pushed past the image he held of her in his mind into the reality beyond mental words and pictures.

Embracing Transcendence

This experience transported Ramakrishna into one of the highest meditative states a human being can achieve. He experienced the living reality of Brahman, the all-pervading essence of awareness that exists beyond thought. Ramakrishna became so firmly grounded in this transcendent state that when Naren challenged him to show him God, the master was able to transmit the actual experience of divine being to the skeptical young man.

Let me hasten to make a point here so you don't get the wrong impression. Unlike Naren, precious few of us go to meet a guru and find ourselves thrown into the highest mystical states. Most of us spend quite a few years performing spiritual practices before we get to a point where we can receive the guru's transmission.

Ramakrishna later explained that Naren was, in fact, a very highly evolved soul who had selflessly entered the physical plane to serve humanity. His European training had temporarily directed him away from his innate spirituality. All Ramakrishna had to do to put him back on track was reawaken a cosmic state of awareness Naren had already achieved in previous existences!

You will understand Hinduism if you can grasp this concept: there is only one Supreme Reality, called Brahman—but Brahman has two modes, nirguna and saguna. Nirguna means "without qualities." Saguna means "with qualities." Nirguna Brahman is the transcendent Supreme Being contacted only in the highest states of meditation. Saguna Brahman is God or Goddess as we know and love Him or Her. This is the deity we can picture in our minds, the one who helps solve our problems and saves us in emergencies, the one whose loving embrace we feel in prayer. Try understanding it this way. If a physicist was paid to describe you, she would list the fields of matter and energy that constitute your body. It would be a very impersonal description. But if a psychologist was given the same job, he would list your many personality character- istics. Some yogis in very deep meditation experience God as an impersonal absolute. Others, whose awareness is focused at another plane, experience God as a loving, car- ing personality.

It's that elephant again. One blind man has it by the tail. The other is running his fin- gers over its flapping ear!

Unthinkable Truth

Nirguna Brahman is the Godhead behind God that the Christian mystic Meister Eckhart experienced in deep meditation. It is Absolute Reality itself, pure self-existent being. Any attempt to describe it falls flat. Even the words I just used are a dim reflec- tion of its glory. The Supreme One is totally beyond our imagination. The human mind can't begin to grasp it.

What we *can* do is transcend our own minds, shift back into the pure awareness within ourselves, and simply experience the living reality itself. It can be known but it can't be communicated in words—though mystics never tire of trying!

Sages Say _____

People of different religions never cease to fight. But think—is religion just another branch of the military? ... The true religion is that in which one becomes aware of one's own Self. That Self is Consciousness, which nothing can surpass. Because it pervades everywhere, Conscious-ness must accept all; it cannot reject anyone. The reli- gion of Consciousness is God's true religion.

—Swami Muktanand

In Hinduism, this transcendent being is symbolized by the sound "Om," which is produced by running the Sanskrit letters *a*, *u*, and *m* together. The Mandukya Upanishad says that "A" stands for the waking state. "U" signifies the dream state. "M" stands for deep sleep. And the slight pause, the little piece of silence that follows your speaking the sound Om and precedes your repeating it again—that pregnant silence is Nirguna Brahman. It's the "nothing" that contains everything.

Om, the Hindu symbol for the primordial reality.

(Hinduism Today)

Seeing the Unseen

The seers of the Upanishads wrestled with words, trying to show us that which cannot be seen. The Katha Upanishad endeavors to explain:

> Beyond the senses is the logical mind. Beyond the logical mind is the intuition. Beyond the intuition is the Inner Self. Beyond the Inner Self is the vast unmanifest reality, the primal energy from which all things emerge. Beyond the unmanifest is the Supreme Being, who exists everywhere yet cannot be seen. One who realizes the Supreme is liberated. Yes, that one becomes immortal.

> No one can see the Supreme with the eye. The only way to know Him is through deep meditation, after the mind has been completely purified. Those great souls who know the Supreme One, they are liberated from suffering and delusion. Yes, they become immortal.

Remember that in Hinduism immortality does not mean immortal life in a physical body. It means the Inner Self becomes free from the process of death and rebirth, relaxing into undying divine consciousness.

The somber Swedish filmmaker Ingmar Bergman liked to compare God to a spider. He meant this to be a creepy image, suggesting a malevolent being who captures us in an inescapable web and eats us alive. The Upanishads use the image of a spider repeatedly but in a different sense.

To the seers, the Supreme spins the entire universe out of its own being, just as a spider generates a web from its own body. At the end of a world cycle, the Supreme One dissolves the universe back into itself. The nature of that awesome eternal being is far beyond the ability of our intellects to understand. Yet the unseeable one is the very one who is peering out through our eyes. It is the all-pervading awareness in which our awareness abides, our own inner-most truth.

> **Sages Say**
>
> There is one Supreme Controller, Who is the Inner Self of all beings. He projects Himself outward, creating infinity from the One. Everlasting joy comes to those wise beings who perceive this great Being within themselves.
>
> —Katha Upanishad

We cannot *see* Nirguna Brahman, yet we *are* Nirguna Brahman!

"Idol Worship": Worshipping an Ideal

Let's shift our perspective from the inconceivable reality to the more user-friendly version of God, Saguna Brahman.

"What I am is utterly beyond the capacity of your mind to conceive," the Goddess tells us in the Tripura Rahasya. "Therefore, worship Me in whatever form appeals to you. I promise, in that very form I will come to you." As you can see, compared to the Judeo-Christian-Islamic God, the Hindu Goddess has a very liberal policy!

To the Hindu, Kali and Krishna are forms in which the divine appears. Yahweh and Jesus Christ are, too. There's no need to convert anyone because the Supreme One is working through "whatever form appeals to you" to help you grow spiritually.

Perhaps the Hindu form of God most poorly understood in the West is the image in the temple, pejoratively called an "idol" by members of monotheistic faiths. From early childhood, my Lutheran Sunday school teachers assured me that the Hindus are hopelessly superstitious—and it's our job to "save" them—because they "worship idols."

Let's get this straight right here, right now. *Hindus do not worship idols.* Hindus worship *God*.

Guidepost

That Hindus "worship idols" is probably the single most common misconception about Hinduism. It's painful for Hindus when Westerners insult their intelligence by suggesting they believe the stone or marble image of a deity in a temple is actually the Divine Being itself. Hindus use images as tools to connect with the Divine. They fully understand that the Divine itself is much greater than the physical image in the temple!

Seeing God

There is the God that can't be seen. And there is the God that can. Hindus visit their temples to see God and be seen by him. Whether it's a statue of the warrior goddess Durga; the ever popular goddess of prosperity, Lakshmi, with her handsome husband, Vishnu; or the powerful South Indian deity Vel, Hindu families come bearing their gifts of coconuts, marigolds, rupees, bananas, or whatever is on hand to offer God or Goddess that day.

The priest draws aside the gate that separates the worshipper from the image, and the family members gaze into the eyes of their beloved deity. This is the process of *darshan*, which means "sight." You see your beloved deity. He or she sees you. A connection is made. A blessing is rendered.

Yet, in spite of what my Sunday school teacher taught, in all my travels through India from one end of the subcontinent to the other, I've never met a Hindu past the age of seven who actually believes the image in the temple *is* God. In fact, if the "idol" should chip or crack, Hindus will take it out and dump it in the river! That's a pretty unceremonious way to treat God, don't you think?

If you look through a telescope, you can clearly see the planets. Yet no one thinks the telescope is actually Mars. The "idols" in the temples, called *murtis* in India, are telescopes to help us see God and Goddess more clearly. The divine comes into focus, comes closer, comes so near we can reach out and touch the divine feet.

Breathing Statues

Still, the Hindu murtis are not just statues. When an image is installed in a temple, the priest performs a special rite called prana pratishtha. Prana is life energy or breath. Pratishtha means "establish." During the ceremony, the living deity is invited to enter the image, to take the statue as one of his or her bodies. The priest breathes onto the image, establishing living energy there, and the statue comes to life.

Once prana pratishtha has been accomplished, the image of the deity is no longer a pretty piece of furniture. From now on, until a priest formally removes the life force, the statue is considered as much alive as any person in the room. Food is brought to the deity throughout the day. The deity is washed and dressed in clean clothes daily and is fanned and presented with incense and tasty desserts. It's treated as an honored guest. Devotees carefully watch what they say, even what they think, in the deity's presence, so as not to cause offense.

Visiting the deity's form in a temple or—as almost all Hindus do—keeping an image of the deity in their own home is a valuable way to practice the presence of God. But it's not just pretend. When the statue is formally brought to life, a tiny fraction of the total awareness of the real deity actually takes up residence in the statue. A fraction of infinity is still infinity. So through the awakened image, the devotee makes contact with the whole of divine being.

Sages Say

How long do small girls play with their dolls? As long as they are not married and do not live with their husbands. After marriage they put the dolls away in a box. What further need is there of worshipping the image after the vision of God?

—Ramakrishna Paramahansa

Divine Outlets

The "real" God or Goddess is beyond form, existing everywhere at once. It is the "real" deity to whom the devotee offers worship. The "real" source of electricity is the power plant. But you don't go to the power plant to get your electricity. You just stick your plug in an outlet in the wall. Because "living" electricity flows through the outlet, that outlet needs to be treated with respect. You don't just casually stick your fingers into it.

In the Hindu tradition, murtis are outlets for divine grace. The priest hooks up the system, and divine energy starts to flow. Since time immemorial, Hindus have energized their spiritual lives using empowered images of divinity.

Speaking from my personal experience, I can report that occasionally a murti is so "juiced up," it's as if a force field surrounds it. You step within several yards of the statue and suddenly feel as if you're walking into a wall of pulsing energy. My guess is that this is an objective rather than purely subjective phenomenon because my fellow travelers, even non-Hindus, would invariably feel the energy field at the same point.

Sages Say _____

In all the worlds you see, and the worlds you don't see, I am there. In all creatures that move, and in beings that don't move, I am there. In every particle of matter, from the grossest to the subtlemost, I am there. Everything you see or hear, in the external world or in the inner world, My divine awareness pervades it.

—Sarva Jnana Uttara Agama

God on Parade

Anyone who's spent time in India has seen God out parading. On special festival days, Hindus take the murti out of the temple and parade it through town. If the murti is too large or unwieldy to take for a ride, a special substitute image goes instead.

The substitute is just as good as the real thing because during a special ceremony, the priest transfers the living presence of God from the main murti in the temple into the smaller portal one. After all, it's the living presence of God or the Goddess that Hindus worship, not the physical idol.

The most famous divine parade happens every June or July (the exact date varies from year to year depending on the lunar calendar) in Puri in the state of Orissa. The murtis from the world-famous Jagannath Temple are loaded onto huge carts to be dragged through town. The murtis are of Lord Jagannath (the name means Lord of the World), his brother Balbhadra, and his sister Subhadra. Lord Jagannath's cart is 14 meters high and 10 meters square. It has 16 wheels, each more than 2 meters in diameter. The carts are so heavy it takes over 4,000 strong men to pull them. Getting them rolling is a real chore. And stopping them once they start moving is tough, too! The English world "juggernaut" came from British observers who watched this procession.

The three murtis are among the best loved in India. You may be interested to know that every decade or two the murtis are destroyed and new ones fashioned from tree trunks replace them. Let me make my point again: it is not the idol itself that is worshipped but the divine presence in it. The physical form is always expendable.

By the way, the European Roman Catholics have a remarkably similar custom. They carry images of Mary, the mother of Jesus, through the city on special feast days.

The Spirit in the Tree

All of nature is sacred to the Hindu. But some locations are especially spiritually potent—a river, a uniquely shaped rock, a particularly beautiful tree.

If you travel through the Indian countryside, you will run across many makeshift "people's shrines." Trees in particular are often centers for community worship. You'll find gifts to the tree's sacred spirit left scattered by its roots. Some of these are offerings of thanksgiving for a healing or other blessing the deity associated with the tree has granted.

The cities have their people's shrines, too. It's not unusual to be walking down a street or alley even in the busiest urban area and suddenly stumble across a little shrine, complete with pocket-size murtis and heartfelt offerings.

Show Me the Devil

You may have noticed that in all this talk about divine unity and everything being one, I haven't mentioned a word about the Devil. Where does evil fit into The Big Picture?

First, there is no Satan in Hinduism, at least not in the Christian sense of a malevolent being so powerful he almost rivals God. Hindus do believe in evil spirits and have various methods for exorcising them. But an ultimate evil being like Satan who is capable of giving God a run for his money cannot possibly exist in the Hindu worldview. God has no rivals.

Second, Hindus can't conceive of a hell in the Christian sense either, a place from which God has withdrawn his grace. To Hindus God is omnipresent—literally. How could there be any place in any dimension of any world where God isn't present?

Hell worlds do exist in Hindu cosmology, but they are more like the purgatory of the Catholics. They are temporary states in which disembodied souls undergo expiation and purification.

Sages Say _____

We have no theory of evil. We call it ignorance.

—Swami Vivekananda

Good and Evil Duke It Out

Christian texts describe a battle between angels and demons that won't end until Judgment Day, when God finally knocks the Devil off his high horse once and for all. Hinduism also frequently refers to the continual struggle between the devas (divine beings) and *asuras* (demons) but the significance is very different.

def•i•ni•tion

Asura in very ancient times meant a god. Later the meaning flipped over, becoming synonymous with selfish, aggressive supernatural beings.

Avidya literally means "non-knowledge." It refers to ignorance of our true spiritual nature.

There are stories of devas like Indra behaving badly and the occasional asura like Prahlada who behaves like an angel. Devas and asuras represent different grades of consciousness. Devas are selfless and serviceful—most of the time, anyway. Asuras are selfish and materialistic—though some of them manage to get their act together. The battle between the forces of egotism and selfless love goes on forever, in all world systems where free will—the ability to choose between right and wrong—is a factor. But Hindus do not believe in evil as something that exists as a living, malevolent force embodied in a Satan.

The Devil in God

In Hinduism, ignorance—not the devil—is the root of evil. Only self-conscious entities can be evil, deliberately choosing to do harm to others or to themselves. When a human being or some other fully conscious entity fails to recognize that everything is interconnected, that we are all one, that harming another is literally harming oneself, then that person is acting out of ignorance of the underlying universal reality.

What Christians call evil is called *avidya* in Sanskrit, which means "lack of knowledge." In mystical states, beginning-level saints first experience the literal unity of all being. They come out of the experience transformed. As Anasuya Devi, the late housewife saint of Jillellamudi, expressed after she became mystically identified with the Mother of the Universe, "I am not anything that you are not. It doesn't appear to me that I am greater than you. The Goddess doesn't exist separately anywhere. You are all the Goddess." Acting from this living realization of primal unity, the saints act for the welfare of all creation. Ignorance has been removed. The choice to commit evil is no longer a viable option in the living light of spirit.

So in a sense, you could say that God is the ultimate source of evil because God granted us the free choice between wholesome and unhelpful acts. But God also set the law of karma into place, ensuring that all of us eventually learn our lesson! In Hindu cosmology, the universe is really a university for souls, and overcoming the evil in ourselves and learning to deal effectively, yet compassionately, with the evil in others is a graduate-level course.

Quick Quiz

1. Nirguna Brahman …

   a. Is the transcendental reality.

   b. Is the personal God worshipped by all Hindus.

   c. Is a type of hump-backed cow common in India.

2. Hindus think the images of the deities in their temples …

   a. Dance around the temples at night after the temple is closed.

   b. Are actual gods and goddesses who control the universe.

   c. Are focal points through which we can see the divine.

3. Out of love for her devotees, the Goddess …

   a. Sends non-Hindus to hell for eternity.

   b. Serves them cookies and ice cream on their birthdays.

   c. Comes to us in any form we choose to worship her in.

4. Hindus believe the Devil …

   a. Will be cast into hell forever on Judgment Day.

   b. Doesn't exist.

   c. Throws great parties.

Answers: 1 (a). 2 (c). 3 (c). 4 (b).

God and the Guru

A very special form of God recognized in Hinduism is the guru. Just as a murti is a physical form through which the power and grace of the divine can manifest, a guru is a human form through which divine wisdom and compassion can flow. As my own gurus took pains to clarify, the person isn't really the guru, no more than a tree trunk painted to look like Jagannath is actually the Lord of the World.

Sages Say _____

That which the guru teaches, you can experience directly through the guru's grace. Therefore fix your mind continually on the guru, just as a loving wife thinks constantly of her husband.

—Guru Gita

During a conference call in which he was simultaneously speaking to many of his disciples at a dozen sites around the world, a swami I studied with explained that considering a person to be the guru is like mistaking the telephone for the person who's calling. In fact there is one divine teacher, called Ishvara or the Supreme Lord, who speaks through innumerable human gurus just as the swami was speaking over multiple phone lines! The real source of truth and spiritual liberation is divinity itself. The human guru is merely its franchise representative.

The Guru Within

Because the human guru represents the divine, he or she is highly honored in Hindu society. The intensity of the devotion many Hindus feel toward their guru is extraordinary. A parent's commitment to a child is for one lifetime. But a guru promises to work with a disciple for as many lifetimes as necessary until the disciple attains God-realization. This is an extraordinary bond.

The guru's job is to introduce you to the guru within. When Ramakrishna touched Vivekananda's forehead, he put him in touch with his own inner guidance. With the guru's grace, Swami Vivekananda was able to change the world.

The Least You Need to Know

- Hindus recognize the Supreme Being as both transcendent and as a loving, immanent God and Goddess.

- God is meant not only to be worshipped but also to be experienced.

- Images of deities are temporarily brought to life so the divine can be worshipped in them.

- Hindus do not believe in the Devil.

- Ignorance of one's spiritual nature is the cause of evil.

11

Meet the Hindu Gods

In This Chapter

◆ A retired creator

◆ The God in charge

◆ God the yogi

◆ The son of God

◆ The inner Sun

When you travel through India, you'll find Hindu gods and goddesses everywhere. Colorful family portraits of a god, his wife, and his children are tacked to the walls in groceries and sari shops. Small shrines to them are set up in every Hindu home and in most Hindu businesses. Even the big Indian lorries, "goods carriages" as they're called over there, are painted with smiling divine faces.

Hinduism has hundreds of gods. It's time for you to meet the most popular.

Brahma: A Retired Creator

Christianity has its Father, Son, and Holy Spirit. Hinduism also has a tri-une God, called *trimurti*. These forms are Brahma the Creator, Vishnu the Protector, and Shiva the Liberator.

Hindus believe that if they can visit the main temples of each of these three deities, all their wishes will be fulfilled. Brahma's temple is in Pushkar in eastern Rajasthan. At Vishnu's main temple in Gaya in the state of Bihar, you can actually see his footprint in a black rock. Shiva's main center is the Vishvanath temple in the holy city of Benares.

In the West, God the Father, maker of heaven and Earth, is our principle deity. While we have innumerable houses of worship to him, in all of India there are only four temples to Lord Brahma, the Creator! It wasn't always this way. Judging from the ancient Puranas, Brahma was once immensely popular in India, but he made a mistake he's still paying for today.

According to legend, Brahma fell in love with his own daughter and tried to make love to her. Incest is a serious crime in India, and Brahma could not be allowed to set such a poor example for humanity. So Shiva cut off one of Brahma's five heads and sent him home to bed without his supper.

Now in Hinduism even the weirdest-sounding myths often turn out to have profound significance. Hindu teachers explain that Brahma was the creative spirit who fell in love with its daughter, matter. When spirit entered matter, the whole world process began. But spirit lost part of itself when this happened. It lost its awareness of its true nature. So here we sit, all we children of Brahma, most of us completely unaware of our divine nature.

Surprisingly, some early Christians had their own version of this story. They were upset with their Creator for "trapping" their souls in the material realm and for pretending to be the only true God when there were other gods far more powerful than he was! Christian Gnostics believed Jesus' beloved Father was not the creator god of the Old Testament but a God of light from a much higher dimension of reality, more like the Hindu god Vishnu.

Vishnu: The Loving Protector

Vishnu is the most popular god in India, as Brahma pretty much retired after he finished creating the world and Shiva spends most of his time sitting around in meditation. So for now, according to his devotees, Vishnu is in charge.

Vishnu maintains law and order in the universe. This sometimes entails getting down and dirty. So from time to time, when things get particularly out of hand down here on planet Earth, Vishnu takes on a human body—or whatever other form works best for him under the circumstances—and sets things straight. Rama and Krishna, the heroes of the *Ramayana* and *Mahabharata* (see Chapter 5), were human incarnations of Vishnu.

I devote most of Chapter 13 to telling you about Vishnu's adventures in his various incarnations. Vishnu preserves the world by ensuring that divine law, including the law of karma, continues to act in the world. He is the great hero, the unbeatable champion, because you can count on his aid when you are acting for the benefit of the world, as Arjuna counted on Krishna during the war in the *Mahabharata*.

Sages Say

Vishnu's supreme form is beyond form, though all forms are projected from it. Of it the sages can only say "It exists." From the self-existent Lord comes this entire universe. Hold the cosmic being in the mental expanse of your meditation. It will burn away all your sins.

—Vishnu Purana

Four Hands for God

You can tell you're looking at Vishnu when you see a *very* handsome blue-skinned Hindu god with four arms. His dark blue color suggests that his nature is as infinite as the sky. Circling one of his fingers is a shining discus that, hurled through the air martial arts style, slices the enemies of goodness in two. That discus also represents the spinning universe, which circles his finger like a toy.

In another hand, Vishnu wields a golden baton. He uses this to flatten our egos when we get too big for our britches. A third hand holds a conch, which is a large seashell Hindus use like a one-note trumpet. This represents Om, the primordial sound from which the universe manifested.

Vishnu's last hand holds a lotus, the symbol of purity in Hinduism. A lotus is a beautiful, delicate flower that grows in muddy ponds. Its roots extend down to the mud but the exquisite blossoms float above the water. Just so, our innermost spiritual nature is not polluted by our problems and desires and negative thoughts here in the material world. It floats above in a world of divine illumination.

The World Axis

The Vishnu Purana tells the story of *Dhruva*, the son of a Hindu king, and one of his girlfriends. One day Dhruva ran to sit in his dad's lap, but the king pushed him away. He preferred to pick up his eldest son instead, who was the legitimate heir to the throne.

def•i•ni•tion

Dhurva is the North Star.

Dhruva was heartbroken and ran to his mother's arms. She explained that due to good deeds performed in previous lives, Dhruva's half brother had earned the right to sit on the throne with his father. Rather than crying, Dhruva should do his best to earn good karma, too, so he could enjoy similar stature in a future life.

Little Dhruva was still very upset. He ran away into the forest, where he met a wandering sage who explained that Vishnu is our real father. He initiated Dhruva in Vishnu's sacred mantra, "Om Vasudevaya Namaha!" which means "With loving reverence, I bow to Lord Vishnu!"

Dhruva repeated the mantra with such innocent sincerity that Vishnu's heart melted like butter in the sun. He lifted the little boy up into his own lap—the highest throne in the world. You can see Dhruva yourself on a clear night. We call him the North Star. All the other stars were so touched by his innocent devotion that to this day they circle around Dhruva to express their admiration.

The Supreme Identity

Many of the stories about the Hindu gods are very charming, but they always point to a higher reality, as the Hindu guru will explain.

The Vishnu Purana tells us who Vishnu really is. The energy substrate of the universe is Vishnu's body. From this are fashioned the Earth, the stars, the many dimensions of reality, and everything that is and ever will be. Vishnu exists in all forms, but he himself is not material. He is intelligence itself. As the Vishnu Purana puts it, "He who knows Vishnu as the unchanging, eternal, universal reality, enters into the Supreme Lord." So you can sit in his lap, too!

Shiva: Lord of the Yogis

If Vishnu is the most popular god in Hinduism, Shiva runs a close second. You won't be able to miss Shiva if you run into him! He's the naked one sitting on a tiger skin with snakes wrapped around his arms. His body is smeared with ashes.

Shiva is naked because he is the stark reality, pure consciousness itself. He sits in meditation rather than holding down a job because Absolute Being makes no effort at all, yet due to its mere existence, all of time and space unfolds. He is covered with ashes because after the entire universe has blown away into cosmic dust, he alone remains.

The Hindu god Shiva.

(Hinduism Today)

The Hindu View

Shiva's primary residence is on the top of Mount Kailash in Tibet. However, his wife Parvati felt the location was too remote. She wanted to live closer to the action in India. So a second residence was established in Kedarnath, Uttar Pradesh. Some Hindus report they've caught glimpses of the god and goddess in the mountains overlooking Kedarnath.

You will also often see beautiful South Indian statues of Shiva dancing gracefully within a halo of flames. This represents the end of the present cycle of time when Shiva will annihilate the universe, not by smashing it to bits but by reabsorbing all existence into his pure awareness. (After some eons, of course, Brahma the Creator will reincarnate in the vast expanse of Shiva's consciousness and start the whole cosmic process all over again!)

Drinking the Poison

Many eons ago the gods and demons, who are always at each other's throats, for once decided to cooperate. If they worked together, they could churn the nectar of immortality out of the Ocean of Milk. Well, everyone wants to be immortal! So they stuck the great mountain *Meru* into the ocean, wrapped the serpent Vasuki around it like a rope, and started churning. For thousands of years the gods pulled on one end, and the demons pulled on the other end.

def•i•ni•tion _____

> **Meru** is the mountain at the center of the world. Astronomically it represents the north/south axis of the Earth. In yoga, it stands for the spinal column.

If you're extremely patient, you can actually see the churning going on. In Hindu astronomical texts, the gods are the stars above the celestial equator, and the demons are the stars below it. Over thousands of years the stars of the lower hemisphere push some of the stars of the upper hemisphere out of the sky. Then the upper stars push their way back. This apparent motion of the stars is due to the wobble of the Earth's axis. The Veda refers to this cycle many times.

Many amazing things congealed out of the churning ocean—magical jewels and horses, that kind of stuff. The nectar of immortality finally came oozing out, but so did a poison so virulent it had the power to destroy the entire world. The gods and demons fought over the nectar but, with Vishnu's help, the pure-hearted gods won the battle and drank the ambrosia of immortality.

But what could they do about the searing poison? Only the god Shiva was powerful enough to solve the problem. He swallowed the poison and through his yoga power held it in his throat. This way it couldn't enter the rest of his system and do any damage. That's why you'll see Shiva's throat stained dark in paintings of him.

Hindu holy men and women explain that, at one level, this is the story of the yogic process. When you "churn" the life energy up and down Mount Meru, the spine, all kinds of wonderful things appear in your consciousness. The nectar of illumined awareness eventually shows up, but so does all the poison in your subconscious. Some yogis advise that you not even try to deal with all that inner poison because it can destroy you. Instead offer it to the Supreme Consciousness, the great being who is far more capable of dealing with powerful negative energy than you are.

The Mark of Shiva

Many statues of Shiva show him in human form. Some of them show Shiva's right side as male and the left side as female. This is to make the point visually that God and Goddess are absolutely equivalent and that male and female are equal. The Supreme Being has both masculine and feminine aspects, whether you see them as pure consciousness and its power, spirit and matter, or justice and mercy.

Everywhere you travel in India you will also see Shiva worshipped in the form of a *linga*, a conical or egg-shaped stone, resting in a base called a *yoni*. Linga means a mark or symbol. While almost all Hindu murtis are shaped into some form, such as a male or female deity, the linga alone remains unsculpted. This is because it stands for God beyond form, pure consciousness itself.

def•i•ni•tion

A **linga** is a shapeless stone representing Shiva, divine consciousness beyond form.

A **yoni** is the base in which a linga rests. It represents the Goddess.

In one famous story from the Puranas, Brahma and Vishnu stumbled upon a pillar of blazing light. Brahma flew upward to try to find the top of the light while Vishnu dug downward, looking for its base. Though they traveled for ages, neither could find the beginning or end of the linga of light. The light of pure awareness is infinite, the Purana is saying. Many yogis take the great meditator Shiva as their ideal and devote their lives to merging in His endless light.

Guidepost

To the Western mind, the linga and yoni, emblems of the god Shiva and his wife, Parvati, immediately suggest, well, sex. Hindus do *not* see the linga and yoni as sex organs and will be horrified if you say you do. Remember the famous quote that ultimately, the male sex organ is just another phallic symbol? The linga represents a cosmic principle to Hindus, not a part of the male anatomy.

Ganesha: The Elephant-Headed God

At Hindu temples throughout the world, priests regularly bring the images of the gods in their temples something to eat and drink. Usually the deities don't actually imbibe; they just bless the food and leave it for us humans to enjoy. But on September 21, 1995, Lord Ganesha drank the milk. Within hours, the news was all over India. Hindus rushed to the temples or to their shrine rooms at home to offer their statues of Ganesha a pitcher of milk.

The Hindu god Ganesha.

(Hinduism Today)

That evening the Milk Miracle was broadcast all over the world on the international news. Camera crews converged on Hindu temples from India to Africa to Canada and filmed the milk actually dematerializing in front of murtis of Ganesha. Thousands of observers, Hindu and non-Hindu alike, who actually watched the milk disappear, described the experience to reporters.

Ganesha has always been known for his delightful sense of humor. On that fall day in 1995, he gently reminded people everywhere that the ultimate purpose of life lies not in serving themselves but in serving God. And that day God wanted to be served milk!

Sages Say _____

Miracles like Ganesha drinking the milk come as a healthy blow to the human intellect. Such incidents stir us out of our deep sleep, at least for a time. It serves as a shock treatment, a wake-up call. An unknown power, beyond the reach of the intellect, constantly maintains a balance in the universe. Those who have experienced it say this power is all-pervading, all-knowing and all-powerful. If God is omnipotent, is there anything He cannot do? If He chooses to drink milk through the statue of Lord Ganesha, it is all His divine play.

—Amritanandamayi Ma

The God with a Trunk

Ganesha is the portly god with an elephant's head. Elephants are not a rare sight in many parts of India. Hindus appreciate them for their high intelligence, extraordinary strength, and exceptional devotion to each other and to their human peers. Elephants will not abandon a friend in trouble but will risk their lives to save those they care about.

Ganesha is the remover of obstacles. After all, if you are lost in thick jungle, just follow an elephant. Wherever it happens to walk becomes a path you can easily follow. Ganesha has very large ears so that he can hear everyone's prayers. He has a huge belly because he contains the entire universe inside himself. His wisdom, strength, and compassion are indomitable.

You'll often see a small mouse darting around Ganesha's feet. Like cowboys riding their ponies and Californians riding their SUVs, Ganesha goes for a ride on his mouse. Gurus explain that the mouse is the human mind, always scurrying here and there, nibbling at this and that. The mouse doesn't realize that riding on its back there's an elephant with unimaginable strength, wisdom, and power. Just so, the mind is often oblivious to the limitless light and power of spirit that "rides around" within its inner recesses.

Throughout history, many Hindus have been illiterate. Their gurus used memorable images like an elephant-headed god astride a mouse to teach unforgettable lessons about the nature of the Supreme Being.

How Ganesha Lost His Head

Many ages ago, Shiva's wife Parvati asked her young son, Ganesha, to guard the door to her hut while she took a bath inside. As fate would have it, Shiva came home from a long meditation retreat just at this moment. He'd been gone so long he wasn't aware his wife had had a child and that Ganesha was his son. And Ganesha had never seen Shiva before and didn't realize he was his dad.

Shiva was extremely irritated at the young boy who wouldn't let him into his own house. He tried to push Ganesha aside, but the boy was incredibly strong. Finally Shiva cut off the boy's head and called out to Parvati, "Honey, I'm home!"

The goddess was beside herself when she saw that her husband had just killed their offspring. Realizing his mistake, Shiva ran up and down the mountain looking for Ganesha's head. It was long gone! Seeing the Divine Mother's grief, an elephant standing nearby volunteered its own head, which Shiva quickly cut off and placed on his son's body, restoring Ganesha to life.

The story is about self-sacrifice. When we sacrifice our selfishness and egotism in service of the divine, as both Ganesha and the elephant did, we gain wisdom and immortality. And, like Lord Ganesha today who helps everyone who appeals to him, we gain the ability to be of service to all beings everywhere.

Hanuman: Monkeying Around

If you step into a Hindu home, odds are high you'll find an image of Hanuman, the monkey god. He has the head and tail of a rhesus monkey and the body of a man. Sometimes you'll see him ripping open his chest to reveal Rama and Sita—God and Goddess—residing in his heart.

It's impossible to exaggerate how much Hindus love this passionate, energetic monkey. In fact, it's a crime to kill a monkey in India. Monkeys are considered sacred due to their association with Hanuman!

God's Army

It's time to return to the cliffhanger I left you with back in Chapter 5, when Rama, the hero of the *Ramayana*, had to attack the military stronghold of Lanka to rescue his wife Sita, who had been kidnapped by the tyrannical king Ravana. Alone in the jungle with his brother, Rama didn't stand much of a chance against Lanka's powerful king. Then Hanuman joined the team along with a makeshift army of monkeys and bears. Keeping the image of his beloved Rama in his heart, Hanuman was able to leap across the strait between India and Sri Lanka to carry a message to Sita, imprisoned in Ravana's fortress.

Moving Mountains

During the battle with Ravana's demonic troops, Rama's brother Lakshman was seriously injured. Unless he could get a particular medicinal herb from a faraway mountain, the local physician explained, he would not be able to save Lakshman's life.

Seeing Rama's grief, Hanuman instantly raced to the mountain, covering huge distances in single leaps and bounds. But once he got there, Hanuman realized he had

no idea which of the many herbs growing on the mountain was the one the doctor needed. So he picked up the entire mountain and brought it back to the battlefield! Lakshman's life was saved, and Rama clasped Hanuman in a famous embrace of gratitude. Hanuman teaches us that when loving and serving God is the focus of our lives, the impossible becomes possible.

Now when you enter a Hindu home and see a picture of a monkey carrying a mountain, you'll know what it means.

Sages Say

Hanuman symbolizes the unfoldment of spiritual strength in an aspirant by the help of which he crosses the ocean of the unconscious and discovers the intuitive faculty which leads him to Rama—the state of Self-realization.

—Swami Jyotir Mayananda

Murugan: The Spear of God

Shiva is immensely popular in South India. So is Vishnu, called Mal, "the Great One," by Tamil-speaking Indians. But Murugan, the youthful warrior god, is uniquely South Indian. He is spectacularly handsome and courageous, not to mention a great dancer! His priests, called Velans, launch into a frenzied dance in an attempt to connect with the god and channel his wisdom and power.

Murugan is usually shown carrying his favorite weapon, a death-dealing spear. He is quick to protect his devotees and generous in granting boons.

As northern and southern Indian cultures amalgamated over the millennia, Murugan became increasingly identified with Skanda, the six-headed warrior son of Shiva.

Skanda has six heads because as an infant he was nursed by six surrogate mothers, the six brightest stars of the Pleiades. The constellation Pleiades is called Krittika in Sanskrit, so Skanda is widely known as Kartikeya.

Skanda is usually shown battling the demon Taraka who had caused an uproar in heaven, throwing the gods out of their rightful place in the sky. The embodiment of youthful male courage, Skanda defeated the arrogant demon and set the world aright. He represents virile male energy directed constructively to helping the oppressed and restoring virtue and order.

Quick Quiz

1. The three great gods of Hinduism are …

    a. Father, Son, and Holy Ghost.

    b. Brahma, Vishnu, and Shiva.

    c. On vacation in Sri Lanka.

2. Vishnu has incarnated on Earth as …

    a. Rama and Krishna.

    b. An elephant-headed deity called Ganesha.

    c. Mahatma Gandhi.

3. The Shiva linga represents …

    a. A dangerous poison churned from the Milk Ocean.

    b. The male sex organ.

    c. Pure consciousness beyond form.

4. Hanuman is honored by Hindus because he …

    a. Leaps tall buildings in a single bound.

    b. Demonstrates perfect devotion to God.

    c. Invented homeopathy.

Answers: 1 (b). 2 (a). 3 (c). 4 (b).

Surya: The Divine Sun

You don't have to visit an Indian temple to see one of Hinduism's most respected gods because he goes galloping over your head in his shining chariot every day of the year. If you ever spent a night freezing in the cold winters of northern India, you'd definitely understand why Lord Surya's appearance over the eastern horizon each morning is so welcome!

Surya, the Sun, is the source of prana, life energy, in our world system. His total selflessness, pouring forth his blessings to all beings day in and day out, without expectation of any reward in return, is the perfect example of true sainthood.

The Sun's Difficult Marriage

Surya's wife, Sanjna, however, was not happy with her husband because he was so bright she couldn't bear to look at his face! So she ran away, but Surya soon noted her absence and went looking for her. She took the form of a mare to escape from him, but he took the form of a stallion, chased her, and impregnated her by breathing on her. Their sons were twin horsemen called the Ashvins, the physicians of the gods.

When Sanjna confessed that she couldn't stand his intense brightness, Surya had his radiance surgically whittled down to a fraction of its original intensity, and the couple lived happily ever after.

The Meaning in the Myth

According to the Hindu tradition, the true light is the Inner Sun, the presence of divine being within us. Sanjna is the soul (her name means "the one with knowledge") who at the dawn of time fled from her divine consort, whose supreme light was too much for her to assimilate. She escaped down into the material world in the form of a horse (horses represent prana, or life energy in Hinduism). When spirit acts through the life force, the Ashvins or healing powers are born.

The Inner Sun yogis experience in deep meditation is only a fraction of a fraction of the light of the Supreme Reality. The Lord of the Universe moderates his brilliance to a level the meditator can withstand. By merging in that inner light, the soul begins its journey home to its true mate, the Lord of Light.

The Least You Need to Know

- ◆ Brahma, Vishnu, and Shiva are the three main gods of Hinduism.

- ◆ Ganesha is famous for the Milk Miracle he performed in September 1995.

- ◆ Hanuman, the monkey god, symbolizes perfect devotion.

- ◆ Murugan is the warrior god of South India.

- ◆ Hindus honor the Sun as an important deity.

Chapter 12

Meet the Hindu Goddesses

In This Chapter

- The Goddess is alive and well
- Wisdom and inspiration
- Prosperity and well-being
- Goddesses at war
- India is a Goddess

In ancient times, the Goddess was worshipped throughout the planet, but over the last 2,000 years, male-dominated religions have stamped out the worship of the feminine face of spirit everywhere in the world. Everywhere, that is, except India. The Hindu tradition is the one world religion where the Goddess is still honored on a massive scale.

Nirguna Brahman, the Supreme Reality in Hinduism, transcends gender. But when the Divine Being takes form, It assumes both male *and* female attributes. In fact, to many Hindus, since the Divine gave birth to us out of its own being and nurtures us like a caring mother, it must be a Goddess. To Hindus, we are not *apart from* God as the Judeo-Christian-Islamic traditions maintain. Instead, we are *a part of* her.

I'd like to introduce you to some of the most popular goddesses in Hinduism. If you travel in India or visit a typical Hindu home, you'll find images of the Mother of the Universe everywhere. To fully appreciate Hinduism, you must understand that the Goddess is alive and well in Hindu culture.

Shakti: Feminine Power

In the West, there is a widespread belief that women are inherently passive and men are naturally active. However, to the Hindu mind, this belief is clearly nonsense. In the Hindu tradition, active power is always thought of as feminine while passive stability is masculine. Hindus know that women get just as much of the work done in the world as men do, if not more. And what male warrior is as fierce and furious as a mother protecting her young?

def•i•ni•tion

> **Shakti** is the Goddess. Shakti also means power, energy, or the illuminating power of consciousness.
>
> A **Shakta** is a devotee of the Goddess.

The Sanskrit word for power or energy is *shakti*. Shakti is also the generic name for the Goddess, so her worshippers are called *Shaktas*. No male deity can accomplish anything without his Shakti, his female consort. She is his strength and power of accomplishment. Some goddesses are married. Others are independent feminine powers of limitless intelligence and capacity.

Sarasvati: The Hindu Muse

The Greeks had their muses, goddesses who inspired music and poetry, drama and science. In Hinduism, this role is filled by Sarasvati, perhaps the oldest goddess in the world who is still widely worshipped. The Veda never tires of praising her.

Artists and scientists have long noted that some of their greatest works or intellectual insights seemed to mysteriously appear fully formed in their minds. Beatle Paul McCartney reports that he first heard the melody for "Yesterday," one of the most popular songs of all time, in a dream. To Hindus, these are gifts from Sarasvati, the divine muse.

Hindu musicians chant to Sarasvati and bow to their musical instruments before beginning a concert. Children pray to Sarasvati for help with their schoolwork. Speakers invite her to "dance on their tongues" before giving a lecture.

Sarasvati is always dressed in white, the color of pure illumination. In one of her four hands she holds a book, showing her command over all intellectual knowledge. Another hand holds a rosary since she is also the source of all spiritual knowledge. Her two remaining hands hold a *vina*, an Indian instrument that looks like a sitar. This means that she is the source of the sound vibrations or primeval waves of energy that form the universe.

Sages Say

You are the swan gliding over the pond of creative energy, waves and waves of creative force emanating from Your form! Radiant Goddess resplendent in white, dwell forever in the Kashmir of my heart!

—Sarasvati Rahasya Upanishad

Sarasvati is the wife of Brahma the Creator. While Brahma's worship has all but vanished from Hinduism, Sarasvati is still worshipped in virtually every Hindu town and village. She is the inner source of creative intelligence, wisdom, and artistic inspiration. When authors experience writer's block, musicians go through dry artistic spells, or speakers' minds go blank, it's because their link with this great goddess has been temporarily broken. For the moment at least, Sarasvati isn't able to use them to complete her creative projects in the world. Her name in Sanskrit means "flowing water." When writers and artists get back "into the flow," they feel inspired again and get back to work!

Lakshmi: Showers of Gold

The goddess of wealth never lacks for devotees, as I'm sure you can imagine! Lakshmi is wrapped in a beautiful red sari. Showers of coins stream from two of her hands, signifying the material blessings that pour out of her. These include not only prosperity but also health and a joyful, harmonious family life. Her two other hands hold lotuses, reminding us that her greatest boons are not material but gifts of the spirit, which are the only blessings of lasting value.

Lakshmi is so well loved because of her extremely kind nature. Her husband, Vishnu, administers justice, but Lakshmi is incapable of punishing anyone. She is so soft-hearted that if you find yourself in trouble with Vishnu, you can run to this sweet-natured goddess and ask her to put in a kind word for you. She'll do everything she can to get Vishnu to ease up on you. In this respect, she's much like Mary, mother of Jesus, in Roman Catholicism. She intercedes for you with God.

In times of crisis, Vishnu incarnates on Earth in human form. In Hinduism, you can't have God without the Goddess. So wherever he shows up, you can count on Lakshmi turning up, too. When Vishnu came as Rama, Lakshmi came as his wife, Sita. When Vishnu manifested as Krishna, Lakshmi came as his wife, Rukmini. Male and female must work together harmoniously in order for universal balance to be maintained.

This gracious goddess will never injure anyone. The worst thing she'll ever do to anyone is ignore them! If Lakshmi's attention is elsewhere, your business starts losing money, debts pile up, the flowers in your garden wither, and your family members get grumpy. That's why it's important to make regular offerings to Lakshmi and keep her in your prayers. That way she remembers to send you her blessings!

Parvati: Divine Wife and Mother

Parvati is the mother of the deities Ganesha and Skanda, who I introduced you to in Chapter 11. She is the great god Shiva's second wife.

What happened to his first wife?

God the Widower

In ages past, the seer Daksha insulted Shiva by not inviting him to a party, even though he invited *all* the other gods and goddesses. Frankly, Daksha thought Shiva was a bum. He didn't have a job; he just sat around naked in the mountains, meditating. Shiva's wife, Sati, was so upset at Daksha's mean-spirited behavior, she jumped into a fire.

The Hindu View _____

This world tears God apart! Egyptians believed Osiris was hacked to pieces by his evil brother Seth. The Greeks believed Orpheus and Dionysus were torn to shreds, too. The Hindus speak of the Goddess being sliced to bits. Hindu gurus believe these stories point to the same mystical truth. As the Veda says, consciousness was once a unified field of awareness that split into units of consciousness like your soul and mine. The goal of spiritual practice is to reunite our awareness with the infinite.

Well, that rocked Shiva out of his meditation! Weeping and wailing, he carried his deceased wife's burnt body around in his arms. Vishnu couldn't allow this sad spectacle to continue, so he kept throwing his whirling discus at Sati's body, lopping off different parts, which fell down here to Earth. Every place a piece of the goddess landed is now a special pilgrimage site.

My guru explained that many eons ago, the World Soul was united with the Universal Spirit, as Sati was united with Shiva. But then the World Soul leapt into the ever-burning sacrificial fire we perceive as the material universe. It caught on fire and started flying in every direction as billions of different sparks like your soul and mine.

How can the human soul get out of the fire pit of material existence and back to her divine lord, the Universal Spirit?

Getting God Back

Our heroine Parvati had been Sati in her previous life! From her childhood growing up in the Himalayas, she'd been hopelessly in love with Shiva. One day she swore she wouldn't let her mind shift away from the lotus feet of Lord Shiva for even an instant until he appeared before her and proposed marriage! So there she sat in the midst of five blazing fires, never moving an inch in spite of monsoon rains, elephant stampedes, and just about every other form of botheration you can imagine.

Then one day, Parvati heard a small child screaming in terror. Immediately she jumped up and raced to help. But there wasn't any child there. Instead Shiva materialized in front of her. "You promised you wouldn't let anything distract you from meditating on me!" Shiva complained. "I created this illusion to test you."

And then the Lord smiled. "You showed that you would give up even what you want most in the world, union with me, to help the helpless. Now I know you truly *are* fit to be my wife!"

Shiva and Parvati are living happily ever after at their mountain retreat in Tibet. But Parvati has shown us the way back to God: continual loving meditation on his divine form and self-sacrificing service to our fellow humanity.

Durga: Take No Prisoners!

At one time, Durga was worshipped all the way from India to Rome. In the Near East she was called Cybele. In Egypt she was called Sekmet. While she has been forgotten in today's Christian and Muslim cultures, she is still the great warrior goddess of Hinduism.

You'll easily recognize Durga because she's always shown riding on a lion or tiger or at least standing beside one. She holds a host of fearsome weapons in her many hands. But look at her face, and you'll notice that even in the thick of battle she's always perfectly calm and centered.

The Glory of the Goddess

The most popular book about Durga is called the *Devi Mahatmyam*, which means "Glory of the Goddess."

It relates a series of stories about Durga's battles with an assortment of evil demons. Blood and gore are described with relish as Durga finishes them off—the poor devils don't stand a chance! These demons represent unhelpful qualities in ourselves, such as hatred, anger, greed, depression, conceit, and selfishness.

> **Sages Say**
>
> When we remember you in times of crisis, you instantly remove the cause of our fear. When we remember you in contemplation, you grant us the highest state of meditation. Oh Mother, you dispel suffering, poverty and fear! Who but you is so compassionate, that you rush at once to help everyone who cries out to you?
>
> —Devi Mahatmyam

The *Devi Mahatmyam* promises that anyone who hears these stories will be cleansed of their sins. This is not just a sales pitch. Many devotees experience a profound sense of catharsis from hearing how the Divine Power purifies the psychic atmosphere of these malignant forces. Even if you don't grasp intellectually that Durga's battle is an inner one, the story is told so vividly that you feel it going on inside you. This has been called "therapeutic myth," the process of resolving your inner conflicts through emotionally charged internal imagery. When the Goddess triumphs in the end, you feel like you yourself have won an important battle.

The Demon Slayer

Durga is especially famous for slaying the buffalo demon Mahisha. But just as she's about to finish him off, he turns into a lion, then a man, then an elephant. When he shapeshifts back into a buffalo, she finally runs him through and restores peace in heaven and on Earth!

If you've ever seen the nearly 5,000-year-old Indus-Sarasvati seals archeologists have discovered, you'll immediately understand what this bizarre-sounding story is really saying. We see the four creatures Mahisha changes into on the seals; they represent the ancient Indus constellations Taurus, Leo, Aquarius, and Scorpio, which marked the equinoxes and solstices when the seals were manufactured. (The next time you look at Scorpio, notice how much it looks like an elephant's head, with the brilliant red star Antares marking its eye!)

Mahisha represents the karmic process which keeps us bound to the cycle of life, death, and rebirth. He is Maha Kala, the great force of time itself. By destroying Mahisha, Durga is freeing us from the bondage of our karma, so that we can live without fear in the material world or step beyond time into eternity should we choose to do so.

Sages Say _____

The people of India do not deny the evil side of the world. They take that also and adorn the Mother on the one hand with evil … on the other hand they represent Her as overflowing with blessings. In times of distress they face danger bravely and pray to Her with unflinching faith and whole-hearted love, recognizing Her grandeur and divine power even behind misfortune and calamity.

—Swami Abhedananda

Kali: The Really Scary One

One of the demons Durga fought in the *Devi Mahatmyam* was called Rakta Bija, which means "drop of blood." Whenever she attacked him, each drop of Rakta Bija's blood turned into a clone of himself the moment it touched the ground.

Rakta Bija was so annoying, Durga actually frowned. From her knit brow leapt the most terrifying Goddess anyone had ever seen: Kali!

Kali stuck out her long tongue and drank up every drop of Rakta Bija's blood before it could touch the Earth. And then she ate him!

Your guru will help you understand that Rakta Bija is your mind's ability to endlessly generate negative thoughts and bad habits. The only way to stop this proliferation is to catch each thought before it has a chance to take root in the fertile field of your unconscious. If you invoke her, Kali will help you clean out the garbage stored in the basement of your subconscious. This process is full of grace, but it's not always pleasant!

The Bloodthirsty Goddess

Kali is a very distinctive-looking goddess. She's half naked, though she does wear a garland of skulls and a belt of hacked limbs. She's waving a lot of very scary-looking weapons around in the air, and her tongue is stuck out to slurp up any negative thought that passes through your mind.

Guidepost

Next time you see a picture of the goddess Kali, look *very* closely at the garland of skulls she wears around her neck. One of those decapitated heads is *yours!* Kali is the bitter enemy of egotism. In the course of each person's life, she finds a way to lop off our conceit and self-importance. *Ouch!*

Westerners will sometimes say, "I'm getting in touch with my inner Kali. I'm really connecting with my anger!" But Hindus don't experience Kali as an angry goddess. On the contrary, they recognize Kali as the slayer of duality. If we're angry at someone, it's because we're seeing him as an enemy, as someone apart from ourselves. It's that sense that anyone or anything exists other than divine consciousness that Kali is determined to destroy. If there's anything less than pure love inside us, sooner or later, in this life or the next, Kali will hack it out of us!

The Divine Protectress

Though she's juggling a lot of terrifying weapons, you'll notice that two of Kali's hands are empty and are making strange-looking gestures. One of those gestures means "Don't be afraid!" The other signifies "I will protect you!"

Though Kali is a scary-looking goddess, Hindus don't think of her as frightening. Instead they see her as their loving mother who corrects them when they make mistakes and who rescues them when they're in trouble. Everyone knows the most dangerous animal is a mother protecting her young. The most dangerous goddess is the Divine Mother—to her children she is the strongest and best mother of all.

Kali's State

According to historians, the state of California is named after a dark-skinned woman warrior named Calafia, who was a character in a famous sixteenth-century Spanish novel. Aggressive, half-naked Native American women reminded the Spanish conquistadors of Calafia, and of Amazons, too, which is why they named the Amazon river after them! But where did the figure of Calafia come from?

This fictional queen was based on an ancient European goddess named Koliada, who represented the winter solstice. She was black-skinned because she symbolized the darkest time of the year and fierce because winters in the Northern Hemisphere are often brutal. But she was honored, too: her festival was celebrated with extravagant feasts and lavish gift giving. When Christianity replaced the old religion in Europe, her winter festival was changed into a new holiday called Christmas.

The name Koliada means "goddess of time," appropriately enough for a solstice deity. Her names in Greek (Kalanda) and Latin (Calenda) are the source of our word "calendar." In antiquity she was worshipped throughout the entire Indo-European world. In Russia she was known as Kolyada. In northeastern India she was called Kalika. Hindus today still worship her as the fierce, dark goddess Kali. Many of my fellow Californians would be surprised to learn the name of our state can be traced back to this ancient goddess!

Lalita: The Supreme Seductress

If you start pursuing serious spiritual practice in a Hindu community, sooner or later you'll hear about the *Dasha Maha Vidyas*, the 10 great goddesses of the Hindu tantric tradition. These are the special forms of the Great Mother worshipped privately by yogis and mystics, as opposed to goddesses like Lakshmi or Durga worshipped more openly by the public.

Lalita is one of these esoteric goddesses. Her name means "She who plays"—and the whole universe is her playground! She's also called Maha Tripura Sundari, "the most beautiful girl in all the worlds"; Raja Rajeshvari, "the supreme sovereign empress of the universe"; and Kameshvari, "the goddess of love."

def•i•ni•tion

The **Dasha Maha Vidyas** are the 10 great goddesses of the Hindu mystical tradition. They are Kali, Tara, Lalita, Bhuvaneshvari, Chinnamasta, Bhairavi, Dhumavati, Bagala Mukhi, Matangi, and Kamala.

The Goddess in the Moon

Kali is worshipped on the day of the New Moon. Its waning cycle represents her action in our lives, as she strips us of anything we value more than her, including finally our life itself. She is dark as the invisible Moon, the embodiment of the destructive power of time. She stands for the loss of every material thing, revealing nothing in the end but the pure existence of spirit.

Lalita, however, is worshipped on the Full Moon. Its waxing cycle represents her activity as she helps us expand the field of our loving awareness to include everyone around us, then all of manifestation in a crescendo of bliss. Kali takes everything away but spirit. Lalita reveals that everything *is* spirit.

With Lalita you have your cake and eat it, too. She is supreme love, supreme beauty, and cosmic consciousness. While Kali takes everything away, Lalita gives us everything we desire. She is the force of desire itself.

You understand, of course, that the New Moon and the Full Moon are not two separate things. There's only one Moon! In the Hindu tradition, we recognize that ultimately Kali and Lalita are the same Goddess. Loss and gain blend together in the epiphany of enlightenment.

Consciousness and Power

Some Hindus speak of Shiva and Shakti, God and his power. Lalita represents a state of consciousness in which there is no distinction between spirit and matter, consciousness and energy. Pure consciousness *is* pure energy and is continually spontaneously pouring forth the "play" of life. Lalita is constantly forming new universes through which her infinite glory manifests. And she is constantly calling back the souls wandering in these worlds into the wonder of her supremely blissful being.

Bharat Mata: Mother India

The Bharat Mata Temple in Benares is one of the most unique temples in the world. Instead of a traditional statue of an Indian deity, it contains an enormous three-dimensional relief map of Greater India from Afghanistan in the west to Burma in the east, from the Tibetan plateau in the north to Sri Lanka in the south. The topographically correct map, made of colored marble tiles, gives a vivid sense of the vast expanse of Hindu culture and the dramatic contrast in altitude between the high Himalayas and the plains of the Deccan.

A colorful poster in the temple shows Bharat Mata, Mother India, in the form of a mature goddess presiding over a satellite image of the Indian subcontinent. The temple, inaugurated by Mahatma Gandhi, is new by Indian standards.

Hindus, like native peoples everywhere, have a profound connection with the land they live on. The planet itself is Bhu Devi, Mother Earth. Bharat Mata is more than the land itself, however. She is the very consciousness of the culture, the magic, sanctity, despair, and self-renewal of the ageless Hindu civilization. At this remarkable temple the people of India honor their own enduring spirit.

Guidepost

Want to pay your respects to Mother India? The Bharat Mata Temple is about a mile south of the Varanasi train station in Benares. Non-Hindus are welcome. While you're in town, stop by the New Vishvanath Temple at Benares Hindu University. There you'll get a full education in Hindu spirituality just by reading the beautifully decorated plaques on the wall. Visit the Shiva linga inside, and you'll receive a special blessing from the priest who worships there all day.

Ganga Ma: Mother Ganges

Hinduism is so incredibly old it remembers a time when the Ganges River didn't exist! The ancient hero Bhagiratha had to go up into the Himalayas and bring Ganga down from her home in the glaciers to the plains of North India.

When the Ganges first came cascading down from the mountaintops (some texts say her source is actually in heaven!), the force of her landing would have destroyed the Earth. So Shiva caught her in the locks of his hair and eased her gushing waters gently to the ground. In many paintings of Shiva, you'll see streams of water pouring onto his head. That's Mother Ganga!

Hindus go to the Ganges not just to wash their clothes but also to wash away their sins. Baptism is an extremely ancient rite in Hinduism, one that people engage in as often as possible since there always seem to be new sins to wash off!

The Hindu View

Can a river fall in love with a city? The Ganges runs eastward about 1,200 miles from her source in the Himalayas to the Bay of Bengal. At only one point does she turn around and head back west. That's at Benares, the city sacred to Lord Shiva, who helped Mother Ganga land gently when she first fell to Earth. The Ganges swings around to lovingly embrace Shiva's holy city and then resumes her course to Bengal.

Visits from Mother

Many of us in the West have heard of the Virgin Mary's many appearances—at Fatima, for example, or Lourdes, or more recently at Medjegorje. What we don't hear about is the Divine Mother's visits to other cultures like China or India. Showing up as the mother of Jesus wouldn't do much good in a Chinese village where many people haven't heard of Mary. So there she'll show up as Quan Yin, a goddess the people instantly recognize.

Some of my American friends and I stopped at a Kali temple in the village of Rajpur in Bengal. As soon as we entered the grounds, we felt electricity in the air. We sat down to meditate, and each of us was transported into extraordinary states of meditation. We all distinctly felt the magic, the tangible presence of spirit, and asked what was going on.

The locals then explained that at this very site the Divine Mother, in the form of the goddess Durga, had been appearing to a Hindu villager named Baba Dulal. They took us to the spot, marked by a sacred tree, where he had repeatedly seen the Mother of the Universe. Her presence was still palpable. It was as if we should still smell her perfume!

To Hindus, the Goddess is not a metaphor or a political statement. She is the Supreme Being itself who gives birth to us, nurtures, educates, and protects us. She lifts us into her lap during meditation and blesses us with shakti, the illuminating power of consciousness, when it's time for us to leave the playground of this world and return home to an inner realm of light.

Quick Quiz

1. Hinduism is the one world religion in which ...

   a. The Goddess is still honored.

   b. Worship of a male God is forbidden.

   c. Women do all the work.

2. Sarasvati is the goddess of …

   a. Wisdom and creative energy.

   b. High-fashion clothing and photography.

   c. Cooking and cleaning.

3. The goddess Durga is poised to attack …

   a. Non-Hindus.

   b. The unwholesome qualities in ourselves.

   c. Lions and tigers and bears.

4. Parvati demonstrates that we can attain union with God by …

   a. Committing suicide.

   b. Sitting alone in the forest.

   c. Meditating and serving others.

Answers: 1 (a). 2 (a). 3 (b). 4 (c).

The Least You Need to Know

- The Goddess is still widely worshipped in Hinduism.
- Sarasvati is the goddess of wisdom and divine inspiration.
- Lakshmi is the goddess of prosperity and well-being.
- Durga and Kali are Hinduism's two fierce warrior goddesses.
- Lalita represents pure consciousness and energy.
- India itself is worshipped as a goddess.

Chapter 13

Visits from God

In This Chapter

- ◆ God incarnates, too
- ◆ The Hindu Noah
- ◆ A killer priest
- ◆ The coming Messiah
- ◆ Modern avatars

Many ancient cultures believed God would visit Earth in human form. (The Greeks and Romans thought the intoxicated, fun-loving Dionysus was a god-man.) Or they believed some men and women were so special they could elevate themselves to divine status. (Hercules and Perseus were two such men-gods.) Christianity picked up the theme, though it claimed that Jesus was the only legitimate instance.

Hindus have long believed in divine incarnations called *avatars*. In fact, much Hindu devotional practice is centered around these beloved figures. Let's look at God and Goddess's interventions in history, when Hindus say he and she assumed a physical form to save the world and to set an example of how we humans should live.

Hindu Saviors

Vishnu's job is to keep the world in good running order and make sure moral laws are enforced. Sometimes he takes a physical body in order to get the job done. He may be born as a human being, but he's also taken other forms depending on what works best at the time. While some other religions believe God would never lower himself to do such a thing, Hindus believe that God can do anything he wants to! The forms in which he embodies himself are called avatars, which literally means "the savior who comes down" to help us.

When the gods and demons decided to churn the Milky Ocean (see Chapter 11), they found a mountain they could use as a churning rod and a gigantic snake they could use to spin the rod with. But they had no base strong enough to rest the mountain on, so Vishnu obligingly assumed the form of a huge turtle, and the churning rod, Mount Meru, was balanced on his shell.

This story may seem weird, but it contains a lot of ancient wisdom. When I was studying ancient Hindu astronomy, I learned that the churning of the heavenly ocean stands for something called "libration," the movement of the north celestial pole back and forth across the sky as the Earth wobbles on its axis over tens of thousands of years. God is the stable pivot point that supports all this celestial commotion.

Another time Vishnu averted a disaster of cosmic proportions. The Earth was disappearing beneath the sea. (They must have had global warming back then, too.) Vishnu took the form of a gigantic boar, plunged beneath the ocean, and used his mighty tusks to heave the land mass back above the water. After all the ice covering Antarctica melts, we may need to call on the divine boar again!

The Fish Who Saved the World

The Puranas tell an amazing story I promise you'll find interesting.

Long ago a kind-hearted king named Manu was bathing in the sea when he accidentally cupped a small fish in his hands. (He just wanted a handful of water to wash his face!) The fish begged him to take him home because a sea full of hungry big fish is not a happy place for a tasty little fish.

Manu placed the fish in a bowl of water, but it quickly outgrew its new home. He kept putting the fish into larger containers until finally it grew so large, it would now be perfectly safe in the sea. As he released it into the ocean, the fish thanked him for his kindness but also warned him, "Very soon the entire planet is going to be destroyed by a flood. Build yourself an ark and lead as many creatures as you can inside it. Then I'll come back and tow it to safety. Better hurry!" (I told you you'd find this interesting!)

Manu thought, "This can't be any ordinary fish! This must be Vishnu himself, come to save the world from destruction!"

The Hindu View _____

You can still find the Flood hero Manu and his big fish today. Go out on a clear night, and you'll see a celestial man pouring a gigantic fish out of a pot. Yes, you will! Look to the constellations Aquarius and the Southern Fish in the part of the sky the ancients called "the ocean of heaven." Manu's boat (Argo Navis) is anchored at the bottom of the sky, where it came to rest after the waters subsided. Many Hindu myths are commemorated with star groupings. India's *Taittiriya Brahmana* even explains which stars represent which deities.

Manu loaded people and animals and seeds of all kinds into the boat. Soon a tremendous flood blanketed the world with raging waters. True to its word, the fish reappeared, and Manu tied his floundering vessel to its head. The fish savior towed the ark to a mountain peak where everyone disembarked safely. When the waters subsided Manu repopulated the world. We are all his descendants!

Children of Manu

Now you know why you and I are called "human," and "man" or "woman." In Indo-European languages, these words can all be traced to the name of our common ancestor, Manu. The word *mankind* actually means "children of Manu." Today we think of the hero who survived the Great Flood by his Jewish name, Noah, but in Indo-European cultures all the way from Bengal to Britain, he was called Manu.

The fish savior appears in ancient Zoroastrian mythology where he advises the first man to release a dove to check if the flood waters have ebbed. In the Hindu Rig Veda, the bird brings Manu back a sprig of soma, the plant of immortality. According to the Babylonian historian Berossos, the fish-man savior Oannes is supposed to have taught humanity the arts and sciences at the beginning of history. Fish-men teachers are often depicted in ancient Assyrian art, too. To this day Christians symbolize their own savior with the sign of a fish! In India this great figure is called the matsya avatar, Vishnu in the form of a fish.

*Manu (Aquarius) and the
Fish Savior (Southern Fish)*

The Tallest Dwarf in the Universe

An extremely ancient myth about Vishnu tells of his famous three steps. The egotistical king Bali had built a huge empire, and it was time to put him in his place! A dwarf showed up at his palace asking for a gift. Bali may have been conceited, but he was also generous. "Ask for anything you want."

"I want as much land as I can cover in three strides," the dwarf said.

Sages Say

Vishnu strode across the universe. Three steps He took, and all the worlds were just the dust raised by His feet. In deepest meditation the great souls look up to that lofty place where Vishnu reigns like an eye in heaven.

—Rig Veda

Bali thought this was the dumbest dwarf he'd ever met. He would have given the dwarf several square miles of land if he'd asked for it. But then the dwarf took one step—and covered the entire Earth. He took a second step—and covered all of heaven. "You owe me one more step," he told the king, "but there's no more space in the universe. Where should I put my foot next?"

Bali was no idiot. He recognized now that he was in the presence of the Lord of the Universe. "Here," he said, offering his own head. The dwarf stepped on Bali's face, crushing it into the Earth.

There is, of course, a moral to the story. Bali is the human ego. Vishnu is all-pervading spirit. Before the Supreme Being, the mature ego must surrender, no matter how great a king or queen it may have imagined itself to be. Because Bali magnanimously admitted defeat, bowing humbly before the power of spirit, Vishnu rewarded him generously.

The Lion Man

Vishnu often incarnates to teach kings gone bad a good lesson. In this story, it's Hiranya Kashipu's turn, an arrogant ruler whose military exploits were terrorizing Earth. Worse, Hiranya Kashipu was also persecuting his innocent son Prahlada, who was a guileless devotee of Vishnu. Well, this was the straw that broke the camel's back!

The evil king had won a boon that he could not be killed at day or night, inside or outside, by man or by god. But no evil king is more clever than Vishnu! At twilight (neither day nor night) as Hiranya Kashipu stepped through a doorway (neither outdoors nor indoors), a statue of a half-man, half-lion (neither human nor god) toppled over onto him, its claws ripping out his heart.

Parashu Rama: An Axe to Grind

Parashu Rama was a hot-tempered fellow. How hot tempered? Well, his name means "Rama with an axe." If that brings to mind a certain genre of movie, you're not far off the mark.

Brahmin priests aren't axe murderers as a rule, but to every rule there's an exception! In Parashu Rama's time, the warrior caste was out of control. They were rampaging through the countryside, killing and exploiting innocent people (a definite no-no in Hinduism's strict code of conduct for warriors). When a soldier assaulted his dad, Parashu Rama had had enough. Though he was a priest and wasn't supposed to fight, Parashu Rama picked up an axe and killed the soldier.

But he didn't just kill *that* soldier. He killed *all* the soldiers. But he didn't just kill all the soldiers; he broke into their homes and killed their wives and children, too. And he didn't just do this once. Anytime he heard there was a warrior anywhere, he rushed there and killed him and his family. Parashu Rama had gone berserk. His goal was flat-out genocide. He didn't just want to wipe out the present evil race of violent men. He wanted to expunge violence forever. But that made him even more evil and violent than the men he was killing!

The story of Parashu Rama may be based on historical fact, perhaps a brahmanical uprising against the corrupt warrior caste. But obviously no ordinary priest could achieve what Parashu Rama did and live to tell the tale. The fact that he was so successful could mean only one thing: he must have been an incarnation of Vishnu, come to rid the world of warriors who had forgotten that they're not supposed to fight to enrich themselves. They're only supposed to use force to preserve the good.

The Himalayan Master

The *Tripura Rahasya* tells the poignant story of Parashu Rama's inner struggle as he realized he was emotionally unbalanced. His anger was out of control, and he was a danger to everyone around him. He approached a number of famous gurus for counseling, but they were all so scared of him, they ran in the opposite direction as soon as they saw him coming. Eventually one wandering sage sent him to the Himalayas to seek help from Dattatreya, the greatest spiritual master of them all.

Dattatreya was so awesome that Hindu tradition would designate him an incarnation of Brahma *and* of Vishnu *and* of Shiva all at the same time! As he approached the master's hermitage, Parashu Rama found other would-be disciples scurrying away. "Don't bother with Dattatreya," they advised him. "He's a fraud!" But our axe murderer had come too far to turn back now.

Entering the ashram, Parashu Rama saw Dattatreya sitting with a jug of wine on one knee and a nubile young woman on the other. No wonder the other seekers had left in such a hurry! But Parashu Rama saw the light of self-realization radiating from the guru's face and wasn't fooled. Instead he prostrated before the master and sincerely requested his help.

Peace of Mind

In passages of extraordinary beauty, Dattatreya introduced Parashu Rama to the Goddess within. By learning to see the Goddess of beauty and bliss inside himself, Parashu Rama overcame his violent tendencies and finally found peace. (Maybe all overly aggressive men could benefit from getting to know their feminine side!)

Parashu Rama is also honored for leading a community of north Indians to colonize the south. The Vedic god Varuna promised him as much land as he could cover with an arrow shot. Belatedly realizing Parashu Rama was so strong that his arrow might fly over the entire Earth, Varuna sent an ant to gnaw loose his bow string. Because the bow was damaged, Parashu Rama's arrow only flew as far as the southern tip of India.

Thousands of years later, Parashu Rama is still honored in South India. I have been told these days he lives quietly in a cave, still occasionally guiding seekers who come for his help, just as his guru Dattatreya once helped him.

Sages Say

A man without spiritual insight is like a frog in a well. The frog thinks its dark, damp well is the whole universe. It never leaps out into the light. In the same way a man who has never developed his spiritual awareness thinks this world is the whole of reality. He dies with this mistaken belief, never having experienced the light.

—Dattatreya

Rama: Avatar Unaware

Could God forget he's God? Amazingly, according to some Hindus, the answer is yes! Remember, God can do anything he wants! He can even conceal his true identity from himself if it serves a good purpose. Here's the story.

Through intense spiritual practices a powerful king named Ravana won a boon from Shiva that no god or any other supernatural being could defeat him in battle. (Spoiler alert: Ravana was so formidable it simply never occurred to him to specify that no mere human should be able to kill him either!) They say power corrupts, and with that kind of power Ravana went a little

Sages Say

A jackass chases a she-ass no matter how many times she kicks it. Just so, the ignorant man pursues worldly pleasure no matter how much grief it causes him.

—Dattatreya

crazy. Like so many of those pesky evil kings in Hindu stories, he started terrorizing heaven and Earth.

So it was up to Vishnu to set matters right. But the only way through the loophole in Ravana's contract with Shiva was that Vishnu would have to renounce his divine identity and come to Earth as a mortal man because only a human could kill Ravana, but no ordinary human could do it!

God and the Flying King

So Vishnu was born as the hero Rama in the city of Ayodhya, where he set an example as the perfect son, perfect husband, and perfect king, all the while not remembering he was God incarnate! Not realizing what he was getting into, Ravana kidnapped Rama's wife, Sita (who was the goddess Lakshmi incarnate, though she didn't remember it either), hoping she would marry him. (She was *very* beautiful.) Rama came after Ravana, but it looked like a lost cause. Ravana had a large, highly trained army at his disposal, as well as all the latest technological breakthroughs in military hardware. He even had a flying machine called a *vimana*, the Vedic equivalent of a helicopter, with which he could drop in unexpectedly on his victims.

The Hindu View

Did the ancients have airplanes? Or hot air balloons maybe? To this day, scholars speculate whether the vimana, the flying vehicle mentioned in early Hindu texts like the *Ramayana*, was just science fiction or whether ancient Indians actually had some kind of airborne transport. No drawing of what a vimana might have looked like has survived.

Rama had only a motley army of monkeys and bears (perhaps this was a colorful way of describing some tribal people of southern India) and bows and arrows. Yet his love for Sita was so immense he managed to defeat Ravana's vastly superior forces and rescue his wife. The story is told in loving detail in a hugely popular Hindu epic called the *Ramayana*.

Who's an Avatar?

Some avatars are full avatars, fully aware of their divine nature from birth. The late Anandamayi Ma, believed by many to have been an incarnation of the goddess Kali, reported that she was fully conscious from the moment she was born. She even described details from her earliest infancy that ordinarily a child couldn't possibly remember. She said she didn't experience the world piecemeal, but all at once, without any limitations on her awareness. She demonstrated again and again that she knew exactly what was happening with her devotees in other parts of India.

Some incarnations, like Rama and Sita, may be partial, where God and Goddess retain some of their divine powers but are not fully aware of their divinity. Others, like Parashu Rama, have forgotten their divine status completely and lost themselves in the drama of life until reawakened by an inspired guru.

Many Hindus sincerely believe their own guru is a special incarnation of one aspect or another of the divine. A guru may be an incarnation of divine wisdom or an embodiment of divine love, for example. Many Hindus feel a number of truly remarkable modern women, like Anasuya Devi from Jillellamudi and Amritanandamayi Ma from Kerala, are actual incarnations of the Mother of the Universe.

An important point to remember here is that in a sense, *we're all avatars*. Each of us incarnates a portion of divine consciousness, though most of us (like Parashu Rama) have completely forgotten our spiritual identity. It's as if Clark Kent totally forgot he was Superman!

The Hindu View

After Rama rescues his wife Sita, he refuses to accept her back till she walks through fire. What an awful ending! But the *Ramayana* isn't a romance; it's a spiritual allegory. God (Rama) will move heaven and Earth to save the soul captured by the material world (Ravana). But the soul (Sita) must purify herself before she can be reunited with spirit.

The fundamental distinction between a great avatar like Rama and the rest of us is that we're working our way *up* to divine status. The great avatars start from the top, working their way *down* to our level of consciousness.

Krishna: He's So Divine!

No Hindu contests Krishna's level of consciousness. He was a full avatar of Vishnu, completely conscious of his divinity from birth. Every day of his life was full of miracles; he embodied Godhood at its most loving, most wise, and most fun.

According to the Bible, King Herod heard of the birth of a future king and was paranoid enough to send out troops to kill all the newborn male infants. The circumstances around Krishna's birth were so similar that Christian theologians at first thought the Hindus had stolen parts of the story of Jesus' birth—till scholars confirmed that Krishna's story was centuries older.

The Butter Thief

A sage had told the malicious king Kamsa that his nephew would kill him and take his throne. No problem: Kamsa simply had each of his sister's children killed the moment it was born. But sister Devaki and her husband Vasudeva managed to slip their eighth infant away to safety. Little Krishna grew up in the village of Vrindavan, where he made a charming nuisance of himself. He was always finding ways to get his little fingers into his foster mother Yasoda's tasty fresh butter, which is why to this day you'll hear Hindus, with tears of affection streaming from their eyes, call Krishna *damodara*, "the butter thief."

Kamsa's assassins were always lurking nearby, but somehow the little toddler turned the tables on them all. Kamsa never did catch the boy destined to be his undoing! If you read the many delightful stories about how Krishna outwits all the people and animals and things Kamsa sends against him, you'll recognize that every one of them corresponds to a constellation! By telling these stories, the ancient masters turned heaven into the *chidakasha* or "spiritual sky." Then every time you'd look at the night sky, you'd be reminded of a story about Krishna!

The Dance of Love

The stories of Krishna's boyhood in Vrindavan are some of the most delightful—and most sensual—in Hindu spiritual lore. It's no wonder Vrindavan is one of the most popular pilgrimage sites in India today! Here Krishna grew up looking after the cattle. In Hindu art, he is often depicted as a loving tender of cows, much as Christians picture Jesus as the good shepherd. Krishna was so devastatingly attractive that all the women of the village fell helplessly in love with him. Most of them were simple milkmaids (*gopis* in Sanskrit), who made their living selling fresh milk. At night, Krishna would wander out into the forest and play enchantingly on his flute. The gopis would slip out of their homes (sometimes out of their husbands' beds!) to rendezvous with their divine lover.

Sages Say

In any place and any time, when good declines and evil rises all around, I descend to Earth. Again and again, I come to rescue the pure of heart and punish the wrongdoers. In age after age, I come to reestablish justice and integrity.

—the avatar Krishna in the Bhagavad Gita

The Rasa Lila is Krishna's mystical dance, a bewitching scene depicted again and again in Hindu art. One night, to satisfy the desires of all the women in love with him, Krishna temporarily cloned himself into dozens of Krishnas. Then he danced through the night with every one of the gopis at the same time.

Each of them innocently believed she alone enjoyed his love! This beautiful story makes the point that while members of different sects and religions believe God is theirs alone, in fact God dances with his lovers everywhere, in all times and all places and all religions.

King of Mathura

As a young man, Krishna left Vrindavan to fulfill his destiny in Mathura, where he overthrew the vicious king Kamsa. But back in his village, the gopis pined for him night and day, especially Radha, his favorite girlfriend. Krishna never returned to Vrindavan, but the gopis ached for him every moment of their lives, until they actually began to see him in everyone and everything around them. Merging into Krishna's true Self, the all-pervading consciousness that sustains all reality, they each attained enlightenment. Many Hindus still cherish the memory of the gopis as the greatest devotees who ever lived.

Krishna eventually became king of Mathura. As the *Mahabharata* relates, he would go on to help his friend Arjuna win the disastrous war against the Kauravas. The Bhagavad Gita, one of the wisest scriptures in the world's spiritual library, recounts Krishna's advice to Arjuna as Arjuna confronts the consequences of serious political errors and the inevitability of death.

Once when hundreds of women from a nearby kingdom were carried off by a pillaging army, Krishna rushed to the rescue. After he'd saved them, the women cried that their husbands and fathers wouldn't accept them back because they were impure since they'd been raped. Krishna called for a priest and married them all on the spot! It's easy to see why Krishna is so popular with women devotees to this day!

Krishna may well be the single most beloved figure in the history of Hinduism. He's more loved than Vishnu himself, even though he's supposed to be just one of Vishnu's 10 major incarnations. The character of Krishna, who combines unsurpassed wisdom with masculine charm and heroic deeds, may actually be the most enchanting figure in world literature.

Quick Quiz

1. Vishnu stepped on Bali's head …

    a. Because Bali's skull was Vishnu's shoe size.

    b. By accident when the lights went out.

    c. To teach him humility.

2. Manu is famous for …

    a. Repopulating the Earth after the flood.

    b. Rajput miniature paintings.

    c. His fried fish recipe.

3. The most beloved figure in Hinduism is …

    a. Ravana, king of Lanka.

    b. Krishna, king of Mathura.

    c. Indira Gandhi, prime minister of India.

4. The boar avatar …

    a. Bore Mount Meru on his back.

    b. Lifted the earth's landmass with his tusks.

    c. Digs for truffles on Full Moon nights.

Answers: 1 (c). 2 (a). 3 (b). 4 (b).

Kalki: The Future Liberator

However, Vishnu's most dramatic incarnation is yet to come. At the end of the Kali Yuga, the cycle of darkness in which the world is presently languishing, Vishnu will incarnate in the form of Kalki the liberator. He will arrive on a white horse, embodying truth and wise leadership. He will liberate the world from injustice and inaugurate a new era of enlightened awareness.

It is difficult to say where the legend of the Kalki avatar originated. It seems to be an extremely ancient myth, shared by the Persians, Jews, Christians, Tibetans, and many Central Asians. Even the Native Americans had their own version, named Kukulkan!

The Least You Need to Know

♦ Avatars are incarnations of God and the Goddess.

♦ Vishnu incarnates to save the world at times of special stress.

♦ Vishnu saved Manu from a deluge that flooded the entire Earth.

♦ The heroes Parashu Rama, Rama of Ayodhya, and Krishna were avatars.

♦ Some of the greatest saints are considered divine incarnations.

♦ The Kalki avatar will restore righteousness at the end of this world cycle.

Chapter 14

The Main Denominations

In This Chapter

- ◆ Major Hindu sects
- ◆ Vishnu's devotees
- ◆ Shiva's nonconformists
- ◆ Goddess myth and gospel
- ◆ Hinduism and its discontents

There are so many thousands of Hindu sects that religious scholars despair of ever getting them all straight. Still, if you walk into a Hindu home, odds are high that the family members belong to one of three major groups:

- ◆ **Vaishnavas:** devotees of Vishnu
- ◆ **Shaivites:** devotees of Shiva
- ◆ **Shaktas:** devotees of Devi, the Goddess

Let's have a look at Hinduism's major denominations. Then we'll take a quick peek at some very important sects that broke from Hinduism to start their own religions.

Vaishnavas: "Hare Krishna!"

The Vaishnavas are the largest denomination in India and have numerous subsects. Devotion to Lord Vishnu and his avatars, especially Krishna and Rama, is their keynote. In addition to the Veda, they hold particularly sacred the Bhagavad Gita, the Bhagavata Purana (which contains many enchanting stories about Krishna), and various compendiums of religious lore, such as the *Vishnu Samhita*. There is also ecstatic devotional poetry, such as the erotically charged *Gita Govinda*, which compares a devotee's yearning for God with a young woman's longing for her lover.

A Personable God

Many Vaishnavas believe God has six special qualities: complete knowledge, total power, sublime majesty, supreme strength, unlimited energy, and full self-sufficiency. He's not just a transcendent undifferentiated mystical blur but an actual divine person. He's something like us, only infinitely better! Vaishnavas like to use one of the oldest Vedic names for God, *Purushottama*, which means "the ultimate person" or, as the Hare Krishnas put it, "the Supreme Personality of Godhead."

Guidepost

In the late 1960s and 1970s, shaven-headed young men in orange robes would approach people at American and European airports chanting "Hare Krishna! Hare Hare!" Bewildered travelers wondered, *Who are these people?* The "Hare Krishnas" were devotees of the late Bhaktivedanta Prabhupada, who showed up penniless in the streets of New York back in the mid-1960s. This Vaishnava guru was already in his 70s when he began his hugely successful teaching mission to the West. He was following in the tradition of the fifteenth-century Bengali saint Chaitanya, who also liked to sing and dance in public streets.

For most Vaishnavas, the divine Self inside ourselves is the same as but not equal to Vishnu. Spiritual liberation means merging into God but not in the same total sense that the philosopher Shankaracharya taught (see Chapter 9). We merge into God without losing our individual nature, for we are meant to be his companions for all eternities. And even though we may enjoy his bliss when our awareness bathes in his, we do not share his infinite power. Only God can create a universe. We merely hang out in the worlds he places us in.

Shankaracharya said a drop of water and the ocean are the same substance, and just as a drop will lose itself completely in the sea, so an individual soul loses its individuality in the great spirit. The Vaishnavas feel that comparing a drop to the ocean is ridiculous. The ocean is infinitely greater!

Hanging Out with Vishnu

While Vaishnavism recognizes the importance of meditation practices, its emphasis lies primarily in religious devotion and morality. The word *bhava* is the key to understanding Vaishnava spirituality. It means emotion or more specifically the overwhelming joy and love that arise from living life in active companionship with God.

While some Hindus focus on deep meditation and others on philosophical contemplation, Vaishnavas are often suspicious of too much head stuff. It's that juice in the heart called love that gives spiritual life its zip. Vaishnavas love to recount the story of Rama's passion for his wife, Sita, or to sit contemplating Krishna's beautiful features and amorous adventures. Deep feelings of religious ecstasy cleanse the mind and propel the heart toward living companionship with Vishnu here and after death.

For some Vaishnavas, God's wife is just as important as he is. This is Lakshmi, who you've already met in Chapter 12. Many Vaishnavas call her Sri (pronounced *shree*), which literally means "auspiciousness" or "all good things." She is the supremely compassionate one, the beloved Divine Mother who looks after us kids and guides us home to Dad.

def•i•ni•tion

Bhava is intense religious emotion or spiritual ecstasy.

Heaven Full of Saints

The spiritual sky of Vaishnavism is alight with a brilliant array of stars: saints of the highest magnitude. Some of the most famous were the 12 *Alvars*, who lived in the eighth and ninth centuries C.E. in the south of India. Their hymns were saturated with love for the divine, bemoaning their separation from the Lord (usually in the form of Krishna) and celebrating those moments of merger when they experienced his living presence.

def•i•ni•tion

Alvar means "one who dives deep" and refers to the 12 great South Indian Vaishnava saints of the eighth and ninth centuries.

The Alvars had such an enormous impact on Hindu spirituality that across the sub-continent Hindu intellectuals were forced to rethink their philosophical systems to accommodate a personable God. They were forced to acknowledge that intense devotion can transport a soul to the highest states of mystical ecstasy.

Closer to our own time the Bauls of Bengal frankly call themselves "madmen for God." Many are minstrels who travel through the countryside singing and dancing. If you hear a Baul even once, you'll never forget the experience. They sing with such passion you half expect their hearts to split open!

Merging in the Temples, Singing in the Streets

Names of certain Vaishnava saints will come up not infrequently in your conversations with orthodox Hindu families, so here is a primer listing a few of the most loved saints from the last 1,500 years or so (the dates given here are historians' approximations):

- **Andal** (725–755). One of the most famous of the Alvars, she so adamantly insisted she would have no husband but God himself that her family actually took her to the Vishnu temple at Srirangam for the marriage ceremony! It's said that there she physically merged into the image in the temple, her love for him was so intense.

- **Jnanadeva** (1275–1296). The child author of the *Jnaneshvari*, which is a commentary on the Bhagavad Gita and perhaps the greatest spiritual classic of Maharashtra. At the age of 21, Jnanadeva had himself entombed alive so that he could close out his life focused exclusively on attaining union with Krishna.

- **Mira Bai** (1498–1546). A Rajput princess whose ecstatic songs to Krishna are still sung throughout India. She caused a stir of divine fervor everywhere she traveled singing of her love. At her death, she merged into a statue of Krishna at Dvaraka.

- **Chaitanya** (1486–1533). Regarded by many Hindus as the incarnation of both Krishna and his lover Radha, Chaitanya made his way through much of India chanting Krishna's name, dancing in the streets, and triggering a massive social movement of religious devotion!

- **Tulsi Das** (1532–1623). A homeless child taken in by the guru Ramananda, he grew up to compose some of the most loved poems in Hindu spiritual literature. His retelling of the story of Rama and Sita, called the *Rama Charita Manasa*, actually replaced the original *Ramayana* in popularity among Hindus.

Sages Say _____

O Lord of all living creatures! Your behavior is so audacious! But who can match Your courage? You remain in bliss even as the stars tumble from heaven and the entire universe disintegrates. Even the sages are stricken with terror as the world systems are destroyed. Yet—all alone—You laugh with delight!

—Shivananda Lahar

◆ **Tukaram** (1600–1650). This destitute farmer became one of Hinduism's most inspired poets. Though physically assaulted by a jealous detractor (who poured boiling water over him!), he forgave the man and later healed him of an incurable illness.

◆ **Anandamayi Ma** (1896–1982). A saint so amazing other saints came to prostrate before her. Illumined from birth, she lived in God consciousness, traveling around India wherever God directed her. From an inner space of luminous clarity, she shared her experience of the unity of all things.

Anandamayi Ma, one of the most extraordinary Vaishnava saints of the twentieth century.

Shaivites: "Om Namah Shivaya!"

You can identify the Shaivites by the three lines of ash running horizontally across their foreheads or by the lingam (a small conical stone) many of them wear around their necks. While Vaishnava holy men may have shaved heads, the Shaivites have a full head of hair, sometimes matted and wrapped around their skulls like a turban.

Even if you've never met a Hindu in your life, you still may have heard friends come home from their yoga classes repeating the most sacred Shaivite mantra, "Om namah Shivaya." It means "With loving reverence, I bow to the Supreme Consciousness." In this tradition, the Supreme Being is called Lord Shiva.

Pashupati: Lord of Beasts

Of the major subsects of Shaiva Hindus, the Pashupatis are the most notorious. *Pashupati* means "lord of domesticated animals" (*pashus* are any animals that are typically bound with a rope). Most people, these Shaivites say, are like cows with rings through their noses. They're led here and there by social conventions and by their own hopes and fears. The Pashupati practitioners break with social norms and often behave in the most outrageous and upsetting ways—on purpose. They're trying to set their inner world upside down so they can shake themselves loose from past mental conditioning and begin to move through the world with true freedom.

There are five stages of practice according to this tradition. Stage 1 marks the conventional spiritual aspirant, who meditates and tries to do good. Eventually this person will reach Stage 2, genuine sainthood. They follow rigorous moral standards and are exemplars of compassion, wisdom, and selfless service. By Pashupati standards, the average saint we recognize in the West functions at the second level.

Guidepost

Some crazy people are, well, crazy. Others may actually be enlightened! In India great saints sometimes act crazy to get supplicants—people who show up demanding miracles and favors—to leave them alone.

The problem with being a Stage 2 saint is that they attract needy souls who waste their time with constant demands and sycophants who inflate their egos with constant praise. So at Stage 3, practitioners are advised to act outrageously, leaping around and shouting as if they're crazy. They make sexual advances on anyone and everyone and break their promises. The crowds of devotees and hangers on who surrounded them in the past now quickly vanish, and the yogi is free to move on to higher practices.

Stage 4 aspirants are more "there" than "here." Though still inhabiting a physical body, their awareness is centered in the world within. To normal people, they may seem distracted or even catatonic. Stage 5 is the level of total mastery, where the adept remains centered in the highest consciousness but now acts in the material world for the benefit of all beings. She has perfectly integrated her experience of complete inner illumination with her awareness of outer reality, and helps to free others from the "nose rings" that control them.

Vira Shaivism: Path of Heroes

The Vira Shaivites also behave horribly by conservative Hindu standards. One of their greatest saints, a twelfth-century brahmin from Karnataka named Basava, was one of the great religious reformers in Hindu history. He led the Vira Shaivites in rejecting caste distinctions (a major no-no in Hinduism), honoring women as full equals of men, and respecting all forms of honest labor including the lowest and dirtiest.

Vira means "hero." A Vira Shaivite is as dauntless and alert in his or her spiritual life as a soldier in the thick of battle.

Vira Shaivites wear a linga, the symbol of Shiva, on their bodies. They consider it his living presence. By keeping it close, they make their bodies Shiva's living temple. A second form of linga exists in the heart. When the kundalini rises from the bottom of the spine illuminating the energy of the heart center, this linga is directly experienced. The third linga is in the brain. When the kundalini activates the center at the top of the head, union with Shiva is experienced. They merge into the linga of pure consciousness.

Vira Shaivites compare the jiva, the individual soul, and Shiva, the cosmic being, to a river and the ocean. There is definitely a difference between the two, as anyone can see. But at the time of enlightenment, the soul merges into Shiva like the river pouring into the sea. At that point, it becomes impossible to distinguish between the two.

Shaiva Siddhanta: Loving Shiva

Shaiva Siddhanta also shows more flexibility in matters of caste, gender, and ethics than the generally more socially conservative Vaishnavas and is the most commonly practiced form of Shaivism in South India today. Devotees of this tradition value the *Tiru Murai* even more than the Veda. This exquisite collection of Tamil hymns to Lord Shiva was compiled by Nambiyandar Nambi in the eleventh century.

Shaiva Siddhanta is famous for its 63 *Nayanars*, Tamil poet saints who lived between 700 and 1000 C.E. Their poetry extols Shiva's extraordinary grace and compassion. Until their arrival on the scene, both Buddhism and Jainism had made substantial inroads in South India. But the Nayanars won back the hearts of the people and reestablished Lord Shiva as South India's premier god. Let me introduce you to a few of these exceptional saints:

- **Appar** (600–681) converted from Jainism to Shaivism. The local Jain king had him thrown into a vat of poison, tried drowning him, and drove an elephant to attack him. But by remembering the holy mantra "Namah Shivaya," Appar survived every assault. The king was so impressed he converted to Shaivism himself.

- **Sambandhar** (644–660) was known for the miracles he accomplished in Shiva's name. It was said he was so adept he could raise the dead even after they were cremated! Like Appar, he taught that ultimately Vishnu and Shiva are the same Divine Being.

- **Sundar** (716–735) went blind as a young man. He complained angrily to Shiva who, according to myth, had three good eyes! Shiva restored his eyesight. In fact, Shiva loved the boy saint so much he is said to have shared his wife, Parvati, with him!

Kashmir Shaivism: The Naked Lady

Kashmir Shaivism is the best known form of Shaivism in the West today, popularized by Swami Muktananda and his successor Gurumayi Chidvilasananda in the second half of the twentieth century. It emphasizes that we're already enlightened. We just need to recognize it!

def•i•ni•tion

Pratyabhijna means Self-recognition, refocusing one's awareness on the divine consciousness in oneself.

Pratyabhijna is the key to the Kashmiri system. At the center of our being lies undying divine awareness. When we clear the impurities out of our minds and stop being distracted by our desires, the light of pure awareness shines through. Then we experience our real nature as Shiva.

Here are a few of the great souls of the Kashmir Shaivite tradition:

- **Vasu Gupta** (ninth century) was directed in a dream to seek out a stone slab on Mahadeva Mountain in Kashmir. Inscribed on the stone were the verses of the Shiva Sutra, one of the most amazing texts on higher consciousness ever composed.

- **Abhinava Gupta** (eleventh century) was one of the most brilliant philosopher yogis in Hindu history. His books on mystical states and how to attain them are among the finest works on spirituality in all world literature. He was one of the greatest tantric masters who ever lived.

- **Lalleshvari** (fourteenth century) is one of the best-known saints of this tradition. She walked out of an abusive marriage and spent the rest of her life wandering naked through the countryside, absorbed in love for Shiva and performing advanced yogic practices.

Shaktas: "Jai Ma!"

There's a famous saying in India: "In public, a Vaishnava. In private, a Shaivite. In your heart, a Shakta." The proverb means when you're in a crowd, behave like a conventional religious person. Within a circle of your close friends, however, feel free to explore your more radical spiritual insights. But when all is said and done, there is no lap more comfortable than Mom's!

Shaktas worship the Mother of the Universe as both the Supreme Consciousness itself and its power. Its power is the will and energy that creates, nurtures, and finally dissolves away the worlds. Some Shaktas, called Kaulas, engage primarily in ritual practice. Others, in the meditatively oriented Samaya tradition, focus exclusively on inner work. The Mishras do some of both: ritual to channel one's physical energy and focus the mind and meditation to plunge into the inner depths where Devi, the radiant goddess, resides.

Sages Say _____

Meditate on the divinity inside you. Drink the nectar of love that pours continually from Shiva's heart.

—Lalleshvari

In heavily Shakta parts of India, like Bengal or Assam, you'll hear Hindus shout "*Jai Ma!*" It literally means "Hurray for Mom!" and has an energy something like "Hallelujah!" Worship of the Divine Mother permeates every aspect of Hindu spirituality. Even Vaishnavas and Shaivites don't worship a male God exclusively like Christians and Muslims do. The feminine divine is always also honored even when the male aspect of the Supreme Being is emphasized.

The Hindu View _____

The sacred scriptures of denominations like the Shaktas and Shaivites are called *agamas*. In their communities these texts may be as highly valued as the Veda itself.

Debunking Indiana Jones

Unfortunately, the little most Westerners know about the Hindu Goddess tradition is what they learn from fiction like *Indiana Jones and the Temple of Doom*. Harrison Ford is called upon to rescue struggling victims about to be sacrificed to a horrible, multi-armed female deity. There is no way to sufficiently express how offensive this depiction of Goddess spirituality is to Hindus!

Guidepost

Ladies, if you're concerned about being carried off screaming to be offered to a bloodthirsty Hindu goddess, relax! Only males are offered to the Goddess. And it's usually male goats at that. At almost all Goddess temples these days, however, flowers and fruit are offered instead.

Europeans of the Victorian era also mistakenly believed that Shaktas engaged in drunken sex orgies. No such luck! These myths got started from rumors based on real tantric practices, though. A Shakta would purify himself or herself for weeks, fasting and chanting a Goddess mantra literally millions of times. Then under the close supervision of a Shakta master, the aspirant would drink high-proof liquor, strong enough to knock the socks off even the sturdiest drinker much less a teetotaler like most Hindus.

The point of the practice was to learn to face death consciously. Most people die in a state of unconsciousness, which is bad news from a Hindu point of view since they want to be alert during the stages of the death process. This allows them to consciously direct their after-death experience. By learning to maintain awareness despite the stupefying effects of strong liquor, the Shakta is training to remain lucid during the process of death itself.

God or Goddess?

Philosophically Shaktism is very close to Shaivism. In fact the two are often considered brother-sister traditions. Their doctrines are essentially identical. However, Shaivism emphasizes the consciousness or Shiva aspect a little more. Shaktism emphasizes the energy or active facet of the divine slightly more.

In the end, Shaivites admit Para Shiva, the highest form of Shiva, contains both Shiva and Shakti, consciousness and energy. Shaktas, too, say Sadakhya, the highest form of the Goddess, contains both Shiva and Shakti. Same difference. Consciousness *is* energy—living self-awareness.

The Lousy Accountant

One of the most famous Shakta saints of recent centuries was Ramprasad Sen, who lived in Bengal in the eighteenth century. He was on fire with passion for the goddess Kali and neglected his work as an accountant so badly his manager fired him! But when his boss read the beautiful lines of poetry Ramprasad had scribbled in the account books, tears came to his eyes. He encouraged Ramprasad to go home and devote his life to spiritual practice—and sent a generous stipend to Ramprasad every month so that he could actually afford to do exactly that! Employers like this are rare and deserve a lot of credit!

Ramprasad is famous for poems in which he approaches the Mother of the Universe like an innocent child or like a petulant child at times! Speaking of his meditation practice, he writes:

> Mother Kali, You dwell in cremation grounds
> so I've made my heart a burning pit
> where You can dance.
> One desire burns in the conflagration of my life:
> To watch Your blazing dance!
> I sit here still as death in my own funeral pyre,
> looking for You with eyes closed.

Quick Quiz

1. The three main sects of Hinduism are …

    a. Buddhism, Sikhism, and Jainism.

    b. Shaktism, Shaivism, and Vaishnavism.

    c. Tantra, yantra, and mantra.

2. Followers of Vaishnavism approach God with …

    a. Fear and trepidation.

    b. Love and joy.

    c. Long lists of complaints.

continues

continued

3. The Shaiva Siddhanta saints taught that Vishnu and Shiva …

   a. Are bitter enemies.

   b. Are ultimately identical.

   c. Are related on their mothers' side.

4. *Indiana Jones and the Temple of Doom* …

   a. Portrays a startlingly accurate vision of Goddess worship.

   b. Grossly distorts Hindu Goddess spirituality.

   c. Was #1 at the box office in Mumbai cinema for nearly a year.

Answers: 1 (b). 2 (b). 3 (b). 4 (b).

Hindu Spin-Offs

From time to time, great spiritual masters left the Hindu fold to start their own traditions. Hindu policy is so liberal, Hindus are allowed to believe just about anything, so what do you have to do to be excluded from Hinduism? Historically, refusing to accept the Veda as divinely inspired and breaking with the caste tradition would usually do the trick.

A number of important Hindu sects splintered from the Vedic fold to form their own faiths. Hinduism has no less than four world-famous stepchildren.

Breaking with Tradition

Buddha was disgusted by the Hindu priestly caste, in whose rituals he had little faith. He rejected the authority of the Veda, the value of worshipping deities, and the concept of an immortal soul. Most of Buddha's teachings and practices, however, retain a strong Hindu flavor.

Mahavir, who lived around the same time as the Buddha and whose life paralleled Buddha's in a number of surprising ways, also rejected the Veda. His spiritual tradition, which strongly emphasizes nonviolence, is called Jainism.

The Sikh tradition started in the Punjab in the twelfth century C.E. It emphasized devotion to God and guru and later to the *Sri Guru Granth Sahib*, the collection of beautiful hymns that eventually took the place of a human guru. Combining Hindu and Muslim ideals, the Sikhs became known for their military valor.

The Hindu View

From the third century C.E. up till just a few centuries ago, Manichaeism was one of the great world religions, practiced from Europe to China. It taught that we are beings of light who must purge ourselves of association with matter in order to merge back into divine light. (Both Christian and Muslim authorities made the extermination of Manichaeism a top priority, which is why you don't see Manichaeans hanging around anymore.) It's startling to find Manichaean literature filled with Sanskrit terminology. This is because Mani, the founder of that religion, traveled to India to study with Buddhist and Hindu masters. Mani, who was born in Babylon in 216 C.E., helped introduce many Eastern ideas into Europe, where they still echo in Europe's Gnostic underground.

The Zoroastrian Connection

Zoroastrianism is immensely ancient. According to the Hindu tradition, Zoroaster would have lived long before 3000 B.C.E. (He is mentioned as an ancient renegade teacher several times in the Rig Veda, which was compiled about 30 centuries before Christ.) Aristotle, the ancient Greek philosopher, confirms that Persians of his time dated Zoroaster to around 6000 B.C.E. However, Western scholars have been extremely reluctant to accept such ancient dates for Zoroaster.

Zoroaster is one of the most important figures in religious history. When he broke with Hinduism, he established a new set of beliefs which much later would work their way into Judaism and from there reincarnate in Christianity and Islam. These ideas include the linear nature of time with history ending on Judgment Day, the resurrection of the physical body, and the promised return of a savior to inaugurate a millennial period of peace on Earth. He also taught the existence of the Devil, a malevolent being nearly as powerful as God.

Hindus accept a modified version of the story of the returning savior. None of Zoroaster's other ideas are accepted in Hinduism.

The Least You Need to Know

- The three major sects of modern Hinduism are Vaishnavism, Shaivism, and Shaktism.

- Vaishnavas believe in the loving personal God Vishnu.

- Some Shaivites are radical in their approach to enlightenment.

- Shaktas worship the Goddess as the active, creative power of Divine Reality.

- Four great religions splintered off from Hinduism: Buddhism, Jainism, Sikhism, and Zoroastrianism.

Part 4

How Hindus Live

Hindus live in a tightly ordered, hierarchical world with clear moral values. Although India is technically a secular state, for practicing Hindus there is no such thing as a secular life. Everything occurs within the context of religion. Sacraments for every Hindu begin before birth and continue after death. Holy days are frequent. Activities are oriented, directly or indirectly, toward the ultimate goal of Hindu spirituality: liberation of the soul from the bondage of karma and rebirth.

Mother India herself is sacred. You can't travel far without reaching one pilgrimage center or another. Temples appear everywhere, though the most familiar one is right in each Hindu's own home.

This part shows how the saints and sages of the Eternal Religion counseled Hindu men and women to structure their society and to live with each other and find peace within themselves.

Chapter 15

A Classy Religion

In This Chapter

- The structure of Hindu society
- Why we're here
- Phases of life
- Women's experience

Hindu culture is tightly structured. Everyone knows where he belongs—and where he doesn't. If you're a Hindu, many of life's choices are made for you: the job you'll have, the person you'll marry, the people you'll hang out with.

For those of us who've grown up in the individualistic West, where our right to self-determination is a paramount value, the hierarchical societies of the East may seem stifling, even inhumane. Yet many Hindus would not trade their way of life for ours. Hindus who move to the West often complain that compared to home, Western culture seems cold and selfish.

So let's take a look at the way traditional Hindu society organizes itself and the religious purpose for this way of life.

What Turns You On?

What turns people on? The Hindu sages noted that basically there are four distinct personality types.

Type 1 is people whose primary passion in life is power. They feel most alive when they're controlling others and would be miserable if they couldn't express their need to be in charge.

Type 2 people are mostly motivated by material things. These folks want to be wealthy, so their satisfaction comes from producing or owning things. Their worst fear is poverty or sometimes simply having less than other people do.

Guidepost

Ever feel like an outcast? Sad to say, the outcastes of India probably feel even worse. Mahatma Gandhi renamed this group of people Harijans, "the children of God." Outcaste status was outlawed in 1950, and today all Hindus are equal before the law.

Type 3 is oriented more toward the inner world. Ideas turn these people on and internal experiences like spiritual visions. Give them a book, ask them to teach a class, or let them sit quietly thinking or meditating, and they're happy as ducks in a pond.

Type 4 is your burger flipper. These people don't particularly want to rule the world, and they aren't money-hungry enough to work their way up to a top-paying job. They don't necessarily long to be the world's leading philosophers either. They're content to wash dishes and sweep the floor, then go home and relax with friends and family.

Four Classes of Hindu Society

The sages gave each of these types a name:

- **Kshatriyas:** motivated by power
- **Vaishyas:** motivated by wealth
- **Brahmins:** motivated by knowledge
- **Shudras:** motivated by work

The kshatriyas are kings and queens and top-level executives and administrators. They're also military and police, the ones who use force to keep order. For most of its history, India was a patchwork of numberless little kingdoms. So the kshatriyas were primarily maharajahs and maharanis, princesses and dukes and their families, and the warriors they retained to help protect those they ruled and conquer those they didn't. Their role is to maintain law and social order.

Vaishyas are business people, trades people, artisans, farmers, and skilled laborers. Their role is to keep the economy booming.

Brahmins are priests, counselors, educators, philosophers. In India until fairly recently, brahmins were primarily responsible for preserving the Veda and were valued as ritual specialists. Today more brahmins are moving into other fields, such as politics, administration, and medicine.

Shudras are laborers. They do the physical work that makes life comfortable and convenient for everyone else.

 The Hindu View

Hindus stay in close touch with their relatives, including those who have died. Spirits of the departed are believed to still take an active interest in family affairs and are even offered meals during special ceremonies!

A Multi-Colored Society

Originally the varnas, or four castes as these groups are called, were somewhat fast and loose designations. But in India as in much of the rest of the world, children learned their trade from their parents. So over the course of time your caste status became something you inherited from your parents rather than an innate inclination you brought with you from your past lives.

Varna can mean color, and the high caste brahmins are associated with white. So when they first started studying India, Western scholars assumed white-skinned people (like themselves) were the most respected classes in India. But white referred to the color of the clothes brahmins wore, reflecting their inner and outer cleanliness. Kshatriyas wore red (as soldiers they dealt in blood), vaishyas wore yellow (as merchants they dealt in gold), and shudras wore brown (as laborers they worked the earth). Varna had nothing to do with skin color!

 The Hindu View

The four basic castes or classes in Hindu society are further broken down into jatis, or subcastes, specific social groups that come with preassigned levels of social status. Much like the guilds of medieval Europe, jatis provide services we Westerners associate with trade schools, unions, and insurance companies.

The Hierarchy of Being

The three upper castes (all except the shudras) are called "twice born" in Hinduism. The first birth occurs when the infant bursts hollering from its mother's womb. The second birth occurs at initiation, the Hindu version of the Christian rite of confirmation. At this time, the child is inducted into formal spiritual practice. Shudras do not receive this initiation probably because originally they were not considered focused and serious enough to stick with a spiritual discipline. In real life, of course, many shudras are highly spiritual. Many great saints have come from the shudra caste.

The four castes are very broad groupings. Most Hindus actually think of themselves in terms of their subcaste and clan. There are over 3,000 human subcastes in Hinduism. This system represents the hierarchical nature of souls in the universe, so there are nonhuman subcastes, too. Animals, plants, even insects have their subcastes—so do gods and demons!

Westerners reflexively condemn the social inequities of the caste system, which also sharply divides diverse classes of people resulting in a disastrous lack of unity that's made India particularly vulnerable to foreign invasion. But the caste system has also served to protect the fantastic diversity of communities in the subcontinent. Nowhere else on Earth can you find so many radically different subcultures in such a confined area. Different groups weren't forced to integrate, so each has retained its unique traditions through the millennia.

Outsiders

Not everyone in the world fits into the four-caste system. Some people left the system voluntarily, and some left involuntarily. Finally, some people were never in the system to begin with.

The panchamas are the famous outcastes of India. These are people, or descendants of people, who committed some serious infringement of caste regulations that led to their being excommunicated from orthodox Hindu society. A person could become a pariah, for example, by marrying outside his social group. (Remember that until the late twentieth century, this kind of social ostracizing based on class relations wasn't unusual in Western countries, either.) Hindus who adopted a new religion, like Buddhism or Islam, met with disapproval, too.

People who performed unsanitary types of jobs were also considered untouchable. These were people who cleaned dirty areas like lavatories or who handled dead animals or dead people. Perhaps the ancients noticed that these people were a source of contagion (of viruses and bacteria we'd say today) and started keeping a distance from them.

While "untouchables" are thrown out of the social order against their will, some people choose to step outside the caste system on purpose. These are the sannyasins, the wandering holy men and women of Hinduism. Sannyasins have given up the comforts and luxuries of home and family to wander freely without any possessions or worldly responsibilities. They are focused only on Self-realization and are considered "in this world but not of it." Caste regulations don't apply to them since they've transcended worldly restrictions. Even though they're outside the caste system like the untouchables, sannyasins are among the most highly respected members of Hindu culture (see Chapter 19).

Mlecchas are foreigners, people who never were Hindus to begin with. Until only recently, many Hindus considered it a calamity to have to leave India and live with mlecchas. This makes sense because for most of their history, Indians enjoyed a high standard of living compared to many other cultures.

Guidepost

If you're meeting a Hindu for the first time, you might be tempted to ask, "What caste are you?" It seems like a natural question, and you're genuinely curious. However, this is an entirely inappropriate question. It's like sitting down next to a stranger on an airplane and asking, "How much money do you make?" It would be interesting to know the answer, but asking is very rude.

What's Life For?

According to Hinduism, human life has four main goals.

- ◆ **Dharma:** Fulfilling your duties honestly
- ◆ **Artha:** Becoming prosperous
- ◆ **Kama:** Having fun
- ◆ **Moksha:** Getting enlightened

Let's take a brief look at each.

Doing Your Dharma

In this context, dharma means doing that which you were meant to do, doing it ethically, and doing it to the best of your capacity. Generally it refers to one's career.

One person's dharma may be to manufacture tires. Another person's dharma could be to sing professionally, lay foundations, or practice medicine.

> **Sages Say** _____
>
> Respect your mother as if she is a goddess. Respect your father as if he is a god. Respect your guest like a deity. Any work you do, do it perfectly. Whatever you do, do good.
>
> —Taittiriya Upanishad

In Hindu culture, often your dharma was determined by the family and clan you were born into. If you were born into a family of stone masons, your fulfillment in life would come from working with stone. If your mother was a washerwoman, you would probably be a washerwoman, too. Though for most women, your primary dharma was being a housewife and mother.

Arjuna's Dharma

In the Bhagavad Gita, Lord Krishna urges Arjuna to pick up his bow and go to war. This was because Arjuna had been born into a kshatriya family of kings and warriors. His brother's kingdom had been illegally taken over by a tyrant, and it was not the dharma of the priest or the stone mason to stop the evil tyrant. As a defender of justice, it was Arjuna's job to ensure that the kingdom was returned to its rightful ruler.

Even though Arjuna didn't want to fight, Krishna insisted he must do his duty; he must fulfill the purpose for which he was born. The Hindu view is that even if a laundryman would rather be an organic farmer, he should stick with the professional responsibility he was born into, an attitude incomprehensible to many Westerners. But in India (as in many Asian cultures), the welfare of society as a whole outweighs the individual's own preferences. Traditional Hindus believe that it is by fulfilling their duty, not by fulfilling their fantasies, that people hold their society together.

Paying Your Debts

There is also a general dharma incumbent on all human beings. Each of us has five duties or debts we need to repay:

- We must fulfill our obligations to the gods for their many blessings by honoring them with the appropriate rituals.

♦ We must repay the tremendous debt we owe to our parents and teachers by supporting them and by having children and passing on our knowledge in turn.

♦ We fulfill our duty to our guests by treating them as if they were deities visiting our home.

♦ We have a debt to all other human beings as well, which we can repay by treating each with the respect he or she is due.

♦ Also we have an obligation to all other living beings including plants and animals. We must offer them food as well as our good wishes and other types of help when appropriate.

Two central preoccupations exist in Hinduism: freedom and responsibility. While tantrics, ascetics, and renunciates launch into the freedom of spirit, Hindus who choose to remain in the workaday world are very conscious of their karmic debts and the profound interconnection and interdependence of the living beings in the many different planes of reality. Dharma defines their place in the world order and shows them how to live together in mutual respect and support.

Making Money

In the Hindu religion, getting rich is considered an entirely appropriate human activity. In fact, some holy texts urge us to use both hands to make as much money as we can and then give it away with *10* hands to those in need!

This emphasis on abundance often surprises Westerners who mistakenly believe Hinduism is a world-denying religion. Keep in mind that for most of its 5,000-year history—right up till the time of the British occupation—India was the wealthiest region in the world. (That's why so many poorer peoples were always invading India! They wanted a piece of the action!) Leading a happy, healthy, prosperous life has always been the ideal for Hindu householders. Many of the hymns in the Veda were chanted to ensure a comfortable lifestyle.

The Hindu View

The Kama Sutra, a manual on aesthetics, etiquette, and sex, is considered a sacred text, not pornography, in Hinduism. It was written by a monk! Kama, incidentally, refers to many forms of sensual pleasure (including, for example, flower arranging), not just sexuality.

There's an important caveat here. Remember how in the list of goals of human life, dharma came first? This means that while we are free, and even encouraged, to make money, we must do it within the context of dharma. Our way of making a living must be ethical. Dharma not only means our duty in life, it also means righteousness. Morality is the framework that holds a successful society together.

Making Love

The Hindus' attitude toward sex is perplexing to many outsiders. No one can fail to notice the expansive variety of sexual postures assumed by half-naked statues that decorate the outside of some Indian temples! Yet to outward appearances, many if not most Hindus are quite sexually conservative. Not only women but also men are often still sexually inexperienced on their wedding night. And it seems overly prudish to Westerners that many Hindu women remain dressed even while bathing! (This was also the practice in much of Europe till fairly recently.)

Sexuality is celebrated in Hinduism but generally within the context of marriage. By confining one's amorous adventures to a spouse, the sexual drive is expressed in a healthy, disciplined manner. There have, of course, always been otherwise outstanding Hindus who did not live by these norms. A few parts of India have been known for their more relaxed attitudes toward sexuality.

Usually though, Hindu couples do not express their affection as openly as we do in the West. They're more like the older generation of Scandinavians I grew up with: very restrained in their behavior in public. This doesn't mean Hindu husbands and wives don't love each other; it's just they don't feel it's appropriate to advertise it!

Today as Western influence becomes more pervasive, sexual experimentation is increasing among Hindus, for better or worse. And yet, as filled with flirtation as India's Bollywood films are, you'll hardly ever see even the most romantic movie stars kissing on screen.

Moksha: The Ultimate Goal

The basic goal of life on which the others are founded is dharma: morality, especially as it expresses itself in the fulfillment of one's duties. But the ultimate goal of life is moksha, enlightenment. The previous three aims are understood in this important context.

This is a wonderful world that can be full of professional fulfillment, delightful material possessions, and passionate love. But death will ultimately take all these things away. Only our relationship with pure spirit is eternal. Therefore, in most Hindu homes God is treated as a family member; he has his altar in a corner of the house, where you can bring him gifts and speak with him.

Hindus believe God and guru will gradually guide them toward spiritual liberation. The universe is a university in which the soul learns many important lessons. When it graduates, it's released from the cycle of reincarnation and finds freedom in the loving embrace of God.

To forget our ultimate goal is to get lost in materialism and lose touch with the very ground of our being. And that's a grievous loss indeed!

Sages Say

Your skin wrinkles and your hair turns grey. Your teeth fall out and your hands shake. Still you are tortured by desire. Your children bring you grief. You find no comfort in wealth. Everything is passing away. Give up clinging to things that disappear. Free yourself to enter the peace and joy within yourself.

—Shankaracharya

Metamorphoses

The Hindu life course is specifically structured so that each individual has an opportunity to go for the gold, to reach for spiritual liberation before death. If all goes according to plan, life metamorphoses through four stages:

1. **Brahmacharya:** Student life
2. **Grihastya:** Married life
3. **Vanaprastha:** Retirement
4. **Sannyasa:** Letting go

Brahmacharya literally means "walking with God." During these years, the student receives cultural, vocational, and religious training. You'll also hear the term brahmacharya used to mean celibacy since Hindus weren't supposed to have sex before marriage.

Marriage is a very big deal in Hindu culture. A small number of individuals renounce the householder life and go directly from brahmacharya to sannyasa (monk-like renunciation), devoting their entire lives to the spiritual quest alone. But the vast majority of people are expected to practice spirituality within the context of home life (grihastya) and raising a family. Remember that having children was one of the five sacred duties required of Hindus. Even parents of some of the greatest saints India has ever known, like Shankaracharya and Ramana Maharshi, tried to pressure them into married life to meet the social norm—and so that they'd support them in their old age.

When a Hindu couple got on in years, they'd retire as we do in the West. But rather than moving to Florida and fishing and boating all day, they'd go live in a hut in the forest to pursue intensive spiritual practices. Vanaprastha literally means "living in the woods."

As death approached, Hindus (especially males) would renounce even the little hut and go wandering on pilgrimages, living on whatever handfuls of food strangers would offer. This was the act of letting go preparatory to final release when the body itself dropped away.

In Western culture, people are very rarely prepared for death. Traditional Hindus spend the last years of their life specifically preparing for this transition. Though these wise customs are gradually losing their hold on the culture, you will still find temples where the aged have gone to spend the last months of their lives chanting God's name. Many temples specifically accommodate these retirees with a minimum of food and shelter so they can close out their lives focused exclusively on God. What a way to go!

Quick Quiz

1. The four castes are …

    a. Earth, Water, Fire, and Air.

    b. Priests, leaders, business people, and laborers.

    c. Tinkers, tailors, soldiers, and sailors.

2. The Hindu goals of life include …

    a. Starring in a Bollywood blockbuster.

    b. Moving to Silicon Valley and starting a software firm.

    c. Enlightenment.

3. As orthodox Hindus get older, they ...

   a. Devote themselves full time to spiritual practice.

   b. Start taking supplements and working out more.

   c. Move to Florida to go boating and fishing.

4. For Hindus, money is ...

   a. The root of all evil.

   b. Prized if it's earned ethically.

   c. Only valuable if it can be converted into U.S. dollars.

   Answers: 1 (b). 2 (c). 3 (a). 4 (b).

Women First

In Hindu India, the role of women is perceived very differently than in North America. Take the first 50 years of India's existence as an independent nation following its emancipation from Britain. For one third of that time, India had a woman prime minister. In the United States, at least up till the moment I'm writing, if Americans so much as had a strong first lady, half the country would become apoplectic!

Perhaps the reason Hindus seem to feel more comfortable with a female commander-in-chief is because they're constantly exposed to images of powerful goddesses. And the Hindu national epics are full of accounts of intelligent, politically influential women. Or maybe it's because the archetypal role for a woman in India is mother rather than sex object as in the West. You might trust your mother to run the country, but you'd probably hesitate to have a sex kitten do so!

If you cross the border from Hindu India into Muslim Pakistan, you'll instantly feel the different cultural climate. In most of India, women can travel comparatively free from fear. In Pakistan, a woman needs to be covered from head to toe in a heavy robe or accompanied by a male guardian. Otherwise she may find herself in serious trouble.

The Hindu View

When Hindus list men and women's names, out of respect for the female gender, they usually list the woman's name first. That's why when Hindus refer to the avatar Rama and his wife, Sita, they'll say "Sita-Ram." Or when they talk about Krishna and his lover Radha, they'll say "Radha-Krishna." Rama himself (Ram in Hindi) is sometimes actually called Sita-Ram, signifying that he's the man privileged to have Sita for a wife.

Declining Status

Nevertheless, there's no question women have lower status than men in Hinduism. The difference in status was almost certainly not so dramatic in the distant past. Hindu scriptures written centuries ago describe women teachers and philosophers and show women receiving initiations they are denied today. The Veda itself includes women among its highest seers.

Some of the unfortunate problems women experience in Hindu culture today may be due to 1,500 years of nearly continual invasions from the north, beginning around 500 B.C.E. To protect mothers, wives, and daughters, women were increasingly confined inside the house, cutting back their wider social roles.

But the worst problems Hindu women experience are due to the horrible practice of selling sons. Though outlawed in modern India, sadly this custom is still widely practiced.

Selling Sons

The dowry system probably did not start out as a bad thing. On the contrary, its original purpose was not to demean women but to support them. In Hindu culture, most women leave the birth home when they marry and become part of their husband's family. The dowry ensured that they brought their own financial resources with them—money they could use to support themselves and their families if their husband died or abandoned them.

Hindu males, however, stay with the birth family. The eldest son is particularly important since he's responsible for looking after the welfare of his younger siblings, for supporting his parents when they retire, and for conducting the parents' funeral rites.

While men receive their inheritance when their parents die, women receive theirs when they marry. This means that each time a daughter marries, her family sustains a substantial loss of income. There's financial loss in both cases, but families only feel it when the girl marries because the son keeps his money within the family.

This system has become grotesquely distorted. It has evolved from sending a daughter away with some worldly goods, to would-be in-laws demanding huge sums of money from parents looking for husbands for their girls. "If she's joining our family, she better bring plenty of income with her!" In other words, these parents sell rights to their sons for exorbitant prices.

The disastrous social consequences are that Hindu families go bankrupt financing the weddings of their daughters. Many families just can't afford to have girls. Now that tests to check the sex of a fetus are available, some Hindus opt for abortion if the fetus is female. That it should come to this is bitterly ironic since Hindu scriptures uniformly condemn abortion.

The opposite practice, of demanding money for a daughter, was strictly forbidden in Hindu law. It smacked too much of prostitution.

The Hindu View

Some parts of India, such as large sections of Kerala, are matrilineal. In these communities, males marry into the wife's family rather than vice versa.

Manu and Woman

Manu, the ancient Hindu lawgiver, was leery of granting women independent status. He preferred they be supervised either by a father or a husband.

But Manu's impression of women wasn't all bad. "Men who wish for good fortune must always honor women," he wrote. "The gods shower happiness and prosperity wherever women are venerated. In those lands where women are not respected, misfortune surely befalls."

New Norms for Modern Times

India is changing at an ever-accelerating rate. In the few decades I've been visiting India, I am stunned at how quickly Hindus are transforming their society. Much of this has to do with the imposition of European and American values. The advance of democracy (India is the most populous democracy in the world) has challenged medieval rules of caste supremacy, and women are demanding a larger role outside the home.

Not all the changes are reassuring. Drug abuse and alcoholism are on the rise. There is a much greater comfort level with violence among the younger generation than I've seen before, perhaps in part due to constant exposure to "cool" violence in popular Western movies. Some young people have adopted the American obsession with material goals to the detriment of traditional spiritual values that sustained their grandparents.

There is profound wisdom in the lifestyle mandated by Hindu seers long ago. I can only hope that in adapting to a new era, Hindus will retain what was best about the past.

The Least You Need to Know

- Hindu society is divided into four castes made up of over 3,000 subcastes.
- The goals of Hindu life are ethical work, wealth, pleasure, and spiritual illumination.
- The four stages of Hindu life are study, marriage, retirement, and renunciation.
- Women are highly respected in Hindu culture but don't always have an easy lot in life.
- Hindu life is specifically structured to accommodate spiritual growth.

Chapter 16

Living Right

In This Chapter

 ◆ Hindu codes of conduct

 ◆ The 10 commitments

 ◆ Championing nonviolence

 ◆ Cultivating good habits

 ◆ Moral flexibility

The ultimate goal of Hindu spirituality is liberation from the wheel of rebirth. But not everyone is capable of becoming enlightened in this lifetime, just as few of us have the stuff to medal in the Olympics. So while we're still riding up and down on the wheel, we need to attend to a practical matter. How should we conduct ourselves?

Moral principles are the foundation of every religion. We all must live together on this planet. And most of us are concerned about living at peace not only with others but also with ourselves and with God. Living ethically makes this possible.

The world's religions hold many moral principles in common. Other ideas about what constitute virtuous action are startlingly different. For example, Christians and Muslims feel morally obliged to convert other people to their religions. Hindus feel respect for other faiths is a more appropriate moral position. Let's look at the basic ethical tenets of Hinduism and see how they agree with or diverge from contemporary Western views.

Doing the Right Thing

Hindu ethics are based on the principle of Rita, laid down over 5,000 years ago in the Veda. It means aligning oneself with reality, living in harmony with God's law as it's expressed in nature and celebrated in religious rituals. Our English words "right," "righteousness," and "rite" are all related to the Sanskrit term Rita. To live according to Rita means to live right!

Laying Down the Law

When Manu, the Hindu Noah, got off the boat after the Great Flood (see Chapter 13), he composed the *Lawbook of Manu*, which explains how orthodox Hindus should live. The book states that a king or his brahmin counselor should enforce laws that reflect the usual practices of decent people, provided these do not conflict with local customs or caste rules. Trustworthy men of any caste can bear witness in a lawsuit, provided they're not motivated by greed. Men are placed in charge of supporting the family, while women control household affairs.

Manu was vehemently pro-environment. Denuding, polluting, or otherwise damaging the environment was considered such a serious offense, a person could be expelled from the community for killing trees!

Manu explains who you can and can't eat with and who you can or can't marry, according to caste rules. He also describes various ways a person becomes psychically polluted. It's inauspicious, for example, to see a corpse. You'll need to perform a rite of purification if you've been in the presence of death.

The Hindu View

The Brehon Laws, which governed ancient Ireland till a thousand years ago, have numerous parallels with the *Lawbook of Manu* from India. Brehon, the old Irish term for "judge," is related to the Sanskrit word "brahmin." In India, brahmins often served as judges.

Living the Good Life

For thousands of years, Hindu sages have offered excellent advice on how to live our lives in the light of spirit. Some of the Upanishads from North India, the

Tirumantiram from South India, and the Yoga Sutra (a short text many Western yoga students study, too) lay out the Hindu code of conduct.

Actions to Avoid

Here are five of the classic Hindu yamas, things no Hindu should ever do:

- **Ahimsa:** Do not harm anyone.

- **Satya:** Do not lie.

- **Asteya:** Do not steal.

- **Brahmacharya:** Do not overindulge.

- **Aparigraha:** Do not be greedy.

Ethics 101

Ahimsa literally means "nonviolence." This Sanskrit term may ring a bell because it was the famous codeword of Mahatma Gandhi's movement of nonviolent resistance against the British occupation of India. Ahimsa means not hurting others and not hurting yourself.

Because ahimsa is a prime moral value, many Hindus are vegetarians. Traditional Hindus, especially Vaishnavas, refuse to incur the bad karma of needlessly killing a defenseless animal. If you're having Hindus over for dinner, avoid serving meat, fish, fowl, eggs, or alcohol. Dairy products are fine and are a staple of the Hindu diet. But serve no beef under any circumstances, please! Cows are beloved animals in India. Killing and eating them is unthinkable to Hindus. To the Hindu, respect for life is not just intended to guide our dealings with other human beings; it extends to all of creation.

Most Hindus, however, are not pacifists. In some situations causing harm cannot be avoided. In the well-known example from the *Mahabharata*, Krishna advises Arjuna to take up arms against an evil prince whose

Guidepost

Most humane people accept ahimsa as a value. But how nonviolent can you be? Some of India's Jains take ahimsa so seriously they wear a cloth over their mouths to avoid accidentally inhaling an insect. They sweep the ground in front of them as they walk to avoid stepping on worms.

illegal actions must be stopped. Note that Krishna makes this suggestion only after multiple attempts at peaceful negotiation have failed.

Hindus are generally peace-loving people. Nevertheless, in cases of self-defense or protection of the innocent, sometimes violence may be the only option. Soldiers and police officers, who put their lives on the line to protect others, are honored for their self-sacrifice.

Some of Manu's harshest language is reserved for men of violence "who cause terror to all living beings." He calls on the king to put a quick end to such aggressive behavior. He repeatedly insists, as did Jesus in the Beatitudes, that it is men of nonviolence who achieve the highest good.

Honest Indian

In Vedic times, a Hindu would rather die than tell a lie. There was nothing more sacred than a person's word. According to the sages, if you never deviate from the truth, *ever*, there comes a time when if you say something, it *must* come true. Blessings from saints are highly prized because their words are imbued with shakti, immense spiritual power, since the saint is fully established in truth.

However, you'll notice that in the list of yamas, Don't Lie comes *after* Rule 1: Don't Harm Anyone. Hindus are very conscious that speech can be hurtful, even when— perhaps especially when—it's true. In a society where so much depends on group dynamics, good Hindus take care to ensure that their speech is kind and helpful, even when this means bending the truth a little bit.

Not Taking What's Not Yours

Taking something that doesn't belong to you is wrong according to Hinduism. (So is hoarding something you don't really need that someone else really does!) Yet the command to practice asteya, nonstealing, was never enforced as strictly in Hinduism as it was in the West. In medieval Europe, a starving man could be hanged for stealing a loaf of bread.

Hindus were a lot more flexible about this kind of thing. In a country with a large number of hungry people, it has long been acknowledged that sometimes you have to do what you have to do to keep body and soul together. Punishment for poor people stealing something they urgently needed like food or clothing was not severe, and sometimes wasn't enforced at all. Gratuitous theft, however, was viewed less tolerantly.

Control Yourself!

All Hindus are supposed to practice brahmacharya, celibacy. Fortunately, celibacy has a broader meaning for married couples! Husbands and wives who are faithful to each other are considered the equivalent of celibate. But brahmacharya means more than avoiding extramarital sex. It also means avoiding any kind of sensual overindulgence. Not giving in to gluttonous impulses for a second or third plate of delicious, sweet *gulab jamin* is a form of brahmacharya, for example.

Unless you're a religious ascetic, Hinduism does not require you to abandon indulgence in life's pleasures. It's *overindulgence* that's the problem!

def•i•ni•tion

Gulab jamins are balls of condensed milk soaked in sweet syrup.

Give Up the Greed

The ancient sages took a dim view of greedy, selfish people. In Hinduism the emphasis has always been on acquiring things of lasting value. In a religion that believes in reincarnation, this means collecting things you *can* take with you.

Everything you own is lost at death. What you *can* carry with you into the next life is generosity of spirit, devotion to God and Goddess, fearlessness, and all the good karma you've acquired through your loving and selfless acts. Greedy behavior can't benefit you for more than one lifetime. Generosity benefits you forever.

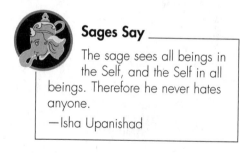

Sages Say

The sage sees all beings in the Self, and the Self in all beings. Therefore he never hates anyone.

—Isha Upanishad

Ten Actions to Practice Daily

You've just learned what a good Hindu avoids. Now here are 10 niyamas, things every Hindu should do, according to the holy texts:

- ◆ **Saucha:** Cleanse yourself.
- ◆ **Santosha:** Be content.
- ◆ **Tapas:** Discipline yourself.

- **Kshama:** Be patient.

- **Daya:** Show compassion.

- **Dana:** Give generously.

- **Puja:** Worship God.

- **Svadhyaya:** Study diligently.

- **Japa:** Repeat God's name.

- **Ishvara Pranidhana:** Surrender to God.

Christianity has its Ten Commandments. You can consider these the Ten Commitments of Hinduism.

Keep It Clean

Hindus strongly believe in internal purity and external cleanliness. It's not unusual to find orthodox brahmins bathing repeatedly throughout the day. (This is more understandable if you keep in mind the heat and dust of India.) But a dirty body is the least of problems on the spiritual path. Meditation is the Hindu method for cleaning out the gunk in the mind, which is a far more serious obstruction to spiritual progress.

Constant Craving

"Be content. But never be satisfied!" my teacher Swami Rama used to say. He was reiterating the old proverb that the wealthiest person is the one who's content with what she already has. Constant craving for more things—more success, more romantic partners, more premium ice cream—shifts us out of the present into a fantasy future in which we hope things will be even better. But God—in the form of the deepest states of consciousness—can be experienced only in the present moment. When the mind stops being distracted by what it hasn't got, it can start attending to what it *does* have already—the living presence of divine being within itself.

Yet complacency is also a spiritual pitfall. So Swami Rama warned against feeling self-satisfied, which can be a form of spiritual laziness. We should be content with what we have, but we should always strive to be better than what we are.

Focus Your Will Power

Tapas actually means heat but is used in the Hindu tradition to signify the red-hot focus of concentrated attention. The Veda says God created the universe through tapas—the force of concentrated will. Hindus practice focusing the will through self-discipline and austerity. A well-disciplined body and mind, like a carefully trained horse, can carry us to the ultimate goal of life, Self-realization.

Ascetic practices are not intended as penances to punish you. Their purpose is to make you strong. Doing without the comforts and conveniences you're used to, or devoting hours a day to mental exercises involving intense concentration, expand your capacity and show you what you're made of. This lays the foundation not only for success in life (which demands focus and self-discipline, too) but also for more advanced spiritual practices you may choose to perform in your declining years, as you prepare for death.

The Hindu View

As part of a program of self-discipline, many Hindus will undertake a vrata, or sacred vow. This may be to repeat a certain mantra 10 million times, go on a difficult pilgrimage to a sacred site, fast on milk and bananas for six months, or some other strict form of penance. This burns away bad karma.

Cultivate Patience

Americans often have a difficult time in India. Things they could accomplish in a few hours at home may take days or even weeks in India. Americans have no patience!

Hindus recognize that reality moves at its own pace. They honor the organic quality of time and are content to let things develop naturally. However, even Hindus sometimes lose patience with misbehaving children or exasperating relatives. The sages remind us that God is fantastically patient with us; we honor him by being patient with others.

Compassion for All

The age-old caste system strongly reinforces social roles. In such a socially segregated culture, it's easy to look down on people we consider beneath ourselves. Over and over the sages remind us that the same great heart beats in all beings. Lack of empathy for others is a form of self-hatred.

Shree Maa of Kamakhya reminds those of us who frequent her ashram not to criticize others. Focusing on the faults of other people fosters a spirit of pettiness. When we open our hearts in compassion to all beings (even ghosts!), accepting each of them in spite of their shortcomings or lower social status, we move closer to perceiving the universe the way the Divine Mother does. Saints don't reject people, and neither should we.

Giving Freely

Hindus are very conscious of punya, which is karmic credit, and papa, which is a karmic demerit. There's no way to build up an excellent karmic credit rating like giving generously to others. There's no way to deplete your account faster than to take what others offer you without giving something back!

I've often been astounded at how generous Hindus are, even the very poorest. The joy of giving has been inculcated in them since earliest childhood. You might as well accept what they're offering because you won't be allowed to leave their home till you do!

The Hindu View _____

Hindus have a saying: "He who eats alone, eats in sin." Food is meant to be shared. Even those who have no choice but to eat by themselves will scatter a handful of grain outdoors for wild animals before eating themselves. Traditional families won't eat before first offering food to the image of the divine in their household shrine and then giving at least a cupful of dahl, a savory dish of curried beans, to the poor or homeless in their community.

Daily Worship

In orthodox homes, Hindus perform rituals before the family altar several times a day. The ancient seers instituted these special practices, called pujas, to help people make worship part of their daily routine. In this way spiritual life and material life are seamlessly integrated.

By physically enacting a ritual, a Hindu householder gives God as much attention as she would to fellow family members. These continual reminders of God's presence and of our obligation to serve him throughout the day make religion a major component of every traditional Hindu's existence.

Self Study

Svadhyaya means "study that leads to Self-realization." This includes study of the sacred scriptures and other books that elevate the mind, such as biographies of saints. Traditionally, though, hearing a scripture recited by a qualified preceptor is considered more auspicious than reading it on your own. That's because an illumined teacher can wrap you in his mind-field, communicating his understanding directly into your mind, almost telepathically. Hearing a text from a man or woman who understands it thoroughly helps you grasp the topic far better than if you study on your own. (This doesn't bode well for students who take classes over the Internet!)

But svadhyaya has another, even more important meaning. You can read holy books for lifetimes without getting Self-realized. Yet Ramana Maharshi lay down on the floor and studied himself intensely for a couple of minutes and achieved enlightenment! By diving deep within one's own self to make the actual connection with divine being, the electricity of inner illumination starts to flow. You start to know your true inner Self at a level most people in this world never ever suspect.

Remember God's Name

Through constant repetition of God's or the Divine Mother's name or of a sacred mantra given by the guru your mind is filled with pure vibrations throughout the day. The sages advised their disciples not to simply occupy their minds with erotic fantasies or gossipy internal jabber. By mentally chanting God's name, you fill your Subtle Body with sacred energy that blesses and protects both you and your family.

Hindus have spiritual bank accounts. Each time they repeat the name of God, a spiritual rupee goes into the account, adding to the karmic merit of the family. Hindus chant their mantras not only for their own welfare but also for the good of their ancestors, children, and grandchildren, too.

Trust in God's Grace

Surrender to God means making God your top priority. Most people surrender their mental attention to their jobs or their relationships or their TV set. Hindu sages suggest we focus instead on inner truth. And don't worry so much! Do your level best, then surrender to God's will and let destiny run where it will. The universe is going to flow its own way anyway, no matter how much you resist!

Hindus believe this universe has its own dharma, its own purpose for existence. It reveals the glory of the Supreme Being—or at least a small fraction of it. If we genuinely try to be the best person we can be, it's safe to trust that we'll be guided to our greatest good.

Antidotes to Bad Behavior

In ancient times, the great yogi Patanjali was only too aware that listing a code of ethical conduct in his famous Yoga Sutras and getting people to actually follow that code are two different things! So he offered some practical advice on how to turn your personality around if it isn't already heading in the right direction.

In Hinduism, it's not enough that you don't harm anyone else if in your heart you'd still really like to smack them. Thoughts are things, and negative thoughts may hurt the person you hate if they're strong enough. And they certainly hurt you! The increased blood pressure, churning stomach, and grinding teeth can't be doing you any good.

Patanjali advises that when you're in the throes of a destructive emotional complex or feel trapped by a bad habit, you "cultivate the opposite." If you can't stand your brother-in-law, for example, make a special point to serve him patiently and speak well of him. If his personality aggravates you so much you can't see his face without frothing at the mouth, then beam your best wishes to his innermost soul, which is free from the personality characteristics that irritate you so much.

Patanjali suggests that rather than wrestling with a bad habit that undermines your spiritual progress, work on developing a good habit—one that counterbalances the unhealthy one. For example, if you're having trouble cutting back your unrestrained indulgence in oily curries and gulab jamins, then go out and get some exercise every day.

The Hindu View

Hinduism actually has a culinary theology! The Veda says, "Food is God." The most widely recited table prayer affirms that food is divine energy being offered back to the divine energy comprising our bodies. Eating is consciousness experiencing itself!

Clearing Your Conscience

Hindu culture is conservative. Alcohol is off-limits. (Hindus prefer chai, sweet, milk-based tea that's recently made its way onto the menu at Starbucks!) Sexual experimentation, divorce, and abortion are not acceptable. Individuals may be expected to sacrifice their personal preferences for the good of the family as a whole.

How can you clear your conscience if you've done something you know is wrong? In his famous lawbook, Manu says, "Confess your misdeed and sincerely admit you're sorry. Then by performing some austerity, giving a generous gift, or by reciting holy mantras, you can free yourself from the evil karma. If your repentance is sincere, your guilt will be erased. But there is one condition. You must never repeat that mistake again."

Sages Say

Refusing to cause harm or to lie, refraining from theft, anger, and greed, and making a sincere effort to do what is beneficial for all creatures, this is the common duty of all castes.

—Uddhava Gita

Quick Quiz

1. Ahimsa means …

    a. Not hurting others or yourself.

    b. Being content but not satisfied.

    c. Telling the complete truth, even when it hurts.

2. Brahmacharya means …

    a. Having sex is a horrible sin.

    b. Sex should ideally be confined to marriage.

    c. Having sex with anyone you want is fine as long as you call it Tantra.

3. The sage Patanjali …

    a. Prescribed a program of ethical living.

    b. Wrote the *Lawbook of Manu*.

    c. Has ashrams around the world where he teaches Tantric Sex.

4. In a traditional Hindu home, beef is …

    a. What's for dinner.

    b. Reserved for tantric orgies.

    c. Forbidden.

Answers: 1 (a). 2 (b). 3 (a). 4 (c).

Moral Challenges

The past thousand years have been the most traumatic in Hindu history. (Hindu history is so long, a thousand-year period is just a short segment!) The Moghul invasions and later the British conquest put Hindus on the defensive and shook their institutions to the core. In some cases, fundamental values flew out the door in the face of violence, oppression, and the resulting massive poverty.

Westerners visiting Hindu areas may not be impressed with some current Hindu values, sad to say. Visitors in past centuries marveled at the peacefulness, prosperity, and moral rectitude of the people. Today unfortunately, corruption is endemic. From government offices to some of the holy temples themselves, you're likely to find a hand thrust at you demanding baksheesh, or bribes, rather than reaching out to help you. The prospects for women in some quarters is truly shocking. Attempts to raise the status of outcastes have met with only modest success. Some gurus—who should all be embodiments of the highest spiritual ideals—are brazenly on the take.

Throughout the subcontinent, Hindu teachers are calling for a return to their religion's eternal values: tolerance, purity, integrity, respect for women, and love for the divine in all its manifestations.

Sages Say _____

The good Hindu should continually recite the holy scripture. He should be self-controlled, kind, and tranquil. He desires to give, not to receive. He is loving toward all living things.

—*Lawbook of Manu*

I can personally attest that Hindus are among the most friendly and hospitable people on Earth. "The guest is God," is a fundamental Hindu belief. Many of us visitors can testify that Hindus behave as if that's literally true! The pure-hearted generosity of our poorest Hindu hosts puts many wealthy Western tourists to shame. Those Hindus who hold to the best in their ancient traditions provide living examples of the guileless spiritual values of India's glorious past—and offer the best hope for India's increasingly bright future.

The Least You Need to Know

- The fundamental value of Hindu ethics is nonviolence.
- Many, though not all, orthodox Hindus are vegetarians and teetotalers.
- The *Lawbook of Manu* defines orthodox Hindu behavior.
- Foreign domination and economic hardship have compromised the high spiritual standards of ancient Hinduism.

Chapter 17

Sacraments and Holy Days

In This Chapter

- ◆ Hindu sacraments
- ◆ Commemorating birth and death
- ◆ Hindu holy days
- ◆ A brother's commitment
- ◆ Acknowledging the guru

For Hindus, one advantage to having so many gods and goddesses is that there are lots of holidays. One deity or another is always being honored. This makes for plenty of festivals, lots of good food, and warm relations between humans and the gods.

In addition to public holidays, Hindus have numerous private holy days. Hinduism has 16 major sacraments and a couple dozen minor ones. So let's have a look at some of the most important days on the Hindu calendar and in a Hindu's life. Then you'll know when to send your Hindu friends "Happy Divali" cards!

Living Life Holy

All of nature and all of time are sacred in Hinduism. Traditional Hindu families make no radical distinction between sacred and secular as we do in the West. In the morning, you get up and put your feet on the Earth, who is a goddess. You go outdoors and greet the Sun, who is a god. You are surrounded by divinity.

The Sanskrit word *samskara* refers to a groove in the mind, a deep impression made in consciousness. The Hindu sacraments, also called samskaras, are special rites in which a Hindu's connection with all pervading divinity is formally reaffirmed. A new groove formed in the soul orients it toward God as another stage of life begins.

Rite from the Start

Sacraments begin before a soul is even conceived. Orthodox couples consider the moment they consciously decide to have a child a sacramental time of great auspiciousness. The Upanishads contain special mantras for would-be parents to recite in order to invite intelligent, devoted, and highly evolved souls into the wife's womb.

Sexual relations then are engaged with full conscious intent to conceive a child. A special rite is actually performed at what the parents assume to be the moment of conception. Many Hindus believe that the state of their minds at the moment they conceive a baby will influence the child's development. Couples whose minds are preoccupied with physical sensations will produce passionate children. Couples who keep their minds in loving and clear states will invoke the entrance of more spiritually advanced souls into their family.

Birth itself is a sacrament. The birth rite is called *jatkarman*, which means the act of birth, the birth of action, or maybe both. Paradoxically, for Hindus biological events like giving birth are both sacred and polluting at the same time. So rites blessing and celebrating the event are joined with rites to purify the physical and mental environment of the suffering and shedding of blood that accompanied childbirth.

Childhood Passages

Several important sacraments are performed during childhood. Usually sometime between the third and sixth week of life, the child is formally given its name. The parents may take the infant to their local temple for this special event or do it at home. Often an astrologer is first consulted to help select an auspicious name reflecting the cosmic energy at the moment of birth. Then the father whispers the child's name into its right ear.

The first time the child is taken outside the house, his universe expands exponentially. The first time he takes solid food marks the beginning of the end of its dependence on his mother's breast. Hindus consider both of these events major rites of passage, and they're witnessed and celebrated by relatives and consecrated with mantras.

Hindus also consecrate their child's first haircut, which would occur sometime before the age of three. The head is shaved, symbolizing purity. Some Hindus like to believe this also helps to shave off some of the bad karma from previous lives.

Ear piercing (for both sexes!) is also a sacramental event and usually is scheduled when the child is around a year old, though it may not occur till age five. Hindus believe that certain points in the physical body relate to particular energy centers in the Subtle Body, much like the Chinese acupuncture points. Therefore, Hindu-style ear piercing is believed to benefit the baby's health.

One of the most important sacraments occurs between the ages of four and seven. This marks the inauguration of formal academic study. A parent, priest, or guru holds the child's finger and guides it through grains of uncooked rice sprinkled across a plate. With the tutor's help, the child spells out a letter of the alphabet for the first time. This is an extremely charming and auspicious event to which Sarasvati, the goddess of education, is invited.

Young People's Initiations

The one Hindu sacrament people in the West have heard of, if they've heard of any of them at all, is the investiture of the sacred thread. This initiation is reserved for boys of the brahmin, kshatriya, and vaishya castes. Without this rite, an upper caste boy cannot study the Veda or marry. The sacred thread is hung over the boy's left shoulder and swings around his right torso, much like the Milky Way—the celestial sacred thread—hangs crosswise across the northern sky. Depending on the boy's caste, this ceremony may take place between the ages of nine and fifteen.

The boy is now initiated in the Gayatri mantra, the most sacred mantra in the Veda. He is then considered twice born, since this spiritual initiation is the equivalent of a second birth. His initiators invoke the gods' and goddess' blessings for this extraordinarily important event.

In olden times, following this critical sacrament, the boy would be sent away to live and study with his guru until he reached marriageable age. In some communities today, the significance of this rite has shifted, and a young man might not receive his sacred thread till his early 20s, immediately before marriage.

Sages Say

With loving reverence we bow to the Inner Sun, the most splendid light in all the worlds. Please illuminate our minds.

—The Gayatri Mantra

Another rite for boys only occurs when the adolescent shaves for the first time. This sacrament is less serious in tone than the investiture of the sacred thread. Gifts are exchanged all around. Once he's relaxed and in a good mood, the boy is asked by his smiling but not joking elders to remain celibate till marriage!

The equivalent sacrament for women occurs at the time of a girl's first menstrual period. She is closed away in a dark room for several days to adjust to her new status as a potential mother and to think seriously about the responsibility this entails. Friends come by to advise and tease her. Then she emerges for a ritual bath and a feast of celebration. Sometimes her female relatives will take the young lady to the local temple and wave lights around her as if she were the Goddess herself. She has just assumed one of the Goddess's most amazing powers: the ability to produce new life.

A Wedding to Last Forever

For many Hindus, the wedding is the most important sacrament of their lives. Hindu weddings go on for days. Even the abbreviated modern versions run on for many hours. The marriage is expected to last a lifetime (at the very least!). Widows seldom remarry in India. Widowers are free to remarry, but since grooms are often a fair bit older than their brides, it's more common for husbands to predecease their wives.

Guidepost

Don't ask a swami to perform your wedding ceremony! Hindus believe you can't give what you haven't got. Since a swami isn't married, he can't give you the state of marriage. In India, it's inauspicious if a swami shows up at your wedding. He represents renunciation of worldly life and infertility—a bad omen for newlyweds!

Hindu marriages are almost always arranged by parents. Even today when many young Hindus are immigrating abroad looking for better job prospects, they'll travel back to their village in India to marry the partner their parents have selected. In North India particularly, the bride and groom may never have met before!

In making a suitable match, parents consider the prospective spouse's subcaste and clan, profession, and financial status. Horoscopes are carefully compared. Then they select an astrologically auspicious date and begin the festivities.

The heart of the long ceremony occurs when the bride steps three times on her in-laws' grinding stone, symbolizing her entrance into their household. Then the couple walks around the sacred fire seven times during which incalculably ancient Vedic mantras are chanted. The groom offers his new wife half of all his good karma. The bride offers back half of her bad karma. As you can see, Hindu women drive a tough bargain. But most Hindu men agree to the deal!

Life After Death

Hindu sacraments begin before a child is born, continue throughout life, and go on long afterward. The dead are not really gone as long as they live on in our hearts—and in their subtle bodies!

Honoring the Departed

A funeral is always a painful and sobering event. Final rites involve bathing and anointing the body and shaving it if the body is male. The corpse is wrapped in a shroud and carried to the cremation grounds, usually within hours of death. Hindus most often burn the dead, then offer the remains to the Earth or a river. Children and sometimes pregnant women are buried rather than cremated. Poorer people, who may not be able to afford the expense of cremation, may also bury their dead. Often saints are buried in special mausoleums rather than cremated. These tombs, the famous *samadhi* shrines of India, often become popular pilgrimage sites.

def•i•ni•tion

A **samadhi** shrine is the burial place of a saint. Samadhi also refers to an intense state of meditative absorption.

Final rites, called shraddha, conclude with the offering of rice balls to the departed. You wouldn't want to send them on their way without something to eat! Some Hindu families continue making food offerings for years after the death has occurred. Attitudes toward the dead can vary greatly from community to community or from home to home. Some people greatly fear hauntings and hope the spirits of the dead will quickly depart. Others rely on the continuing advice and blessings of the dead, as indicated in the omens spirits use to signal their recommendations to loved ones left behind.

Linking Up

There are numerous other Hindu sacraments besides those I've described here. Some are rarely practiced anymore; others are performed only regionally. Yet the sacraments are an extremely important expression of Hindu life. Not every Hindu is versed in the intricacies of Upanishadic philosophy or can chant whole books from the Veda. Yet every one feels connected to the wider Hindu community and to the fountain of blessing force flowing from higher levels of reality through these ancient holy rites.

Sacred Time

Next I want to tell you about the most popular Hindu holidays, but I have a problem because I can't tell you exactly when these holidays are! That's because most Hindus use a lunar calendar based on the phases of the Moon, which is different from our Western solar calendar, which is based on the solstices and equinoxes, pivotal points in the Sun's yearly journey through the ecliptic.

Because of this discrepancy, dates from the Hindu calendar seem to hop around on our Western calendar. This is why your Hindu friend who celebrates her birthday in October one year may have a birthday party in November the next year! I'm tacking in an East/West calendar wheel, so you'll have at least a general idea how the two calendars interface.

The Festival of Lights: Divali

According to legend, it was on this night thousands and thousands of years ago that the hero Rama and his wife, Sita—freshly rescued from the tyrant Ravana—returned to their home capital of Ayodhya after 14 years of exile. The city exploded with joy! Citizens came racing into the night carrying portable lamps to celebrate the safe return of their dearly loved king and queen.

The Hindu View _____

During the enormous Tamil celebration of Thai Pusam each January or February, Hindus pierce their bodies with hooks or small spikes in honor of Murugan, the youthful spear-carrying demon-slayer. Remarkably, the devotees don't bleed and claim to feel no pain!

If you can only attend one festival in India, Divali is the one to see. Like many Hindu holidays, it actually goes on for days. Why celebrate one day when you can party all week? Though this holiday isn't all play and no work. For many Hindus, it's a time for cleaning out the house and buying new things for the home. Business people start up new ledger books on this holiday. It's time to move out the old and start afresh!

Divali, or Diwali or even Dipavali as it's also called, occurs in October or November and means "the festival of lights." You'll see why on the New Moon night. As the Sun slips over the western horizon, all over India villagers light small clay lamps, leaving them on their windowsills and in the roads. They also float millions of make-shift lamps down the rivers. In the cities, Hindus hang out strings of electric bulbs. The entire subcontinent is lit up with cheerful twinkling lights. The effect is so spectacular—and so heartstoppingly beautiful—you'll never forget the sight till the end of your days.

Firecrackers (and these days fireworks) go off everywhere. Dainty foods, especially sweets, are offered to the deities. This is a night to connect with Lakshmi, the goddess of prosperity and domestic happiness, and Ganesha, the elephant-headed god of wisdom and success.

Divali is now a formally recognized holiday in nine countries: India, Nepal, Sri Lanka, Trinidad, Singapore, Fiji, Mauritius, Guyana, and Malaysia.

Sages Say

Clothed in light, glittering like priceless gems, You, the grace-filled World Mother, uphold the entire universe! To Goddess Lakshmi I bow again and again with gratitude and awe!

—Maha Lakshmi Stotram

Holi Day

Holi is New Year's Day for many Hindus. (But not for all Hindus, as some communities have their own unique calendars!) But for all Hindus, it's time to celebrate. This is the craziest, most carnival-like of the Hindu holidays and happens in late February, early March.

How did Holi get started? Well, once there was a demoness named Holika who was so mean-spirited she ate a little boy or girl every day! Finally a sannyasin passing through the area saw a poor widow weeping bitterly and asked what the problem was. "Holika is going to eat my only son!" she wailed.

The holy man devised a plan. When Holika showed up that day, he brought all the children together to shout obscenities and throw mud at her. The ruse worked. Holika was so humiliated she dropped dead of shame!

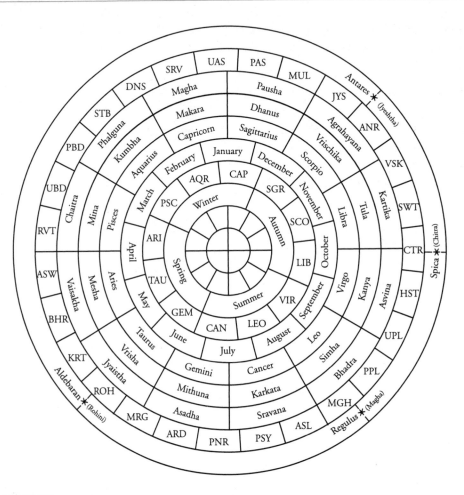

Calendar Wheel

Western Seasons

Western Sun Signs

Western Months

Constellations

Hindu Sun Signs

Hindu Months

Hindu Moon Signs

Bright Zodiac Stars

Moon Sign Abbreviations

"P." is for "Purva", "U." for "Uttara"

ASW	Ashwini	MGH	Magha	MUL	Mula
BHR	Bharani	PPL	P. Phalguni	PAS	P. Ashadha
KRT	Krittika	UPL	U. Phalguni	UAS	U. Ashadha
ROH	Rohini	HST	Hasta	SRV	Shravana
MRG	Mrigashiras	CTR	Chitra	DNS	Dhanishtha
ARD	Ardra	SWT	Swati	STB	Shatabhishaj
PNR	Punarvasu	VSK	Vishakha	PBD	P. Bhadrapada
PSY	Pushya	ANR	Anuradha	UBD	U. Bhadrapada
ASL	Ashlesha	JYS	Jyeshtha	RVT	Revati

© 2001 Johnathan Brown

The Western solar-based calendar in relation to the Hindu lunar-based calendar.

Anyway, that's the reason everyone's running around shouting insults and throwing dirt and red powder at each other on Holi! There's lots of singing and dancing. And mean old Holika gets roasted in a roaring bonfire!

While all Hindus participate in these festivals, Divali has a vaishya feel, as if it was originally thought up by business people. Its focus is on prosperity, happiness, and success. Holi has more of a shudra atmosphere. It's time for the working class to let loose a little and vent. They shout their real feelings at their employers and neighbors. The next day everything is forgiven and forgotten!

Guidepost

I hope you're not wearing your good clothes if you're with Hindus during Holi! Out come the water guns, and you're covered from head to toe with colored water or red powder. Let me tell you from personal experience, it's not easy to wash out!

Honor Thy Sibling

In ancient times, the gods got themselves in a pickle. They were losing their war against the demons so badly that Indra, warrior king of the deities, was completely unnerved! But Indrani, his peerless wife, saved the day. She tied a beautiful magical bracelet around Indra's wrist, and the next day Indra led the gods to an easy victory.

Rakhi Bandhan is celebrated around July or August and means "bond of protection." On this day, sisters tie multicolored bracelets around the wrists of their brothers, which means from now on, their brothers will have to protect them, no matter what!

While the festival is lighthearted, the commitment signified by the *rakhi*, or protective bracelet, is not. Stories tell of women who, being harassed by amorous suitors, ended the problem by sending the man a rakhi. It means she sees him as her brother and from now on he's responsible for protecting her virtue, not trying to make off with it!

In some parts of the country, women tie the colorful bracelets around their uncles' wrists, too. A few pockets of Hindu culture are matrilineal, which means uncles, even more than fathers, are responsible for a woman's welfare.

def•i•ni•tion

A **rakhi** is a bracelet girls tie around the wrists of their brothers, uncles, or other nonromantically involved males, asking for their protection.

Celebrating Spirit

Some holidays like Holi are raucous. Others like Divali have a mercantile flavor, somewhat like our Christmas, which also involves making lots of purchases and hanging out strings of light. Rakhi Bandhan is more private, a family rather than a community event. Still other festivals are devoted to spirit and are celebrated with fasting rather than feasting, with meditation rather than merrymaking.

Shiva's Night

Maha Shiva Ratri, the night sacred to Shiva, occurs on a Moonless night in February or March. Devotees honor it by sitting in meditation with Lord Shiva himself. They fast all day (they may take some fruit and water) and hold vigil all night.

The Shiva linga at the temple or in one's home shrine is bathed with milk, honey, and water and offered particular types of fruit and leaves that Shiva especially likes. Celebrants chant holy mantras like "Om namah Shivaya!" They sing hymns, often accompanying themselves on the hand organ. You may find some devotees seated around the sacred fire, tossing offerings of grain into the flames as they chant Shiva's name. Many simply meditate all night. Shiva is the lord of dissolution. If you worship him with full commitment on this long, dark night, he will dissolve away your sins!

Guru Purnima

The full Moon night of July (or sometimes June) marks Guru Purnima, the night all Hindus honor their spiritual preceptors. The sage Vyasa, who compiled the Vedas and wrote many other important scriptures like the *Mahabharata* and the Puranas, is also remembered with affection and respect.

If their guru is physically present, Hindus like to wash his or her feet as a token of their deep appreciation for the teachings and guidance they've received. If the guru isn't there in person, his or her sandals may be washed instead. Hindus don't use soap and water for this auspicious occasion, by the way, but milk mixed with honey, sandalwood paste, and pure water. The sandals don't just get cleaned, they become positively fragrant!

No human being is more special than the one who leads you to God. You'd follow her footsteps anywhere! No wonder her sandals are so magical!

Happy Birthday, God!

Just as Christians celebrate the birth of their savior Jesus Christ, Hindus celebrate the days their most popular divine incarnations were born. The birthdays of the avatars Rama and Krishna are cause for special festivities. The delightful elephant-headed deity Ganesha also gets his own special festival.

Rama Navami

Rama Navami, Lord Rama's birthday, is a huge pan-Indian celebration celebrated in or around April. Some Hindus will fast for the nine days leading up to the big day. In many communities, recitations of the *Ramayana* are organized. Folk dramas enacting favorite scenes from the lives of Rama and Sita are enthusiastically staged.

Krishna Jayanti

Krishna's birthday, called Krishna Jayanti, occurs in July or August and is an enormous national celebration. Much as Jesus was born rather humbly in a manger, Krishna was born in a prison cell! His parents were being held captive in a Mathura jail by the tyrant Kamsa. Krishna's father managed to get the baby to safety while the prison guards slept.

Krishna was born at midnight. At the stroke of midnight on every Krishna Jayanti, Hindus blow their conches, clang their bells, and shout Krishna's praises at the top of their lungs! Then they break their fast, sitting down to a feast including plenty of sweets.

Ganesha Utsava

You'll remember Ganesha from Chapter 11. He's the god with the elephant head who asked, "Got milk?" His special day, Ganesha Utsava, is held in August or September and is a time of great rejoicing, especially since Ganesha is so adept at removing our problems if we ask him nicely!

On the final days of the celebrations, statues of Ganesha, which were made specifically for worshipping during this festival, are carted down to a nearby river. Then they're immersed till the lightweight materials they're made of dissolve away. The ritual immersion of images of deities is a reminder that at the end of the universal cycle even the gods themselves will dissolve into the all-pervading consciousness of the Supreme Reality.

Quick Quiz

1. For Hindus, marriage is …

    a. The most important sacrament.

    b. Arranged over the Internet.

    c. An excuse to get drunk.

2. Hindus wash their guru's feet …

    a. But he has to polish his shoes himself.

    b. Out of respect for the guru's guidance.

    c. To prevent athlete's foot.

3. The Festival of Lights commemorates …

    a. The destruction of the demoness Holika.

    b. Rama and Sita's return home.

    c. The discovery of electricity.

4. On Holi you're likely to …

    a. Be squirted with colored water.

    b. Sit up all night meditating.

    c. Deck the halls with boughs of Holi.

Answers: 1 (a). 2 (b). 3 (b). 4 (a).

Victory on the Tenth Day

Dasara isn't just a holiday. It's a whole holiday season, 10 straight days of celebrations held in September or October! The first part is called Nava Ratri ("Nine Nights"). Three days and nights each are devoted to the worship of the great goddesses Durga, Lakshmi, and Sarasvati. Nava Ratri commemorates, among other things, Rama worshipping the warrior goddess Durga before setting off to battle the evil king Ravana. Rama won Durga's favor, which made him invincible even though he was vastly outnumbered by Ravana's better trained troops.

The final day of the holiday is called Vijaya Dashmi ("Victory on the Tenth Day"). Rama's fantastic victory over Ravana is celebrated with parades and fanfare. Enormous, odd-looking effigies of Ravana (after all, he had 10 heads!) are set on fire to signal the triumph of justice over injustice. Nava Ratri is the favorite festival of the year in Goddess country—the northeastern part of India. This is an especially auspicious time to approach the Divine Mother for blessings and special favors.

Saris for Spring

Hindu communities have their own regional festivals as well. In Tamil Nadu in the South, sometime around January, there is Pongol, celebrating the rice harvest. During Naga Panchami, also held in the south, snakes are honored and fed. (Few Hindus use pesticides. Snakes have always done just fine for pest control.) In the North, Vasant celebrates the arrival of spring. You'll know it's Vasant when all the women you see are wearing bright yellow saris!

In one month it's time to plant. In another it's time to harvest. But in Hinduism it's always time for God. Sacraments and holy days help keep mortals and eternity in close touch. That's something to celebrate!

The Least You Need to Know

- Hinduism has many sacraments, beginning before conception and ending after death.

- Marriage is the most important sacrament for most Hindus.

- Favorite Hindu holy days include the Festival of Lights and Rama and Krishna's birthdays.

- On Maha Shiva Ratri, Shiva's devotees stay up all night meditating and worshipping.

- Hindus devote one holiday each year just to honoring their guru.

Chapter 18

Temples and Sacred Sites

In This Chapter

- The sacred subcontinent
- Visiting a Hindu temple
- Divine possession
- Pilgrimage points
- Biggest party in the world

Few North Americans have a sense for the sanctity of the land. A few places like the Grand Canyon or Niagara Falls do evoke a sense of awe. But an appreciation of the inherent holiness of the land itself—such as the Native Americans have—is largely missing from the children of immigrants who now dominate North America.

The Hindu attitude is dramatically different. To them the planet itself is Bhumeshvari, "Mother Earth"—a living Goddess. And India is Jambu Dvipa, "Rose-Apple Island," the holiest place in the world.

The entire Indian subcontinent is dotted with temples and sacred sites. Within a day's walk of virtually any spot in India, you'll find at least one holy center. Hindu renunciates spend their lives circling India, stopping at another pilgrimage point or famous temple each evening. These places are magnifying lenses for the spiritual energy of the land itself, the Hindus' beloved Mother India.

Take Off Your Shoes!

You'll have to take off your shoes before you enter a Hindu temple. You're not allowed to drag in the dirt from the outside world, either on the soles of your shoes or in your own soul. Outside all large temples you'll find a shoe stall where you can store your shoes for a few pennies. You're expected to leave your worldly thoughts behind, too, though there's no convenient place to store them!

Any visitor should also dress modestly. Ladies, in Hindu culture this means the bosom, upper arms, and legs should not be exposed, so no halter tops or shorts. Gentlemen, clothes should be clean and untorn, with your legs covered. Please leave leather items at home, as it is considered a desecration to bring objects made from butchered cows into a Hindu temple.

Guidepost

It's appropriate to circumambulate a Hindu temple several times before you enter. This means walking around it, keeping the temple to your right. You're going to meet God or the Goddess inside, so use the time to prepare yourself for a beautiful experience.

Come bearing gifts! God and Goddess have filled your life with blessings, so it's only appropriate that you bring a present as an expression of your gratitude. Fruits like mangoes, coconuts, or bananas are good. So are handfuls of flowers. Rupee notes go down particularly well. Foreign currency will not be turned away! If it wasn't convenient to bring anything with you, don't fret. Plenty of helpful vendors will meet you at the temple door and cheerfully sell you every kind of offering appropriate at that temple.

Be careful not to stumble as you walk in. There's a raised step right before you enter. (After you've tripped over it a couple of times, you'll start remembering it's there!) You may want to bow, touch this step with the fingers of your right hand, and then touch your fingers to your forehead and heart. Even the dust from the steps of a holy temple carries a blessing!

Worshipping in a Hindu Temple

If you've timed your visit right, Goddess or God will come out and greet you. Ask in advance what the deity's office hours are. You don't want to get there before the murti, the divine statue, has had a chance to bathe, dress, and have a bite to eat—with a little help from the priests. Dressed up in fresh clothes and weighed down with numerous garlands of fragrant flowers, the deity will see you now.

You are admitted into the holy of holies, and a screen is pulled away so you can see the deity, and he or she can see you. At busy temples, you may have only a moment in the divine presence before you're waved out so the next group of devotees can squeeze in. At smaller community temples you can stay for the full service, however, which may include devotional singing and devotees dancing before the divine image. These slow, very stylized dances are quite restrained by Western standards.

A priest or devotee will offer objects like a fan, a fly whisk, and incense. If it's a Goddess, a few accessories she especially enjoys may be brought out, like a mirror to help her check her makeup!

The main event is *arati*, the ritual waving of lights before the deity. A brass tray filled with camphor candles is waved in circles before the deity. Then a temple officiant carries the tray around to each worshipper. Pass your hands quickly through the flames (it doesn't hurt!) as you waft the sacred fire's blessings toward yourself.

Receiving Your Blessing

The temple assistant will come around with several more items for you. He or she will pour some holy water into your cupped right palm. Hindus drink the water, then run their right hand over their heads, distributing the blessing force. Don't tell anyone I said this, but if you're in a Hindu temple in India, as opposed to another country where you're sure the water is amoeba-free, you may be better off discretely pretending to drink it and then rubbing it into your hair. You'll get the blessing just the same!

Temple personnel will also come around to mark your forehead. This *tilak* is a sign that you've received the deity's blessing.

Don't leave without *prasad*. Some of the gifts devotees have brought to the temple will be returned to you, blessed by the deity.

 The Hindu View _____

Devotees of Vishnu mark their foreheads with sacred designs etched with white clay. Followers of Shiva streak ash across the top of their faces. If the temple priest marks your forehead with red cosmetic powder, he's a devotee of the Goddess.

def•i•ni•tion _____

A **tilak** is the mark Hindus wear on their foreheads.

Prasad is food or some other offering you've brought to the image of a Hindu god or goddess. It's returned to you with blessings.

Usually this is an article of food or a handful of flowers and is a token of the Goddess or God's affection for you. It's considered quite holy. Amazing healings have been attributed to the power of prasad!

Inside and Outside the Temple

Let me give you just a point or two about the Hindu temple itself. Westerners sometimes find older traditional Indian temples a bit hard on the eye. The outside of many temples is covered with so many figurines it's exhausting to look at. At the bottom are demons and animals, at the middle story humans are portrayed, and higher up are numerous figures of gods and goddesses at work and play. Then you walk into the temple itself—and it's practically empty!

Do you get the point? The outside of the temple represents our outer life and the infinitely varied external manifestation of the divine. The inside, or garbha (which literally means "womb"), stands for the interior of the soul and for the unmanifest reality, in which only Pure Consciousness is present. In some temples, there's nothing inside but the image of the God or Goddess itself.

Outside the many. Inside the One.

Altar in the Living Room

In the West, we think in terms of the separation of Church and State. Most of us also tend to think of a church, synagogue, or mosque as the place we go to worship and home as the place we go to watch TV. The situation is *totally* different for Hindus. The center of the Hindu religion is *not* the temple. It's the home.

Hindus go to the temple for festivals or consecrations or to ask for special favors from the deity. But no sermons are delivered there. You don't go to the temple to get lectured at or be educated in your religion. You just go to pay your respects to the temple deity. The real worship goes on right in your own house. So does your religious education, which comes from your parents and elders. Or you may go to your guru's home to study with him or her.

Every Hindu home has its own shrine where images of the favorite family deities are installed. The family (or at least the women, who are in charge of household activities) worship before these deities every day, waving lights and offering incense and food. In fact, good Hindus won't touch their meals till the food has first been blessed by the household gods.

The home shrine may contain small statues of popular deities like Krishna, Lakshmi, or Shiva. Or there may be pictures and even inexpensive color posters of the Hindu gods and goddesses. These are not considered less holy than metal or stone statues. The divine presence has been invoked in these articles, and Hindus treat them as living representations of the deity.

The household shrine saved Hinduism during the Muslim takeover. Fanatic Muslim leaders destroyed almost every major temple in northern India in an effort to exterminate Hinduism, but they failed because the most important temples were in peoples' homes. Most Hindus remained faithful to their religion despite tremendous pressure to convert to Islam. When calmer Muslim governors, and later the British, headed the country, the great Hindu temples were rebuilt.

Hindu Hot Spots

If this entire book were devoted just to listing holy sites in India and I somehow managed to limit myself to only two paragraphs for each one, we still could barely skim the surface of the thousands of pilgrimage spots in India. When Hindus talk about India as a holy land, they're not kidding!

But I want to take a quick tour of the subcontinent, so I can introduce you to a few of the most special places in India and explain what each one represents for Hindus.

The Navel of the World

Let's start at the extreme north, a little way across the present Indian border into Tibet. Ironically, the ancients considered this northernmost tip of Hindu culture the *center* of the Hindu world. I'm talking about Mount Kailash, an amazing mountain that seems to spring up out of nowhere in the Tibetan plateau. Its striking conical shape reminds Hindus of a Shiva linga. Lord Shiva and his wife, Parvati, are said to have their main residence at the top of the mountain. It's so sacred no one would even think of climbing it. You might disturb Shiva in his meditation!

Within walking distance from Kailash are two sacred lakes. Remarkably, Manasarovar is shaped just like the Sun. And Raksas Tal is shaped like a crescent Moon. In a way, Kailash really is the center of the world. Remember how the Bible says four rivers run out of the Garden of Eden? Well, the Indus, Sutlej, Brahmaputra, and Karnali rivers—four of the greatest rivers of Asia—begin virtually at the foot of Mount Kailash. This really is the Hindu paradise, or I should say *paradesh*, which means "supreme land" or "highest region," an appropriate designation for the holiest site at the roof of the world!

Kailash is the holiest mountain in the world. It's sacred not just to Hindus but also to Buddhists, Jains, and the native Tibetan Bonpos. Even during the most brutal part of the Chinese occupation, Hindu pilgrims risked their lives trying to reach this legendary mountain. Today, the political situation has calmed down somewhat. But the mountain rises from a barely breathable altitude of 15,000 feet (add 22,028 feet on top of that if you want to measure the peak). In addition, the plateau is riddled with killer hail and sandstorms, making this one of the most dangerous sacred sites in the world to travel to. Perhaps that's why pilgrims who actually reach this holy place are said to gain tremendous merit.

City of Light

One of the best things about being a tour guide is I get to pick our stops. The next point on our itinerary is Benares, my favorite city in India. Archeological evidence suggests this is the oldest continuously inhabited city in the world. Kashi, "the City of Light," as Benares is also called, is mentioned even in the ancient Veda!

Benares has been one of the intellectual capitals of India since time immemorial. Today it's home to four universities, including the largest residential university in Asia.

Even more important, it's Lord Shiva's favorite city! Hindus fortunate enough to die here are shuttled directly to the highest heaven, thanks to Shiva's gracious intervention. This is the final stop for many of Hinduism's elderly, who stream into the city hoping to take advantage of Shiva's good nature and pass away here on Shiva's deluxe train to heaven. If you take the spectacular boat ride down the Ganges here, you'll see the famous burning *ghats* on the west side of the river where older pilgrims who got their timing right are being cremated.

On some maps, Benares is still called by its older name, Varanasi. The ancient city was bounded by the Varuna River on its north and the Asi River (now a creek) on its south, with the Ganges running along its western shore. Here's a secret the yogis will share with you. The Varuna stands for the right *nadi*, or "inner river of energy" in the subtle body. The Asi is the left nadi. The Ganges stands for the central canal in the subtle body through which the kundalini energy flows. If at the moment of death you can balance the subtle energy flowing through these nadis, then you will indeed enter the city of Shiva. This is the center of highest consciousness at the top of the brain. If you hold your awareness here throughout the death process, you'll experience the light of liberation. Then your karmas will burn away in the cremation ghat of divine awareness.

def•i•ni•tion

A **ghat** is a set of steps leading down to a river. Many Hindus bathe, wash their clothes, worship, and perform cremations at ghats.

A **nadi** is a current of energy in the subtle body. It's the equivalent of a nerve in the physical body.

City of Tents

What if you threw a party and 70 million guests showed up? In India it happens! Every three years a festival called the Kumbha Mela is held at one of four sites: Prayag at Allahabad in north-central India, Nasik on the West Coast, Ujjain a little northeast of Nasik, and finally at Hardwar in the Himalayas. The festival rotates between these four centers, so each city gets to sponsor the Mela every 12 years.

Tens of million of Hindus attend these fairs with every possible Hindu sect represented. They get together in an atmosphere of mutual respect to worship in their own way. Holy men and women pour out of their retreats in the Himalayan mountains and forests to join the common people in a celebration of spirit.

The Kumbha Mela at Prayag, where the Ganges and Yamuna rivers meet, is the biggest of all. It's generally held in January and February when the two rivers partly dry up. The Indian army is sent in to construct a city of tents in the dry river basin. Pilgrims live in the tents for free. Spiritual leaders from all over the country build makeshift ashrams there for the six-week festival. Programs go on 24 hours a day, and food is distributed free to all comers.

The Hindu View

Kumbha Mela means "Festival of the Pot." Ages ago the celestial physician (the constellation Aquarius, called Kumbha in India) accidentally spilled his pot of divine nectar. A few drops splattered in Nasik, Ujjain, and Hardwar, but most of it poured out in Prayag. At the astrologically auspicious time of the Kumbha Mela, you can taste the nectar of immortality as it drips from heaven!

Seventy million people turned up for the Kumbha Mela at Prayag in January 2001. It was the biggest collective event in world history! Ordinarily you can't see even the largest cities (like Tokyo with a population of a mere 34 million) from outer space. This Kumbha Mela was so huge that satellite photographs picked up the massive crowds!

I attended the 2001 Kumbha Mela, and it was absolutely one of the most powerful spiritual experiences of my life. I can hardly begin to express the effect of having 70 million human beings together in one place, all praying, chanting, and meditating with each other in an atmosphere of harmony and mutual support. It was like spending a month in heaven!

The Busiest Temple in the World

What is the one most visited pilgrimage site in the entire world? Rome? Mecca? Guess again! If you guessed Tirupati in Andhra Pradesh in South India, you win a cookie and a bowl of ice cream!

The Sri Venkateshvara Temple at Tirupati is the wealthiest in the world, bringing in about $6,000,000 *per day*. Some 30,000 devotees show up every day of the year. They climb 10,000 steps (you read right—I said *10,000* steps) to reach the temple at the top of the hill. There they are offered the opportunities to donate all their gold and valuables and have their heads shaven clean. (Both men and women leave Tirupati bald.)

Devotees then shuffle forward in an agonizingly slow line leading to the inner sanctum. Many of them are singing hymns, chanting holy texts, or repeating their mantra. Finally they reach Vishnu himself, who is appearing as Sri Venkateshvara in the form of a black stone statue covered with priceless jewels.

It's said that any wish you make before Sri Venkateshvara *must* come true. Stories abound of extraordinary miracles and healings experienced by Hindus who visit this shrine. Many devotees return with even more expensive gifts for Sri Venkateshvara to express their gratitude for the boon he granted on their last visit. There's no stronger endorsement for a Hindu deity than this kind of repeat business!

The Statue of Liberation

The United States has the Statue of Liberty, and India has Saint Tiruvalluvar. At Kanya Kumari, the very southernmost point of India, you can see the Indian Ocean, the Arabian Sea, and the Bay of Bengal with one sweep of the eyes. You'll also see the spectacular 133-foot statue of Tiruvalluvar towering over the shoreline.

At 151 feet, the Statue of Liberty is a bit taller, but it's only a third the weight of the 7,000-ton Indian statue, which over 150 stone workers sculpted by hand.

Tiruvalluvar wrote a Tamil spiritual classic called the Tirukural ("Holy Verses") some 2,200 years ago. One of the greatest masterpieces on religious ethics in world literature, the 1,330 verses of the text are inscribed around the pedestal of the statue.

The Statue of Liberty represents American's highest value and its lasting contribution to world culture: the commitment to personal freedom. The stone statue on India's southern shore represents India's greatest value and *its* greatest gift to the world: a religious tradition devoted to freedom from ignorance, suffering, and the wheel of rebirth.

While we're here, take note of the Vivekananda Memorial a few hundred yards away. Swami Vivekananda was sitting on this rock when he had a vision of his late guru, Ramakrishna, standing out on the water, urgently signaling him to step out into the ocean. Vivekananda took this as a sign that he was supposed to cross the Atlantic and begin teaching Hinduism in America. In 1893, he made the crossing and first introduced modern Westerners to Indian religion.

> **Sages Say** _____
>
> The satisfaction of getting revenge lasts only for a moment. The glory of forgiveness lasts forever.
>
> —Tirukural

Krishna's Playground

Swinging back up the western side of India, we have to pause in the holy cities of Mathura and Vrindavan, where many of the enchanting episodes in the life of Lord Krishna unfolded. Krishna was born in Mathura and later reigned there as king. But his childhood romances all occurred in Vrindavan (Brindavan in Hindi), about 6 miles to the north.

Mathura has been a great city for thousands of years and was known even to the ancient Greeks following Alexander's visit. But it's hard to get a feel for what the rural area of Vrindavan must have been like thousands of years ago when Krishna was tending cows there and devastating the milkmaids with alluring glances from his foxy eyes.

Sages Say _____

There is just one place where man meets God—right within the heart He dwells as the innermost self. He who seems to be the farthest is the nearest of all.

—Swami Satprakashananda

Now so many temples and shrines are built in his honor that he wouldn't recognize his old town if he dropped by!

About three million Krishna devotees make the pilgrimage to Vrindavan every year. It's a very active center for religious devotion with singing, ecstatic dancing, worshiping, and meditating going on at all hours of the day and night as pilgrims seek to recapture the feeling of being in Krishna's living, loving presence.

Guidepost _____

Don't be offended if you're denied entrance to a Hindu temple. A number of non-Hindus have behaved so disrespectfully in some temples that the priests have closed the doors to foreigners. The problem isn't you, and it isn't the priests. It's immature foreigners whose disdainful behavior spoils the experience for everyone.

Seeing the Saints

If Westerners are going to make a pilgrimage all the way to India, often it's the saints, not the temples, they're going to see. Connecting with great yogis and sages is not as easy as you might think. Contrary to popular mythology, you're unlikely to get off the plane at Delhi and find a guru waiting for you, calling out breathlessly, "My child, at last you have come!" Most real gurus play hard to get because life is short and they only have time for serious students. Trusting the flow of karmic forces, they know the legitimate devotees will be guided to the right teacher.

But if it's holy people you want to see, I recommend you make your way to Rishikesh in Uttar Pradesh. There no matter how bad your karma is, you're sure to run into at least a couple of saints.

Rishikesh is about a dozen miles north of the holy city of Hardwar, where the Ganges bursts through a breathtaking gorge to begin its descent into the Indian plains. Rishikesh is less congested than Hardwar, so more sadhus congregate there. It's also where pilgrims come to begin the long trek up to the holy sites of Badrinath, Kedarnath, and Gangotri. These three areas are tougher to get to, but serious spiritual practitioners make their way there to bask in the beauty and purified atmosphere of the Himalayas while they worship and meditate.

You'll find plenty of ashrams in Rishikesh. However, for a place that used to be awfully secluded, a lot of construction is going on these days, and it's not as quiet as it used to be. With the modern world encroaching on all sides, it's getting harder to find a quiet, isolated cave to do your spiritual practice in the traditional manner.

The Goddess Drops In

Divine energy doesn't just center itself in places; it also comes through people. Divine possession is commonplace in Hindu culture. The Goddess in particular is fond of selecting special women as her mouthpiece.

When people in the community experience a crisis, they may go to the Goddess's franchise representative, a local village woman who then goes into a trance. The Goddess speaks through her, offering advice and blessings. The woman temporarily becomes a living temple through which divine grace emanates.

Divine being is not a theoretical abstraction to Hindus. It is really present in the temple and in the land. It even speaks to Hindus directly through a human oracle when receiving specific instructions is critical. While temples and sacred sites can be focal points for divine energy, the most fluid conduit for divine grace remains the human heart.

Quick Quiz

1. Camphor candles are waved in Hindu temples …

   a. So you can see your way in the dark.

   b. To express devotion to the deity inside.

   c. To send messages to priests hiding behind a screen.

2. The most popular pilgrimage place on Earth is …

   a. Mecca.

   b. Tirupati.

   c. Graceland.

continues

continued

3. At the southernmost tip of India is an enormous statue of ...

    a. Mother Teresa.

    b. Swami Vivekananda.

    c. Saint Tiruvalluvar.

4. Hindu temples are mostly empty inside ...

    a. Symbolizing the unmanifest reality.

    b. To make them easier to clean.

    c. Since Hindus never mastered the art of interior decorating.

Answers: 1 (b). 2 (b). 3 (c). 4 (a).

The Least You Need to Know

- Hindu temples are constructed to represent inner and outer realities.
- Hindus worship primarily not in temples but in their own homes.
- India contains the most popular pilgrimage sites in the world.
- The Kumbha Mela attracts as many as 70 million pilgrims for a six-week festival.
- "Divine possession" allows people to channel advice directly from the Goddess.

Part 5

God's House Has Many Doors

According to Hinduism, there are many entrances to God's house. There's the door for people with dynamic personalities who always have to be doing something. Another door is for people who are all heart, and still another for those who are mostly in their heads. Then there are entrances for technique-oriented people who prefer a systematic approach to spirituality. You can take your time moseying up to the door or sprint right through like India's yogis and swamis.

Hinduism is not a "one size fits all" religion. Whatever your personality, whatever your circumstances in life, whatever your skills and abilities, the Divine Being will find a way to guide you home. In God's house, everyone is welcome.

Chapter 19

A Robe of Fire

In This Chapter

- ◆ God's hobos

- ◆ Walking away

- ◆ Death before dying

- ◆ The spiritual quest

- ◆ Freedom to serve

They're the crown jewels of Hinduism, the men in bright orange robes wandering the Indian subcontinent with little more than a walking stick and a begging bowl. In other countries penniless vagrants like these, unkempt and unemployed, might be considered undesirables. If one camped in front of your home, you might call the police to shoo him away. But this is India, where the lens of spiritual insight turns everything topsy-turvy. These men aren't the least respected people in society—they're the most honored of all. These are Hinduism's sannyasins, the renunciates who have given up everything they ever had—including their personal identity—to attain enlightenment.

These remarkable men, with their piercing eyes that seem to see through you into eternity, are the human embodiment of the Hindu tradition. They walk the path of fire and light without regard for heat or cold, hunger or thirst, safety or danger. Supporting their quest for God is the duty and privilege of every Hindu householder. Free of social obligations and free of himself, the wandering sadhu becomes a conduit for the flow of divine grace. The presence of an enlightened sannyasin, with his singular focus on God, radiates blessings to everyone who approaches him. That's why he's the most valuable person in the community!

Meetings with Remarkable Men

Backpacking through northern India one winter, I really thought I was going to freeze to death. It was the coldest January in decades. Four layers of clothes, two wool blankets, and an Arctic-rated sleeping bag barely got me through the night. A group of sannyasins stopped near my campsite. Each was wearing only a thin sheet of cotton cloth covering their loins and lightly tossed over one shoulder. Not even bothering to light a fire, they sat down to chant God's name. They looked as comfortable as if they were sipping a mango *lassi* on a warm summer evening!

def•i•ni•tion

A *lassi* is a light, frothy, chilled Indian beverage made with yogurt or buttermilk and flavored with spices or fruit.

I interviewed them about their lifestyle, though this wasn't easy with chattering teeth! Amazingly kind and patient, they answered my questions about life on the road to God-realization.

Why They Wander

Many of us feel fundamentally dissatisfied with life. We have a haunting feeling that there's something more, something better, just out of reach. Some of us may even have had genuine mystical experiences, a spontaneous sense of universal oneness or a numinous sense of the immediate presence of something higher. In Western culture this usually means it's time for a good, stiff drink! Often we shrug off these feelings or turn to drugs, alcohol, TV, or computer games to snuff out the sense that something fundamental is missing in our lives.

The sannyasins I spoke with had these feelings as children. They saw that their relatives were frustrated and unhappy despite achieving prosperity and success. But they also grew up hearing stories about great saints and seeing holy men wander contentedly through the villages and forests. Sooner or later they felt an intense inner call to an active search for mental peace and spiritual understanding. Following the example of seekers for thousands of years before them, they decided to become itinerant monks, often to the horror of their families.

Mothers and fathers are rarely delighted to lose a son to a life of renunciation. Who will take care of them when they get older if their son is gone? Hindus in India don't have Medicare! But there is spiritual compensation: the tradition says when a man becomes enlightened, blessings accrue to his relatives backward in time through seven generations! Benefits like this help, because a would-be sannyasin needs to get his parents' permission (or his wife's, if he's married) before he's inducted into the life of spiritual asceticism. There is a very human paradox in the Hindus' enormous respect for authentic renunciates and grief in seeing a beloved family member leave home forever to become one.

I know you're wondering if women can become renunciates, too. Yes they can! They're called *sadhvis* (female sadhus), *swaminis* (female swamis), or *bhairavis* (female tantrics). Most Hindu women, however, prefer to do their spiritual practices at home, in the context of family life.

Guidepost

Is that Hindu holy man you just met an enlightened master? Or is he an impostor? Unfortunately, some of the sannyasins you see are not genuine spiritual aspirants but people who don't want to work. They know that posing as a holy man can be a ticket to a free meal. Some just spend the day smoking hashish and soaking up the Sun.

Sages Say

Why don't you understand you really are absolutely One, the single awareness looking out through billions of eyes? You are the irrefutable awareness in which all reality abides, the one self-evident truth that cannot be denied. Why do you divide that which can't be split into pieces?

—Avadhuta Gita

Many Monks

Ochre-robed swamis are India's most famous renunciates. Many of them belong to the order of monks founded by the great yogi and philosopher Shankaracharya centuries ago (see Chapter 9). You can tell a swami belongs to this prestigious tradition if his name ends with any of these words:

◆ Tirtha, a place of refuge like a holy site

◆ Ashrama, a source of spiritual family like an ashram

- Vana, self-disciplined as an ascetic living in the forest

- Aranya, nonattached like a yogi living alone in the woods

- Giri, firm in spiritual practice as a hill

- Parvata, unshakably established in truth like a mountain

- Sagara, immersed in knowledge as in an ocean

- Saraswati, an ever-flowing river of wisdom

- Bharati, full of spiritual knowledge

- Puri, vibrant as a city with spiritual realization

Swamis have formally taken vows in one of the renunciate orders. Don't expect to go to their headquarters and get a list of all the swamis, though. Things are not done in an organized way in India but rather in an organic way. Someone who's a swami initiates you in his or her order without necessarily registering your name anywhere. You put on the orange robe of a swami, and you're in business. Recently there was an attempt to begin keeping order in the orders, but the resistance was so fierce the effort collapsed. How can you expect someone who's renounced the world to worry about whether his name is listed in the ledger in some administrative building?

Performing Your Own Cremation

How do you actually become a swami? By celebrating your own death!

There are two major types of rites for the dead. One kind is for dead people who've left their bodies (see Chapter 17). The other is for dead people who're still very much alive. When Hindus take formal vows of renunciation, they perform their own cremation, burning themselves in effigy.

The Hindu View

When Hindu renunciates physically die, they are usually not cremated because when they took their vows of renunciation, they already cremated themselves. They can't burn twice! Most often their corpses are offered to a river.

From the point of view of their families, swamis really are dead. The cremation marks the end of the old personality with all its ties of friendship and family, all its attachments and responsibilities. The renunciate then enters a river and emerges naked, symbolizing his or her spiritual rebirth. The guru waiting at the bank gives the renunciate a new name and the orange robe of a world-renouncer.

The orange robe is the color of fire. It stands for the fiery immolation of the person this individual used to be and for the fire of spiritual awareness in which he or she now lives. Most sannyasins then begin a homeless life of incessant pilgrimage, poverty, and one-pointed focus on Self-realization. Others, however, join ashrams or welfare organizations and commit themselves to a lifetime of teaching or selfless service. Shankara, the founder of this order of swamis, established four pithas, or spiritual centers, one in each corner of India, where swamis could study, meditate, and teach. Since his time, the number of mathas, or monasteries, has expanded exponentially.

Sages Say

Everything we enjoy in this world, we're sure to lose one day. What difference does this make to the man who has already renounced them? Clinging to the things we enjoy ultimately leads to grief. Renouncing them leads to self-control and contentment.

—Vairagya Shatakam

Renouncers

Besides swamis, many other types of renunciates are found in Hinduism. If you travel around India, you may run into the nagababas, 100 percent naked ascetics you don't want to mess with because they cultivate extraordinary physical strength and spiritual power. Other Hindus often are justifiably intimidated by them. There are tapasvins, who perform superhuman penances. There are ash-smeared Shaivite tantrics with matted hair who smoke a lot of ganja (hashish) to help them sit still for hours on end, dissolving their consciousness in Shiva. Avadhutas are extremely unconventional and may appear crazy to ordinary people. (I hear that's because their awareness is focused at much higher planes of reality than the rest of us are attuned to!) There are hundreds of different types of renunciates.

As you can see, quite a few of the sannyasins wandering India are not technically swamis. Some wear a white loincloth instead of orange robes. Others wear nothing at all. (Hindus discreetly say this last group is "clothed in pure sky.") But all of them have renounced worldly life with the blessing of their guru. They beg for food once a day or get a free meal at a local temple. Typically they move along from one pilgrimage spot to the next, since staying in any one place for longer than a few days is seen as a potential source of unwanted attachment. During the monsoon season, however, travel just isn't practical, and even the most itinerant ascetics settle down in a shelter especially constructed for pilgrims to wait out the heavy rains.

A Carefree Lifestyle

What a great life! No 9-to-5 job, no mortgage payments, no screaming kids. You just sit around and think about God all the time!

But the renunciate lifestyle is no picnic. He's almost always on the move, often in terrible heat and sometimes in freezing cold. Lots of nights he's sleeping outside on the ground. He may only have one meal a day, and if he's meditating in a particularly remote area, he may not even get that!

He travels light, with maybe one extra loincloth, a small pot for carrying water, a begging bowl, and maybe a stick with a bar at the top to lean on during long hours of meditation. (Pressed against your armpit, the bar helps regulate your breathing pattern so you can meditate more deeply. I'm not kidding; this really works!) Does he have a sleeping bag? No. An extra blanket or two? Probably not. An iPod? Sorry!

The Hindu View

Do yeti, the "abominable snowmen of the Himalayas," really exist? My guru assures me they do! But yeti is a mispronunciation of *yati*, a mountain-dwelling yogi! Scruffy-looking yogis wandering the mountains of north India have sometimes been misidentified as mysterious ape creatures.

Everywhere he goes, he's followed by well-meaning but pesky hangers-on who imagine he's already enlightened and can cure their arthritis or find a husband for their daughter. Maybe mortgage payments and screaming kids don't sound so bad anymore!

A person needs great courage and a lot of dispassion to spend his life under conditions like these. Part of his training is learning to live with hunger and thirst, extremes of temperature, insects, and illness—and still maintain his psychological equilibrium. Hindu ascetics develop phenomenal inner strength, faith, and focus, living under such tough conditions.

Rules for Renunciation

If you can take the heat (asceticism is called tapas in India, which literally means heat), Hindu culture will support your spiritual work as much as it can. Many temples and hostels will offer you free food. Villagers are often happy to share part of their meal with you—it's a good way to earn karmic credit points! You can ride free on public transportation if your feet ache from walking all day.

Although you're free from the social rules that control most Hindus' lives, you're now bound by another set of regulations. Many renunciate traditions have strict regimes of daily spiritual practice, including many hours of meditation and rituals. Other rules may include never touching money (you can only accept donations like food) or never looking a woman in the eye. (If a woman speaks to you, you direct your gaze to her husband or another man nearby while replying. You're supposed to be celibate, and looking at an attractive person of the opposite sex can lead to difficulty.) Some sannyasins never sleep under a roof. Some go for years, even decades, never uttering a word.

Why would anyone go to all this trouble?

Shipwrecked Aliens

When talking with people who have a deep interest in spiritual life, whether the person is from India or Indianapolis, I frequently hear one comment. "I feel like I don't belong on this planet. My soul must have made a wrong turn, and I landed on Earth by mistake! I don't fit in here. I'm not into what everyone else is into. I don't fit in!"

These people aren't satisfied with the things their relatives, friends, television, and magazine ads all tell them should make them happy. Anti-wrinkle creams don't do it; sexual experimentation is surprisingly disappointing; drugs are a desperate temporary fix. More and more, these people suspect that what everyone else seems to want in life is just a distraction from facing an underlying sense of anxiety and spiritual homelessness.

Two thousand years ago Christian gnostics described the feeling of being an illegal alien wandering through a hostile foreign country with unfamiliar and self-destructive customs. They just wanted to get back to the world of light they intuitively felt was their real home!

If you're a Hindu and you have this feeling, you don't go to a psychiatrist for a prescription of Prozac. Instead, you set out on a spiritual quest to find the real truth that everyone else seems to be missing. You find a guru who can point you in the right direction. Then you head out on the road to find your way to your true home.

Letting Go

People who feel like strangers in a strange land intuitively sense that while prosperity and pleasure are great (and sure, just about everybody wants them!), they don't last forever. After eight or nine decades at the most, the soul loses everything it has gained in this life as its physical body crumbles away. If our pursuit of the good things in life hasn't been from the perspective of the supreme good, then death can be a horrendous experience. Being cut off from the people and things we're attached to can be wrenching.

Death is less of a trauma if during our lives we've been practicing the premier Hindu spiritual discipline of vairagya or dispassion. Western students sometimes think vairagya or nonattachment means stifling our emotional nature and cutting ourselves off from relationships when in fact it means *expanding* them.

Truly dispassionate people are the most loving folks you'll ever meet. They don't just love their family members and friends; they love everyone and everything. The divine inner nature, which is love itself, is allowed to shine in all directions, embracing everyone without particular attachment to one individual or another. Just as the Sun shines on every person alike without favoritism, the seeker renounces his ties to a small group of people, like family and friends, or a particular place, like his home or village. Now the entire universe is his house, and everyone he meets is a relative.

This is a radical lifestyle. As human beings we naturally love our children, our family, and close friends. Hinduism suggests though, that we not get overly attached to our attachments. At some point, we will have to let every one of them go. If we bear this in mind through life, death becomes an expansive experience, not a fearful ending. We look forward to—and actively work toward—an illumined state of consciousness that enfolds all our fellow beings in a state beyond time.

Inner Attainment

Sannyasins devote all their energies to the process of detaching from things of lesser value, perishable things, in order to lock onto things of infinite value, imperishable things. Their focus is not on the gifts of the world but the gifts of spirit.

Sages Say

I am the universal awareness that experiences the waking state and the sleep state; I indeed am the cosmic dreamer. I am the state beyond these states. I am the universal mind and, indeed, the universe itself. I am the Self of empty space. Everything, anything, indeed I am. I am pure self-existence.

—Ribhu Gita

Renunciates are giving up things we all ultimately lose anyway. Abandoning the particular, they move toward the universal. Their life outside conventional boundaries allows them the freedom to drill through the mind to the bedrock of existence, the common awareness that unites us all.

Those who succeed in this goal are said to gain extraordinary powers like telepathy, precognition, past life recall, and perhaps even the ability to transfer their consciousness to another body. Hindus believe this is possible because "universal awareness" isn't just a metaphor for them, it's a real state attainable to those who work hard to achieve it. Those who attain this level of consciousness are no longer limited by the perceptions of the five senses. They experience a level of extrasensory awareness the rest of us can barely begin to imagine. For thousands of years, the yogis' psychic powers have been legendary. Yet some of them renounce even this! Others use these abilities to guide and protect humanity. These are the spiritual masters who lead the rest of us forward in our own evolution.

Renouncing Renunciation

Since the beginning of its history, India has looked to its sages not only for spiritual advice but also for personal and social guidance. When Apollonius of Tyana visited India in the first century C.E., he noted how both kings and commoners sought out spiritual adepts for help with their practical concerns (see Chapter 3). The extraordinary level of insight the sages had attained made them the best all-purpose counselors possible! Maybe now you can understand why Hindus believe supporting sannyasins, who go on to become enlightened masters, is such a wise investment!

In the late nineteenth century, the role of swamis and sannyasins in serving the masses greatly intensified. Vivekananda, the swami you met in Chapter 10, was disturbed at the extent to which the Hindu tradition had sunk in India after centuries of foreign domination. A culture that had once been one of the most prosperous, respected, and dynamic in the history of the world had been reduced to physical poverty and psychological slavery. He realized the sannyasins still had the freedom, power, and prestige to rescue India from its morass of self-doubt and despair.

So Vivekananda called upon the Hindu renunciate orders to renounce renunciation! He asked them to meditate with eyes wide open. "Look around instead of closing your eyes. There are hundreds of poor and helpless people in your neighborhood. You will have to nurse and procure food and medicine for the sick. You will have to feed those who have nothing to eat. You will have to teach the ignorant. My advice to you is that if you want peace of mind, you will have to serve others."

Thousands of swamis have responded to the call. Today many sannyasins work in colleges and universities, hospitals and hospices. Free from the demands of supporting a family or raising children, they devote themselves to selfless service and social activism.

The Fortunate Few

The twentieth-century Himalayan yogi Swami Rama always referred to his fellow sannyasins as "the fortunate few." Only a fraction of the billions of people on Earth, he said, are cut out for the rigorous lifestyle and intense inner work of the traditional renunciate.

The yogis in his lineage spend part of the year in cave monasteries in the Himalayas. Some of the caves have several compartments, which were enlarged by hand over the centuries so that a growing community of ascetics could live in them. During the rest of the year these monks travel the subcontinent, Tibet and Nepal, visiting sacred pilgrimage sites and studying with adepts from affiliated traditions. Sister lineages are based in forest hermitages or other remote areas where the sannyasins can have privacy.

There the ancient knowledge of the spiritual adepts is passed down to new generations of seekers over the millennia. These forest academies and mountain monasteries have preserved the spiritual heritage of enlightened masters from eras long past and have given birth to many of the illumined adepts of our own time.

These sannyasins are not just philosophers; they're practical mystics who guard the secrets of the subtle body and research the powers of consciousness with a thoroughness we usually associate with Nobel Prize–winning scientists. Their monasteries are the Harvards and Yales of spirit.

Hinduism has always nurtured these kings of the inner realms. Hindu culture has fed and clothed these adepts, even organizing its society so men and women of spirit are sheltered, supported, and honored. In too many other civilizations great mystics have been persecuted, their schools attacked, their books burned, and their disciplines mocked. In Western culture today the situation is no less insidious. These custodians of humanity's spiritual heritage are blithely dismissed as anachronisms, human fossils from a supposedly more superstitious age. Perhaps our modern bias to dismiss these ancient traditions is only a reflection of our own ignorance. It is to the everlasting credit of the Hindu religion that during its greatest flowering and even at its lowest flounderings, it has always provided a home for the fortunate few, spiritual heroes on the greatest quest of all.

The Hindu View

Imagine backpacking across the country—but without a backpack. You don't have a dime—or a credit card either. All you know is you have to discover the meaning of life. And everywhere you go, people help you and feed you because they recognize your search is the most important thing any human being can undertake. That's Hinduism!

Quick Quiz

1. Sannyasins are ...

    a. Hindu hippies.

    b. Wandering holy men.

    c. Ottoman Turks who terrorized the Crusaders.

2. Sannyasins perform their own cremation ...

    a. By burning themselves alive.

    b. In order to assume a new spiritual identity.

    c. To avoid making payments on their credit cards.

3. To the Hindu, nonattachment means ...

    a. Not marrying your girlfriend after you get her pregnant.

    b. Spending money freely since tomorrow will take care of itself.

    c. Valuing all things equally rather than some things more than others.

4. Hindu society's response to renunciates who abandon their social duties is ...

    a. Anger and disgust.

    b. Overwhelming relief.

    c. Respect and support.

Answers: 1 (b). 2 (b). 3 (c). 4 (c).

The Least You Need to Know

◆ Some Hindus are not at peace with conventional reality and actively seek a higher truth.

◆ Religious renunciates "die" to their former life, assuming a new, spiritualized identity.

- The renunciate's life is difficult and highly self-disciplined.

- Some renunciates commit their lives to social activism.

- Hindu culture actively supports sincere renunciates on their spiritual quest.

Chapter 20

The Rewarding Life

In This Chapter

- God's original sacrifice
- Life without expectations
- Selfless service
- Duties, not rewards
- Unconditional love

Usually when we in the West picture Hindus, we think of orange-robed swamis or naked *babas* meditating alone in a cave. But the vast majority of Hindus are ordinary lay people raising children within the context of the extended family system, getting up each morning and going to work just like us.

In Hinduism, working people are just as capable of enlightenment as swamis. Most of the Vedic rishis, the sages who composed the holy Veda, were married and had full-time jobs. Even great avatars like Rama and Krishna had their hands full with administrative duties and family obligations.

Renunciates are free to devote their full attention to the quest for Self-realization. Lay people have more balls to juggle. Sacred texts like the Bhagavad Gita explain how working men and women can transform their daily duties into spiritual discipline—how housewives and washerwomen can become saints and how farmers and shopkeepers can become spiritual masters.

The Supreme Sacrifice

According to the Veda, at the beginning of time, Prajapati, the Supreme Being, performed the first religious act when he sacrificed himself in order to create us. He sacrificed his original state of perfect unity and bliss, splitting his body into the component parts of the material and subtle worlds and splitting his consciousness into the infinite number of souls inhabiting these worlds.

God set the example for how we ought to live. We also should base our lives on the principle of self-sacrifice. For yogis who want to return to him, this means reversing the process and sacrificing their individual selfhood back into his Supreme Consciousness. For the rest of us, it means performing our actions for the greater good, as if our activities are offerings to God. God sacrificed himself to bring us into being so he could express his creative power and his limitless love. When we imitate him by sacrificing our time and energy in the selfless performance of our duties, we reflect our Maker's love back to him.

def•i•ni•tion

Baba is an affectionate term for any Hindu holy man.

Into the Fire Pit

In ancient times the Vedic seers aligned themselves with God's law by re-enacting the primordial ritual. They didn't sacrifice themselves, though! During the fire sacrifice, called a *yajna*, they offered items of real value nonetheless. This sometimes included livestock, which constituted wealth back in the days before credit cards and ATM machines.

Rams and billy-goats were commonly sacrificed in India (as they were in Old Testament times in the Bible). Usually male animals were humanely slaughtered, then offered to the ritual fire. But other valuable commodities, like clarified butter, grain, or a milky drink called *soma* were offered, too. It was Agni the fire god's responsibility to carry these items to heaven, and one could see him doing his job as smoke from the fire pit rose to the sky.

Today animal sacrifice is rare in India, and many Hindus are vegetarian. But the original concept was based on the observable fact that life feeds on life: herbivores feed on grasses and grains; carnivores feed on herbivores; insects and bacteria feed on carnivores; insects and bacteria become nutrients in the soil which sustains grasses and grains; and so on in a continuous cycle of life and death. Performing a sacrifice meant we as humans acknowledge the living intelligence in nature and offer our fair share back into the system. We feed the forces of nature, and they sustain us. It's a reciprocal exchange that benefits everyone involved.

For many of us Westerners today, sacrifice seems barbaric. Instead of feeding life force back to nature, we feed nature an incessant stream of pollutants. Is that really more enlightened?

Sages Say

The gods need our worship as much as the Sun needs us to hold up a candle to light its way. The real reason we make offerings to the gods is to cultivate the spirit of self-sacrifice. We contemplate the divine qualities of the gods and goddesses in order to become more like them: generous, pure and selfless.

—Amritanandamayi Ma

The Limits of Sacrifice

The practical benefits of ritual actions were immense. If an individual sacrificed to the gods, they would ensure he had good weather, his cows were fertile, his children stayed healthy, and he lived to a ripe old age. Even better, if a deity was happy with a person's offerings, he or she would make sure he enjoyed a long, pleasant vacation in svarga, or heaven, after death. Then he'd return to Earth in a new physical body and enjoy all the pleasures life has to offer, all over again. Fortunately, there was never a shortage of priests willing to take a person's money and perform sacrifices for him!

Yet in some sacred texts there is a deep ambivalence about the value of these ancient Hindu rituals. The famous Mundaka Upanishad says,

> Rituals actions were prescribed by the seers in the Veda. Perform these rites correctly and you'll certainly enjoy the results, even rising to heaven to join the Creator. But rituals are a leaky boat because the benefits they deliver don't endure. Fools flatter themselves that they have accomplished something great by all their sacrifices. Due to their attachment to pleasure, performers of religious rites fail to recognize the supreme truth. Therefore they fall from heaven when the good karma produced by their pious deeds is exhausted, and once again fall prey to suffering and death.

Heaven is highly overrated, according to some spiritual masters. Even the special souls in the most comfortable bungalows in heaven glance anxiously over their shoulders. They know that when their pool of karmic credit runs dry, it's back to the salt mines on Earth. A comfortable stay in the afterlife is only temporary according to Hinduism if we're still attached to the things of this world below. When our karmic merit runs out, our visit to heaven comes to a halt, and rebirth is inevitable.

Breaking the Cycle

Birth, measles, school, puberty, years and years of hard work, disease, death, decay, birth …. According to the Hindu sages, the cycles keeps spinning like a dog that never gets tired of chasing its tail.

When you get tired of chasing after one thing you desire, then another, and then another, and constant loss and lack of fulfillment wear you down, then you start to ask, "Is there a way off the treadmill?" Hinduism teaches how you can short-circuit the karmic cables that bind you to the endless, repetitive, and ultimately futile attempt to find lasting happiness in the material world. There *is* a way out of the fire pit of suffering.

Acting in God's Play

As I said a moment ago, the universe is God's sacrificial pit. He has nothing to sacrifice but himself—what else exists but the self-existent Supreme Being? He has no one to sacrifice to but himself.

So God has immolated himself in a cosmic sacrifice. God remains God—perfect and whole—but he's now also *us*, imperfect, fragmented parts of himself. It's as if you looked at yourself in a cracked mirror. You'd see multiple versions of yourself, but you'd still be yourself! You wouldn't be altered in any way; you'd simply be entertained by the spectacle! The universe, in a way, is God's TV set. He's the producer, director, screenwriter, and actors, and he watches all the channels at once.

To keep the shows from becoming boring (where's the suspense if you know how it's going to come out?), God gives each of his actors free will. Each can rewrite his part in the script if he wants to, though God retains the rights to the script as a whole. Free will is the key to the whole process, and it's what makes humans so special. Of all the creatures on Earth, we're the ones with a fully developed will, should we choose to use it.

Most animals don't really generate karma because they're not acting of their own free will—nature is acting through them. That's what behaving instinctually means. But we humans have the unique ability to use our free will to stop karma, the cosmic process, and take ourselves beyond sorrow and fear. We can go back to the place God was before he created the universe, the place where in fact he is right now, whole and unfragmented. That marvelous place is beyond space and time and, therefore, beyond the reach of karma. It's even better than heaven!

Better Than Heaven

The path of Karma Yoga, explained by Lord Krishna himself in the Bhagavad Gita, is not about working with the law of karma to create a happy and fulfilling future. It's about throwing out the karmic process altogether. Its goal is *mukti*, not *svarga*.

Krishna explained you can't get out of doing things. Even renunciates have to go to the toilet! Yet your actions have karmic consequences you must experience sooner or later. Karma Yoga gets you out of this bind. It's simple to understand, but it's tough to practice. It involves cutting the link between cause and effect. You snap the chain of causation in two.

> **def•i•ni•tion**
>
> **Mukti** means liberation—freedom from karma.
>
> **Svarga** is the Hindu heaven, a temporary after-death state reserved for virtuous souls.

> **Sages Say**
>
> Not to do what you feel like doing is freedom.
> —Swami Chinmayananda

"Surrender the fruits of your actions to Me," Krishna told the warrior Arjuna. He was speaking to us, too! "Perform your duty without any expectation of reward. Do what you have to do because it's the right thing to do. Not because there's something you want out of it."

If we renounce the fruits of our actions, sacrificing the results to God, we are no longer emotionally bound to suffer or benefit from our actions. We do our job to the best of our ability because that is the work God has put before of us, not because we want to be successful or because we need a paycheck. We don't worry about money or success because we've given our lives to God. Let him worry about it!

The Hindu View _____

Some Hindus do believe in a heaven world like Brahma Loka, where you reside with the Creator, or Vaikuntha, where you live with Krishna for limitless amounts of time—as long as you want! You don't need to return to Earth if you can reach those high heavens through your good acts and devotion. Yet from those worlds you can launch into the supreme state beyond space and time if you so choose.

Then when our biweekly paycheck arrives or we get credit for our excellent work, we count these as gifts from God, not as something that we somehow inherently deserve. God gave us the intelligence and energy to do the job in the first place. Why shouldn't *he* get the credit? The troops out on the battlefield do the fighting, but the general gets credit for winning the war.

Conquer Through Surrender

Karma Yoga involves actively engaging in life, fulfilling our dharma whether that's being a website manager, a police officer, a flight attendant, or a stay-at-home dad or mom. We do the best we can because our everyday actions are our form of worship. Our work—be it ever so humble—is no less valuable spiritually than the inner work a yogi does sitting in meditation—provided that we do it with awareness and without demanding anything in return.

The key to transforming work into worship and external activity into internal sacrifice, is attitude. When we simply do the best we can and leave the results to God, we become free. We raise our children to the very best of our ability, but how they turn out is in God's hands. We sow a crop of grain and tend it carefully, but whether there's a bountiful harvest or a flood that wipes it all away is up to God. He carries the burden of our existence. We are free!

In Karma Yoga, we sacrifice our attention. Thoughts that would ordinarily run toward fantasies about the future or romantic liaisons or irritating memories are instead directed to God. "This action is for you, Lord. And this one. And this one, too."

At Peace with Life

Karma Yoga brings peace through action. The paradox is that while the surrendered soul becomes free from worry about the results of his or her actions, those results still occur. The most rewarding life, ironically, is one where we don't seek rewards. Then if they come, they come.

The law of karma still operates in the outer world. But we are psychologically free because our inner world remains unpolluted by the aggravation caused by unrealized expectations or delayed rewards. We're not haunted by fear about what may or may not happen. If we're karma yogis, our bodies go through the motions of fulfilling our duties and reaping the consequences. But our souls remain at peace, leaving our fate to God or the Goddess, in whose providence we trust implicitly. We do the work; God manages the outcome.

Sages Say _____

Duty done out of selfish motives is far inferior to that done with a detached attitude. When the mind is yoked to the ultimate good through cultivation of detachment, which is the highest form of love, then one takes delight in loving all and excluding none.

—Swami Rama of the Himalayas

Yoga, not bhoga, is the desire of the karma yogi. Yoga here means union with the Divine Will. Bhoga means enjoyment in the world. We may well still enjoy life (with Krishna's help Arjuna won the war and enjoyed the victory, such as it was), but the good things that come to us are now seen as gifts of God's grace—not as the rightful results of our work, as something we have coming.

Hindus consider Karma Yoga a legitimate path to spiritual liberation because it cultivates a state of desirelessness and egolessness. And when selfishness and desire drop away, so does the depository of past life karma we carry around with us in our causal body. There's no emotional glue to make it "stick" to our soul anymore. We are now free from the wheel of rebirth and don't have to reincarnate again, unless we want to for the sake of helping others.

Guidepost _____

Why not experiment with Karma Yoga? If you're intensely aggravated by your job, for example, decide you're simply going to do the very best you can and that's it. It doesn't matter if your boss approves, if you get a raise, if there's a write-up about you in the company newsletter. Do your job well, and surrender the results. You may find that you're in a much more relaxed frame of mind and that you work more effectively and efficiently.

The Potter's Wheel

By surrendering to God and acting from the space of the Inner Self, the soul is freed from karma. Inside you remain tranquil no matter how good or how bad circumstances are. But the body may still go through tribulation. Though he totally surrenders to Krishna in the Bhagavad Gita, Arjuna suffers horrendous losses in the war, including the death of his son.

In Hinduism, a person who's achieved liberation is called a jivanmukta, which means "a soul who's free." In India, where to this day saints aren't rare, you'll see great men and women who go through life in an amazingly tranquil and composed state of mind. Nothing seems to throw them off their center. Yet karma still plays through their lives: they still get sick, still have enemies, may still be unusually lucky or unlucky.

Sages Say _____

Karma Yoga teaches us how to work for work's sake, unattached. The karma yogi works because it is his nature ... and he has no object beyond that. He knows that he is giving, and does not ask for anything in return, and therefore he eludes the grasp of misery.

—Swami Vivekananda

The sages say this is because the life of an enlightened person is like a potter's wheel. When the potter finishes work, she gets up and walks away. Even so, the potter's wheel keeps spinning for a while because it still carries some momentum. Just as the potter is no longer continuing to spin the pot, a jivanmukta is no longer adding to his store of karmic merits and demerits through his desires and expectations. Yet his body keeps moving and his karma keeps playing out because of the karmic momentum of the past. Inside, however, the jivanmukta is free.

Everyone's Mother

Seva—selfless service—is a major component of Hindu spirituality and an important expression of Karma Yoga. "Our quest for the Self starts with our selfless service in the world," says Amma, the great "hugging saint" from Kerala. She elaborates:

def•i•ni•tion _____

The **third eye** is the center of intuitive consciousness in the subtle body. Find the point between your eyebrows, then move your awareness about 3 inches backward toward the center of your brain. This is the focal point of your inner vision.

If all we do is sit in meditation with our eyes closed, anticipating the *third eye* will open, we will be disappointed. We cannot escape from the world by keeping our eyes closed. Spiritual practice is the effort we make to see the oneness of all beings in creation with open eyes. When that vision becomes spontaneous, that is Self-realization.

Amma (a.k.a. Ammachi or Amritanandamayi Ma) was born in a poor fishing village in southwestern India in

1953. From earliest childhood, she was completely devoted to God. If she caught herself walking several steps without repeating Krishna's name, she would run back and take those steps again keeping the Lord foremost in her mind.

When Amma was in her late teens, the Goddess herself in the form of blazing light appeared before her, commanding her to serve humanity, and then merged into her body. Extraordinary miracles began occurring all around her. A small bowl of water suddenly contained enough rice pudding to feed the entire village. Patients with serious diseases, such as leprosy or malignant cancers, were suddenly healed. Men addicted to gambling or alcohol mended their ways after just one visit to the radiantly loving young saint.

Unconditional Love

Many Hindus believe Amma is an incarnation of the Mother of the Universe. If you have a chance to see her in action, you'll see why. Her ability to connect with every single soul who comes before her is phenomenal. She radiates love, making each person feel like he or she is the one person Amma loves most in the world.

But here's the really strange thing. At every stop in South India, a minimum of 40,000 people are waiting in line for Amma's blessing. The lines are literally miles long. She doesn't get up, not even to eat or go to the bathroom, till she's seen—and physically embraced—every person, which can take days! And when Amma finally does get up, she's still as fresh and radiant as she was when she first sat down. I've seen this with my own eyes and can still scarcely believe it. Where does this lady get her batteries? I get exhausted just watching her!

Hinduism Today calls Amma "a supernova of spirituality." In 1993, she was named one of the top three Hindu leaders of our time. She embodies unconditional love in the most dramatic way possible, in her every action. When I interviewed her, Amma explained that she actually sees God in the face of every person she meets. Her limitless love and equally limitless energy arise from her delight in serving God in each of us.

Selfless Service

In the past two decades, Amma's charitable projects have expanded to include orphanages, shelters for battered women, a huge hospital complex in Kerala that provides medical care free to the destitute, schools and vocational training institutes, and temples and ashrams. One of her current projects is building thousands of new homes each year to be given free to poor families.

Ammachi, Hinduism's "supernova of spirituality."

How can a penniless woman from a tiny Indian village inspire millions to help her build huge institutions or give up their jobs to work unpaid for the benefit of the poor? Amma is the quintessential karma yogi. People see her walking her talk. She lives a life of selfless service, working 22 hours a day. Hindus—and increasingly admirers from around the world—are so inspired by her example that they want to join her work.

Hindu culture is perhaps the last place on Earth where many children still dream of being a saint, like Amma, when they grow up. Charitable organizations abound. There is hardly an ashram that doesn't help provide free food and free medical care for the poor. Seva, selfless service, is an integral part of the Hindu tradition.

Action in Inaction

Hindus believe that even the sages who appear to be doing nothing at all immensely enrich society by their mere presence. One of my mentors, Swami Rama of the Himalayas, was a philanthropist who built a huge hospital facility for the impoverished villagers of the state of Uttara Pradesha, as well as providing scholarships for numerous poor students (including me!). Yet he bristled at the suggestion that his own teachers, who spent their lifetimes meditating in the Himalayas, were turning their backs on humanity. "The sages protect the world!" he insisted. "The human race would have destroyed itself long ago if not for the blessings the sages send out in their meditation! You have activists who protect the outer environment. Through their pure thoughts and well wishes the Himalayan sages clean out the pollution in the inner environment!"

In deep states of meditation, the yogi's will takes on laser-like intensity and benefits the entire world. This is the supreme Karma Yoga of the masters who appear to be doing nothing at all.

Quick Quiz

1. Karma Yoga is …

    a. Doing your duty without desiring any reward.

    b. A series of physical postures such as the headstand.

    c. The result of our evil actions.

2. The goal of Karma Yoga is …

    a. Making as much money as possible.

    b. Scored only if the goalie can be lured from the net.

    c. Freedom from the bondage of karma.

3. Renouncing the fruits of our actions …

    a. Leads to irresponsible behavior.

    b. Frees us from worry.

    c. Is fine if we can still have the vegetables.

Answers: 1 (a). 2 (c). 3 (b).

Get Up and Fight!

In the Bhagavad Gita, Krishna describes several paths to God-realization. These are the paths of devotion, knowledge, and action. Yet given the emergency of impending war, Krishna's specific advice to Arjuna is, "Get up and fight!" But Arjuna is not to fight out of anger or desire for revenge. To fight in this mindset would incur terrible karma. Instead he must go to war because it's his duty to stop an evil tyrant from taking over the country. Whether he ultimately wins or loses isn't as important as taking the action he knows is right.

"People are trapped in the web of their own karma except when they perform their actions as worship of God," Krishna explains. "Therefore do your work as if it is a sacrament. Don't be concerned about the results. Always do your duty, but without attachment. By working honestly without anxiety about the future, you will reach the supreme state."

The Least You Need to Know

- Karma Yoga means performing your work to the best of your ability without concern for reward.

- Karma yogis rise above the karmic process by not engaging psychologically with the consequences of their actions.

- Selfless service is a huge component of Hindu spirituality.

- Hindu saints like Vivekananda and Ammachi taught selflessness through their living examples.

- Even sitting alone in meditation, yogis are able to transmit blessings throughout the world.

Chapter 21

An Ever-Expanding Heart

In This Chapter

- ◆ Hindu devotionalism
- ◆ Relating to God
- ◆ Love makes saints
- ◆ The holy name
- ◆ Religious ecstasy

What's the most intoxicating liquor of all? Southern Comfort? Sake? According to the Hindu sages, it's love for God. Devotion is the divine nectar that makes even the most bitter life sweet.

Throughout the millennia, in the same way other countries have been rocked by earthquakes, India has been rocked with convulsions of religious ecstasy. Waves of bhakti, massive movements of devotion for God or Goddess, have swept through the subcontinent in shockwaves of joy. Hinduism is a religion of bhaktas, of devotees who deeply and truly love their Maker.

Love, Hindu sages claim, is the quickest path to the Lord of Light, whose own infinite love embraces all the beings in all the galaxies in all dimensions of time and space.

The Heart and the Head

Recently a student asked the South Indian Saint Amma (see Chapter 20) what is the most dangerous spiritual path. He was expecting her to say "Tantra" and to warn him away from the alleged sensual pitfalls of "the left-hand path." Instead she instantly answered, "The path of the intellect."

The student was astonished. Many Hindu spiritual masters have been intellectuals of the highest caliber. "Reasoning is necessary, but we should not allow the intellect to eat up our heart," Amma went on to explain. "Too much intellectual knowledge too often leads to a big ego. The ego is a burden, and a big ego is a big burden."

"Devotion without spiritual knowledge cannot free us," Amma continued. "But knowledge without devotion is like eating stones." She pointed to a nearby jackfruit tree, a tree that produces fruit near the bottom of the trunk where one can easily reach it. "On the path of devotion we can enjoy the fruit from the very beginning," Amma concluded. On other paths to God you do a lot of spiritual work first before you begin to experience the divine presence. It's like other trees, which you have to laboriously climb to reach the sweet fruit.

And how sweet the fruit of devotion is! The Goddess's loving presence suffuses our lives the moment we open our heart. Instantly she takes us into her lap, and we feel at home in the very heart of the universe. This is Bhakti Yoga—reaching straight for the cup of joy.

Intellectuals spend a lot of time discussing the nature of Divine Being. Is it conscious or unconscious? Is it one unitary reality, or is matter different from spirit? How does the One split into the manifold universe we see in front of us? Bhaktas aren't overly concerned with these nit-picking details. They just want to hang out with God!

The Divine Relationship

You can't hang out with an abstraction—at least most people can't. But you can easily relate to another person. So most bhaktas imagine the Divine Being as a sort of Super Person. In the Judeo-Christian-Islamic tradition, there's basically one type of relationship you can have with God—He's the father, you're his child. Hinduism, however, includes many different ways we can relate to the Supreme. For example, we may picture the Divine Being as our:

◆ Father   ◆ Master   ◆ Lover   ◆ Enemy

◆ Mother   ◆ Friend   ◆ Child

Consider the many different ways people looked at Lord Krishna during his lifetime. To Yasoda, who raised Krishna in the tiny village of Vrindavan, the Lord was her little baby. To Radha and the other milkmaids in Vrindavan, Krishna was their lover. To Arjuna, Krishna was his closest friend.

Hindus still relate to Krishna in these ways. Some Hindu women keep a statue of Krishna as a small child in their homes and tend it as if it's their baby! Others look on their own children as baby Krishnas. Still other Hindus carry on a continual internal dialogue with Krishna as if he is their best friend. They feel he is actually present, listening to their problems and providing guidance as he did for his friend Arjuna.

Sages Say _____

Five minutes of sincerely crying to God is worth more than hours of unfocused meditation.

—Amritanandamayi Ma

To the Bengali saint Ramprasad Sen (the failed accountant from Chapter 14), Divine Being was Mom. He would plead with her and argue with her as if she were his real life mother! Some Hindu saints look at Vishnu or Shiva as their divine father, much as Christians and Jews do.

Many Hindus think of themselves as the servants—even the slaves—of God. Their lives are totally in his hands, and they live only to do his will. Hindu names like Ram Das or Bhagavan Das literally mean servant of God.

Hating God

You may be surprised to hear that Hindus consider people who hate God to be in better shape spiritually than those who never think about God at all. This is because at least those who see God as their enemy think about him continually. That's all the hold God needs in order to begin doing his transformative work in their lives. He just needs their attention! Remember Valmiki, who in Chapter 5, chanted "Mara, mara" ("Evil, evil") and became a saint because unwittingly he was chanting God's name ("Rama, Rama").

Hindus even believe that being killed by God is the greatest possible blessing! For example, remember that Rama, who was God in human form, killed the cruel king Ravana. At that moment, Ravana went straight to heaven! That's because he'd been obsessing about Rama constantly. Even though his mind was filled with animosity, Ravana was totally focused on Rama at the moment of his death, so God was able to reach into his soul and liberate him instantly. God's grace really is amazing!

The Divine Lover

For Hindus, one of the favorite ways to picture God is as the divine lover. Krishna and Shiva particularly lend themselves to this role—Krishna because he had so many girlfriends and Shiva because he is Kameshvara, the Lord of Desire. When Shiva makes love to his wife, Parvati, he has such perfect yogic control that he never ejaculates. So according to the holy texts, when Shiva and Parvati start getting it on, the action continues for years!

Shaivite saints, like Lalla and Antal, pined for the love of Shiva. The Vaishnava saint Mira Bai literally considered herself married to Krishna—a fact her real-life in-laws didn't appreciate. Some male saints, like Chaitanya, would think of themselves as spiritually female in order to imagine being brides of Krishna.

In the Shakta tradition some images of the Goddess, such as Lalita, are breathtakingly voluptuous. If you're filled with erotic energy, why not redirect that drive toward the divine? Then instead of dragging you off into steamy fantasies, your romantic desires actually help increase your sense of intimacy with the Supreme Being.

God in the Guru

As I mentioned in Chapter 10, for many Hindus, the guru is the physical embodiment of Divine Being. "The water in which the guru's feet are bathed is the holiest water in the world," says the Guru Gita. "This water can wash away your sins, ignite the fire of Self-realization, and carry you to safety across the stormy ocean of this world."

Devotion to the guru is another popular form of Bhakti Yoga. If you're not lucky enough to be living at a time and place when an avatar like Rama or Krishna are physically present, the guru is for all practical purposes your equivalent of Rama. And you don't have to use your imagination to visualize a relationship with God. If you honor your guru as a divine embodiment, then God or the Goddess is standing in front of you in the flesh, walking with you and giving personal guidance.

Obviously, care must be taken to ensure the guru truly is Self-realized and is able to actually handle such powerful projections. My personal observation is that the occasional guru lets the adulation go to his or her head, but most of them take the job of spiritual mentorship very seriously. They are ultimately

Guidepost

Has your guru gone bad? Occasionally a Hindu teacher begins abusing his or her power. Out of respect for the teacher's spiritual lineage, Hindus rarely publish embarrassing exposés. Instead, they quietly withdraw their support and go find another guru!

servants of the Supreme Guru whose wisdom manifests through them when they align themselves with their Highest Self. Being someone's guru is a huge responsibility with major karmic implications.

The guru lineage is a safety valve built into the Hindu system. If one is a guru, he has his own guru and the other masters of his lineage to answer to if he messes up. The disciple answers to the guru, but the guru answers to the lineage.

The Saint Factory

The Hindu tradition is a virtual saint factory, having produced more holy women and men than any other religion. In fact, at any one moment, there are far more fully acknowledged Hindu saints than Catholicism has recognized in its entire 2,000-year history!

What transforms an ordinary person into a saint? Does it happen spontaneously or can a person actually go into training to become a saint? Some people are born saints. The Hindu sages explain that this is either because these people have tons of great karma from previous incarnations because they spent lifetimes purifying themselves and serving others. Or it's because they're visitors dropping in from higher planes of reality.

The Hindu View

Hindu psychology focuses mostly on higher states of consciousness. Western psychology focuses mostly on dysfunctional states. Only a few Western psychologists, like Abraham Maslow, have emphasized the value of "peak states" or mystical experiences.

And other times, well, it just kind of seems like the Goddess picks someone out of the crowd and zaps her!

Spontaneous Combustion

Let's talk about the divine zap. In all cultures, in all times, certain people—with or without any previous interest in spirituality—spontaneously have extremely powerful mystical experiences. They can have incredible feelings of self-transcendence, a tremendous sense of unity with all things, and the feeling of melting into all-pervading awareness. These experiences seem to come out of the blue, but they're so vivid and powerful they shake an individual to the core.

In some cases, the experience is drug induced. In other cases, it's triggered by an accident, a major shock, or even by seeing or hearing something mind-blowingly beautiful. There have been numbers of reports in recent years of people having extraordinary mystical sensations during a near-death experience. In other cases, there doesn't seem to be any precipitating factor at all. Someone is just walking across the room when—*zap!*—his awareness explodes out of his body and he experiences himself merging into the universe.

Yogis attribute these events to the sudden temporary triggering of kundalini, the energy underlying consciousness, which causes an abrupt awakening to mystical awareness. It could be a fluke and never occur again. Or it may be that the person did lots of meditating in a previous incarnation and is just now reawakening to inner life. Then again, it may just be the whim of God. "He chooses whom He chooses," the Upanishads say rather wistfully.

But for the vast majority of people, mystical awareness is something they have to work at developing, like any other skill. What turns average people on to God as opposed to football or mineral powder cosmetics or real estate development?

Four Motives for Devotion

In the Bhagavad Gita, Krishna says there are four conditions under which people turn to God. First, there are those who are in trouble. There's nothing like a life crisis to turn the mind to religion! Someone's sick or dying, his house is in foreclosure, or he's about to lose his job, and suddenly the devotee is on his knees pleading to Krishna to save him from calamity.

Sages Say

If I say God is within me, it sounds like blasphemy. If I say He's not in me, it's a lie. In God the inner and outer worlds are one world. He rests His feet on both.

—Kabir

Then there's the person who wants something really badly but can't get it on her own. It could be a potential boyfriend who hasn't yet noticed she exists or a new house that's out of her price range. She's on her knees begging the Lord for the blessing she desires so desperately.

Next there's the type who just wants to understand. Who is God really? How does karma operate? What are worlds in other dimensions like? The quest for knowledge is his burning motivation. He's so boggled by the beauty and complexity of the universe that he spontaneously turns to its living source in worship and wonder.

The final type is the one who loves God for God's sake alone. God is just so lovable! She has no ulterior motive, just love. Krishna says he's delighted to accept the prayers of each kind of devotee. But the soul who delights him most is the one who comes to him out of pure, unselfish devotion.

Deepening Devotion

Once an interest in spiritual life is aroused, how do we increase our enthusiasm? The pressing affairs of our mundane life intrude from all sides. Diverting our attention to a nonphysical entity like God comes naturally to a handful of innately mystically inclined individuals, but for most of us it takes some effort. Here are some of the tried-and-true methods bhaktas use to deepen their connection with the divine.

Satsang: Spiritual Fellowship

Satsang means keeping company with fellow devotees. The mutual support of others with similar interests, especially those further along the path, can be a continual source of inspiration. Seeking out the company of a God-intoxicated mystic is the best form of satsang short of the ecstatic experience of God's presence itself. Reading books about gods and saints and keeping their pictures nearby is a second-tier form of satsang.

Kirtan: Making a Joyful Noise

Kirtan means singing about God or the Goddess. Frequently bhaktas get together to chant the glories of the Divine and sing beautiful hymns of love and longing composed by the saints. Devotional music is a particularly soul-stirring form of worship. "Kirtan is the calling, the crying, the reaching across infinite space—digging into the heart's deepest well to touch and be touched by the Divine Presence," says singer Jai Uttal.

Smarana: Divine Obsession

Smarana means remembering God throughout the day. One constantly thinks about the superlative attributes of the Divine: his strength, nobility, and purity or her power, love, and grace. Reading the inspiring stories in Hinduism's holy scriptures helps. So does chanting a mantra. Eventually even one's dreams are imbued with divine remembrance.

Puja: Ritual Practice

Puja is ritual worship. Several times a day a person sits down before his home altar to make a living connection with the Supreme by enacting a short ceremony of worship and prayer. It's like making a telephone call to God, keeping in regular contact. Going through the physical motions of a ritual is especially helpful for people who need something concrete to focus on in order to keep their minds concentrated.

Atma Nivedana: Surrendering Your Attention

Atma Nivedana means offering our innermost being to God. This is total self-surrender, offering not just our stream of thoughts but our continual awareness back to its source in Divine Being. Staying in a state of spiritual balance like this isn't easy at first, but it's like learning to ride a bicycle. Once we get the hang of it, it feels natural.

Guidepost

Don't waste time sleeping! Yogis worship and meditate even in the dream state. In laboratory experiments, advanced yogis, hooked up to EEG equipment, have proven they can remain fully conscious while their brains are sleeping.

Good Company

Satsang, spiritual fellowship, is the root practice of Bhakti Yoga. As anyone who's tried to start a fire by rubbing two sticks together knows, fires don't start easily! But if someone brings you a burning stick from their campfire, you can ignite your pile of twigs and dried leaves effortlessly.

The guru, and other devotees farther along the path, already have their fires roaring. When you spend time with them, you see love for God actually happening. You see spirit being lived. For many the effect is galvanizing. Saints who are enlivened with shakti, with divine energy, transmit it to others as if they're spiritual tuning forks.

Some people's spiritual batteries have run down so low that they have to be repeatedly jump-started before they're able to keep their inner light glowing. Once your own light starts burning night and day, whether anyone's there to pump you up or not, you are now a bhakta, a genuine devotee.

What's in a Name?

Who's your God? The form of God or Goddess you relate to most naturally, the face of the divine you love most dearly, is your Ishta Devata, your beloved deity, your personal divine contact. Hindus relate to their Ishta Devata somewhat as Christians think of their guardian angels. The personal deity shields you from harm and guides you through life by supplying just the right information or just the right experiences at just the right time. In another sense, the Ishta Devata is your own Higher Self.

An important technique many Hindus use to cement their relationship with the deity is to chant the God or Goddess's name constantly. Nama Japa, or "chanting the name," purifies the mind, opens the heart, makes the subtle body vibrant and the physical body healthy, and surrounds the devotee with a vibratory aura of protection and blessing.

For Hindus the name of God *is* God. To name him or her is to invoke the Divine's living presence. It's said that in the beginning you chant the name. Then the name chants you. You no longer have to make a conscious effort to repeat it; it repeats itself in the echo chambers of your mind. This doesn't mean you're continually distracted by the syllables humming in your head! When you have to focus your attention on the job in front of you, the divine name shifts into the background of your awareness. You no longer hear the sound, but the *feeling* doesn't stop resonating in your heart.

A teacher of mine told me about an elderly Hindu woman who locked herself in her room to spend the last few years of her life doing Nama Japa, chanting the name of her Ishta Devata. Her devotion was extraordinarily intense. After her death, people claimed they could still hear the mantra sounding in her room. My teacher thought they were exaggerating. But when he stopped by her room and pressed his ear to the wall, he swears he could actually hear God's name sounding over and over again!

All Blissed Out

Hinduism has manuals for everything, even for love. Two of the famous manuals for lovers of God are the Narada Bhakti Sutras and the Shandilya Bhakti Sutras. Bhakta literature lists certain signs that a person is entering higher and higher grades of spiritual ecstasy. Some of these signs are:

- The bhakta spontaneously weeps with love.

- The hair stands on end. (With joy, not horror!)

- The bhakta collapses or rolls on the ground in ecstasy.

- The devotee sings or dances in total self-abandonment.

- The devotee slips into ecstatic trance.

- The devotee is always radiant.

- Miracles occur in the bhakta's presence.

It's important to note that there's a distinction between genuine states of spiritual ecstasy and mental illness or epilepsy! Unbalanced or physically sick people often emerge from similar sorts of fits frightened and unable to cope. Bhaktas experience fits of divine love and come out refreshed, joyful, and transformed in the most positive ways.

Advice from the Source

In the Bhagavad Gita, Krishna distinguishes between three levels of devotees. The purest, he says, worship the one God in any of his manifold forms out of sheer love. The middle group is really only using God, hoping he'll help them in their quest for wealth and power. The lowest type worships ghosts and evil spirits. Lower types may also practice asceticism to such an extreme that they practically destroy their bodies, a practice of which Krishna strongly disapproved. He taught that the body was the temple of spirit and must be kept in good health.

The appropriate practice for bhaktas, Krishna said, is "respect for the gods and goddesses, the forces of nature, the saints, sages and gurus. You should be guileless, honest, clean, and have your sex drive firmly under your control. Speak the truth but without causing pain to others. Study the holy books every day. And don't talk too much!"

"Remain calm and tranquil," Krishna continued. "Be kind to others. Always act with the highest integrity. And for some time every day pull your awareness away from the outer world. Pull it even out of your body, and focus on your Inner Self. When you act in the world, dedicate all your actions to the Supreme Being. In this manner you will come to me."

Quick Quiz

1. When your kundalini is suddenly activated, you may …

    a. Spontaneously experience the unity of all being.

    b. Be able to receive satellite TV programs in your brain.

    c. Be eligible for disability benefits.

2. According to Hinduism, hating God …

   a. Leads straight to the lowest pit of hell.

   b. Is a legitimate form of relationship with the divine.

   c. Can be perfected through Hatha Yoga and vegetarianism.

3. One sign that a bhakta is entering higher states is she …

   a. Stops watching so much TV.

   b. Is radiant with love.

   c. Starts running full-color ads advertising her seminars.

4. Ishta Devata is …

   a. India's leading hip-hop artist.

   b. Torturing your body in order to experience your Inner Self.

   c. The God or Goddess you're mostly closely linked to.

   Answers: 1 (a). 2 (b). 3 (b). 4 (c).

The Easiest Path—Or the Hardest?

Hindu saints frequently recommend Bhakti Yoga as the easiest and most enjoyable path into the Divine presence. Often when you attend bhakta gatherings, you find all kinds of sweets laid out on the table. They're a reminder that God's love is sweet and that walking the path of devotion is life's greatest pleasure.

But when you read the requirements for Bhakti Yoga Krishna spells out in the Bhagavad Gita, you begin to suspect the path of devotion isn't all singing, dancing, and dessert! "Don't hate or harm any creature. If you truly love me, you'll love everyone," Krishna says. That's easier said than done! "Don't kid yourself that anything belongs to you. Everything in this universe is mine alone." He continues:

> A real bhakta is serene, forgiving, content, and self-controlled. My devotee is constantly engaged in meditation. Nothing disturbs the one who trusts in me. My bhakta is unswayed by fear or jealousy, and doesn't desire anything in this world but me. Whatever occurs in life, he remains relaxed. He doesn't dread the difficulties of life, or waste time grieving over what he's lost.

Friend and enemy—My bhakta honors them both. Praise and blame—they're both the same to him. His thoughts are always running toward me, and his heart is always brimming with love.

True bhakti is a tall order. God is present in everyone and everything. If you *really* love God, you love the Divine everywhere it appears, even in your worst enemy or in your worst nightmare. The lightness of heart that comes from such total surrender is moksha: freedom and enlightenment.

Pitfalls on the Path

Could a path that's all about love possibly have any pitfalls? There are plenty, actually. Unfortunately there *is* an all-too-common shadow side to bhakti.

Some of the serious problems people on the path of devotion need to watch out for are …

- ◆ Imagining your surging emotions are the highest possible state of spirituality.

- ◆ Mistaking your own opinions for the will of God.

- ◆ Fanatic devotion to your ideal that excludes and condemns others.

- ◆ Developing a fortress mentality. "Anyone who isn't with us is against us."

The Yoga Vasishtha explains that devotion to the Divine and selfless, ethical actions— Bhakti Yoga and Karma Yoga—are the two wings of the bird of authentic spiritual life. Without both wings, the bird can't fly. But the tail feathers, the "rudder" the bird uses to navigate, are reason and common sense. Without the guidance of the intellect, religious emotionalism can spill over into blind and destructive fanaticism.

The Least You Need to Know

- ◆ Bhakti Yoga is the spiritual path of devotion.

- ◆ Some people have spontaneous flashes of cosmic consciousness due to the abrupt activation of kundalini.

- ◆ More typically, people turn to God out of fear, desire, wonder, or love.

- ◆ Bhakti Yoga offers methods to help deepen one's relationship with the Divine.

- ◆ Emotionalism that abandons rationality completely can lead to trouble.

Chapter 22

The Razor's Edge

In This Chapter

- ◆ Facing reality
- ◆ Intellect transcending itself
- ◆ Methods of Self-realization
- ◆ Mind-shattering truth
- ◆ Egolessness and arrogance

Imagine a tornado. It sweeps through a neighborhood with devastating force. But what is this monster, really? It's just air—like the air inside it and the air outside it. Looking at it, you'd think the funnel had some kind of independent reality. Yet as the currents feeding it simmer down, the killer storm dissolves into its source—thin air.

Part of the magic of a tornado is its eye. If you could sit in the center of the swirling storm, you'd find that the air there is motionless. It's calm, peaceful, and perfectly safe! And when the tornado dies, that tranquil eye merges seamlessly into the atmosphere around it, which it really was part of the whole time.

Jnana Yoga, the path of Self-awareness, is the mind's attempt to understand the storm of life and the calm eye of the Inner Self. When intellectual understanding matures into experiential realization, the tornado ends. The Inner Self merges into the all-pervading consciousness from which it was never *really* separate in the first place.

Lead Me from the Unreal

At the ashram where I lived, several times a day we'd chant one of the oldest prayers in the world. It comes from the Rig Veda, and in English it says, "Lead me from unreality to truth. Lead me from darkness to light. Lead me from death to immortality."

Sages Say _____

There's no difference between the air in a jar and air everywhere else. Nor is there any difference between the consciousness within you and the consciousness that pervades the universe. Stop imagining that you're separate from the Supreme Consciousness! Enter the inner stillness where truth resides!

—Viveka Chudamani

Jnana Yoga, the spiritual path of discriminating awareness, leads from ignorance to Self-knowledge. The metaphor usually used to explain this transition involves a snake that's not a snake. Walking through the forest on your way back to your village on a moonless night, you suddenly see a cobra coiled in the path before you. You freeze. One false move and it could strike. And that would be the end of you!

You stand there for minutes that seem like hours, paralyzed with fear. Eventually you notice that the snake hasn't moved. I mean, it hasn't moved *at all*. You build up your courage, take a tentative step forward, and look more closely. It turns out it's not a snake at all, just a piece of coiled rope someone left on the path.

You're giddy with relief but also feel a little foolish. You reacted as if your life was in jeopardy when in fact there was no danger at all. The master jnana yogi Shankaracharya says that's what enlightenment is like. At first you think this world is a big, scary place that sooner or later is going to kill you. Then you finally realize it's all God. It's absolutely nothing but Divine Consciousness. When you *really* see that, when you know it in your gut, fear vanishes forever and you're a jivanmukta, a liberated sage.

Confronting the Snake

Here's another way to look at it. You're walking through the forest on a moonless night. Apparently someone's dropped a coiled rope in the path. You stop to kick it out of the way when instantly the snake you mistook for a rope sinks its venomous fangs into your leg. And that's the end of you!

You can't be too careful because ignorance is a dangerous thing. Ignorance, called avidya or "lack of knowledge" in Sanskrit, leads from death to death. "Everything you see here is that one Supreme Reality. That one Being is everything everywhere. He travels from death to death who imagines otherwise," warns the Katha Upanishad.

Most of us are caught up in maya, the illusion that the snake is a rope or the rope is a snake. But the illusion itself is an illusion! Because never at any point in the process were the snake or the rope anything other than themselves. The entire cosmos is not and never has been anything other than Divine Being. We need to get this straight. And straightening out our misperception is what Jnana Yoga is all about. It helps us see the universe *as it really is*. As God sees it, you might say.

Got What It Takes?

Jnana Yoga is a tough path and not for everyone. The path is straight, but it's awfully steep. Centuries ago, the great philosopher-yogi Shankaracharya traveled around India setting up monasteries where monks could devote themselves to this form of spiritual practice. But the entrance exam was rough.

As Shankaracharya explained, you have to meet four prerequisites before you can think seriously of getting on this path.

Requirement 1. You need to be able to discriminate between the eternal and the non-eternal. Okay, what's that mean? It means you have to recognize that everything in this world, including your life, is fleeting but that behind this world, there's an abiding Reality that endures forever. If this isn't 100 percent clear to you, another path like devotion or selfless service might be more appropriate for you.

 Guidepost

Think you're smart? Surprisingly, Hindu gurus often advise bright people to cultivate devotion. That's because very intelligent people often benefit more by learning to open their hearts. The more mental path of discriminating awareness is not so much for intellectuals as for people with a strongly developed mystical sense and a burning desire for the actual experience of God-realization.

Requirement 2. If you're still craving fame or success, sex, drugs, or rock 'n' roll, forget it! Jnana Yoga requires intense concentration. Desires will distract your mind, and this intensely mental path demands freedom from distraction. You must fully surrender all your actions and all your desires to the divine so that you can focus not on the noneternal, like just about everyone else, but on the eternal, like the great masters and mystics.

Requirement 3. You must have your psychological and ethical act together. In other words, virtue must be your second nature. You're already tranquil, even-minded, honest, and self-controlled. If you're not, you could misuse the power that comes with the superior will power and laser-like mental focus developed on this path. This is the sort of thing that happened to Ravana, the treacherous king in the *Ramayana*. He started out as a yogi focused on Lord Shiva, but he wound up misapplying the tremendous mental power he developed through his spiritual practices and started exploiting others.

Requirement 4. Your desire for liberation must be real. If it's not incredibly strong, there's no way you'll reach the goal on this difficult path. Jnana Yoga is not for dabblers. Nor is it for intellectuals who want to read all about spirit but aren't prepared to make the sacrifices necessary to actually experience it. Anyone with reasonable intelligence can become a pandit, but very few have what it takes to become a Self-realized sage.

Study, Think, Act!

Once you and your guru have decided Jnana Yoga is the right path for you, you don't have far to go. According to Shankaracharya, there are only three steps on the path to spiritual illumination.

Step 1 is *shravana* or intensive study, which begins with listening to the words of the guru and reading the scriptures carefully. But the point is to develop the intellect as a tool for Self-realization, not just for shooting the breeze with fellow eggheads. If you're able, proceed to Step 2.

Step 2 is *manana*, which means contemplating what you've learned. You chew on it until you digest it, till you deeply understand and live it. You can't just sit around reading scriptures; you must assimilate what they say. It's easy enough to parrot, "My Inner Self is one with the eternal Reality." But do you really grasp what that means? Do you sense its actual truth? When you start to get it, really get it, proceed to Step 3.

Step 3 is *nididhyasana*, which is your practicum. Stop worrying about what your guru says; stop memorizing Sanskrit texts; stop focusing on anything outside yourself. It's time to actually get to know that Divine Reality the teachers and the texts are talking about. This means diving deep into your own spirit, paying attention to your inner states, going beyond the thoughts and images in your mind to the pure awareness behind them, and finally going beyond your own consciousness into cosmic consciousness, the divine light that holds you and every other thing in its illumined awareness. This inner act turns the truths voiced in the Upanishads into your actual living experience.

def•i•ni•tion

Shravana is listening to the words of the guru and carefully studying the scriptures.

Manana means deeply contemplating the spiritual truth you've been taught.

Nididhyasana means deeply contemplating your own Inner Self.

Truths to Chew On

The sages pulled four great sayings from the scriptures, one from each of the four Vedas, for *jnanis* to chew on. These are …

- **Prajnanam Brahma:** The Supreme Reality is illumined awareness.

- **Aham Brahmasmi:** I am the Supreme Reality.

- **Tat Tvam Asi:** You are that Divine Being.

- **Ayam Atma Brahma:** The Inner Self is Self of all.

def•i•ni•tion

Jnani literally means "knower." This is someone who knows the truth from direct experience, not just a person who knows about it. (Think of the related English word "gnostic.")

 Sages Say

The divine fragrance of the Inner Self is overwhelmed by the awful stench of our petty thoughts and desires. But foul odors disappear when you rub a stick of sandalwood, which fills the air with its own sweet smell. Rub your mind with the thought, "I am Brahman. I am the Supreme Reality," and your mind will be become pure and fragrant.

—Shankaracharya

Some Buddhist monks contemplate koans, perplexing statements designed to shatter the rational mind and carry human consciousness to a higher level of clarity. These four statements are the koans of the Vedic tradition, except that they're not perplexing at all. In fact, they're the simplest statement of the ultimate truth, "I and the Supreme are One."

Jnanis contemplate these truths until the living reality they point to unfolds itself in their experience. They shut everything out of their awareness except awareness itself and ride it to its source. By stabilizing their attention in the unchanging eternal reality of Divine Consciousness, these adepts transcend birth and death and achieve true immortality. The drop is assimilated into the ocean. The spark falls back into the fire. The racing wind of the tornado dissolves into still air.

Living Like a Tortoise

In the Bhagavad Gita, Krishna spells out the essentials of Jnana Yoga. "That which truly exists will never stop existing. The Supreme Reality which pervades the universe has always existed and always will. You are that Reality. Bodies die but the awareness which inhabits the body lives on. It is impossible to kill it." Krishna continues:

> The Inner Self was never born. It will never die or ever change. You, the Inner Self, drop one body and put on another like a change of clothes. This Inner Self is not harmed by weapons or affected by the elements. That which is born must die. That which dies must be reborn. But the One who dwells within is never born and never dies.

> Like a tortoise drawing its legs back into its shell, draw your attention out of your body and into your innermost spirit. He who controls his senses and withdraws his mind into the undying spirit, who lives beyond birth and death, him I call enlightened.

Krishna tells Arjuna to dive into the changeless heart of Reality and experience deathless awareness. At the same time, he had to keep his day job! Enlightenment doesn't just mean sitting around like a couch potato merged in infinite consciousness (although that option is available). For Krishna, it means living an active life, fulfilling his duties and responsibilities, while merged in cosmic consciousness. Now that's real mastery!

The Hindu View

Jnana Yoga is an extremely ancient path going back to the time of the Upanishads at the very least. But the form in which it's best known to Hindus today was popularized more than 12 centuries ago by Shankaracharya and his main disciples, Mandana Mishra, Sureshvara, Padmapada, and the rather dull Totaka, who in the end turned out to be the smartest student of them all.

Knowing the Unknowable

Jnana Yoga is a mental path, yet the mind can never know the truth. The truth is too big. The mind is too small. When the *Apollo* spacecraft bound for the Moon blasted off, the bottom stage of the rocket—filled with the fuel needed to blow the space vehicle off the Earth's surface—was ejected and fell back to Earth. Think of intellect as the booster rocket for soul. Intellect helps propel inner awareness into the vast, still cosmos of consciousness. Intellect can't go there itself, but it can point you in the right direction and give you a lift upward.

Reality is mind-blowing. God/Goddess is utterly beyond human comprehension. But because the innermost core of human awareness comes straight from the heart of divine awareness, all it needs to do is relax back into its true nature. The mind shatters itself to free the inner spirit.

Junior-Level Masters

Does spiritual illumination happen all at once or in stages? Some sages report the moment of liberation is like flipping on a light switch. The light doesn't come on gradually—the room fills with illumination instantaneously. It's like the moment you realized Batman and Bruce Wayne were the same guy. The realization comes in a flash.

Other sages outline varying levels of mastery. Depending on the intensity of your level of practice and how much spiritual work you've already done in previous lives, enlightenment may come quickly or slowly. And, disconcertingly, it may not stay! The Tripura Rahasya describes three levels of jnanis. Which level you're at depends on how fully you've established yourself in the radiant field of enlightenment.

Level 1: Remembering and Forgetting

Manda yogis have experienced spiritual illumination, but they're not yet able to remain fully focused in that state. It's like going to see a movie. If it's a good film, most of us completely forget ourselves and get wrapped up in the plot and characters. This is exactly analogous to the way the mind forgets its true nature, Divine Consciousness. It gets caught up in the drama playing in the external world. Level 1 jnanis sit in the theater remembering who they really are, experiencing their inherent divine nature. And then the drama gets so exciting they forget their real nature and are caught in the maya again.

These beginning-level jnanis remember and forget. Sometimes I sit with them, and I'm convinced they're fully realized masters. The next time I see them, they seem like average people. Their attention fluctuates between the inner and outer worlds. Treading the path of Jnana Yoga is like walking on a razor's edge, the Upanishads say, because the mind can slip so quickly from its focus on the inner reality.

Level 2: Mad Mystics

Eventually the jnani reaches a stage where she becomes almost totally engrossed in the Inner Self. At this point, it becomes as difficult for her to bring her attention back to the external world as it is for most of us to center our awareness in the inner world. These saints, called madhyama yogis, may seem crazy or dysfunctional. They may sit without moving for hours on end or lose the ability to speak comprehensibly.

Sometimes jnanis at this stage have to be taken care of like small children. Ramakrishna and Anandamayi Ma both temporarily lost the ability to feed themselves and had to be force-fed by disciples. Neem Karoli Baba had to be reminded to go to the bathroom, or he would forget about his bodily functions altogether!

Level 3: Full Mastery

In the highest state of realization a person can attain while still in a physical body, he gains full mastery of both the inner and outer worlds. "He remains in the world, but above it," as my teacher Swami Rama would say. His awareness never leaves the Supreme, yet he's able to function quite normally in the world. This adept, called an uttama yogi, becomes a fountain of blessings as the Higher Self pours its grace through him in the form of inspiration, healing, and blessings that engulf those fortunate enough to enjoy his company.

Finding What You Never Lost

Karma yogis want to live in the world without anxiety and, at the end of life, to be free from the bondage of karma that keeps drawing people back to death after death. Bhakti yogis want God or the Goddess's company. Love is its own reward, and nothing is better than divine love!

Jnana yogis want to actually *be* God. This doesn't mean they think they're now lord of the universe and everyone else will worship them. It means they recognize their innermost nature is identical in essence with God's, just as the air in a tornado is the same as the air outside the tornado. To attain Self-realization is not to obtain anything new. It's simply to consciously recognize what has always been true anyway: that you and the Supreme Being are, always have been, and always will be one in essence.

 Sages Say

Rama didn't remember he was an incarnation of God till the sages helped reawaken him to his true identity by praising him as Lord Vishnu. We also are identical to the Highest Being. We also have to be reminded who we really are.

—Totaka, disciple of Shankaracharya

Some Western psychologists mock this goal as a desire to "return to the womb," which only shows they miss the point entirely. Jnanis aren't negating themselves in a retreat from life but expanding their awareness to the ultimate extent possible. They seek to literally embrace the living cosmos permeated with Divine Consciousness. They're not running away from reality but running toward its fullest possible expression.

Center of Joy

In the famous Hindu tale, a musk ox searches everywhere for the heavenly fragrance it smells all around itself and doesn't realize the fragrance comes from its own body. Just so, jnanis say, most people search everywhere for happiness, everywhere but where happiness really lies, which is in one's own Self.

Hindu texts like the Vijnana Bhairava point out that in moments of rapt ecstasy like during sexual climax or while eating premium ice cream, our mind isn't running to the future or the past. It's totally focused, and it's totally present. At that moment the nature of the Self manifests in our awareness, and we experience rapture.

According to Shankaracharya, the Inner Self and the Supreme Reality, to the extent that they can be characterized at all, have three qualities: being, awareness, and bliss. We imagine that objects outside ourselves make us happy. But really they're just serving as focal points that enable us to experience the rapture that's always already inside us though we're usually not focused enough to feel it!

From the point of view of duality, Shankaracharya admitted, universes appear to come and go. Our minds superimpose them on Divine Being the same way the fellow in the forest superimposed a snake on the rope. But what exists forever is absolute being, awareness, and bliss.

The Most Dangerous Path

The Upanishads say that to walk the path of Jnana Yoga is to tread the razor's edge. The intellect can lead us toward the Supreme, or it can lead us astray. Avidya, Self-delusion, is an ever-present danger.

The Hindu tradition is filled with tales of warning. There was the pandit with a huge following who continually repeated, "Everything is One. I am that one Supreme Reality. You are that one Supreme Reality." Then one day his wife forgot to add salt to the curry. The pandit was furious. "If everything is consciousness and there's no distinction between anything, how can you even tell there's no salt in the beans?" his wife taunted.

Even Shankaracharya himself slipped up from time to time. In one very famous episode, he was about to enter a Shiva temple when he discovered a dead body on the steps. The dead man's widow was wailing with grief. For Hindus, corpses are psychically polluting. Shankaracharya gruffly ordered the low-caste woman to get her husband out of the way so people could enter the temple without contaminating themselves.

"Aren't you the teacher who says there's nothing but Divine Consciousness anywhere?" the woman cried. "What is it you see in my husband's dead body that isn't divine?" Shankaracharya was a great enough soul to recognize words of truth when he heard them. So he prostrated before the widow and thanked her for the lesson.

Confronting the Elephant

Then there was the disciple who took the teachings so seriously that when he saw a charging elephant, he stepped out into the street anyway, thinking, "I am the Reality.

The elephant is the Reality. It's all Divine Awareness." The elephant's owner screamed at him, "Get out of the way!" But the disciple remembered his guru's instructions about maintaining perfect fearlessness and walked straight in front of the elephant.

Needless to say, the disciple spent months flat on his back recovering from his injuries. "This is what I get for believing your teaching!" he yelled at his guru. "I should never have listened to you!"

"What you should have done, you idiot," his guru answered, "was listen to the man who owned the elephant and get out of the way. He was the Supreme Reality, too!"

Quick Quiz

1. Jnana Yoga leads to …

    a. Intellectual brilliance.

    b. The living experience of Self-realization.

    c. Getting bitten by a snake.

2. Jnana Yoga consists of …

    a. Studying, contemplating, and meditating on the Self.

    b. Making other people feel dumb.

    c. Uncoiling a rope.

3. If an elephant charges, a jnani should …

    a. Merge in the elephant's consciousness.

    b. Call the local zoo.

    c. Get out of the way.

4. The Inner Self is like …

    a. A really good movie.

    b. The eye of a tornado.

    c. The eye of a potato.

Answers: 1 (b). 2 (a). 3 (c). 4 (b).

Practical Transcendence

There are two common problems that arise on the path of discriminating awareness.

The first is gaining some intellectual knowledge and then thinking you know something. Immature jnanis are frequently criticized for their arrogance. Jnana is not knowledge *about* Reality; it is the living experience *of* Reality. People with a lot of facts in their heads can be quite vain about it. But real jnanis, those who actually live in Divine Being, are noted for their deep humility.

Fully realized masters don't just see the divine in themselves—they see it in everyone. This is not an ego-inflating experience. On the contrary, it opens the heart to all living things. This is why universal love is a quality Krishna and the other sages so often associate with real jnanis.

The second problem half-baked jnanis may run into is lack of practicality. From time to time, the Jnana tradition has come under criticism for contributing to a sense of otherworldliness and a lack of concern for the horrible suffering and injustice in the material world.

Different saints have different missions. It may not be the purpose of all sages to solve our social problems. But it's clear from the Bhagavad Gita that Krishna himself saw Jnana Yoga as an adjunct to effective and successful life in the world, not as a retreat from it. One of the most famous jnanis of all time, King Janaka of Videha, remained in a state of God-realization while ruling a kingdom. He did a really good job, too! Spiritual illumination ultimately increases the soul's ability to bring light to the whole world.

The Least You Need to Know

- Jnana Yoga is a mental path leading to the actual experience of Self-realization.

- The path of knowledge has three steps: intensive study, contemplation of the truths you've studied, and meditation.

- Jnana Yoga simply makes us aware of who we really are and always have been.

- Jnani yogis have to be careful not to confuse intellectual knowledge with genuine Self-realization.

Chapter 23

The Royal Road

In This Chapter

- The deluxe path
- Unlocking the nervous system
- Developing mental focus
- E.S.P.
- Self-absorption

Around the beginning of the twentieth century, Swami Vivekananda wrote a series of highly influential books called *Karma Yoga*, *Bhakti Yoga*, *Jnana Yoga*, and *Raja Yoga*. These popular little volumes introduced the West to Hinduism's time-tested methods of God-realization.

Raja Yoga, the royal path to realization (*raja* means "king"), is traditionally known as Ashtanga Yoga in Hinduism. (*Ashtanga* means "eight limbs.") Just as the Hindu deities have many arms so does this type of yoga. It doesn't have rungs you climb up one at a time like a ladder, rather it has eight separate arms that all work together to lift you to your true Self.

The Eight Limbs of Yoga

The eight components of this form of spiritual practice are …

1. **Yama,** morality.

2. **Niyama,** ethics.

3. **Asana,** posture.

4. **Pranayama,** control of the breath.

5. **Pratyahara,** control of the senses.

6. **Dharana,** concentration.

7. **Dhyana,** meditation.

8. **Samadhi,** transcendent awareness.

You met the first two, yama and niyama, in Chapter 16. These are the elements of a decent and humane life—not injuring others, being honest, not stealing, expressing sensual desires appropriately, not being greedy, practicing inner and outer purity, being content, disciplining yourself, learning about God/Goddess, and surrendering to the divine will.

Sitting Still

It makes sense that ethical behavior is the very root of spiritual practice, but what does posture have to do with spirituality? Plenty, it turns out. All the rest of the components of Raja Yoga involve controlling the mind so you can begin your inward journey toward Self-realization. This is extremely difficult if the body is out of order. If you're sick or physically restless, it's tough to concentrate. The key to successful meditation, and to some extent to health itself, lies in how you hold your body.

The optimal condition for intense concentration is to sit upright with your head, neck, and trunk straight. Don't sit bolt upright in a strained position; instead, sit up straight in a relaxed manner! Try this next time you have to study for an exam or listen to a lecture. You'll be amazed at how much clearer your awareness is. This is because the nerves running between your spine and brain aren't being obstructed or constricted.

The classical meditation postures involve sitting cross-legged on the floor. But a whole system of more varied postures, called Hatha Yoga, eventually developed to help keep the body healthy and supple, in perfect shape for meditation. These involve exercises ranging from the head stand and shoulder stand to twists, stretches, and balancing poses. Unlike aerobic workouts, which exercise the cardiovascular system, Hatha postures work more with the endocrine system (the endocrine glands are associated with the chakras in the subtle body) and tone the internal organs. A lot of emphasis is placed on keeping the spine limber. A flexible spine, the yogis say, helps ward off problems associated with aging.

People who've been practicing Hatha conscientiously for some time can often sit comfortably in a meditation posture for hours on end. The original purpose of Hatha postures was not to promote beauty and a youthful appearance but to promote meditation!

When you say the word "yoga" to a Hindu, he or she will automatically think of meditation. Yoga literally means "union with Divine Consciousness," which typically happens in deep states of meditation. In the West though, when you say "yoga," most people think of standing on their heads!

Sages Say _____

Hatha Yoga without meditation is blind, and meditation without Hatha Yoga is lame. The combination of the two is called Raja Yoga—the balanced path.

—Swami Rama of the Himalayas

Hold Your Breath!

"Breath is the flywheel of life," my teacher Swami Rama would insist. The yoga masters have an amazingly advanced understanding of how the body operates. It wasn't until yogis like Swami Rama began coming to the West in the early 1970s and allowing scientists to experiment on them that our physiologists even began to suspect how profound the link between the breath and the nervous system is.

Swami Rama called breathing a flywheel because it's one physical function that's both voluntary and involuntary, and it affects every other system in the body. That means although the breath runs by itself, we can easily override its automatic function. We can breathe faster, slower, or even stop our breathing temporarily just by willing to do so.

Guidepost _____

Please don't experiment with yogic breathing exercises without the close supervision of an experienced teacher. People have done serious damage to their heart and nervous system by practicing some of the more advanced techniques prematurely.

The yogis noticed that how we breathe has an enormous impact on our emotional state and also affects our heart rate, blood pressure, and other bodily functions. If, for example, you make yourself take rapid, jagged breaths, you'll start feeling anxious. If you breathe slowly, evenly, and smoothly, you'll relax. If you hold your breath, you'll be awfully uncomfortable, but your mind will become incredibly focused.

The great Hindu masters studied the breath so intensively they created a whole science of breathing called *Svarodaya*. By applying its principles, they could manipulate functions in their bodies that otherwise wouldn't be possible to control through the power of thought, such as heart rate and the involuntary nervous system. This led to control over brain states, which led to the attainment of focused states of awareness beyond the imagination of nonyogis.

The Hindu View _____

There's an entire class of Hindu scriptures whose characteristic feature is that nobody can understand them! Sutras are the guru's lecture notes, a list of often meaningless words and phrases that the guru "unpacks" for the students during class. Disciples memorized these sutras as a way to keep the course material organized in their minds.

Western linguists have asked how it could be possible that Panini achieved an understanding of the mechanics of grammar that modern researchers couldn't duplicate even with advanced computers. To Hindus the answer is obvious. It's because Panini was a yogi! States of awareness that seem like genius to the rest of us are available to yogis who master the science of breath, which gives them amazing control over their brain and tremendous powers of concentration.

Diving Deeper: Controlling the Senses

By clearing the conscience through ethical behavior, stabilizing the body through correct meditative posture, and controlling the breath in order to calm and steady the nervous system, the yogi is getting ready to meet God. Not the deity in the temple but the deity in the body, shining splendidly from behind the physical, subtle, and causal bodies. That deity the Tripura Rahasya calls "Her Majesty, the Supreme Sovereign Empress, Pure Consciousness Herself." In Raja Yoga, the Divine One is called *Purusha*, the Higher Self.

Through breath control, the body and mind become quite still, so we now can move on to pratyahara or sense withdrawal. This means drawing the attention away from the body, away from the breath, and focusing it entirely in the nonmaterial realm of pure mental awareness. In Hinduism, this is accomplished in a number of different ways. One is to move the awareness up through the spine, severing your connection with the elements Earth, Water, Fire, Air, and Ether as you move upward toward pure awareness. The steps of the inward journey are detailed in the sage Patanjali's notes on Raja Yoga, called the Yoga Sutras.

The Flight to God

You're heading from Los Angeles to New Delhi. Your jet starts slowly taxiing down the runway at LAX, going faster and faster until suddenly you're in the air. As you move higher, you encounter some unsettling turbulence, but the jet keeps rising. You race into the clouds, through the clouds, and suddenly—poof!—you're above the clouds at 35,000 feet, and the rest of the flight is smooth sailing.

The last three components of Raja Yoga are exactly like that. You take off slowly as you begin to concentrate. You move higher into the state of meditation, quickly passing through the mental turbulence of thoughts and emotions on the way to a state of tranquil clarity. Finally you enter a realm above space and time where you float unperturbed in the horizonless atmosphere of consciousness. This process of moving from concentration to meditation to total absorption, soaring from 0 to 600 mph in your mind, is called *samyama* in Sanskrit. It's the portal to higher dimensions.

def•i•ni•tion

Samyama is the movement of attention from concentration through meditation into total mental absorption.

Degrees of Attention

What's the difference between concentration, meditation, and absorption? When you concentrate, you think about one subject. There may be numerous thoughts in your mind, but they're all about the same topic. "Krishna is so handsome. He's so compassionate. He's incredibly wise."

In meditation, you have only one thought in your mind. You're not thinking *about* Krishna, you're thinking only Krishna. His form (his smiling face or his holy feet, for example) or one of his qualities (such as

 Guidepost

Worried that meditation masters take over their disciples' minds? It's mistaken to confuse deep stages of meditation with hypnotic states. Hypnosis and trance are passive conditions. A meditator, on the other hand, is fully lucid and alert. She is directing her own experience, not being "taken over" by any entity outside herself.

radiant divine love) is the only image or feeling in your awareness. Hindu sages compare this state to pouring oil into a bowl. The flow of your attention toward God, or whatever object you're meditating on, is as unwavering and unbroken as the stream of oil.

Samadhi—total meditative absorption—takes your mental focus to the highest level. When you're in samadhi, you erase yourself. You're no longer present. The only thing present is Krishna or whatever the object of your meditation is. Your focus is so total that you, the process of meditation, and the thing you're meditating on fuse into one experience. Krishna totally dominates your field of awareness, not you. In a sense, you have become Krishna.

Merging With What You Love

If you can catch hold of Divine Being in meditation, then through samadhi you can actually merge into it. Your own being fuses with the Divine. This is what yoga technically means. Your awareness becomes "yoked" or united with its object. If that object is the Supreme Being, you are now in a very high state indeed.

Psychic Science

Not everyone meditates on God. Some people focus intently on sex, which leads them to a state of bliss. Others focus intently on art or music or poetry, which leads them to another kind of blissful experience. Many people these days experience "computer samadhi" as they sit in front of their computer screens in a state of full mental absorption. One of my mentors, Shree Maa of Kamakya—a saint who's capable of shifting effortlessly into the highest states of consciousness—recently commented that computers are actually good because they teach people to concentrate. That's an important step on the road to Self-realization!

In the Yoga Sutras, Patanjali admits that many inner explorers focus on developing psychic powers. His sutras list some of the supernatural abilities you can develop through intense mental control, such as …

◆ Remember your past lives.

◆ Gain knowledge of past or future events.

Sages Say

If you practice regular meditation, you are bound to get some psychic powers. You should not use these powers for base and selfish purposes. I again and again seriously warn you! Desire for psychic powers will act like puffs of air which may blow out the lamp of Yoga.

—Swami Sivananda

- Read other people's minds.

- Become invisible.

- Gain the strength, swiftness, or skills of certain animals.

- Gain full knowledge of cosmology—no telescope required!

- Communicate with higher beings in the subtle worlds.

- Enter someone else's body after that soul has vacated it.

- Travel without dragging your physical body along.

- Pull any information out of the universe that you may have use for!

Spiritual healing, talking with beings in parallel universes, materializing objects, teleporting from one place to another, astral traveling, sending messages telepathically—these things are viewed as spiritual realities, not superstition, in Hinduism. Even average people experience extrasensory perception from time to time. In India, saints, sages, and yogis demonstrate so-called miraculous powers routinely. After all, becoming a sage means one's normally limited human consciousness is expanding to superhuman proportions. So of course you develop extraordinary mental powers!

Don't Worry, I'm Here!

Late one night the great Bengali saint Anandamayi Ma abruptly announced to her astonished devotees that she was leaving for Sarnath. Her disciples trotted after her as she boarded a train that was not scheduled to stop at Sarnath. At Sarnath, however, the train pulled to a halt. Anandamayi Ma jumped off, trailed by her disciples, and started walking through town obviously looking for something.

When they arrived at the Birla Hotel, Anandamayi Ma walked in without bothering to stop by the reception desk. She burst into a guest room, and there sat her devotee Maharattan, who was stranded in town and had been crying to Anandamayi Ma for the past several hours. "It's all right!" Ma said. "I'm here!"

Sages Say

The kingdom of consciousness is a unity, and until you experience it in its totality, you will never be content. You, a child of immortality, can never feel at home in the realm of death. Man's true nature—call it what you will—is the Supreme Self of all.

—Anandamayi Ma

This was back in the 1930s—there were no phones in Sarnath at the time. So how did Anandamayi Ma know Maharattan was in trouble? And how could she have known where to find her? "There is only one all-pervading consciousness everywhere," Ma explained. "In reality, appearance, continuance, and disappearance occur simultaneously in one place." Anandamayi Ma was constantly in the highest state of samadhi whether she was sitting in meditation or interacting with others in the physical world. She experienced her unity with all being so completely that, like other advanced meditation masters, she seemed to know everything that was going on everywhere all at once!

Caution! Psychic Power Alert!

In the West, we make a distinction between the natural and the supernatural. In Hinduism, this distinction doesn't exist. The so-called supernatural is just a higher octave of the scale of consciousness. As we continue to grow spiritually, we also experience these siddhis or psychic powers.

To cavalierly show off one's siddhis is considered a sign of spiritual immaturity in Hinduism. But this is not to say Hindus don't get as much of a thrill out of watching siddhas, or spiritual adepts, display their special powers as we do in the West!

Yet in the Yoga Sutras Patanjali carefully distinguishes between psychic powers that can enhance spiritual development and those that may actually sabotage it. The appropriate use of intense states of concentration, he says, is to learn to distinguish between the eternal Purusha—the Self within—and the transient things of the world. He discourages disciples from pausing on the path to play with psychic powers. Patanjali encourages them instead to keep their eyes on the prize: spiritual liberation.

Spiritual Expansion

You can't force yourself to relax; you can't make yourself sleep. You "slip" into relaxation; you "fall" asleep. Just so, you "fall" into meditation. When you're really meditating, it's effortless. When you rise from meditation, you're as refreshed and invigorated as if you've had a good sleep. You're not any wiser when you climb out of bed in the morning. But if you've truly made contact with your Higher Self in meditation, you get up from your meditation cushion brimming with intuitive insight, creative energy, and healing power.

As your consciousness continues to expand through the practice of Raja Yoga, you begin to link with other entities everywhere. Swami Rama explained that each of us is like a light bulb while the cosmic mind is like the electric current that sets all the individual bulbs glowing. "The cosmic mind is very subtle, and it is in close contact with other minds," he said. "As one's mind evolves one enters into a conscious relationship with other minds. Numerous minds are linked in this way, and this network forms part of the cosmic mind."

For Christians, mature faith is the key to salvation. For Hindus, actual *experience* of higher realities is what spirituality is really about. By advancing in meditation we can personally experience the living reality our faith points us toward.

Quick Quiz

1. Raja Yoga begins with ...

   a. Moving to the Himalayas.

   b. Moral and ethical principles.

   c. Standing on your head so you get a fresh perspective on life.

2. Raja yogis control their breathing in order to ...

   a. Turn their faces a dark shade of blue.

   b. Diminish the symptoms of allergies and asthma.

   c. Calm and steady their nervous system and mind.

3. Developing psychic powers ...

   a. Is the whole reason for practicing Raja Yoga.

   b. Allows yogis to mentally bend forks and spoons so they don't have to eat with their fingers.

   c. Can be a distraction on the spiritual path.

4. Hatha Yoga postures were originally designed to ...

   a. Help you sit in meditation comfortably for hours.

   b. Make you look and feel great!

   c. Torture prisoners in Soviet gulags.

   Answers: 1 (b). 2 (c). 3 (c). 4 (a).

Inner Enemies

Raja yogis hate and harm no one, but they are not without enemies. And real power, as any politician knows, comes from conquering one's enemies. The five enemies of the Raja yogi are …

- **Avidya,** spiritual ignorance.

- **Asmita,** self-centeredness.

- **Raga,** attachment.

- **Dvesha,** aversion.

- **Abhinivesha,** fear of death.

Avidya, ignorance of one's true nature, is the root cause of all suffering. No one would harm anyone else if he saw into the heart of reality. In the experience of cosmic consciousness, we literally experience every living being as we ourselves. Avidya leads to asmita, the sense that we exist apart from others. We might begin perceiving them as a threat or as competitors, which is to fundamentally misunderstand the unified nature of all things.

Attachment and aversion, desire and repulsion, are offshoots of avidya. So is clinging to life, mistaking our physical body for our self.

Sages Say

Yoga means control of the contents of your mind. When your thoughts are stilled, your consciousness experiences only itself. But when thoughts begin to flow, you get caught in them and the images they present to you.

—Yoga Sutras

These enemies are really tough to conquer. But by expanding our consciousness through deeper and deeper states of meditation, we pass the knot in consciousness we call "me" and move into a wider experience of reality.

Patanjali says that when we reoriented our lives so that we're established in the highest state of meditative absorption, we become free from karma. Our past karmas are roasted like seeds fried in a pan and can never germinate again. What this means in our practical experience is that we're no longer governed by our habit patterns, cravings, and fears. Instead we now live in the pure wisdom of the Higher Self.

Divine Isolation

Patanjali, author of the Yoga Sutras, was a great yoga master. He was an ascetic type who didn't believe this world had much to recommend about itself. Most people might be prepared to put up with disease, suffering, and death—but not him.

For Patanjali, the ultimate aim of Raja Yoga was retreat from the outer world into the undying reality of the Inner Self. In the highest state of consciousness, he wrote, your consciousness subsides into itself. It locks itself away from the surging and heaving of matter and energy and from the fluctuations of thought. It rests instead in its own nature, pure consciousness alone, remaining aware of nothing but itself and absolutely content!

Another, very large group within Hinduism sees life differently. Life—including suffering and death—is the play of consciousness and, therefore, is sacred and deserves our respect, not our contempt. For these people, called tantrics, Patanjali's highest state—consciousness resting in itself—was not the end point of spirituality but the beginning of an even more extraordinary journey into mystical awareness (see Chapter 24).

Is Yoga Hindu?

What if you're not a Hindu? What if you're a Christian or a Jew? Should you practice yoga? Or is that being untrue to your faith? Is yoga a universal set of physical and mental exercises anyone can practice, or is it only appropriate for Hindus? Most people in Western culture have no problem with going to church in the morning and to yoga class in the afternoon. Yet this issue is often raised by fundamentalist Christians and Roman Catholic authorities. It was even debated on CNN! Here is my personal perspective on this continuing controversy.

Tools for the Spirit

Hatha yoga postures and meditation practices are tools for enhancing physical and mental health. They can also be tools for developing higher awareness. Yoga-like practices have long been embraced by non-Hindu religions like Buddhism, Jainism, and Sikhism.

What many people don't realize is that yoga-like techniques are nearly universal. The ancient Greeks had yoga practices. If you don't believe me, read Plotinus' *Enneads*.

The Hindu View

Psalm 46:10 in the Bible says, "Be still, and know that I am God." That's easier said than done! Many of us can barely still our thought stream for two consecutive seconds! Yoga practices teach us how to still our body and mind so we can feel the living presence of a Higher Power.

This third-century Western spiritual master led his students through the exact same stages of meditation Patanjali outlined in the Yoga Sutras! The Native Americans also had yoga-like practices and even shared some of the cosmology described in India's ancient Puranas! In addition, early Christian ascetics practiced many yoga-like techniques, including breathing exercises.

These universal techniques for enhancing spirituality were particularly nurtured and systematized by Hindus in India. Hindus deserve a lot of credit for doing such a fine job! But when yoga masters began arriving in the West, starting with Vivekananda in 1893, they never demanded Western students convert to Hinduism. Instead they offered yoga as a free gift that anyone could use in the context of his own culture, to deepen his connection with spirit.

Hinduism really is like a mother, as it offers its wisdom without strings attached. (Though perhaps a little respect for the Hindu tradition would be refreshing!) This is very different from a missionary showing up at your door offering you food or a job if only you convert to his religion.

Accepting the Gift

True spirituality, from a Hindu point of view, gives freely. Spirit is the opposite of ego. Ego says, "I want …! Give me …!" Spirit, on the contrary, looks for the opportunity to share. So it should surprise no one that Hinduism's great spiritual masters offer us the gift of yoga simply because it's the divine thing to do. In my opinion, it would be a little foolish to refuse a gift that does so much to enliven our spiritual lives, no matter what our own religion may be.

The Least You Need to Know

- ◆ Raja Yoga is a systematic meditative path to Self-realization.

- ◆ Breath control is an important tool for mastering the body and mind.

- ◆ The deepest states of mental absorption lead to merging in the object being contemplated.

◆ Psychic powers are a natural but potentially distracting result of developing intense inward concentration.

◆ The goal of Raja Yoga is to establish yourself in your true nature: Pure Consciousness.

Part 6

A Timeless Tradition

Hindu science emerges from a worldview radically different from ours in the West. Hindus see our universe as the living expression of divine intelligence, not as a random, meaningless product of atoms and physical forces. For over 5,000 years, Hindu sages have investigated subtle dimensions of the cosmos that Western science has yet to explore.

While Hindu India faces tremendous challenges in its homeland and with its Communist and Muslim neighbors, Hinduism abroad is meeting with increasing success. Basic Hindu tenets such as reincarnation and karma, as well as Hindu practices such as vegetarianism and yoga, are being enthusiastically embraced in the West. The value of Hindu techniques such as meditation and hatha postures, as well as some aspects of ancient Hindu history and cosmology, have been validated by Western scientists.

The most ancient religion in the world is still as fresh and relevant as it was 5,000 years ago. While adapting to the ever-changing conditions of the present day, it preserves the eternal vision of humanity's greatest mystics and visionaries.

Chapter 24

The Interwoven Universe

In This Chapter

- ◆ The structure of reality
- ◆ Living enlightenment
- ◆ Tantric tools
- ◆ Raising your kundalini
- ◆ The merit of self-discipline

Like it or not, we have incarnated into a physical universe. It's quite beautiful in many respects, but terrible suffering, injustice, disease, and death are never far away.

Hindu tantrics believe the world is an expression of God's delight. They explore its every nook and crevice fearlessly, learning its laws so they can deal effectively with whatever life throws at them. By understanding—and mastering—the cosmic principles underlying manifestation, they make themselves at home in the universe, come what may. After all, this is where their Divine Mother has placed them for now. They have no reason to be afraid.

When you see the universe not as a product of *matter* and energy as we do in the West, but as a projection of *consciousness* and energy as tantrics do in Hinduism, you relate to the cosmos in a very different way!

Warp and Weft

For much of human history, people have manufactured cloth by running thread lengthwise and crosswise over a loom. This weaving became an important metaphor for many Hindus. They sensed that the cosmos itself had been made the same way, sewn together by a superb seamstress, the Mother of the universe. If one tugs at any bit of thread in one section, the entire piece of fabric is affected.

In Hindu cosmology, each particle in the universe is interlinked with every other one, though some links are closer than others. Understanding these links is the key to cooperating with, and consciously manipulating, nature's finer forces. Understanding how these interconnections operate in your own body and mind leads to self-mastery. And self-mastery is the passion of Hindu tantrics.

Wine, Women, and Song

We think we know what Tantra is all about—sex orgies with God's permission! But how much do we know, really? Western ideas about Tantra are so outrageous, Hindus hardly know whether to laugh or cry. The myth that Tantra is "the yoga of sex" says more about the projections of the repressed Victorian Europeans who took over India a few centuries ago and first started circulating these stories than it does about Hinduism!

Today a whole industry is built around "tantric sex," complete with numerous provocatively illustrated paperbacks and "spiritual sex" seminars in Hawaii. A few Hindu businesspeople, who know how to make a buck as well as the next person, have gotten in on the act. Some professional artists in India even produce paintings of couples having "tantric sex" to sell to the naive Westerners who actually believe this is a common Hindu practice!

Tantra in Real Life

Most of the Hindu teachers I've studied with over the decades have been practicing tantrics. People who believe the sensationalized stories would be disappointed to meet them. Rather than being masters of exotic sexual postures, most of them live lives of extraordinary austerity. Some have engaged in disciplines the Western mind can hardly imagine—such as meditating in a cramped Himalayan cave without any light for 11 months straight or surviving in the jungles of Assam for months on end with little or no food.

In fact, there are still tantrics today who live without any food at all. In addition to an occasional sip of water, all they eat is sunlight. They assimilate prana, or vital energy, directly out of the atmosphere. Others sit for hours without breathing (do *not* try this at home!), their bodies in a state much like hibernation while their minds remain absorbed in meditation.

Stories such as these about tantric adepts sound like they are adapted from science fiction or fantasy novels. Yet those of us who've spent time in areas of India where ancient tantric techniques are still practiced can verify that we've seen these things with our own eyes. In some ways, the *true* story of Tantra is far more fantastic than the garbled tales of spiritual eroticism you hear in the West.

Sages Say

After Self-realization you become absolutely fearless. You can only be afraid if you think there's something *apart from* you that threatens you. When you become Self-realized you see that everything is *a part of* you. There can't be fear in that state, anymore than there can be darkness after sunrise.

—Tripura Rahasya

Liberation or Enlightenment?

The vast majority of people practicing Tantra are not miracle-working adepts, however. They're ordinary Hindus with an extraordinary goal: enlightenment in this lifetime. Some Hindus, including many of the renunciates we met in Chapter 19, believe the highest state of awareness we can experience is *liberation from* this world. Tantrics believe the highest state is *enlightenment in* this world. Their goal is *sahaja* samadhi, which means to remain in the highest state of consciousness not just while withdrawn from the world in meditation, but also while active in the world, fulfilling one's duties, supporting one's family, and enjoying life.

def•i•ni•tion

Sahaja means the natural state. Sahaja samadhi, therefore, means in the highest state of consciousness continuously, both in meditation and out of it. Enlightenment has become one's natural condition.

A story in the Tripura Rahasya tells about a prince who achieves samadhi, a blissful state of mental absorption, while on a meditation retreat. "Don't bother me," he tells his wife when she stops by to pick him up. "I'm experiencing the supreme state of consciousness."

The princess, who is secretly a tantric master—not a beginner like her husband—can't resist teasing him. "What kind of supreme state vanishes when you open your eyes? You're still as far from the true supreme state as the stars are from their reflection in the sea. When you're permanently in that state, you'll enjoy the same bliss whether you're sitting in a cave meditating or sitting on your throne governing the kingdom."

The prince got the message. He returned to his day job but kept working with himself till he could remain balanced in the highest state whether he was awake, dreaming, or asleep, in meditation or out, inspecting the provinces he ruled.

Ladder to Unity

These days people with a spiritual orientation often talk about getting in touch with their Higher Self. In very advanced states of meditation, though, tantrics found that the Higher Self is not the highest reality. The Inner Self is a stop on the way to the final goal, not the destination itself. The ultimate reality is the Supreme Consciousness and its limitless knowledge, power, and peace.

Here's how tantrics explain the nondistinction between your innermost Self and God. Beyond the Higher Self lies maya, the force that leads the Self to mistakenly feel it exists in its own right, apart from God's all-pervading divine awareness. Maya operates through five restraining factors:

♦ **Niyati** limits omnipresence, creating the illusion that you exist in one particular place in space.

♦ **Kala** limits eternity, creating the confusion that you exist in this fleeting moment rather than in all times at the same time.

♦ **Raga** limits your innate sense of complete fulfillment, creating the desire to acquire objects you mistakenly believe exist apart from yourself.

♦ **Vidya** limits omniscience, generating the illusion that you don't already know everything!

♦ **Kala** (pronounced with a long "a" at the end, unlike the kala in Item 2 of this list) limits omnipotence, creating the false sense that you can't effortlessly will things into existence.

Beyond these five facets of maya lies your true identity. And that's not jiva, the individual soul, but Shiva, the Universal Spirit.

Divine Identity

For tantrics, the universe is not a vale of suffering, a place you must escape from. Rather, it's a divine realm projected by the Supreme Being, in which we all exist together as seemingly separate entities—when in fact we are one unified whole, a single piece of fabric.

Most Hindus share the tantric perspective that all of nature is holy, and all deserves our reverence. And by learning to control the living energies inherent in the cosmos, we can live in the universe like benevolent angels rather than helpless victims crushed beneath the wheel of nature's erratic moods and inexorable cycles. We can become companions of the Divine, exercising the compassion, intelligence, and creative power that is our birthright as divine beings.

Guidepost _____

So you think you're God? Hinduism claims that each of us is an actual part of God, just as a spark is part of a fire. But it never confuses God-realization with megalomania. Megalomaniacs see God only in themselves. Genuine saints see God in everyone. That's why genuine saints are the humblest people you'll ever meet!

Mantra, Yantra, Tantra

The tool kit Hindu tantrics use to expand their consciousness and navigate the sea of energy we misperceive as the physical world is extremely extensive. All the methods of selfless service, rituals, devotion, intellectual inquiry, yoga, and self-understanding are called into play. But other techniques are applied, too, including ones that would be considered "magic" in the West. Two of the most important of these tantric practices are mantra and yantra.

Chant Your Mantra!

Tantrics use mantras to create a link between our limited human awareness and the unimpeded cosmic awareness we can link into, deep inside ourselves. According to Hindu tradition, the sacred syllables of a mantra create a vortex, like a wormhole between worlds that links the subconscious, conscious, and superconscious parts of our mind. We can use this vibratory gateway to bring guidance and healing power from the depths of our being. Tantrics also use it to move consciously into their subconscious and operate on the unhealthy aspects of themselves, their complexes and neuroses. They literally replace "bad vibes" with "good vibrations"!

The Hindu View

Ancient Hindu sages divided the celestial ecliptic into 27 sectors called nakshatras or lunar mansions. Each of these in turn was divided into four equal quarters, 108 in all. Each nakshatra is governed by a different Vedic deity. When you chant the 108 beads on your Hindu rosary you're invoking the blessings of all the gods in heaven.

You will often see Hindus using a mala or rosary to keep track of the number of times they've repeated their mantra. Most malas have 108 beads, which may be made of sandalwood, crystal, lotus seeds, or the rudraksha seeds sacred to Shiva and Shakti. They chant a mala of mantras and give themselves credit for 100 repetitions. The extra eight beads cover the moments when their minds strayed from the mantra. If they were completely focused while chanting, then they donate the extra eight mantras to the universe for the welfare of all beings.

It's not unusual for pious Hindus to commit to repeating a sacred mantra hundreds of thousands or even millions of times! These practices can take years, and sometimes lifetimes, to complete.

The Hindu View

The ancient Greeks and Egyptians used mantras, too. In the fourth century C.E., the Neoplatonic master Iamblicus complained that Greek mantras didn't work nearly as well as Egyptian ones—because the Greeks would make up mantras off the cuff. Egyptian mantras, on the other hand, had been empowered by thousands of years of repetition and had immensely powerful effects.

Draw Your Yantra!

A yantra is an abstract geometric diagram that represents the structure of the universe. It starts from the center point of consciousness and radiates out via all the shaktis or universal energies through every plane of manifestation. Yantras may be drawn on paper or fabric, carved in wood, or inscribed on metal.

Various yantric designs represent different cosmic energies or deities. Tantrics empower yantras with sacred mantras and enliven them by transferring the center point of their own awareness into the yantra to be worshipped. Yantras can transmit strong blessings and healing vibrations when they're properly "turned on."

Yantra literally means "machine." They're machines for consciousness, with each square and triangle, petal and circle in the drawing representing not only a cosmic force but also an energy in the tantric's own body and mind. By aligning physical, mental, and cosmic circuits, tantrics aim to achieve specific effects such as enhancing their awareness, creating a protective aura, or attracting prosperity.

The most powerful yantras are those tantrics draw in the subtle matter of their own minds. These become internal maps they follow to the center of the inner universe. Their innermost point is the source of the worlds—of all manifestation, in fact. It's also the point you travel through on your way out of these worlds into a place beyond space and a moment beyond time.

Sri Yantra, a geometric design representing the powers of the Goddess.

Kundalini Rising

Most of us think we know what kundalini is, too. We've heard rumors about a "serpent power" that lies dormant at the base of our spine and, when properly activated, travels upward into our brain to produce amazing mystical experiences.

Kundalini is actually the power of consciousness, whether it's in our body or in the universe at large. Most of us are so preoccupied with the objects or entities we perceive in the world around ourselves or in our thoughts or emotions that we fail to attend to the force of consciousness within us that is doing the seeing, thinking, or feeling. That inner light is the kundalini. In most of us it's only operating at 40 watts. In great saints and tantric masters, it functions at a thousand gigawatt amperage. They're veritable power stations of kundalini!

The Inner Pilgrimage

One way to activate your kundalini is to go on a pilgrimage. However, the sacred sites tantrics visit are inside the body, not outside it. The inner journey proceeds from the bottom of the spine upward through six more pilgrimage sites:

1. **Muladhara Chakra:** Base of the spine

2. **Svadhishthana Chakra:** Near the genital organs

3. **Manipura Chakra:** Behind the navel

4. **Anahata Chakra:** At the heart

5. **Vishuddha Chakra:** At the throat

6. **Ajna Chakra:** Behind the point between the eyebrows

7. **Sahasrara Chakra:** Corresponds to the cerebral cortex

There are hundreds of other smaller chakras, such as the vortices of subtle energy in the hands and feet through which saints can direct blessing power.

Sages Say

That which is the general characteristic of the Indian systems, and that which constitutes their real profundity, is the paramount importance attached to Consciousness and its states … And whatever be the means employed, it is the transformation of the "lower" into "higher" states of consciousness which is the process and fruit of Yoga.
—Sir John Woodroffe

The Inward Gaze

Jokes about the yogi who sits around contemplating his navel actually refer to meditation on the manipura chakra. According to Patanjali, who wrote the famous Yoga Sutras, intensely focused concentration here can lead to extraordinary insights and powers.

Each chakra is associated with a different set of psychic powers and spiritual experiences. Mastering the heart chakra, for example, brings the experience of universal love. Controlling the throat chakra bestows the powers of telepathy and prophecy. Opening the "third eye" chakra brings universal knowledge. When the "lotus" of the "thousand-petaled" chakra at the top of the head blooms, the tantric merges in Shiva, divine consciousness.

Getting High on Meditation

Tantrics use many other paths to mystical awareness. Drug enthusiasts in the West like to point out that the Rig Veda, India's most ancient sacred text, speaks approvingly of an intoxicating drink called *soma*. For years Western pharmacologists have been trying to identify which chemical substance soma may have been, hoping to recreate the long lost recipe. Some speculate it was a hallucinogenic mushroom called *amanita muscaria*. Others think it may have been the drug harmaline. Identifying it is difficult because ancient descriptions of what it looked like and how it was prepared are confusing and obscure.

Interestingly, the Rig Veda itself says that anyone who believes soma is really a beverage is a fool. Brahmins still drink soma during some of their rituals today, and it has no intoxicating effects at all!

Drinking the Nectar

The Hindu yogis I studied with told me Western scientists will never uncover the secret of soma because they're looking in the wrong direction. The answer lies within, not without. In the esoteric Hindu tradition, soma is understood as a type of inner experience occurring in the soma chakra, which lies between the third eye and the chakra at the very top of the brain. The psychoactively harmless soma prepared by brahmins for their rituals is just a symbol of this inner nectar tasted by yogis in high states of meditation.

Drug use is a controversial topic in Hinduism as everywhere else. Some sannyasins told me they used hashish to help calm the mind and dissolve their mental boundaries, as well as to help them sit still for long hours at a time. It is used sacramentally in some rituals, something like tobacco or peyote are used among American Indians. Marijuana must never be abused, however. Like all natural substances it has a devata, a living spirit or natural intelligence. If you abuse the devata, the devata begins to abuse you. Drug abuse can lead the unwary to disaster.

A Path Without Light

For most Hindus, drug use (as well as alcohol) is strictly forbidden. Many Hindu teachers point to Vyasa's classic commentary on the Yoga Sutras, in which the ancient master explains that although use of "herbs" is one way to alter consciousness, it is not recommended because "it leads to a path without light." Several prominent swamis also advised me to avoid psychedelics since they alter brain chemistry without promoting lasting clarity of consciousness, as meditation does. Worse, I was told, powerful mind-altering drugs can damage the nervous system.

Guidepost

Want to expand your consciousness? Try meditation—not drugs. Yogis say that drugs weaken the will, damage the nervous system, and stupefy consciousness. One yogi told me he'd seen heavy-duty drug users so internally damaged they would need *lifetimes* to detoxify their subtle body.

In the stricter tantric lineages, aspirants are instructed to avoid crutches like drugs. Instead they need to develop mental focus and inner strength— something drugs can't give. Advanced yogis alter their consciousness by manipulating the internal energies of the subtle body and getting "high" on consciousness itself.

Yogis think ahead, considering not just this life but also existences to come. They note that once they're dead, no physical drug can help them! Self-control and mastery of the processes of the subtle body will serve them well in the after-death state. Hashish and other psychoactive drugs are worthless to disembodied spirits!

Indulging in Self-Discipline

The amount of effort and self-discipline required to become a tantric adept is the equivalent of what an athlete needs to do to win an Olympic medal. I myself have watched tantrics sit for half an hour or more without breathing as they shifted their awareness into the increasingly high states that breath retention makes accessible. If you've tried holding your breath for even 30 seconds, you can well imagine how difficult these practices are to master.

I've also watched naked tantrics sitting outside in freezing weather as if they were sunning themselves on a beach in Hawaii! In the Hindu tradition, adepts like these have mastered the yogic science of generating internal heat from the chakra in the solar plexus.

If you spend time with genuine tantric masters, you'll quickly be cured of your doubt that tantric science isn't real. While most of the tantric techniques remain unknown to Western science, practitioners in the East have refined and preserved them for thousands of years. Still, the number of Hindus who actually master these techniques is small since the amount of self-discipline they require is so rigorous. Lots of kids play baseball—very few grow up to play in the Major Leagues!

It's ironic that Westerners think of tantrics as libertines! The adepts know that one doesn't become a master by doing things that are easy. A person becomes a master by doing things that are hard. Self-discipline is hard, but no one achieves greatness in any field without it.

Sages Say

The Moon has a blemish on his face he can't get rid of. I can't get rid of my attachment to the things I own. I throw myself at Your feet, O Lord. They're the only force strong enough to help me overcome my weaknesses!

—Tulsi Das

Tantric Sex Orgies

Rumors of men and women having sex while consuming intoxicants led Europeans to believe tantrics engaged in wholesale orgies, just as stories of Christians eating "the body and blood of Christ" during Holy Communion originally led to charges that Christians were cannibals!

What was really happening was that in sacred tantric rites, participants raised their awareness together through extraordinarily demanding concentration exercises. Elevating consciousness—raising the kundalini to the top of the head—is a major focus of the practice. They practice this so that at the time of death, they can consciously exit the body through the top of the skull. A conscious yogic exit leads to a conscious after-death experience and also, if the tantric wants, to a choice of which world he or she wants to explore next! Tantric adepts are no longer driven willy-nilly by the force of their karma but can now consciously direct the course of their spiritual evolution.

Western Tantra is generally about releasing one's guilt and inhibitions while indulging in life's pleasures. In India, tantric practice is geared toward developing courage, self-control, and self-knowledge. Traditionally, only students who demonstrated true worthiness in the form of spiritual intelligence, high ethical principles, and commitment to rigorous disciplines were initiated into the tantric lineages. This could include women

The Hindu View

Tantric scriptures, called *Agama* in Hinduism, often take the form of dialogues between the god Shiva and his wife, the goddess Parvati, with one lovingly explaining secret tantric teachings to the other.

and members of lower castes who were often excluded from more orthodox Vedic practice.

For the Hindu tantric, to be enlightened means to live—and die—fearlessly, honoring nature's forces without forgetting one's true identity as a spiritual being rooted in all-pervading awareness. For them life is not a horror of suffering from which we must flee as rapidly as possible, but an amazing adventure in the echoing corridors of spirit.

Quick Quiz

1. Tantra is a path to higher consciousness involving …

   a. Complicated sex postures.

   b. Mantras and yantras.

   c. Expensive seminars in Hawaii.

2. Chakras are …

   a. Centers of consciousness in the subtle body.

   b. Geometric diagrams representing college sororities.

   c. Vegan but high in cholesterol.

3. The purpose of Tantra is …

   a. Guilt-free sex.

   b. Liberation from the world.

   c. Enlightenment in the world.

4. Drug use is …

   a. Unknown in India.

   b. Generally not advisable according to many tantrics.

   c. Okay with a doctor's prescription.

Answers: 1 (b). 2 (a). 3 (c). 4 (b).

The Least You Need to Know

♦ Tantrics seek spiritual mastery in the midst of worldly life.

♦ Mantras and yantras are used to master cosmic energies, both within the mind and outside it.

♦ Kundalini is the illuminating power of consciousness as it manifests in the body.

♦ The chakras represent increasingly higher levels of awareness within the subtle body.

♦ Mastering advanced tantric techniques gives extraordinary powers and requires a commitment to ethical behavior.

Chapter 25

Spiritual Science

In This Chapter

- Directing evolution
- The science of consciousness
- Adventures in awareness
- Reality inside out
- The mental climate

For the last 2,000 years of Western history, religion and science have been at war. But that's not so in India. The Hindu approach to spirituality has always been scientific: search for universal truths, then test and verify them. Hindu sages are the scientists of spirit. They explore the metaphysical terrain, then lay out systematic routes others can travel to reach the same destination. "Here are my findings," says the seer. "Check the evidence for yourself."

Hindus have always been scientists, leading the world in mathematics, physics, medicine, linguistics, and psychology. Yet for thousands of years to this very day, Hindu India has been most famous for its spiritual science.

A Brilliant Design

How did our planet, teeming with millions of life forms, come into being? How did *we* get here? Is there a Creator? Or was the world shaped by blind forces, as Western scientists claim?

The holy texts of Hinduism explain that at the beginning of the present cycle of space and time, Brahma the Creator crafted our world system out of the debris left over from the last manifestation of the universe. It was shaped like a great shining egg, very much like the glowing ball of plasma and atomic particles Western scientists claim seeded our early solar system.

The Hierarchy of Creation

Then Brahma called in his assistants, the Vishvadevas, who refined this creation, adding an atmosphere, ocean, dry land, all the things we need to make our planet inhabitable. Today we would call the Vishvadevas "natural forces," although to Hindus these great beings are far from blind or random in their actions. Indeed they are inherently intelligent, custom designing the planet so that life can flourish here.

Next Prajapati took over. His name means "father of progeny," since all living beings are his children. He developed creatures that had prana (life force) and manas (the ability to consciously respond to forces outside themselves)—including us!

Did Brahma (Stage 1) or the Vishvadevas (Stage 2) or Prajapati (Stage 3) sit around with compasses and calculators, agonizing over their blueprints? Nope! According to the Hindu sages, these great forces are *inherently* intelligent—intelligence is their very nature. A brilliantly designed cosmos appears spontaneously, with no forethought at all, the way a new tune pops, fully formed, into the mind of a musician.

A fourth stage of creation is going on right now. Prajapati passed the baton to the rishis, the great seers. These sages are guiding us towards the next level of our evolution. They teach us to transcend the animal nature we share with Prajapati's other creatures, to become moral beings who exercise our free will for the good of all. And they direct us toward the state of enlightenment, when we will no longer be bound by a physical body but can transverse the universe at will, subside into the essence of our being, or continue to serve God through service to his creation, whichever destiny we freely choose!

Sounds like a plan!

Intelligent Direction

Modern science claims the universe stumbled blindly toward intelligent life. Hinduism says the universe was projected out of intelligence. A Supreme Intelligence lies at the root of all things, though its level of awareness is virtually inconceivable to those of us who are less than fully enlightened. Its breath is the universal prana, or life force, that actively guides the development of biological forms on worlds prepared by natural forces to receive life.

At first, I was shocked when my Hindu teachers insisted the Darwinian theory of evolution was incomplete. Like many others in the West, I uncritically accepted the scientific views I had learned in school. Gradually I came to appreciate the Hindu perspective: that we can't find "missing links" in the fossil record because the universal prana can radically reshape biological forms with extraordinary rapidity when the need arises. Think of an ordinary grasshopper. When environmental factors give the signal, within hours it transforms itself into a radically different-looking and different-behaving creature called a locust.

 The Hindu View _____

The Hindu Puranas speak of other races of humanity who lived on Earth in remote times but eventually perished. Today paleontologists collect fossil evidence of extinct human races like Neanderthals, Cro-Magnons, and Homo erectus.

Today, textbooks say Fizeau and Foucault discovered the speed of light in 1849. Yet the Hindu pandit Sayana gave the correct figure centuries earlier in his commentary on the Rig Veda.

The Babylonians are credited with formulating the foundational principles of modern astronomy and dividing the sky into 12 double sectors (the basis of our 24 hours), in the first millennium B.C.E. Yet over 2,000 years earlier, the Rig Veda speaks of a celestial wheel with 12 spokes and 720 segments (2 × 360 degrees of a circle or days of a year).

Each new design is perfect in its own right. DNA, from the Hindu perspective, is simply a biological code shuffled by the inherently intelligent, nonmaterial life force that directs it. Matter is not intelligent. The prana or living energy that organizes it and manifests through it, *is*. This is why the Prashna Upanishad says, "As spokes are fitted in the hub of a wheel, so all living things are fixed in prana. Everything that flourishes on Earth is controlled by the life force. Everything in heaven also is ruled by that living intelligence."

Western scientists speak of the conservation of matter and energy. To that the Hindu scientist would add the conservation of life force and consciousness. These can pass into a nonactive phase when a cycle of manifestation (individual or collective) comes to an end, but they cannot be destroyed.

Humans Come and Go

Western science says Homo sapiens sapiens ("the smartest of the smart humanoids"), a.k.a. *us*, are not the first humans to exist on this planet. Hinduism says the same thing! The Puranas say we're seventh in a line of humans who've appeared on Earth, but we're not necessarily the smartest!

In fact, some Hindu texts suggest that people in the past had much better memories, a much greater understanding of nature, and far deeper spiritual vision than we do today. While other cultures have tried to exterminate the past, burning libraries, executing scientists and scholars, and rewriting history, Hindus have done everything in their power to preserve the memory of our distant ancestors as well as their great wisdom and spiritual nobility.

Guidepost

Blind faith is not a virtue in Hinduism. The Upanishads warn that when the blind lead the blind, everyone wanders in darkness. In Hinduism, shraddha, faith in God, guru, or scripture, is for beginners only. Hindus are expected to do their inner work so that direct personal experience of a higher reality can replace faith.

Hindu scriptures agree with Western science that the Earth is billions of years old and that humans have been around for a few million years. But they disagree with modern scientists that our life here is a fluke. The closest Hindus come to admitting a random component in evolution is when they acknowledge this universe is the lila, or "play," of the Great Goddess, who is matter and energy herself.

The Hindu View

Hindu scriptures say the Earth goes through cycles when it flourishes and other periods where it's virtually uninhabitable. Sometimes things get so intolerable the souls who live here flee to other world systems entirely. But don't start packing yet! The texts say these cycles occur over eons.

Reports from Inner Space

Many of Hinduism's great spiritual masters had a profound understanding of the science of consciousness and how to manipulate its many powers. They understood the workings of prana and how to activate their kundalini. Let's look at some examples of the practical application of Hindu spiritual science.

Once the great yogi-philosopher Shankaracharya was having a debate with a very famous scholar named Mandana Mishra. In those days, public debates were serious business because whoever lost had to renounce his own views and become a disciple of the person who won. (Imagine if during our presidential debates, the losing candidate had to join the political party of the winner!)

Shankaracharya defeated Mandana, which meant Mandana had to renounce the world to become a wandering monk like Shankaracharya. Needless to say, Mandana's wife Bharati wasn't particularly thrilled! She went to Shankaracharya and demanded, "The Vedic tradition says husband and wife are one being, doesn't it? Then you haven't won the contest till you've conquered me, too!"

So Shankaracharya and Bharati started to debate. Well, the long and short of it is Bharati was winning. When she argued for the value of married life, Shankara had to acknowledge he couldn't respond based on personal experience because he'd been a renunciate since the age of eight. He asked for a six-month time-out. Knowing that Shankaracharya would never break his vows of celibacy and that he, therefore, would never be able to adequately respond to her arguments, Bharati granted his request.

Sages Say

Nothing exists apart from Divine Being, which is an undivided whole without parts, existing now and always. There is no more difference between the Supreme Being and the world than there is between you and a city you see in your dream.

—Yoga Vasishtha

Guidepost

If you're a fan of fun short stories, check out a Hindu classic called the *Pancha Tantra* at your library. It's a collection of tales about talking animals and the practical life lessons they learn the hard way. You probably know this book as *Aesop's Fables*, as the *Pancha Tantra* was called when it arrived in the West.

Borrowing a Body

Fortunately for Shankaracharya, a local maharajah had just passed away. Shankaracharya asked his disciples to keep an eye on his physical body, then flew off in his subtle body to borrow the king's corpse. Just before his family was about to cremate him, the king suddenly got up from his pyre and headed home!

Now maybe you think borrowing a used body is an easy thing. (Or maybe you don't!) But even advanced yogis like Shankaracharya face complications. One is that a cast-off body is still hard-wired for its previous occupant, so the yogi winds up struggling with a nervous system programmed with the ex-owner's habits and desires. Shankaracharya started living in the maharajah's body in the maharajah's lavish home, with his numerous gorgeous courtesans and every other luxury and convenience a man of that era could desire. I'll leave the consequences to your imagination.

Back at their campsite, Shankaracharya's students began wondering why their master was taking so long to complete his research and return to his own body. Asking around, they heard that a raja from a nearby kingdom had died a few months ago, then suddenly revived during his funeral. The disciples immediately realized, "That's our guru!" and rushed off to see what had gone wrong.

Rescuing the Guru

At the maharajah's palace the disciples were shocked to see the "king" having a wonderful time partying with his girlfriends and enjoying the good life. This wasn't like the sternly ascetic teacher they'd once known! These disciples were sneaky guys, though. They innocently sat down near the king and began to sing one of the songs Shankaracharya himself had composed about the ultimate emptiness of sensual indulgence and the everlasting glories of spiritual life.

Sages Say _____

Souls are in bondage because they mistake their body for themselves! They take good care of the body, believing that's who they really are. They become enmeshed in it like a caterpillar in its cocoon. And so they get swept here and there, rising and sinking in the ocean of death and rebirth. In reality, only the body dies. The Inner Being is forever.

—Shankaracharya

A stricken look appeared on the raja's face. Suddenly, to his family's horror, the king once again dropped dead. The disciples raced back to their campsite where, sure enough, Shankaracharya had already picked up his physical body and gone back to finish his debate with Bharati Mishra. Shankaracharya won the debate, and the Mishras were forced to become his students.

In the end, Mandana Mishra was so blown away by Shankaracharya's wisdom and yogic power that he became his leading disciple. As for Bharati Mishra, Shankaracharya had so much respect for her that he named one of his monastic orders after her.

Stories about advanced yogis temporarily abandoning their bodies to travel abroad are quite common in the Hindu tradition. In one famous incident some years ago, a yogi—a disciple of the legendary adept Bengali Baba—left his body in a locked room in a hospital in India. The doctor who had promised to look after it was called away on an emergency, and the hospital staff found the "dead" body and carted it away. The yogi was startled to wake up several hours later in the morgue. But not as startled as the staff in the morgue when he got up and walked away!

Tales from Today

Recently my husband and I were fortunate enough to spend Guru Purnima—the holiday in which Hindus honor their spiritual teachers—with Shree Maa of Kamakhya, one of the greatest saints of northeastern India. She'd just returned to her ashram and was disappointed to find that in her absence the ground had baked dry and her garden had withered away. And the rainy season was still months away!

Shree Maa of Kamakhya.

(Devi Mandir, Napa, California)

Shree Maa told Parvati, one of her disciples, to go into the temple and recite mantras to Lord Indra, god of thunder and rain. Unfortunately Parvati obeyed immediately, rather than waiting till after lunch. Many of us devotees were enjoying a picnic on the ashram grounds when abruptly the temperature plummeted, dark clouds gathered, and suddenly we found ourselves and our plates of curry and chapattis getting soaked!

Later I asked Parvati about the unseasonal shower. "It wasn't me!" she protested. "It was Shree Maa. She just wills it, and it manifests." Welcome to the magic of Hinduism, to the sympathetic connection between us and the universe. In the Hindu worldview, all nature is alive and is literally "all one." If Shree Maa needs her garden watered, she simply goes into that part of her consciousness that's one with the atmosphere and turns on the rain like we turn on a faucet in the kitchen sink!

Bringing Back the Dead

I could tell you zillions of true stories, but let me throw this one into the mix because it's so well documented in India. While these events were going on in the mid-twentieth century, they were headline news in Indian newspapers. Movies have been made about it. The story is about Bengali Baba, one of the legendary holy men of the Himalayas, who left his last known physical body in 1982.

The prince of Bhawal had just died and was taken to the riverbank to be cremated. As his pyre started burning, monsoon rains poured so fiercely they put out the fire and swept the body into the river. It washed up on shore miles downriver where Bengali Baba and a group of his disciples were staying. Baba asked his students to unwrap the body, which was sealed in linen sheets. Then he asked the recently deceased prince to get up—and he did!

The prince of Bhawal spent some time studying with the yoga master. Baba advised him to forget his worldly life and devote the rest of this incarnation to spiritual growth. But the call of worldly pleasure was too strong, so the prince headed home.

The Hindu View

Hindus believe the climate in the world is affected by the climate in our minds. Droughts, cyclones, floods, and other natural phenomena may be caused by our collective karma. If a change in weather is needed, ritual specialists can be hired to make offerings to the subtle intelligences who control the atmosphere. These priests work to improve the community's relations with the gods and request them to send better weather.

Reclaiming Your Identity

The prince was anything but welcome when he got home. He'd been filthy rich, and his money had already been distributed to his relatives. His wife had also taken a lover. And besides, they just couldn't believe it was him. He was supposed to be dead!

The prince had to go to court to prove he was himself and get his land holdings back. It was one of the most publicized cases in Indian judiciary history. His relatives did everything in their power to prove the old prince had really died—including providing the testimony of the physician who had pronounced him dead! The prince, on the other hand, did everything in his power to prove he was still the same man he'd been before he "died."

This was Hindu India where, you will recall, all kinds of different versions of the truth can be true at once. The jury decided the prince had in fact died. But since Bengali Baba was a bona fide spiritual master, it didn't seem unlikely to them that he could recall the prince's soul to his body. The well-known yogic practice of transferring someone's consciousness into a particular body is called *parakaya pravesha* in Sanskrit. So the jury pronounced in the prince's favor, and he got his property back!

Emergency Medicine

Recently K. N. Rao, a prominent Vedic astrologer in India, was glancing over a friend's horoscope when he noticed the man was about to enter an extremely dangerous planetary cycle. Death was imminent! Rao didn't mention what he'd seen but strongly advised his companion to chant the Maha Mrityunjaya mantra faithfully every day.

The Maha Mrityunjaya mantra is the great Vedic mantra for staving off death. Translated into English it goes something like, "I honor the All-Seeing One, whose grace is all-pervading like the fragrance of a flower. May he release me from the grip of death as easily as a ripe fruit is released from a vine!"

A few weeks later this gentleman was conducting an inspection in a warehouse. A girder suddenly gave way and several tons of cement bags came tumbling down over his head!

Sages Say

Do not be frightened by God's cinema. Movies, whether enjoyable or disturbing, are merely movies. Is it not wiser to place our attention on that Power which is indestructible and unchanging? Make God the polestar of your life.

—Paramahansa Yogananda

Workers rushed to drag the heavy bags off him, but they were certain he'd been killed. If he hadn't died instantly from a blow to the head or been crushed, he should have suffocated in the time it took them to free him. It turned out that although Rao's friend had been knocked unconscious, once he came to, he was no worse for the wear. He had a hairline fracture to a leg bone but was otherwise okay!

I guess most of us in the West would think this was just dumb luck. But Hindus take this kind of story as evidence for the protective power of mantras—and as proof that we can even change our destiny with a little boost from God's grace.

Tales from the Lab

Christianity has always had an uneasy relationship with science. Some of the medieval Christians' fundamental beliefs, such as that the universe is about 6,000 years old or that the Sun circles the Earth, have taken a beating at the hands of scientists. Although the Church is no longer allowed to burn scientists at the stake, the relationship between science and religion in the West remains embittered. In fact, scientists continue to wash their hands of so-called "supernatural" phenomena, which they refuse to research at all. And Christian fundamentalists still seek to keep some aspects of science, such as the theory of evolution or the explanation of human reproduction, out of public school education.

The relation between modern science and Hindu spirituality has gone more smoothly. Although Western researchers were initially even more hostile toward Hindu teachings than Christian ones, many Hindu beliefs have stood the test of laboratory research and demonstrated their real value.

"We're Not in Kansas Anymore!"

The fireworks started in 1970 when Swami Rama of the Himalayas, who had been a high-ranking monk in the Hindu tradition, showed up at the Menninger Foundation, a leading research institute in Topeka, Kansas. He'd been recruited to serve as a human guinea pig in the Foundation's experiments on voluntary control of internal states.

Carefully monitored on some of the most advanced scientific equipment available at the time, Swami Rama quickly showed that he could control his heart rate, brain waves, and body temperature to a degree that up till that day had been considered impossible by Western physiologists. He could effortlessly mimic brain death, for example, as well as alter his heart and breathing rates to barely perceptible levels. These were skills any yogi who had mastered the state of deep meditative absorption could demonstrate, Swami Rama explained.

The results of these amazing experiments were written up in science journals and encyclopedias. But there was one experiment the researchers didn't report for years. The results were so unbelievable, they feared telling anyone would destroy their careers.

The Hindu View

In recent years, a spate of bestsellers and documentaries have explored the astonishing similarities between the most advanced thinking in Western physics and the ancient tenets of Hindu spiritual science. Hindus aren't afraid of Western science. They're just waiting for it to catch up!

In that painstakingly controlled experiment, Swami Rama moved a metal spindle *just by looking at it.* Of course telekinesis—and even teleportation—are just two of the many abilities ascribed to advanced masters of Hindu science. But no one in Kansas, or just about anywhere else in the West, was ready to hear about it!

Researching the Impossible

I actually got to know Swami Rama fairly well over the years. He often complained how frustrating it was to work with Western scientists. They were only interested in what Swami Rama considered the most superficial aspects of yoga, the physical stuff. The real juice, he claimed, lay in what yogis could do *in consciousness.* But Western scientists refused to go anywhere near the fabled nonphysical skills of the yogis—not even with a 10-foot pole!

Quick Quiz

1. According to Hinduism, the world is …

   a. A senseless realm of random genetic mutations.

   b. Shaped and directed by intelligent forces.

   c. Going to hell in a hand basket.

continues

continued

2. Hindus feel that honest scientific inquiry …

    a. Threatens the foundation of their faith.

    b. Is what their ancient sages were doing.

    c. Is irrelevant to spiritual life.

3. Hindus believe you can generate rain by …

    a. Washing your car.

    b. Seeding clouds with ice crystals.

    c. Propitiating the deities who control the weather.

4. In science labs, the claims of yogis have …

    a. Held up remarkably well.

    b. Been utterly disproven.

    c. Led to bitter lawsuits over patents.

Answers: 1 (b). 2 (b). 3 (c). 4 (a).

Nevertheless, over the years Hindu mystical techniques scored again and again in the laboratory—yes, meditation delivered as promised in terms of enhancing physical and mental well-being. So did Hatha Yoga postures and a balanced vegetarian diet.

Only a handful of Western scientists, such as Dr. Ian Stevenson of the University of Virginia Medical School, dared to venture into the realms of consciousness that Hindu mystics explored. Dr. Stevenson produced a large number of thoroughly researched case studies suggesting that reincarnation might possibly be a reality.

So reports about incredible achievements made possible by Hindu science continue even into our own time. And still most folks in the West refuse to believe them!

The Least You Need to Know

◆ Hindus believe the force behind evolution is inherently intelligent.

◆ While Western culture has excelled in studying the external world, Hindus have thoroughly investigated consciousness.

◆ Hindus believe the human mind has extraordinary potentials that great saints and yogis can tap.

◆ Hindu adepts use their physical bodies as launching pads into higher dimensions.

◆ Scientific studies have verified some miraculous-sounding Hindu stories about human potential.

26

Ancient Religion in Modern Times

In This Chapter

- ◆ The best and the worst of ancient traditions
- ◆ The Hindu/Muslim conflict
- ◆ Hinduism's impact in today's world
- ◆ The East heads West
- ◆ The message of the sages

Hinduism is by far the oldest of the world religions; no other faith even comes close. While other cultures around the world have aggressively stamped out their ancient traditions, Hindu civilization has preserved the wisdom of the ancients. When we listen to brahmin priests chanting the Veda today, we are hearing the echoing voices of seers who lived 5,000 years ago. When we read the myths and cosmology recorded in the Puranas, we glimpse legends that may have taken root in the last Ice Age.

Archeologists have confirmed what Hindus themselves have always claimed: in thousands of years, their faith has changed little. The Hindu tradition is extremely conservative, having held its basic shape for millennia. This religion has a lot of baggage, some of which, reformers claim, it's time to toss out.

Can such an old tradition meet the challenges of modern times? Can a religion so resistant to change accommodate the realities of technological progress and progressive social ideas? Will a faith so rooted in the past continue to flourish in the future?

Let's look at the problems Hindus wrestle with today. And let's look at the extraordinary gifts "the Eternal Religion" offers our present-day world.

From Bullock Cart to Computer

The Western world made the transition into the modern era relatively gradually, taking about two centuries to shift from a predominantly rural culture into an urban civilization. The Industrial Revolution heaved the West into a new technological era that ultimately catapulted astronauts to the Moon and put radios, then televisions, then computers, then iPODs in nearly everyone's home.

India is making the same jump at light speed. When I visited India in the early 1990s, Hindu children shared with me their dreams of moving to America. They hoped to find better paying jobs there and a wider array of opportunities. By the early 2000s, migrating to the United States or United Kingdom had nearly dropped out of the conversation. The new buzz word was "IT" (information technology). Bangalore is the new Silicon Valley, and Mumbai has plenty of good jobs, too. Who needs the United States?

The Impact of the West

Against all odds, since expelling the British, India has pulled itself up by the bootstraps and put itself back on the map. In the early 1990s, finding a working telephone in India was a day-long project. Less than 10 years later, almost everyone had access to a phone. Five years after that, much of India was online.

There is no underestimating the impact that TV, cinema, and the Internet have on a culture. Contentment and a lack of aggressive materialism have long been the signature of Hindu culture. These values could blow away like dust before the onslaught of Western TV programming, commercials, and pornography now being broadcast into Hindu villages.

Along with rampant consumerism, the media has brought a whole range of new ideas into Hindu communities. Imagine women actually getting university degrees, supporting themselves, and living on their own! Imagine the children of sweepers, even of butchers, growing up to take jobs that make them virtual equals of priests and princes. This is radical stuff for Hindus!

Most of the founders of modern India, men like Jawaharlal Nehru, were British educated. Their essentially Western worldviews inspired them to declare India a secular, democratic state. Western democratic ideals have not always sat well with Hindu orthodoxy and its entrenched belief in social hierarchy. (It's useful to bear in mind that democracy was not eagerly embraced by the upper classes of Europe, either!)

Sages Say _____

The tragedy of human history is decreasing happiness in the midst of increasing comforts.

—Swami Chinmayananda

Wisdom and Inertia

Hinduism has preserved both the best—and the worst—of ancient culture. Prejudices cherished for 5,000 years are unlikely to change overnight. In fact, they're unlikely to be recognized as prejudices at all. And practices that have been in effect since before the dawn of history, such as dumping one's garbage in the river, are difficult to change now when a billion Indians are throwing their refuse into the waterways. The horrifying consequence is that today even the holy Ganges itself is choking with pollution.

The rapid changes of modernization are forcing Hindus to begin looking at many issues that even the most prescient sages could hardly have foreseen. But as changes begin to occur, particularly among the younger generation, which craves more of the material goods and freedoms of the West, there's the very real danger that the baby will float away down the river with the bath water. Down through the ages, Hinduism's most brilliant religious leaders have helped Hindus adjust to changing conditions. But today's more material-minded Hindus may be less inclined to listen to their spiritual elders.

As Swami Vivekananda pointed out, rather astutely I think, "This is the only country where poverty is not a crime." In olden times, Hindus evaluated their quality of life based on the qualities they held in their hearts. Increasingly Hindus are joining the West in judging themselves and others by how expensive their cars are or how fashionable the cut of their new clothes.

Sages Say _____

Shall India die? Then from the world all spirituality will be extinct; all moral perfection will be extinct; all sweet-souled sympathy for religion will be extinct; all ideality will be extinct; and in their place will reign the duality of lust and luxury as the male and female deities, with money as its priest; fraud, force, and competition its ceremonies; and the human soul its sacrifice.

—Swami Vivekananda

In the rush to change, ancient spiritual wisdom preserved in India—wisdom that once existed everywhere but has been forgotten in almost every other culture around the world—could be lost forever. Hindus may gain materially but, like much of the rest of the modern world, they could lose their soul in the process.

Hindu Reformation

For all its strengths, Hinduism is burdened with all-too-evident weaknesses. First there is the overpopulation spurred in part by the preoccupation with producing sons. Then there is the treatment of women and people of the lower classes, which too often fails to reflect the loftier vision of the more equal-minded Hindu sages.

Throughout Indian history, social reformers have emerged to challenge overly inflexible, and even inhumane, distortions of Hindu doctrine. In the nineteenth century, groups like the Brahmo Samaj, Adi Samaj, and Arya Samaj were leading advocates for human rights. In their zeal for a revitalized Hinduism, however, reformers sometimes attacked essential institutions that define Hinduism, such as the use of images in worship. Perhaps some of these well-meaning leaders had become too Europeanized, to the extent that they could no longer see the authentic wisdom in these ancient practices.

Guidepost _____

How do you define happiness? I've often been impressed by Hindu villagers, who are dirt poor by American standards but are healthy and cheerful. They haven't learned yet that they can't be happy because they don't drive a Lexus. Having enough food and shelter, combined with a rich culture, warm family relationships, and a satisfying spiritual life is enough to make most traditional Hindus quite happy.

Amritanandamayi Ma is a remarkable example of an exceptionally successful twenty-first century reformer. She begins by calling for a reformation of the human heart. She calls on her hundreds of thousands of devotees to love all and serve the needy. By modeling a life of selfless service herself (see Chapter 20), Amma, (mother), as she is called, has connected with the masses in a way the more intellectually minded leaders of the Brahmo Samaj were unable to. Saints walk their talk.

In the presence of saints like Amma, the orthodox priest sits down to eat with the untouchable. When a "supernova of spirituality," as *Hinduism Today* has called Amma, calls for fair and respectful treatment of women or the lower castes, men are inspired to listen. It's impossible to argue with the universal love and astonishing wisdom of one of Hinduism's greatest living saints.

Toe to Toe with Islam

The relationship between Hindus and Muslims has not always been a happy one. Many Muslim rulers in India were relatively tolerant, and a few, such as Akbar the Great (1556–1605), were practically half-Hindu. But other fanatic Islamic rulers laid waste to India in a deliberate attempt to eradicate Hinduism. At the beginning of the second millennium, Mahmud of Ghazni virtually annihilated whole cities, as did the Emperor Aurangzeb, who ruled from 1658 to 1680. They demolished practically every major Hindu temple in North India. Tens of thousands of Hindus who refused to accept Islam were put to the sword. These activities did little to improve Hindu-Muslim relations.

A Clash of Cultures

Muslims say there is one God whose name is Allah and Mohammed is his final authenticated prophet. Hindus say there is one God whose name is any name you want to give him or her, and prophets—even divine incarnations—appear on Earth all the time, including right now! Muslims say God is formless and should never be worshipped—or even imagined—in any form. Hindus say God is formless and can be worshipped in any form whatsoever since God pervades them all.

Hindus have made room for outsiders who came to stay, often gradually absorbing invaders and immigrants into their culture. But Hindu and Muslim worldviews appear irreconcilable. Mohammed Ali Jinnah tried to solve the problem by calling for the splitting up of India when the British left in 1947. This led the Brits to partition India into two countries: India proper and East and West Pakistan. (East Pakistan is now independent Bangladesh.)

Jinnah's idea was that Muslims would live in the two Pakistans in the far north and Hindus in India. Mahatma Gandhi fought the Partition, as it came to be called, but his worst fears came to pass. The forced evacuation of millions of Hindus from the newly created Pakistan and of millions of Muslims from India led to some of the worst massacres in human history. Both sides participated in atrocities. The horrendous karma of the bloody Partition haunts India and Pakistan to this day.

Nuclear Tensions, High Stakes Hope

As the twenty-first century progresses, the stakes have never been higher. India and Pakistan are fighting over Kashmir, the ancient stronghold of Shaivite religion. Both countries now have nuclear weapons. While both have promised to show restraint, emotions run high.

Sages Say

The path of true nonviolence requires much more courage than violence.

—Mahatma Gandhi

In an effort to promote healing between the two belligerent religions, saints like Kabir, Lokenath, Ramakrishna, and Shirdi Sai Baba publicly acknowledged the value of both traditions, in some cases, even to the extent of adopting spiritual practices from both religions! The saints dramatized through their lives that Hindus and Muslims can set hostility aside, forgive the past, and meet in spiritual community.

Hindus Abroad

In the past two centuries, the population in India has increased by an astonishing 500 percent. In 1800, 200,000,000 people lived on the Indian subcontinent. By 1900, the figure rose to nearly 300,000,000. But by the year 2000, with the world population hitting 6,200,000,000, India now held one fifth of the human beings on the planet: 1,200,000,000 souls.

It may be possible to churn out that many babies that fast, but feeding and creating jobs for that many new people is no simple feat. A massive exodus in the second half of the twentieth century saw Hindus heading for ports abroad. More than a million Hindus live in England now, working alongside the people who used to be their masters. Another 60 million Hindus are scattered across the globe.

Losing My Religion

A serious problem for Hindus abroad has been finding spiritual support. If there is no Hindu temple or cultural center nearby, children born in foreign countries can lose their sense of religious identity within a single generation. Kids want to fit in with their peers. For Hindu teenagers in North America that's often meant trying to seem a lot less "Hindu" in order to fit more smoothly into a predominantly Judeo-Christian culture.

I can't tell you how often I used to hear Hindus in the United States bewailing the fact that their children didn't know a thing about their religious heritage. The problem was compounded by the fact that often those Hindus motivated to leave India in search of economic opportunities elsewhere were the very ones least educated in their own tradition—and therefore, least qualified to pass it on to the next generation.

The Hindu View

Until recently, in Canada the word "religion" applied only to Christianity and Judaism! When a Hindu couple tried to open a temple there, they ran into enormous legal obstacles because the government didn't recognize their religion! Because of their efforts, religions like Hinduism, Buddhism, and Islam finally achieved legal status in Canada in 1973.

A Spate of Temples

Thankfully, the situation is changing rapidly. Is there a Hindu temple near you? If not, there may soon be. They're popping up all over! The two million or so Hindus in North America have responded to their crisis in cultural identity by raising tens of millions of dollars for temple construction—and thousands more to import brahmin priests from India. The priests conduct their age-old rituals for them and also, in some cases, teach classes on the Bhagavad Gita and other sacred texts.

I am thrilled to visit the new Hindu temples and community centers materializing throughout the United States. Since the Immigration Department relaxed its quotas limiting the influx of South Asians, Hindus have poured onto our shores. Most are professionals, placing the American Hindu population among the best educated and most prosperous ethnic groups in the Western hemisphere.

When Hindus reacted with horror at how insensitively and inaccurately their religion was portrayed in California grade school and high school textbooks, the state was forced to make corrections. American Hindus are reclaiming their tradition and earning the affection and respect of their neighbors in the West.

The Perennial Philosophy

One peaceful evening in 1876, a Canadian physician named Richard Bucke had a sudden, inexplicable mystical experience. He was relaxing quietly when, without warning, he felt an incredible sense of exultation and in "one momentary lightning-flash of Brahmic splendor" he actually experienced, to the core of his being, that "the Cosmos is not dead matter but a living Presence" and that "the foundation principle of the world is what we call love." The universe was actually consciousness itself! This was not a whim or an intellectual insight but an actual explosion of awareness that knocked his socks off!

> **Sages Say**
>
> [Cosmic] consciousness shows the cosmos to consist not of dead matter governed by unconscious, rigid, and unintending law; it shows it on the contrary as entirely immaterial, entirely spiritual and entirely alive; it shows that death is an absurdity; ... it shows that the universe is God and that God is the universe.
>
> —Richard Bucke, M.D.

def•i•ni•tion

> **Bodhi** is the experience of enlightenment. It's fully illumined awareness.

The experience lasted only a moment, but it radically transformed his life as he spent the rest of his life investigating the extraordinary phenomenon he called "cosmic consciousness." His book, *Cosmic Consciousness: A Study in the Evolution of the Human Mind*, came out at the beginning of the twentieth century. It catalogued descriptions of similar experiences recorded by historical figures such as Jacob Boehme, Plotinus, Jesus, Mohammed, Swedenborg, Ramakrishna, and a friend of Bucke's, an American newspaper reporter named Walt Whitman.

At the time of his mystical experience, Bucke knew virtually nothing about Hinduism. Yet in one moment of illumination he rediscovered the central truths of India's ancient seers. This is the reason Hinduism can justifiably be called "the Eternal Religion." The experience of divine illumination on which Hinduism is based keeps reasserting itself. At any moment, at any place, someone somewhere spontaneously *awakens*. Hindus would call this the experience of *bodhi* or enlightened awareness. Dr. Bucke speculated that all humanity is evolving toward cosmic consciousness—a view many Hindu texts support.

In the early 1940s, Aldous Huxley explored similar themes in his classic work, *The Perennial Philosophy*. Huxley quoted at length from the Upanishads and the Bhagavad Gita as well as from Hindu sages like Shankaracharya. He pointed out the astonishing similarities between reports of mystical experiences in many different spiritual traditions. Perhaps you noticed the title of Huxley's book is an alternate translation of the Hindus' name for their tradition, Sanatana Dharma, "the eternal religion."

Ancient Wisdom Is Eternally New

Just about everywhere its teachings have been presented fairly, Hinduism has been a hit. Some of the important cultural components of Hinduism, such as the caste system, have failed to make a favorable impression in today's increasingly democratic world. But the mystical beliefs of the Vedic sages—from karma and reincarnation and the essential unity of all things, to the mind-expanding powers of meditation—have been enthusiastically received wherever they've traveled. As Hinduism leaves home and expands outward from India, it is winning increasing interest and support.

Western Minds, Eastern Truths

From at least the time of the ancient Greek sage Pyrrho, who entered India in the entourage of Alexander the Great, some of the finest minds of the West have turned to Hinduism for inspiration. Many recognized in the Hindu tradition the clearest explanation of the perennial philosophy underlying the great mystical systems of the world. Some of the twentieth century's most progressive thinkers, such as Franklin Merrell-Wolff and Aldous Huxley, were avid students of Hindu philosophy.

From philosophers like Arthur Schopenhauer to scientists like J. Robert Oppenheimer, leading American and European intellectuals have been inspired by Hinduism. Top writers have been involved, too. William Butler Yeats helped translate several of the major Upanishads, the crown jewels of India's spiritual heritage. Christopher Isherwood helped translate the Bhagavad Gita and wrote extensively on the Hindu saint Ramakrishna. Alan Watts's *The Book: On the Taboo Against Knowing Who You Are* was one of the best introductions to Hinduism thought available in the 1960s.

Innocents in India

Mark Twain is perhaps the best-loved American writer of the nineteenth century, well known for books like *Tom Sawyer, Huck Finn,* and *Innocents Abroad.* But few of his American admirers know Twain traveled extensively in India. He called it the "cradle of the human race, birthplace of human speech, mother of history, grandmother of legend, great-grandmother of tradition."

Twain, usually quite a cynical fellow, was genuinely awed by the Hindu tradition. India, he said, was "the one land that all men desire to see, and having once seen, by even a glimpse, would not give that glimpse for all the shows of all the rest of the globe combined."

Joseph Campbell, the immensely popular American mythologist, traveled widely in India and was a good friend of the radical Hindu teacher J. Krishnamurti. He also assisted in the translation of one of the greatest spiritual classics of modern times, *The Gospel of Sri Ramakrishna*. At one point, he admitted that discovering the Mandukya Upanishad affected him more profoundly than the beginning of World War II!

Hinduism in the New Age

While Hinduism deeply affected some of the leading Western thinkers, scientists, and artists, its most pervasive influence has been on Western popular culture. Today Hatha Yoga classes are taught at just about every physical fitness center throughout the world. Hatha was shaped into its present form over a thousand years ago by Hindu adepts in Bengal, such as Gorakh Nath and Matsyendra Nath. Its original purpose was to keep the physical body in optimal shape for advanced spiritual practices.

The "New Age" movement, which arose in the West in the latter half of the twentieth century, grew out of an increasing disenchantment with orthodox Western religions and a craving for a richer personal experience of spirituality. "New Agers" were sometimes satirized as superficial and superstitious. What their critics missed was the New Agers' open-mindedness, willingness to experiment, and heartfelt sincerity.

Hinduism, directly and indirectly, contributed immensely to the New Age movement. The quest for understanding the Inner Self, meditation, visualization and stress-reduction techniques, vegetarianism, a fascination with occult powers, openness to the religious beliefs of indigenous peoples, certain healing methodologies, recognition of past lives and the role of karma, and the search for the spiritual master were all adopted by New Agers from the Hindu tradition. In some respects, the New Age movement is virtually a beginning-level form of Hinduism.

Surveys show that over the past half-century, the number of Westerners who believe in past lives and who take the concept of karma seriously has skyrocketed. Most of these people would never identify themselves as Hindu, yet their worldview has been profoundly altered by the great Hindu masters, whether they realize it or not.

Something for Everyone

Hinduism appeals on so many levels. It recalls the respect for nature and the communion with natural forces, so pervasive in ancient pagan religions. It reactivates reverence for the Goddess, whose worship was stamped out throughout the Western world but is still a living force in Hinduism where the profound mysticism of her tradition has been lovingly preserved from prehistory. There is the singing and dancing and worshipping before the images of the Divine, where one's love for God and Goddess find full expression. There are the physical and mental exercises that expand one's capacity to directly experience spirit. And there is the guru. Having a realized guru is for Hindus like walking with Christ himself for Christians.

Whatever you call the Supreme Being, however you picture him or her, whatever name you give your faith, an inner core of genuine mystical experience links your faith with every other authentic tradition. Hinduism, the oldest world religion, has preserved the wisdom of the ancients and their techniques for transcendence. That's why Hinduism is still as vital and vibrant today as it was 5,000 years ago.

The Launch Pad

I'd like to close with a few lines from my favorite American poet. In "Passage to India," Walt Whitman wrote:

> O Thou transcendent,
> Nameless, the fibre and the breath,
> Light of the light, shedding forth universes, thou centre of them …
> Athwart the shapeless vastnesses of space,
> How should I think, how breathe a single breath, how speak, if, out of myself,
> I could not launch, to those, superior universes?

Some blue-eyed Hindus like me have made our hearts a beachhead for Hinduism because we recognize in the Eternal Religion a launching pad for spirit. As the Goddess herself says in the Tripura Rahasya, between our own heart and the limitless being of infinity, there is no distance whatsoever. We have only to turn within to find the Divine One who exists everywhere. The Hindu sages show us how.

I hope this book has given you a little taste of one of the most delicious religions around. I offer my loving respect to the Divine One, to the saints and sages of all traditions, and, my patient reader, holding this book in your hands, especially *to you!*

Quick Quiz

1. "IT," a booming industry in modern India, stands for ...

    a. International terrorist.

    b. Information technology.

    c. Inner truth.

2. The Hindu saints Lokenath and Ramakrishna ...

    a. Taught that Hindus and Muslims can live together in mutual respect.

    b. Urged the Indian government to expel Muslims from India.

    c. Wore milk moustaches in a prodairy ad campaign.

3. The Partition ...

    a. Is the name of a popular television game show in India.

    b. Refers to the creation of India and East and West Pakistan.

    c. Divides the shower stall and toilet in an average Hindu home.

4. The experience of cosmic consciousness ...

    a. Has never been reported in the West.

    b. Is the exclusive domain of astronomers and astrophysicists.

    c. Lies at the very heart of Hinduism.

Answers: 1 (b). 2 (a). 3 (b). 4 (c).

The Least You Need to Know

- ◆ The rapid transition into a modern, democratic culture is challenging fundamental Hindu values.

- ◆ Hindu-Muslim hostilities have a bloody thousand-year history with no resolution in sight.

- ◆ The population of India has soared from 200,000,000 to 1,200,000,000 in just 200 years.

- ◆ Hindus abroad are actively building more temples in order to preserve their heritage.

- ◆ Hindu spirituality, though not necessarily Hindu culture, has found enthusiastic adherents in the Western world.

Appendix A

Glossary

Here's some advice on Sanskrit pronunciation.

Hindus pronounce vowels something like Italians do. Depending on whether the vowel is short or long:

> a is pronounced like the u in "but" or the a in "father"
>
> e is pronounced like the a in "say"
>
> i is pronounced as in "it" or like the ea in "eat"
>
> o is pronounced as in "no"
>
> u is pronounced like the u in "push" or "brute"

A couple of vowels in Sanskrit are almost impossible for Americans to pronounce because we have no corresponding letter in the English alphabet. To save you trouble, I've transcribed them as "ri" and "lri," which is probably as close as we English speakers will get to pronouncing them anyway.

A few more tips:

> bh is pronounced like the bh between "club house"
>
> chh is pronounced like the chh between "church hill"
>
> dh is pronounced like the dh in "adhesive"
>
> gh is pronounced like the gh between "dog house"

kh is pronounced like the kh between "work house"

ph is pronounced like the ph in "uphill"

th is pronounced like the th in "anthill"

But:

sh is pronounced as in "ship"

There are four different letters each corresponding to four different ways to pronounce the letters "d" and "t" in Sanskrit. Though Indians can easily hear the difference, we English speakers have a lot of trouble making them out. There are also two letters representing two ways to pronounce the sound "sh" as in "shoe." These depend on exactly how you hold your tongue as you make the sound. Since most English speakers can't hear the difference, in this book I've transliterated them for you as just plain "d," "t," and "sh."

There is no "f" sound in Sanskrit, nor is there any "th" as in "that" or "thing."

For more information on Sanskrit, consult Judith M. Tyberg's wonderful *First Lessons in Sanskrit Grammar and Reading* (Los Angeles: East-West Cultural Center, 1964.)

Abhinavesha   Desire for life; fear of death.

Acharya   An especially learned teacher.

Adharma   Unethical behavior; unrighteousness.

Adhibhautika karma   Group karma.

Adhidaivika karma   Karmic cycles of the forces of nature.

Adhyatmika karma   Karma we generate ourselves.

Adridha karma   Karmic consequences that can easily be changed.

Advaita   Nondual; unitary; one without a second.

Agama   Sacred texts of the tantric tradition.

Agni   The god of fire; fire itself; matter in the process of combustion.

Ahankara   Self-identity; the sense of me and mine.

Ahimsa   Nonviolence; nonharming.

Ajna Chakra   The center of awareness found several inches behind the point where the eyebrows meet.

Akasha Extremely attenuated physical matter. The "stuff" of which "empty" space is made.

Akriti Uncreated, eternal. Beyond time, space, and causation.

Allah Muslim name for God.

Alvar "One who dives deep." The 12 great South Indian Vaishnava saints of the eighth and ninth centuries.

Anahata Chakra The chakra at the heart.

Ananda Spiritual bliss.

Ananda Maya Kosha The subtlemost body made of very rarified energy.

Angirasas Ancient fire priests.

Anna Food.

Anna Maya Kosha The physical body.

Aparigraha Nongrasping; not being greedy.

Apas Physical matter that's fluid (such as water).

Arati Ritual waving of lights before a Hindu deity.

Aranya A forest.

Archana Ritual worship involving offerings to a deity (usually of flowers and fruit) and chanting the deity's name.

Artha Wealth, material well-being.

Arthaveda Politics, a subsidiary science regulated by religious texts.

Ashram A group home where the central focus is spiritual practice.

Ashtanga Yoga "Eight-limbed yoga." A form of yoga practice with eight components.

Asmita Egotism and selfishness.

Asteya Not stealing.

Asura A selfish, aggressive supernatural being; in very ancient texts, a god.

Atma Nivedana Surrender of the Inner Self to the Self of All.

Atman The Inner Self; the immortal spirit.

Avadhuta   A highly unconventional renunciate.

Avatar   An incarnation of God or the Goddess.

Avidya   Ignorance, especially of our true spiritual nature.

Ayurveda   Indigenous Hindu medicine.

Baba   An affectionate term for a Hindu holy man.

Baksheesh   Money or a bribe.

Bhagavan   "Bestower of good fortune." God.

Bhairavi   A female tantric practitioner.

Bhajan   A spiritual song, often extolling the divine qualities of God or the Goddess.

Bhakta   A person who's in love with the Divine.

Bhakti   Love for God or the Goddess; spiritual devotion.

Bharat   The Indians' own name for India.

Bharati   A Hindu scholar renowned for her wisdom.

Bhava   Mood. Feeling of spiritual ecstasy.

Bhoga   Worldly enjoyment.

Bodhi   Illumined awareness.

Bodhisattva   A Buddhist seeker who aspires to benefit all beings.

Brahma   Creator deity.

Brahmacharya   Celibacy. Avoiding unhealthy extremes of sensual indulgence.

Brahman   The Supreme Reality, the one all-pervading consciousness.

Brahmins   The caste of priests.

Buddha   An enlightened person or, specifically, the Hindu prince who founded Buddhism.

Buddhi   The mental capacity to make judgments. The higher intellect, intuition, and conscience.

Chai   Indian tea, usually steeped in milk with spices.

Chakra   A center of spiritual energy in the body.

Chakshu   The sense of sight.

Chandas   The sacred science of meter, used to help in pronunciation of mantras.

Chappati   A flat slice of fried, unleavened wheat bread.

Chidakasha   The spiritual sky or "sky of mind."

Chit   Consciousness.

Dahl   A dish of curried beans.

Damodara   Butter thief. This is an affectionate name for the mischievous, divine child Krishna.

Darshana   "Seeing." Any one of Hinduism's schools of theology, which are different ways of "seeing" God. Also having the direct vision of the Supreme Being yourself, for example, when you see His or Her image in a temple.

Dasha Maha Vidyas   The 10 great Goddesses of the Hindu mystical tradition.

Deva   Radiant being; a divine being or deity.

Deva Loka   The heaven world where exceptionally pure souls dwell.

Devata   A nature spirit. The inherent intelligence of an object or energy.

Devi   A Goddess.

Dhanur Veda   The Hindu martial arts, particularly archery.

Dharma   The best possible course; righteousness; the fulfillment of one's true purpose; virtue.

Dharma Megha   The last hoop a yogi has to jump through before achieving enlightenment. When pierced by the kundalini, it releases a torrent of divine knowledge and bliss.

Dhruva   The North Star.

Dosha   One's constitutional type according to Ayurvedic medicine. There are three doshas: fiery, phlegmatic, and nervous.

Dridha karma   Inevitable karmic consequences.

Dridhadridha karma   Karmic results that can be averted with effort.

Durga   The warrior goddess.

Dvesha   Hatred and aversion.

Gandha   Matter that can be smelled.

Gandharva Veda   The Hindu sacred arts of music and dance.

Ganja   Hashish.

Garbha   Womb, matrix, or the inner sanctum of a temple.

Ghee   Clarified butter, an important ingredient in Hindu cooking and ritual offerings.

Ghrana   The sense of smell.

Giri   A hill or mountain.

Gita   A song or chant. Specifically, the Bhagavad Gita.

Gopi   Milkmaid. The gopis of Vrindavan are legendary as Krishna's most lovelorn devotees.

Gulab Jamin   Indian dessert made of condensed milk, soaked in sweet syrup.

Guna   One of the three modes in which energy operates: rajas, sattva, or tamas.

Guru   Teacher. Specifically, the spiritual preceptor.

Guru Shakti   Illuminating power; the energy of enlightenment.

Indriyas   The five senses.

Isha   God. Also an Indian pronunciation of the name Jesus.

Ishta Devata   One's personal deity; the god or goddess with whom you form an intimate relationship.

Ishvara   "Lord," a common name for God.

Ishvara Pranidhana   Remaining focused on God and surrendering to divine will.

Japa   The continual repetition of God's name or of a sacred mantra.

Jatkarman   The sacramental rite performed at the birth of a Hindu baby.

Jinva   The sense of taste.

Jiva   The individual soul.

Jivanmukta   A liberated soul who's still in a physical body.

Jnana   Knowledge, particularly experiential knowledge.

Jnani   A "knower"; a Self-realized sage.

Jyotisha   The sacred science of Vedic astrology.

Kala   Time. Also the force that limits the soul's omnipotence.

Kali   Fierce mother goddess.

Kalpa   Ritual science.

Kalpataru   A "wish-fulfilling tree" or a saint who generously grants boons.

Kama   Sexual desire or desire in general; pleasure.

Karana Sharira   The causal body or "seed" body. The body that reincarnates.

Karma   The law of action and reaction at work in the moral universe. "As you sow, so shall you reap."

Karmashaya   Karmic residue we carry from past lives—our old memories, habits, and desires—which are stored in our subtle body.

Kaya Kalpa   The technique for regenerating the physical body.

Kirtan   Devotional chanting.

Kosha   A sheath or covering. Any of the soul's five increasingly subtle bodies.

Kripa   Divine grace.

Kriyaman Karma   Our actions; the karma we're producing in this lifetime.

Kshatriya   The warrior caste: rulers, administrators, police, and military.

Kundalini   A subtle form of psychic energy, latent in most people, that lies at the bottom of the spine. When it rises into the brain, extraordinary states of mystical awareness are produced.

Lakshmi   Goddess of prosperity.

Lassi   A light, frothy, chilled Indian beverage made with yogurt or buttermilk and spices or fruit.

Lila   Play, or a joyful, spontaneous action performed without thinking first.

Linga   A conical or egg-shaped stone representing Shiva, Divine Consciousness beyond form.

Madhyama   Verbal thoughts heard with your inner ear.

Maha Deva   A "Great God" like Brahma, Vishnu, or Shiva, in charge of many minor gods. Most commonly refers to Shiva.

Mahamandaleshvara   A specially acknowledged Hindu leader.

Mahat   The cosmic mind, the network of intelligence through which all living creatures are interlinked.

Mala   A Hindu rosary.

Manana   Deeply contemplating spiritual truth.

Manas   The part of the mind that processes sensory data and thinks.

Manipura Chakra   The chakra behind the navel.

Mano Maya Kosha   The subtle body made of mental energy, the mind (as opposed to the more subtle soul).

Mantra   A sacred sound, word, or phrase that leads the mind to a higher state of consciousness.

Manu   The forefather of the present race of humanity.

Mara   Evil; wrongdoing.

Maranatha   "Lord of Love."

Matha   A Hindu monastery.

Matsya   Fish.

Meru   The mountain at the center of the world. Astronomically it represents the north/south axis of the Earth. In yoga, it stands for the spinal column.

Mlecchas   Non-Hindu foreigners.

Moksha   Liberation from the bondage of karma and from the wheel of death and rebirth.

Mukti   Liberation. Another word for moksha.

Muladhara Chakra   The chakra at the base of the spine.

Murti   A statue of God or the Goddess, sometimes mistakenly called an idol by non-Hindus.

Nadi   A current of energy or "nerves" in the subtle body.

Nagababa   A naked, militant renunciate.

Nakshatra   A constellation, or a 13°20' sector of the Hindu zodiac.

Nama Japa   Continual repetition of the name of God or the Goddess.

Nayanar   The 63 great Tamil poet saints of the Shaivite tradition.

Nididhyasana   Deeply contemplating one's own Inner Self.

Nirguna   "Without qualities"; not having shape or form.

Nirguna Brahman   The transcendent God beyond the reach of thought.

Nirukta   The sacred science of etymology.

Niyama   A moral observance. Something you really ought to do.

Niyati   This force limits the soul's inherent omnipresence.

Pada   The ability to move around.

Panchama   Outcastes; people excommunicated from Hinduism.

Pani   The ability to handle objects.

Papa   Bad karma; actions that generate unfortunate consequences.

Para Vak   Unmanifest meaning inherent in silence. The truth abiding in deep meditative states.

Paradesh   The highest or supreme land. This is the Tibetan plateau above Uttarapradesh, India's northern region.

Parakaya Pravesha   The yogic practice of transferring an adept's consciousness into another soul's vacated body.

Param Anu   An atom.

Parvata   A mountain.

Parvati   Hindu goddess; the wife of Shiva.

Pashupati   "Lord of animals that have been bound with a rope." Shiva.

Pashyanti   Abstract concepts perceived in your higher mind.

Patala   Hell; a transient after-death state of mental terror and anguish.

Payu   Excreting.

Pitha   A seat of spiritual energy; an important religious institution or pilgrimage site.

Pitri Loka   The after-death realm where average souls meet their family members who died before them.

Prajapati   The divine intelligence who called animate beings into existence.

Prakriti   Primeval energy, the energy matrix from which organized matter emerges.

Prana   The breath or life energy, vital force, *chi*.

Prana Maya Kosha   The subtle body made of life energy.

Prana Pratishtha   The process of infusing the image of a deity with life breath so the image becomes spiritually enlivened.

Prapatti   The devotional path of total surrender to God.

Prarabdha Karma   That portion of our total karma destined to manifest in our present lifetime.

Prasad   Food or some other offering brought to the image of a Hindu God or Goddess and returned to the giver with divine blessings.

Pratyabhijna   Self-recognition; recollecting the Divine Consciousness in oneself.

Prithivi   Dense physical matter. The Earth.

Puja   A religious ritual, usually involving making offerings to an image of a deity.

Punya   Past life credit. Actions that generate fortunate consequences.

Purana   "Ancient chronicle" or "book of the ancient times." There are 19 major Puranas and an ever increasing number of minor ones.

Puri   A town or city.

Purushottama   "The Supreme Person." God, Vishnu.

Raga   Different styles of classical Indian music; also desire and attachment.

Raja   King. Raja Yoga is therefore the "royal" yoga.

Rajas   The quality of being in motion, active and energetic.

Rakhi   A magical bracelet or "band of protection."

Rasa   Matter that can be tasted.

Rasa Lila   The dance of divine love.

Rasayana   Ayurvedic rejuvenation. Hindu medical techniques for prolonging longevity.

Rishi   Seer. The Vedic seers were saints and sages of the highest caliber. One Hindu, tradition notes seven different levels of seers. Ranging from highest to least advanced they are the Deva rishis, Brahma rishis, Raja rishis, Maha rishis, Parama rishis, Shruta rishis, and Kanda rishis.

Rita   The laws of nature; the natural flow of reality. Righteous behavior.

Rupa   Matter that can be seen; form.

Sadhu   A man who has renounced the material world and wanders from place to place without any possessions, immersed in meditation and spiritual practice.

Sadhvi   A woman renunciate.

Saguna   "With qualities"; having shape and form.

Saguna Brahman   The personal God who responds to our appeals.

Sahasrara Chakra   The chakra at the top of the head.

Samadhi   An intense state of concentration. Also the burial shrine of a saint.

Samskara   A habit or tendency. Also a sacrament.

Samyama   The movement of attention from concentration through meditation into total mental absorption.

Sanatana Dharma   The Hindu's own word for their spiritual tradition. It means "the eternal religion."

Sanchita Karma   The karma we've accumulated in all our previous incarnations.

Sannyas   Renunciation.

Sannyasin   A Hindu renunciate.

Santosha   Contentment.

Sarasvati   The goddess of education and the arts.

Sat   Pure beingness; absolute truth.

Satsang   Keeping company with the guru or other devotees; spiritual fellowship.

Sattva   The quality of harmony. Sattvic energy is light and clear.

Satya   Truth; honesty.

Saucha   Inner purity and external cleanliness.

Seva   Selfless service.

Shabda   Matter that can be heard; sound.

Shakta   A devotee of the Goddess.

Shakti   The Goddess. Shakti also means power, energy, or the illuminating power of consciousness.

Shaktipat   The transmission of spiritual knowledge and power. Usually the energy of enlightenment is channeled to an aspirant through the guru.

Shiksha   The sacred science of phonetics.

Shiva   Supreme God or god of dissolution.

Shraddha   Faith, or a sacrament performed for the dead.

Shravana   Listening to the teachings of the guru and assimilating their truth.

Shruti   "That which is heard." Divine revelation imparted directly from God. The holy Veda and its direct auxiliary texts like the Upanishads.

Shuddhi   Purification. The shuddi rite restored Hindu status to ex-Hindus who had converted to Christianity or Islam.

Shudra   The working class; laborers.

Siddha   An advanced spiritual adept.

Siddhi   Supernatural power.

Smarana   Continuously remembering the Divine and its characteristics.

Smriti   "That which is memorized." Sacred scriptures authored by enlightened sages.

Soma   The divine nectar drunk by gods and yogis. The Moon.

Sparsha   Matter that can be felt.

Sthapatya Veda   Hindu sacred architecture.

Sthula Sharira   The physical body and its life energy or vital force.

Stotra   A holy hymn or prayer. Also the sense of hearing.

Sukshma Sharira   The astral body.

Sutradhara   A master architect who ensures that buildings are designed according to sacred principles.

Sutratma   The cosmic mind which pervades the world like a thread running through all the flowers in a garland.

Svadhishthana Chakra   The chakra near the genital organs.

Svadhyaya   Study and self-analysis.

Svarga   Heaven.

Svarodaya   The yogic science of breath.

Swami   An orange-robed Hindu renunciate.

Swamini   "Master of herself." A female swami.

Tamas   The quality of inertia: heavy, stupid, lethargic.

Tapas   Self-discipline; austerity.

Tapasvin   A person who performs rigorous austerities.

Tilak   An auspicious mark some Hindus wear on their forehead.

Tirtha   A ford or religious site.

Trimurti   "The three forms of God." This refers to the three main gods of Hinduism: Brahma, Vishnu, and Shiva.

Tvak   The sense of touch.

Upa Veda   One of the four sacred sciences not directly related to scriptural study.

Upastha   The ability to procreate.

Vaikari   Physical sound one hears with his ears.

Vairagya   Dispassion; nonattachment.

Vaishnava Shakti   The force that stuns the soul at the time of rebirth, so it loses conscious memory of its past life.

Vaishya   The merchant caste: business people, trades people, and farmers.

Vak   The ability to speak. The goddess of speech. The divine word.

Vana   A forest.

Varna   The four castes of Hindu society.

Vasana   Unconscious thoughts and tendencies.

Vastu   The Indian science of sacred space, Hindu *feng shui*.

Vayu   Gaseous matter; wind. The god of wind.

Veda   The Bible of Hinduism.

Vidya   Knowledge. Also the force that limits omniscience, cutting universal knowledge down to human knowledge.

Vijnana Maya Kosha   The subtle body consisting of intelligence.

Vimana   An airborne vehicle mentioned in ancient accounts.

Vira   Hero.

Vishnu   Loving God who maintains justice.

Vishuddha Chakra   The chakra at the throat.

Vishvadevas   The forces of nature understood as intelligent entities.

Vrata   A vow to complete a spiritual discipline in a certain time period.

Vyakarana   The sacred science of grammar.

Yajna   A fire sacrifice.

Yama   A moral restraint. Something one shouldn't do. Also the God of death.

Yantra   A geometric diagram into which the living presence of the Divine has been invited.

Yati   A swami in one of the Shankara orders.

Yeti   A Himalayan snowman.

Yoga   Union with the Divine. Also a path to that union.

Yoni   The base in which a linga rests. It represents the Goddess.

Yuga   A cycle of time. Yugas are of different lengths varying from five years to many billions of years.

Appendix B

More to Read

In the happy event that you're inspired to learn more, here's a listing of some of the top books on Hinduism for you. I realize you don't have unlimited free time to sit around reading, so I'm also marking with an asterisk the books I most strongly recommend for a newcomer to the subject. These are the books you might want to pick up first.

Histories and Surveys

Here are some fine general introductions to the Hindu tradition and issues related to Hindu history. *Warning:* Archeological finds in the last 20 years have thrown the investigation of Hindu origins into an uproar. Be advised that many books contain badly outdated information about early Hindu history. Also be aware that any dates you find for events up to about 1000 C.E. may be wrong by centuries. Dates for events before 1000 B.C.E. may be off by more than a thousand years!

Basham, A. L. *The Wonder That Was India.* London: Sigwick & Jackson, 1985.

Bryant, Edwin. *The Quest for the Origins of Vedic Culture.* Oxford: Oxford University Press, 2001.

Flood, Gavin. *An Introduction to Hinduism.* Cambridge, MA: Cambridge University Press, 1996.

*Frawley, David, and Navaratna S. Rajaram. *Hidden Horizons: Unearthing 10,000 Years of Indian Culture*. Amdavad, India: SwamiNarayan Aksharpith, 2006.

*Jagannathan, Shakunthala. *Hinduism: An Introduction*. Mumbai, India: Vakils, Feffer and Simons, Ltd., 1984.

Johnson, Gordon. *Cultural Atlas of India*. Oxfordshire, England: Andromeda Oxford Limited, 1996.

*Klostermaier, Klaus K. *Hinduism: A Short History*. Oxford: Oneworld Publications, 2000.

*———. *A Survey of Hinduism*. Albany, NY: State University of New York Press, 1989.

Michaels, Axel. *Hinduism: Past and Present*. Princeton: Princeton University Press, 1998.

Subramuniyaswami, Satguru Sivaya. *Dancing with Siva: Hinduism's Contemporary Catechism*. Concord, CA: Himalayan Academy, 1993.

Hindu Saints

The Hindu tradition has more acknowledged saints per capita than any other religious tradition. The following books offer a tiny sampling of the remarkable lives of India's spiritual giants.

*Amritanandamayi, Mata. *Awaken Children!* (nine volumes). San Ramon, CA: Mata Amritanandamayi Center, 1988–1998.

Chetanananda, Swami. *They Lived with God: Life Stories of Some Devotees of Sri Ramakrishna*. St. Louis: Vedanta Society of St. Louis, 1989.

Dehejia, Vidya. *Slaves of the Lord: The Path of the Tamil Saints*. New Delhi: Munshiram Manoharlal Publishers, 1988.

*Gupta, Mahendranath. *The Gospel of Sri Ramakrishna*. New York: Ramakrishna-Vivekananda Center, 1969.

Johnsen, Linda. *Daughters of the Goddess: The Women Saints of India.* St. Paul, MN: YES International Publishers, 1994.

Hallstrom, Lisa Lassell. *Mother of Bliss: Aanandamayi Ma.* New York: Oxford University Press, 1999.

Hawley, John Stratton, and Mark Juergensmeyer. *Songs of the Saints of India.* New York: Oxford University Press, 1988.

Mahadevan, T. M. P. *Ten Saints of India.* Bombay: Bharatiya Vidya Bhavan, 1961.

Muktananda, Swami. *The Play of Consciousness.* San Francisco: Harper & Row, 1978.

Nikhilananda, Swami. *Vivekananda: A Biography.* New York: Ramakrishna-Vivekananda Center, 1989.

O'Brien, Justin. *Walking With a Himalayan Master.* St. Paul, MN: YES International Publishers, 1998.

*Rama, Swami. *Living with the Himalayan Masters.* Honesdale, PA: Himalayan Institute Press, 1999.

Ranade, R. D. *Mysticism in India: The Poet-Saints of Maharashtra.* Albany, NY: State University of New York Press, 1983.

Saraswati, Swami Satyananda. *Shree Maa: The Life of a Saint.* Napa, CA: Devi Mandir Publications, 1997.

Shuddhananda, Swami. *Yogavatar Baba Lokenath.* Calcutta: Lokenath Divine Life Book Trust, 1986.

Venkataraman, Sri T. N. *Bhagavan Sri Ramana: A Pictorial Biography.* Tiruvannamalai, India: Sri Ramanasramam, 1981.

*Yogananda, Paramahansa. *Autobiography of a Yogi.* Los Angeles: Self Realization Fellowship, 1979.

The Living Tradition

These books transport you into the heart of the living tradition, explaining Hindu thought as it's actually understood and practiced by ordinary—and some quite extraordinary—people.

Dass, Ram. *Be Here Now*. Boulder, CO: Hanuman Foundation, 1978.

*Huyler, Stephen P. *Meeting God: Elements of Hindu Devotion*. New Haven, CT: Yale University Press, 1999.

Johnsen, Linda. *The Living Goddess: Reclaiming the Tradition of the Mother of the Universe*. St. Paul, MN: YES International Publishers, 1999.

*Lonnerstrand, Sture. *I Have Lived Before: The True Story of the Reincarnation of Shanti Devi*. Huntsville, AR: Ozark Mountain Publishers, 1998.

Svoboda, Robert E. *Aghora: At the Left Hand of God*. Albuquerque, NM: Brotherhood of Life, Inc., 1986.

Yoga and Hindu Mysticism

Here are some particularly readable introductions to various fascinating aspects of the Hindu mystical tradition.

Feuerstein, Georg. *The Yoga Tradition: Its History, Literature, Philosophy and Practice*. Prescott, AZ: Hohm Press, 1998.

Rama, Swami. *The Royal Path: Practical Lessons on Yoga*. Honesdale, PA: Himalayan Institute Press, 1999.

*Tigunait, Pandit Rajmani. *From Death to Birth: Understanding Karma and Reincarnation*. Honesdale, PA: Himalayan Institute Press, 1997.

*———. *The Power of Mantra and the Mystery of Initiation*. Honesdale, PA: Himalayan Institute Press, 1996.

Hindu Scriptures

You would have to reincarnate many times if you hoped to read all the scriptures of Hinduism. Here are a few special gems from the enormous mass of spiritual literature.

Dimmitt, Cornelia, and J. A. B. van Buitenen. *Classical Hindu Mythology: A Reader in the Sanskrit Puranas*. Philadelphia: Temple University Press, 1978.

Nikhilananda, Swami, trs. *The Upanishads*. New York: Bell Publishing Company, 1963.

Panikkar, Raimundo. *The Vedic Experience, Mantramanjari: An Anthology of the Vedas for Modern Man and Contemporary Celebration*. Pondicherry, India: All India Books, 1977.

*Prabhavananda, Swami, and Christopher Isherwood, trs. *The Song of God: Bhagavad-Gita*. New York: New American Library, 1951.

Prabhavananda, Swami, trs. *Srimad Bhagavatam: The Wisdom of God*. New York: Capricorn Books, 1968.

*Rajagopalachari, C. *Mahabharata*. Bombay: Bharatiya Vidya Bhavan, 1977.

*———. *Ramayana*. Bombay: Bharatiya Vidya Bhavan, 1976.

Saraswathi, Swami Sri Ramanananda, trs. *Tripura Rahasya or The Mystery Beyond the Trinity*. Tiruvannamalai, India: Sri Ramanasramam, 1980.

Shearer, Allistair, trs. *Effortless Being: The Yoga Sutras of Patanjali*. London: Unwin Paperbacks, 1989.

Tapasyananda, Swami, trs. *Sivananda Lahari or Inundation of Divine Bliss*. Madras, India: Sri Ramakrishna Math, 1985.

Venkatesananda, Swami. *The Concise Yoga Vasistha*. Albany, NY: State University of New York Press, 1984.

Hindu Philosophy

The Indian tradition is not only deeply devotional, but it's also robustly intellectual. Hinduism boasts an extraordinary legacy of philosophical and theological thought going back to the dawn of human memory. If you're a pandit at heart, you'll enjoy these books.

Larson, Gerald J. *Classical Samkhya*. Delhi: Motilal Banarsidass, 1979.

*Mishra, Kamalakar. *Kashmir Saivism: The Central Philosophy of Tantrism*. Cambridge: Rudra Press, 1993.

*Puligandla, P. *Fundamentals of Indian Philosophy*. New York: Abingdon Press, 1975.

Radhakrishnan. *Indian Philosophy* (two volumes). New York: Humanities Press, 1971.

Radhakrishnan, Sarvepalli, and Charles A. Moore. *A Sourcebook in Indian Philosophy*. Princeton: Princeton University Press, 1973.

Woodroffe, Sir John. *Principles of Tantra* (two volumes). Madras, India: Ganesh & Company, 1991.

If you have trouble locating any of these books, remember that your local librarian would be delighted to help you track down a book through the Inter-Library Loan service. Or try contacting South Asia Books; their contact information is in Appendix C.

Hindu Resource List

Want to learn more about Hinduism? These contacts will guide you on your way to exploring any and every facet of the Eternal Religion.

Websites

Hindu Universe
www.Hindunet.org

This is one of the leading Hindu websites in the world. It's so immensely popular, sometimes it's difficult to log onto! It's well worth the effort, however!

BBC
www.bbc.co.uk/religion/religions/hinduism/index.shtml

Count on the BBC to offer all kinds of valuable information about Hinduism!

Hindu Wisdom
www.HinduWisdom.info

A warm and easy-to-digest introduction to the wisdom of India's saints and sages.

The Heart of Hinduism
www.Hinduism.iskcon.com

A wonderful summary of Hinduism by Hindus.

Hindu Temples
www.indiantemples.com

Answers many of your questions about Hindu temples and worship.

Ancient India
www.ancientindia.co.uk/hinduism

This website brings ancient Vedic deities to life.

Magazine

Hinduism Today
107 Kaholalele Road
Kapaa, HI 96746
Phone: 1-800-850-1008
Website: www.HinduismToday.com

Hinduism Today is a superb, full-color bimonthly magazine covering current events in Hinduism. It features excellent interviews with leading Hindu spiritual teachers and engaging historical and educational articles on Hinduism. Informative, funny, inspiring. *Highly* recommended!

Books

South Asia Books
P.O. Box 502
Columbia, MO 65205
Phone: 573-474-0116
Website: www.SouthAsiaBooks.com

If you can't find the book on Hinduism you're looking for from your usual sources, South Asia Books can usually track it down for you. They stock thousands of hard-to-find books from major Indian publishers.

Organizations and Training Programs

The following are a few of the best contacts in North America for learning about Hinduism, yoga, and Ayurveda.

American Institute of Vedic Studies
P.O. Box 8357
Santa Fe, NM 87504
Phone: 505-983-9385
Website: www.vedanet.com

Arsha Vidya Gurukulam
P.O. Box 1059
Saylorsburg, PA 18353
Phone: 570-992-2339
Website: www.arshavidya.org

The Ayurvedic Institute
11311 Menaul Blvd. N.E.
Albuquerque, NM 87112
Phone: 505-291-9698
Website: www.ayurveda.com

International Vedic Hindu University
113 N. Econlockhatchee Trail
Orlando, FL 32825
Phone: 407-275-0013
Website: www.ivhu.edu

Index

W–X–Y–Z